A COMMENTARY ON
JAMES

KREGEL EXEGETICAL LIBRARY

A COMMENTARY ON
JAMES

Aída Besançon Spencer

KREGEL
ACADEMIC

A Commentary on James

© 2020 by Aída Besançon Spencer

Published by Kregel Academic, an imprint of Kregel Publications, 2450 Oak Industrial Dr. NE, Grand Rapids, MI 49505-6020.

Unless otherwise noted, the English translations of the original Greek or Hebrew texts of the Bible are the author's own. Emphases in Scripture quotes added by the author.

The Hebrew font used in this book is NewJerusalemU and the Greek font is GraecaU; both are available from https://www.linguistsoftware.com/lgku.htm, +1-425-775-1130.

ISBN 978-0-8254-4461-6

Printed in the United States of America

20 21 22 23 24 / 5 4 3 2 1

The one who teaches, learns the most,
and the one who studies, grows the most.

I dedicate this book to the Creator of lights
who has given me generously through this creative letter
many insights into the wisdom coming down from above,
which have gathered together and filled up my desire
to love and obey the good, compassionate, and just God.

Aída Besançon Spencer
March 2020

CONTENTS

LIST OF ILLUSTRATIONS

LIST OF TABLES

LIST OF EXCURSUSES

PREFACE

The Kregel Exegetical Library is a wonderful series aiming to provide a close exegetical-literary reading of the text that explores the thematic emphases of each major literary unit in a way that is exegetically helpful for the scholar but theologically accessible and homiletically useful for the pastor and teacher. I am honored and delighted to contribute to this series. I particularly want to show the thematic unity of the Letter of James, since the unity is not always readily apparent to the reader. My goal has been to demonstrate the subtle progression of themes in order to show how the parts of the letter interrelate to create a coherent whole. I have done the majority of the translation from Greek and some from Hebrew; if I preferred the wording of another version, it is indicated. My desire is to reflect the original language as a basis for the exposition to follow. The New Revised Standard Version has often been used as a complementary translation since it is a more literal version than others.

My specialty is literary and historical analysis. My work on my doctoral dissertation, Paul's Literary Style, has helped me to recognize and evaluate James's stylistic features and images. He uses many delightful and descriptive illustrations from nature and daily life. I also take seriously the historical background of James, Jesus's earthly brother, in his Jewish and Roman settings. James appears to rely throughout on Jesus's teachings, as well as on the Old Testament, as indicated. I have focused attention on the relationship between verses and, as well, on the meaning of words in their paragraphs. Words are the building blocks of meaning, as they are stacked into clauses, sentences, and paragraphs. Words and phrases studied are indicated in **bold** font for easy recognition.

As a former Hispanic community organizer, born and reared in the Dominican Republic and New Jersey, I have empathized with James's sympathy for the poor. And as a Presbyterian minister with more than forty years of experience, I have included some specific contemporary pastoral applications, as well as considered issues of language and gender.

I have enjoyed teaching the Letter of James for many years to graduate students at Gordon-Conwell Theological Seminary in South Hamilton, MA. Gordon-Conwell has been a supportive place for scholarship with its sabbatical programs, complimentary computers, extensive Goddard Library holdings, helpful library staff, and active interlibrary loan system. The current director, Jim Darlack, was particularly helpful in confirming the chart on "Unusual Words and Phrases in James," as was my Byington Scholar (teaching assistant) Jihyung Kim. David Shorey, the Director of Support Services, was most diligent and efficient in duplicating the different manuscript versions over the years. The Kregel editorial team has been most gracious, giving me much freedom in my approach. I am especially grateful to my husband, the Rev. Dr. William David Spencer, who as a grammarian and theologian teaching theology and the arts at Gordon-Conwell's Boston campus, graciously read in depth the first draft of the manuscript, despite his own busy writing schedule.

I have had a community of resources to bolster my own thoughts as I requested God the Trinity to enlighten me so I could help enlighten others. My overall goal has been to increase the reader's confidence in God's reliable and authoritative revelation, which is applicable through the Holy Spirit to everyone in every place in every era.

—Aída Besançon Spencer

ABBREVIATIONS

CURRENT LITERATURE

AfrJ   *Africanus Journal*

BBR   *Bulletin for Biblical Research*

BDAG   Bauer, Walter, Frederick W. Danker, William F. Arndt, and F. Wilbur Gingrich. *Greek-English Lexicon of the New Testament and Other Early Christian Literature*. 3rd ed. Chicago: University of Chicago Press, 2000.

BDB   Brown, Francis, S. R. Driver, and Charles A. Briggs. *A Hebrew and English Lexicon of the Old Testament*. Oxford: Clarendon, 1907.

BDF   Blass, F., and A. Debrunner. *A Greek Grammar of the New Testament and Other Early Christian Literature*. Translated and edited by Robert W. Funk. 10th ed. Chicago: University of Chicago Press, 1961.

BECNT Baker Exegetical Commentary on the Greek New Testament

BHGNT Baylor Handbook on the Greek New Testament

BibInt   Biblical Interpretation Series

CEB   Common English Bible

CEV   Contemporary English Version

CT   *Christianity Today*

ESV   English Standard Version

FC   The Fathers of the Church

HBT   *Horizons in Biblical Theology*

HCSB   Holman Christian Standard Bible

HNTC   Harper's New Testament Commentaries

HPA   House of Prisca and Aquila Series

IBC   Interpretation: A Bible Commentary for Teaching and Preaching

ICC	International Critical Commentary
IDB	*The Interpreter's Dictionary of the Bible.* Edited by George Arthur Buttrick. 5 vols. Nashville: Abingdon, 1962, 1976.
JB	Jerusalem Bible
JBL	*Journal of Biblical Literature*
JETS	*Journal of the Evangelical Theological Society*
KJV	King James Version
LCC	Library of Christian Classics
LCL	Loeb Classical Library
LEC	Library of Early Christianity
LSJ	Liddell, Henry George, Robert Scott, Henry Stuart Jones. *A Greek-English Lexicon.* 9th ed. With revised supplement. Oxford: Clarendon, 1996.
LXX	Septuagint (the Greek Old Testament)
MM	Moulton, James Hope, and George Milligan. *The Vocabulary of the Greek Testament.* Grand Rapids: Eerdmans, 1930.
MT	Masoretic Text of the Hebrew Bible
NASB	New American Standard Bible
NCCS	New Covenant Commentary Series
NCV	New Century Version
NET	New English Translation
NICNT	New International Commentary on the New Testament
NIGTC	New International Greek Testament Commentary
NIV	New International Version
NLT	New Living Translation
NRSV	New Revised Standard Version
NT	New Testament
NTME	The New Testament in Modern English
NTS	*New Testament Studies*
OT	Old Testament
REB	Revised English Bible
RevExp	*Review and Expositor*
RSV	Revised Standard Version
TDNT	*Theological Dictionary of the New Testament.* 10 vols. Edited by Gerhard G. Kittel and G. Friedrich. Translated and edited by Geoffrey W. Bromiley. Grand Rapids: Eerdmans, 1964–76.
Thayer	Thayer, Joseph Henry. *Thayer's Greek-English Lexicon of the New Testament.* Marshallton, DE: National Foundation for Christian Education, 1889.
TLG	Thesaurus Linguae Graecae

ABBREVIATIONS

TLNT	Spicq, Ceslas. *Theological Lexicon of the New Testament.* Translated and edited by James D. Ernest. 3 vols. Peabody, MA: Hendrickson, 1994.
TNTC	Tyndale New Testament Commentaries
UBS	*The Greek New Testament.* Edited by Barbara Aland, Kurt Aland, Johannes Karavidopoulos, Carlo M. Martini, and Bruce Metzger. 5th ed. Stuttgart: United Bible Societies, 2014.
WUNT	*Wissenschaftliche Untersuchungen zum Neuen Testament*
ZNW	*Zeitshrift für die Neutestamentliche Wissenschaft*

ANCIENT LITERATURE

Ancient Greek and Latin Writings

Disc.	Epictetus, *Discourses*
Eloc.	Demetrius, *On Style*
Geogr.	Strabo, *Geography*
Georg.	Menander, *Georgos*
Hal.	Oppian, *Halieutica*
Lives	Diogenes Laertius, *Lives of Eminent Philosophers*
Morb.	Hippocrates, *Diseases*

Apocrypha and Pseudepigrapha

Ep. Jer.	Epistle of Jeremiah
1 Esd.	1 Esdras
Jub.	Jubilees
LAE	Life of Adam and Eve
1 Macc.	1 Maccabees
2 Macc.	2 Maccabees
3 Macc.	3 Maccabees
4 Macc.	4 Maccabees
Sir.	Sirach/Ecclesiasticus
T. Ab.	Testament of Abraham
T. Sol.	Testament of Solomon
Wis.	Wisdom of Solomon

Early Christian Writings

Bapt.	Tertullian, *Baptism*
Barn.	Barnabas
1–2 Clem.	1–2 Clement
Comm. Jo.	Origen, *Commentarii in evangelium Joannis*
Cult. Fem.	Tertullian, *The Apparel of Women*

Haer.	Irenaeus, *Against Heresies*
Herm. Mand.	Shepherd of Hermas, Mandate(s)
Herm. Sim.	Shepherd of Hermas, Similitude(s)
Herm. Vis.	Shepherd of Hermas, Vision(s)
Hist. eccl.	Eusebius, *Ecclesiastical History*
Hom. Josh.	Origen, *Homilies on Joshua*
Pol., *Phil.*	Polycarp, *To the Philippians*
Strom.	Clement of Alexandria, *Miscellanies*

Josephus

Ag. Ap.	*Against Apion*
Ant.	*Jewish Antiquities*
Life	*The Life*
J.W.	*Jewish War*

Mishnah (m.) and Babylonian Talmud (b.)

ʾAbot	Avot
B. Mes.	Bava Metziʹa
Ber.	Berakhot
Bik.	Bikkurim
ʿEd.	Eduyyot
Git.	Gittin
Ketub.	Ketubbot
Maʿas. S.	Maʾaser Sheni
Mak.	Makkot
Maks.	Makhshirin
Meg.	Megillah
Ned.	Nedarim
Qidd.	Qiddushin
Sanh.	Sanhedrin
Sebu.	Shevu'ot
Seqal.	Sheqalim
Sot.	Sotah
Yad.	Yadayim

Philo

Creation	*On the Creation of the World*
Embassy	*On the Embassy to Gaius*
Moses 1, 2	*On the Life of Moses 1, 2*
Sobr.	*On Sobriety*

DEFINITION OF TERMS IN GRAMMATICAL ANALYSIS

The Greek is divided into sentences. Each sentence is identified as one of the following:[1]

initial: the first sentence of a paragraph;

additive: a proposition that has no organic relationship with its predecessor; not essential; an addition (e.g., introduced by "and");

adversative: a proposition that changes the direction of the argument; almost a negation ("but, however, yet, on the other hand, only, still");

alternative: a proposition that may be substituted for the previous one ("or, in other words");

causal: any proposition that provides the cause of a preceding conclusion ("for");

explanatory: a restatement, definition, or expansion of the previous proposition ("in other words, that is");

illustrative: an illustration or instance ("for example, for instance"); or

illative: the conclusion ("therefore, consequently, so, thus, hence").

---

1.   See further Spencer 1998a, 30–32; Trimmer 2004, 480–81.

Each grammatical sentence begins with the letter "a." The punctuation and numbering of the sentences follow the fifth revised edition of *The Greek New Testament* (2014), except for phrases in apposition. The translations of the Greek text aim to reflect the Greek word order whenever possible.

Each Greek sentence is separated into clauses.

A clause contains a subject and a finite verb. The verb can be elliptical (implied). Greek participles and infinitives are not finite verbs unless they function as genitive absolute,[2] accusative absolute,[3] infinitive with its own subject in the accusative case,[4] or imperatival infinitive.[5] Clauses are identified as one of the following:

A *main clause* is an independent clause, a complete sentence that makes an independent statement. A sentence must have at least one main clause, but a sentence can have more than one main clause.

A *subordinate clause* is a dependent clause. By itself it does not make an independent statement. There are four types of subordinate clauses: adverbial, adjectival, noun, and parenthetical (see definitions below).

A *relative clause* may be an adjectival, adverbial, or noun clause (see definitions below).

An *adjectival clause* is a subordinate clause modifying a noun or pronoun. Adjectival clauses answer "which, that, who."

A *noun clause* is a subordinate clause serving as subject, object, or complement in a sentence. Noun clauses answer "who, that, about, what."

A *parenthetical clause* is a clause placed as an explanation or a comment within an already complete sentence. It is the rarest of all clauses.

---

2. A genitive absolute has a noun or pronoun and participle in the genitive cases disconnected from the rest of the sentence, e.g., Matt. 9:33.
3. An accusative absolute has a noun or pronoun and participle in the accusative cases disconnected from the rest of the sentence, e.g., Acts 26:3.
4. E.g., James 1:18; 3:3; 4:15.
5. Infinitive as a command, e.g., James 1:1; Phil. 3:16.

An *adverbial clause* is a subordinate clause modifying a verb, adjective, or adverb in a way that is:

causal: the clause states or implies the cause, ground, or reason for the assertion contained in another clause, beginning with words such as "because, since";

comparative: the clause introduces an analogous thought for the purpose of elucidating or emphasizing the thought expressed in the principal clause, beginning with words such as "like, such as, just as";

conditional: the clause introduces a condition or supposition and, if fulfilled, leads to certain results, beginning with words such as "if";

final: the clause explains aim and end and may be divided into purpose (aim, intention of the action of the main verb, beginning with words such as "in order to, with the purpose that") or result (that which is consequent upon or issues from the action of the main verb, beginning with words such as "so that, with the result that");

local: the clause is introduced by a relative adverb of place indicating "where"; or

temporal: the clause defines a thought by means of its temporal relations indicating "when." Adverbial clauses answer "how, in what manner, where, when, because, as, if, since, though, why, whether, that, just, than, before, even, until, so, while." It is the most common type of subordinate clause.

INTRODUCTION

AUTHORSHIP

Determining authorship is a foundational issue for the letter of James. Who the author is affects dating and setting. We will begin our search with data from the letter, then look at early church traditions about authorship, and then compare this data to the New Testament and extrabiblical information. I will present my conclusions on authorship, date, and setting, and then look at alternate theories on authorship and explain why I think what I accept is to be preferred. Several possibilities for authorship have been proposed: James, the Lord's brother (which I prefer); James, the brother of John; James, the son of Alphaeus; James, the Lord's brother, plus an editor; and a pseudonymous author using the name "James."

The Letter of James on Its Author

The letter begins: "James, a slave of God and of the Lord Jesus Christ" (1:1). The Greek form, Ἰάκωβος, replaces the Hebrew Ἰακώβ[1] and was applied to other Jews in the first century, such as James son of Zebedee (Ἰάκωβος, Matt. 4:21). The James of our letter humbly describes himself simply as a "slave" (δοῦλος), emphasizing of whom he is a slave: "of God and of the Lord Jesus Christ" (1:1). Thus, he is a disciple of Jesus, whom he describes as equal with God (see also 2:1).[2] He also describes himself as a teacher (διδάσκαλος, 3:1) who exhorts his readers to be wise (1:5; 3:13, 15–17), guarding their speaking.[3] Truth is important to him (3:14). Maturity and

---

1. E.g., Gen. 25:26 LXX; Matt. 1:2; Robertson 1933, 10.
2. See exposition of James 1:1.
3. James 1:19, 26; 2:12; 3:2, 5–10; 5:12.

integration in faith are major issues.[4] He is impatient with ambivalence (1:8; 4:8), evil,[5] self-deception (1:16), and slander (3:17; 4:11–12).

He is a Messianic Jew who describes Abraham as the "father" or ancestor of himself and the readers (2:21). He uses many Old Testament people as positive illustrations: Abraham, Rahab, Job, Elijah, and the prophets as a group.[6] The Old Testament is authoritative for him,[7] and he has a positive view of the law of freedom.[8] He believes in only one God (2:19) who is generous, fully good, compassionate, and worthy of blessing, full confidence, and love.[9] Humans should exhibit humility and dependence toward such a great God.[10] Trusting prayer is very effective with God (5:13–18).

James's language is direct. After his introductory sentence, he immediately begins with a command: "consider for yourselves" (1:2). His letter has many imperatives: sixty-seven.[11] Twenty-five percent of all finite verbs in James are imperatives (sixty-seven out of 264 finite verbs). His use of imperatives is similar to Paul's use in the letter to the Philippians (16 or 23 percent of Phil. 3:2–4:13). Only with a receptive as well as intimate audience can a person be so "bold" as to exhort so directly. The readers need exhortation and encouragement, and James the author has a claim on those to whom he writes.[12] Therefore, although James may be humble, he writes in a familial and an authoritative manner.

Paul and James address their readers as equals, as "brothers and sisters," frequently and in an affectionate manner. But James uses it a total of fifteen times, the most of any New Testament writer.[13] The total number is surpassed by 1 Corinthians (twenty times); however, 1 Corinthians is a letter with sixteen chapters, more than four times as long as James's letter (437 verses vs. 108). In addition, James's affection is shown by his frequent use of the modifiers "my" and "beloved" (eleven times), more than any other New Testament letter.

---

4. James 1:4, 12, 19, 22–26; 2:14, 17, 20, 22; 3:2; 5:15–16, 19–20.
5. James 1:14–15; 2:9; 3:15–16; 4:1–4, 8, 17; 5:15–16, 19–20.
6. James 2:21–25; 5:10–11, 17–18.
7. E.g., James 2:8, 11, 23, 25; 4:5–6.
8. James 1:25; 2:9–12; 4:11–12.
9. James 1:5, 12–13, 17–18, 27; 2:5; 3:9; 5:11.
10. James 3:13; 4:6–10, 14, 16.
11. See Appendix.
12. Spencer 1998a, 126–27, 184. In contrast, the use of imperatives in Romans 8:9–39 and 2 Corinthians 11:16–12:13 is much less—respectively, two and zero.
13. First Thessalonians is close, with fourteen references to ἀδελφοί in five chapters.

	Use of "Brothers and Sisters" as Address (Vocative)[14] (Total number, followed by specific passages)			
Letter	"brothers & sisters" 'αδελφοί	"my brothers & sisters" 'αδελφοί μου	"(my) beloved brothers & sisters" 'αδελφοί (μου) 'αγαπητοί, 'αδελφοί 'ηγαπημένοι	Total[15]
Rom.	8 (1:13; 7:1; 8:12; 10:1; 11:25; 12:1; 15:30; 16:17)	2 (7:4; 15:14)	0	10
1 Cor.	16 (1:10, 26; 2:1; 3:1; 4:6; 7:24, 29; 10:1; 12:1; 14:6, 20, 26; 15:1, 31, 50; 16:15)	3 (1:11; 11:33; 14:39)	1 (15:58)	20
2 Cor.	3 (1:8; 8:1; 13:11)	0	0	3
Gal.	9 (1:11; 3:15; 4:12, 28, 31; 5:11, 13; 6:1, 18)	0	0	9
Eph.	0	0	0	0
Phil.	4 (1:12; 3:13, 17; 4:8)	1 (3:1)	1 (4:1)	6

14. See also the table "Gender Language in James Chapter 1."
15. Figures are from the UBS 4th ed. Greek text.

	"brothers & sisters" 'αδελφοί	"my brothers & sisters" 'αδελφοί μου	"(my) beloved brothers & sisters" 'αδελφοί (μου) 'αγαπητοί, 'αδελφοί 'ηγαπημένοι	Total[15]
Use of "Brothers and Sisters" as Address (Vocative)[14] (Total number, followed by specific passages)				
Letter				
Col.	0	0	0	0
1 Thess.	13 (2:1, 9, 14, 17; 3:7; 4:1, 10, 13; 5:1, 4, 12, 14, 25)	0	1 (1:4)	14
2 Thess.	6 (1:3; 2:1, 15; 3:1, 6, 13)	0	1 (2:13)	7
1, 2 Tim., Titus	0	0	0	0
Philem.	2 (7, 20)	0	0	2
Heb.	4 (3:1, 12; 10:19; 13:22)	0		4
James	4 (4:11; 5:7, 9, 10)	8 (1:2; 2:1, 14; 3:1, 10, 12; 5:12, 19)	3 (1:16, 19; 2:5)	15
1 Peter	0	0	0	0
2 Peter	1 (1:10)	0	0	1
1 John	1 (3:13)	0	0	1
2, 3 John	0	0	0	0
Jude, Rev.	0	0	0	0

James is concerned for the poor among his readers and exhorts people in the community to demonstrate humility, respect, impartiality, and justice toward them.[16] He values physical as well as spiritual health (5:13–16). His use of images and illustrations are creative and fresh. He uses many metaphors, similes, and illustrations from nature, including references to water,[17] winds (1:6; 3:4), fire (3:5–6), plants (1:10–11; 3:5, 12), animals (1:8; 3:7–8), horses (1:26; 3:2–3), the home (1:23–25), birth (1:15, 18), farming and agriculture (1:17–18, 21; 3:17–18; 5:7, 18), boating (3:4), landowners and laborers (5:4–7), and merchants (4:13). He also coins many new words.[18] In summary, as a prophet, he calls for repentance (5:1–6); as a teacher, he educates (3:1–4); as a pastor, he exhorts; as an artist, he creates.

Early Church Traditions about the Letter of James

The internal data from the letter suggests a humble Messianic Jew who writes in an authoritative and didactic yet pastoral and prophetic manner to other Jews. The early church traditions support James, the Lord's brother, as the author. Even critics of the traditional view, such as James Hardy Ropes, concede: "In general there was no departure from the traditional view; and down to the sixteenth century, if nothing to the contrary is indicated, a reference to 'James the apostle' as author of the epistle is to be taken as meaning James the Lord's brother. . . . Modern Protestant criticism of the epistle begins with the first edition of DeWette's *Einleitung*, 1826."[19]

Origen, who lived in the second-third century (AD 185–253) is the earliest writer to cite "the apostle James," the Lord's brother, as author, specifically quote the letter, and describe the letter as canonical. He cites passages such as "faith apart from works is dead" (James 2:17).[20] Portions of James are retained in early papyri[20] and p[23], which date from the third century. Papyrus[23], dated AD 250–300, contains James 1:10–12, 15–18, and papyrus[20], dated 275, contains James 2:19–3:9. Both are Alexandrian text-types, which are considered the most

---

16. James 1:9–10, 26–27; 2:1–9, 15–16; 5:1–4.
17. James 1:6; 3:11–12; 4:14; 5:7, 17–18.
18. See "Unusual Words or Phrases in James" in the Appendix. See also Mayor's fine summary of James's style (1913, cclix): "Whatever he says, he says forcibly. . . . He wastes no words . . . richly endowed with a high poetical imagination and all a prophet's indignation against wrong-doing and hypocrisy, is now softened and controlled by the gentler influences of the wisdom which cometh from above."
19. Ropes, 1916, 45, 46.
20. *Hist. eccl.* 6.14.1; *Hom. Josh.* 10.2; *Comm. Jo.* 19.6; and others, cited by Mayor 1913, lxxxi–lxxxii.

accurate.[21] Careful professional scribes copied these manuscripts for churches to be read aloud.[22] Papyrus[100] from the third-fourth century, also Alexandrian, contains James 3:13–4:4 and 4:9–5:1. Papyrus[20] and p[23] are some of the earliest Greek New Testament manuscripts.[23] The third-century *Epistles to Virgins* (1.11.4) also cites James.[24]

But even before Origen, unusual words in James were cited by Christians in the first and second centuries (see Appendix). Clement of Rome (ca. AD 95–97) and Shepherd of Hermas (1–2 c.) use the word "two-willed" (δίψυχος, James 1:8; 4:8).[25] Polycarp, writing to the Philippians (ca. 117), cites "to bridle" (χαλιναγωγέω, James 1:26; 3:2) and "partiality" (προσωπολημψία, James 2:1) (Pol. *Phil.* 5:3; 6:1). Shepherd of Hermas (1–2 c.) refers to "compassionate" (πολύσπλαγχνος, James 5:11).[26] Barnabas (ca. 70–135) probably alludes to James 1:21 when he refers to "the one who placed within us the *implanted* [ἔμφυτος] gift of his covenant" (Barn. 9:9).

By the third and fourth centuries, many well known Christians quote James directly, such as Dionysius of Alexandria (264), Gregory Thaumaturgus (270), Methodius of Olympus (3rd c.), Lactantius (300), Hilary of Poitiers (367), Athanasius of Alexandria (373), Cyril of Jerusalem (386), Gregory of Nazianzus (390), Didymus (398), and John Chrysostom (407). J. B. Mayor cites as well numerous allusions to James's letter from AD 95–394.[27]

The historian Eusebius of Caesarea (AD 260–339), who collected the early traditions about the church, states that few ancients quote James and thus its authenticity is denied by some, but "we know that these letters have been used publicly with the rest in most churches" (*Hist. eccl.* 2.23.24–25). He also notes it is "the first of the Epistles called Catholic." When he summarizes the New Testament canon, he lists two categories of "disputed" books. James, Jude, 2 Peter, 2 and 3 John, although disputed, were "known to most" and "according to the tradition of the church" were also considered "true, genuine, and recognized." Other "disputed" books were neither "genuine" nor canonical

---

21. They may be found in Grenfell and Hunt 1912, 1914, 9:9–11; 10:16–18.
22. Comfort 1992, 21, 57, 63–64, 67.
23. Comfort 1992, 31–33.
24. James 3:1–2; Dibelius 1976, 51; Ropes 1916, 94.
25. 1 Clem. 11:2; 23:3. Δίψυχος is a frequent word in Herm. Vis. 2.2:4; 3.4:3, 7:1; 4.2:6. *Commandments* and *Parables* use this noun thirteen more times. See also Laws 1980, 22–23.
26. Herm. Sim. 5.7:4; πολυσπλαγχνία: Herm. Vis. 1.3:2; 2.2.8; 4.2:3; πολυεύσπλαγχνος: Herm. Mand. 4.3:5; 9.2.
27. Mayor 1913, lxviii–lxxxiv.

but familiar to most of the writers of the church: the Acts of Paul, the Shepherd of Hermas, the Apocalypse of Peter, Barnabas, and Teachings of the Apostles. None of these fit under the "heretical" books category, "put forward by heretics under the name of the apostles," such as the Gospels of Peter, Thomas, Matthias, and Acts of Andrew and John: "To none of these has any who belonged to the succession of the orthodox ever thought it right to refer in his writings" (*Hist. eccl.* 3.25.3–7). Thus, although James was not included in Eusebius's category of "Recognized Books," Eusebius did consider it "true, genuine, and recognized" (*Hist. eccl.* 3.25.6).[28] All the books included in his disputed section are short books. In addition, the second fall of Jerusalem in AD 135 must have seriously disrupted the presence of Jews in Jerusalem, which may have affected the promotion of James's letter written to diaspora Jews. The placement of the letter of James as the "frontispiece" of the Catholic Epistles, some suggest, is best explained by the "decisive role played by James at the conference in Acts 15."[29]

The letter of James was affirmed as canonical by Origen (253/54), Cyril of Jerusalem (386), Gregory of Nazianzus (390), Athanasius (373), Epiphanius (403), Jerome (419/420), Augustine (430), the Synod of Hippo (393), the Third Council of Carthage (397), and the Apostolic Constitutions (380).[30] Mayor has noted the similarities between the letter of James and James's words at the Jerusalem Council (Acts 15:13–29). The parallels do not prove the letter of James is by the speaker in Acts (a large sample of writing, 100,000 words, is needed for that),[31] but they do confirm the historical data assigning authorship to the same person. Donald Guthrie concludes that the parallels are "indisputable" and "remarkable in that they all occur within so short a passage attributed to James in Acts and because they are of such a character that they cannot be explained by the common accidents of speech."[32] For instance, both letters begin with "greeting" (χαίρειν, James 1:1; Acts 15:23), and both use words such as "brothers and sisters" (ἀδελφοί, Acts 15:13, 23; James 4:11; 5:7, 9, 10), "beloved" (ἀγαπητοῖς, Acts 15:25; James 1:16, 19; 2:5), "called by name" (ἐπικαλέω ὄνομα, Acts 15:17; James 2:7), "hear my brothers and sisters" (ἀκούσατε, ἀδελφοί, Acts 15:13; James 2:5; 5:10, 14), "visited"

---

28. Mayor also notes that Eusebius himself cites James as Scripture spoken by the holy Apostle (1913, lxvii).
29. Goswell 2016, 78.
30. Mayor 1913, lxviii–lxix; lxxxiii–lxxxiv; cxliv; Goswell 2016, 78.
31. Spencer 1998a, 149.
32. Guthrie 1970, 742.

(ἐπισκέπτω, Acts 15:14; James 1:27), and "turn" (ἐπιστρέφω, Acts 15:19; James 5:20). Two hundred and thirty words in the speech and letter in Acts 15 reappear in the letter of James.[33]

New Testament Information on James

The New Testament refers to three men by the name of "James" (Ἰάκωβος) who might have authored the letter of James: two are members of the twelve; all are "apostles."[34] James, son of Alphaeus, is mentioned but is not prominent.[35] James the fisherman, brother of John and son of Zebedee and Salome, is prominent in the Gospels but is killed by Herod Agrippa (Acts 12:2). James, the brother of Jesus, is mentioned by name at one incident in the Gospels, but after the resurrection his prominence increases. When Jesus is in his hometown of Nazareth, his brothers are specifically named (James, Joseph, Simon, and Judas) and his sisters are mentioned (Matt. 13:55–56; Mark 6:3), as well as the fact that their father Joseph worked as a carpenter or builder.[36] James is mentioned as one of the siblings in five other incidents reported in the Gospels. Jesus traveled with his disciples, his mother Mary, and his brothers (and probably sisters) to Cana in Galilee for a wedding and returned together with them to Capernaum (John 2:1–12). This means that James witnessed Jesus's first sign, his miraculous changing of water to wine. Later, James, his brothers (and probably sisters), and mother Mary were in the midst of a large crowd hearing the questions directed to Jesus by some Pharisees and teachers. While they waited to speak to him, Jesus tells their messenger that his real mother, brothers, and sisters are those who do the will of his heavenly Father (Matt. 12:38, 46–50). When some teachers of the law were claiming Jesus was possessed by Beelzebub, the family went to seize him because people were saying he was out of his mind (Mark 3:20–35). After Jesus finished teaching about the parable of the sower and the importance of listening, again his family wanted to see him. Probably three times Jesus repeated in their presence that his real mother and siblings were those who heard the word of God and did it (Luke 8:4–21). Hearing and doing God's word will become a major theme of James's letter. If Jesus's family may have been more positive

---

33. Mayor 1913, iii–iv.
34. Not relevant are James, Judas's father (Luke 6:16; Acts 1:13), and James the younger, the son of the "other" Mary and brother of Joseph (Matt. 27:56; Mark 15:40; 16:1; Luke 24:10).
35. Matt. 10:3; Mark 3:18; Luke 6:15; Acts 1:13.
36. Τέκτων, LSJ, 1769; BDAG, 995.

in his early ministry, the gospel writer John notes that eventually they did not believe in Jesus and, as a consequence, his siblings chided him to go with them to Judea at the Festival of Booths to show himself to the world (John 7:3–10).

The many allusions to Jesus's teachings in James's letter[37] indicate that James heard many of his brother's teachings, even though he may not have believed all his claims at the time. A radical change is witnessed in Acts 1:14 when Mary and her children are included with the eleven apostles in an upper room in Jerusalem (a crowd of 120) gathered in prayer waiting for the "promise of the Father," baptism with the Holy Spirit (Acts 1:4–5, 12–15). The apostle Paul adds the key missing incident: Jesus appeared to James after his resurrection (1 Cor. 15:7). Sometime after Pentecost, James becomes an authoritative figure in the church in Jerusalem. When Peter is released from prison by an angel and describes this event to the household of Mary, mother of John Mark, he tells the crowd to inform James and the others what happened (Acts 12:17). When Paul first goes to Jerusalem for two weeks, he visits only Peter and James (Gal. 1:18–19). He describes James, Cephas (Peter), and John as the "acknowledged pillars." They affirm Paul's ministry to the Gentiles while James and Peter would themselves prioritize outreach to Jews. They ask only that Paul remember the poor (Gal. 2:9–10). James's letter is indeed a letter to other Messianic Jews, with emphasis on care for the poor. When Paul and Barnabas want to resolve the issue of whether converted Gentiles had to be circumcised, they again go to Jerusalem to see the "apostles and elders." James becomes the spokesperson for the group in replying to Peter, Barnabas, and Paul. He proclaims that he has passed this judgment on the matter: "We should not trouble those Gentiles who are turning to God" (Acts 15:19). He proposes a compromise to maintain fellowship between believing Gentiles and Jews. The concluding solution from the group is almost identical to James's original proposal (Acts 15:1–29; 21:25). After Paul arrives in Jerusalem, before his arrest, within a day he visits James and the elders. The group affirms Paul and his team's ministry among the Gentiles, but they do not want the converted Jews zealous for the law to think that Paul himself does not observe the law (Acts 21:17–26).

Thus, the New Testament view of James, the Lord's brother, is commensurate with the James of the letter. He is someone who has undergone a phenomenal transformation, which has resulted in

---

37. The exposition of James will indicate these many allusions. Also, see excursus "James Shows Christ."

humility. Yet, as a leader of the church, he is comfortable with his own ecclesial authority. Even his own brother Jude defines himself with respect to James (Jude 1). But both of them humbly describe themselves simply as "slaves" of Jesus Christ. James's ministry is mainly to fellow Jewish converts. He is gracious and compassionate, yet firm. As Jesus's brother, he has heard Jesus's preaching and Mary's teachings, as illustrated in the Magnificat, which he echoes throughout his letter.[38]

Eusebius and Josephus on James

James's ecclesial authority is affirmed in early writings outside the New Testament, and many of the qualities seen in his letter were observed. Eusebius mentions many times that James was the first elected to be bishop of the church in Jerusalem.[39] Repeatedly, he was called the "Just" (δίκαιος), a quality he esteems in his letter.[40] Eusebius summarizes that James was "believed to be most righteous because of the height which he had reached in a life of philosophy and religion" (*Hist. eccl.* 2.23.2). His fluid Greek style is evidence of his scholarly aptitudes. He was known also as no respecter of persons (*Hist. eccl.* 2.23.10). James was renowned for his prayer. Hegesippus wrote that James used to be found in the temple "kneeling and praying for forgiveness for the people, so that his knees grew hard like a camel's because of his constant worship of God, kneeling and asking forgiveness for the people" (*Hist. eccl.* 2.23.6). At his death, although dying because he confessed that "our Lord and Savior Jesus Christ is the Son of God," he prayed for his killers: "Forgive them, for they know not what they do" (*Hist. eccl.* 2.23.2, 16).

James was the first Hebrew bishop in Jerusalem, but, after the second Jewish revolt, Hebrew bishops ceased (*Hist. eccl.* 4.5), and thus their important testimony was missing from the great councils of Nicaea and Chalcedon. But his witness remains in the canon for Jew and Gentile to read today.

DATE AND SETTING OF THE LETTER OF JAMES

If James, the Lord's brother, is the writer of the letter of James, then the date of the letter must precede his death. James's death is one of the more firm New Testament dates because he died shortly after Roman governor Porcius Festus died, and therefore before his replacement Albinus arrived. Festus is mentioned in Acts 25–26; he died in

---

38. See exposition of James 1:9–11.
39. *Hist. eccl.* 2.1; 2:23; 3.5; 4.5; 7.19.
40. James 1:20; 2:21, 23–25; 3:18; 5:6, 16.

AD 62.[41] Hegesippus, in agreement with Clement, cited by Eusebius, gives a full account of his martyrdom at the temple in Jerusalem (*Hist. eccl.* 2.23.10–19).

The dispersion to which James refers is probably the earliest one that affected the Messianic Jews in Jerusalem (Acts 8:1).[42] Since James writes to a Jewish church still meeting in synagogues (2:2) and does not refer to any of the issues that become so important later (e.g., must the converted Gentiles be circumcised and follow the Old Testament laws of cleanliness?), most likely, then, he wrote his letter between Acts 8:1–14:28, ca. AD 34–48, before the Jerusalem Council cited in Acts 15. The Roman emperors during that time period were Tiberius (AD 14–27), Gaius (Caligula) (AD 37–41), and Claudius (AD 41–54). Herod Agrippa I was king in AD 37, 40–44 and Herod Agrippa II in AD 50–92/93. Procurators were: Marullus (AD 37–41), Cuspius Fadus (AD 44–46), and Tiberius Iulius Alexander (AD 46–48).

From James's letter we learn that the Jewish readers were in diaspora and in trials (1:1–2). Economically, the churches had both rich and poor, teachers, merchants, landowners, and farm laborers.[43] The poor included orphans and widows (1:27) and those without sufficient food to eat or water for cleaning (2:2, 15). Jeremias includes in the category of "wealthy" those who had property both in Jerusalem and the countryside, rulers, merchants, landowners, tax-farmers, bankers, Jews of private means, temple officials, and the priestly aristocracy. Nicodemus and Joseph of Arimathea are examples of wealthy landowners. The middle class included retail traders and craftsmen.[44] The majority of the priests lived in poverty, as did widows, slaves, and day laborers.[45] There was often animosity between the high priests and the ordinary priests. Josephus cites an incident, during the time of Governor Felix, when the high priests sent "slaves to the threshing floors to receive the tithes that

---

41. Hammond and Scullard 1970, 435; *Hist. eccl.* 2.23.21–24; *Ant.* 20.9.197–203.
42. See exposition of James 1:1.
43. James 1:9–10; 2:2–3, 6, 15; 3:1; 4:13; 5:1–4.
44. Jeremias 1969, 95–100.
45. Jeremias 1969, 108–11. Gerhard Lenski suggests up to 10 percent of the population in the first-century Mediterranean world could have been poor and/or sick enough for their lives to be in jeopardy (Blomberg and Kamell 2008, 30). Some divide ancient society into five levels: 3 percent truly wealthy—political and military elite; 7–15 percent well-to-do veterans, merchants, and traders; 22–27 percent economically stable merchants, traders, farmers, and artisans; 30–40 percent subsistence-level workers and wage earners; 25–28 percent truly poor (Verbrugge and Krell 2015, 108–11).

were due to the priests, with the result that the poorer priests starved to death" (*Ant.* 20.8.8.181). Jesus's family was probably between the lower and middle class. Joseph, as an artisan, may have fit in the middle class, but Mary's sacrifice for Jesus's purification was that offered by the poor (Luke 2:22–24; Lev. 12:6–8).

The spiritual difficulties mentioned in James's letter include sinful internal desires, anger, hearing but not doing the word, partiality to the wealthy, the need for mercy, not controlling the tongue, cursing people, envy, selfish ambition and competition, asking for wrong desires, friendship with the world, haughtiness, lack of perseverance, and swearing.[46] Their doctrine about monotheism was correct (2:19), but not their practice.

If it is true that James writes to diaspora Jews before the issue of the inclusion of Gentiles becomes prominent, then the letter needs to be set between Acts 8–15. Acts 8–15 can be divided into several stages, as seen from the perspective of the apostles in Jerusalem. Even though James is not mentioned until Acts 12:17, he would most likely be present whenever "apostles" (and probably "elders") in Jerusalem are mentioned.

Early Stages in Development in Acts 8:1–15:35

1. *Persecution of the church in Jerusalem after Stephen is martyred, led by Saul* (8:1–40, ca. AD 34)
   a. The "apostles" remain in Jerusalem while other Messianic Jews disperse to Judea and Samaria (8:1–3).
   b. Philip preaches in Samaria. When the "apostles" hear of the Samaritans becoming believers, they delegate Peter and John to check them out. They return to Jerusalem (8:4–25).
   c. Philip goes to Azotus and Caesarea (8:26–40). This must have been a time of great shock and mourning at the death of Stephen (8:2) and fear and anxiety, particularly fear of Saul coming to one's house (8:3). Yet also it would be a time of excitement as the good news is spread (8:4), miracles of exorcism and healing are witnessed (8:6–7, 13), and people are led by the Holy Spirit (8:39).
2. *Saul extends persecution of Christians outside of Jerusalem* to places of "safety," such as Damascus, but then returns to Jerusalem a follower of Christ (9:1–29; ca. AD 35). The terror

---

46. James 1:14–15, 20; 2:3, 9, 13, 22; 3:2, 8–9, 13–14, 16; 4:1–6, 16; 5:8, 12.

of Saul's extension of persecution of women as much as men (8:3; 9:2) throughout the provinces is then followed by the shocking rumors of his change. Saul is then persecuted himself by Hellenists (9:29).

3. *The church experiences a time of peace* in Judea, Galilee, and Samaria after Paul leaves for Tarsus (9:30–43). Peter travels to Lydda and Joppa (9:32–43). The church grows.

4. *Gentiles begin to be converted* in Judea with Cornelius in Caesarea (10:1–11:18). Peter's views about Gentiles are transformed. The "apostles" hear that Gentiles have converted and the circumcision party criticizes Peter (11:1–3), but his testimony is positively received in Jerusalem (11:18).

5. *The diaspora Messianic Jews spread out, traveling to Phoenicia, Cyprus, and Antioch* (11:19–30). They preach to Gentiles, who are converted, in Antioch. When the church in Jerusalem hears of this, it sends Barnabas to Antioch to check it out. Barnabas brings Paul from Tarsus to teach with him at Antioch (11:25–26). Agabus warns the church in Antioch of a future famine in Judea. Barnabas and Paul bring relief to elders in Judea (11:27–30). The famine occurs in AD 46–47.

6. *King Herod initiates persecution against Messianic Jews in Jerusalem* (12:1–25, AD 37–44). James, the brother of John, is killed and Peter is arrested (12:2–3). James is told of Peter's release (12:17). The church must have been terrified of this return to persecution. Food is scarce in Tyre and Sidon (12:20).

7. *Barnabas and Paul are sent by the Holy Spirit from Antioch to Cyprus and South Galatia* (13:1–14:28, AD 47–48). They first preach to Jews, then to Gentiles (13:46–47). They learn that hardship precedes entrance into God's reign (14:22).

8. *The earlier criticism from the circumcision party* (11:3) *escalates*, as Pharisee Christians insist that Gentiles must be circumcised and obey the laws of cleanliness in order to be saved (15:1–35, AD 48–49). Paul and Barnabas travel to Jerusalem to resolve the issue. James affirms their ministry but recommends guidelines.

The issue of Gentiles begins to become prominent in stage 4 (Acts 10), but it escalates at stage 8 (Acts 15). Thus, Acts chapters 8–9 (stages 1–3) fit the context of James's letter best, although stages 4–7 are possible. By stage 8, the place of Gentiles in the church has become a major issue. The "trials" the Jewish church endures appear to change at this period.

During these years (AD 34–48), Israel has had to experience brigands, crucifixions, friction with Roman authorities about the temple, and uprisings (*Ant.* 20.1, 2). There was also a major famine in Judaea (AD 46–47). During Gaius Caligula's reign, the Jews in Alexandria, Egypt, were persecuted by Gentiles. Gaius wanted to install statues of himself in the synagogues in Alexandria and in the temple in Jerusalem. But Emperor Claudius restored religious rights to the Alexandrian Jews.[47] Before the war in AD 66, there was a chasm between the rich and poor. Landowners were able to amass much land and were harsh with hired laborers. After the war against Rome, all were affected economically. By the end of the war, the countryside and Jerusalem were destroyed.[48]

Since James stayed in Jerusalem, the letter was written from that city. Israel was a land of springs, figs, and olives (3:11–12),[49] near the sea (1:6; 3:4). It was renowned for its early (October) and late (April) rain (5:7), characteristic of Israel, not Egypt, Italy, or Asia Minor.[50]

Alternate Theories on Authorship

Although many commentators agree that James the Lord's brother wrote the letter early in his ministry,[51] some commentators have proposed alternate theories.

1. James the son of Zebedee and Salome, brother of John, wrote the letter. This view was proposed by Isidore of Seville (d. AD 636) according to a subscription in a tenth-century Latin Codex Corbeiensis. This theory was followed through the seventeenth century by Spanish writers and assumed in Dante's *Paradise* 25 and by Martin Luther.[52]

   Since Herod Agrippa I (who killed this James) himself died in AD 44, the letter would be very early (before Acts 12). This theory has no early church attestation. Acts does not present this

---

47. *J.W.* 2.10.1–5.184–203; Schürer 1973–79, 1:389–94, 446.
48. *J.W.* 5.12.3.511–26; 6.1.1; 7.1. See also Davids 1982, 30–32.
49. Olive trees abounded in Galilee, Samaria, and Judea. The fig is prominent in Mediterranean countries (Zohary 1982, 56, 58).
50. Joel 2:23; Vlachos 2013, 4; Davids 1982, 14.
51. E.g., McCartney 2009, 30–32; Hiebert 1979, 25, 41; Robertson 1933, 4–5; Vlachos 2013, 5–6; Kistemaker 1986, 19; James 2005, 1738; Mayor 1913, cxliv–cl; Guthrie 1970, 758, 764; Maynard-Reid 1987, 8. A few argue for James writing the letter after the Jerusalem Council, such as Witherington 2007, 401. Foster 2014, 24, leaves the date open.
52. Ropes 1916, 45; Dibelius 1976, 55; Manton 1693, 13.

James as prominent in the early church. Therefore, even Martin Dibelius declares that James, the brother of Jesus, is the "only *one* person of reputation in primitive Christianity who could have been suggested by the way in which his name appears."[53]

2. A few suggest that James the son of Alphaeus, one of the Twelve, wrote the letter. This view was proposed by Thomas Manton (d. 1620): "No epistle but theirs [of apostles] being received into the rule of faith."[54] John Calvin was inclined to agree: "I am therefore rather inclined to the conjecture, that he of whom Paul speaks was the son of Alphaeus. I do not yet deny that another was the ruler of the Church at Jerusalem." Yet, he goes on, "The ancients are nearly unanimous in thinking that [the author] was one of the disciples named Oblias and a relative of Christ, who was set over the Church at Jerusalem."[55] Calvin himself admits that the view that James son of Alphaeus was the author of the letter has no early attestation. Acts does not present this James as prominent in the early church. In addition, the New Testament does not limit "apostles" to the Twelve, but rather the term includes witnesses of Jesus's resurrection.[56] Therefore, James can be called an "apostle" (Gal. 1:19).[57]

3. James, the Lord's brother, plus an editor[58] or an unknown author wrote the letter, possibly called "James," or writing in James's name.[59]

---

53. Dibelius 1976, 12. Vlachos adds that James the son of Zebedee did not have "the authoritative influence to issue an encyclical of this tone. . . . Only this James [the Lord's brother] would have been well enough known to have required no identification beyond his mere name in the letter's greeting" (2013, 3). Also, Paul mentions James first in the list of pillars of the church in Jerusalem (Gal. 2:9, 12).
54. Manton 1693, 12.
55. Calvin n.d., 2552. Jerome identified the son of Alphaeus as brother of the Lord in *De perpetua virginitate B. Mariae* (Dibelius 1976, 12, 54; Ropes 1916, 57–58).
56. E.g., Acts 1:21–22; 1 Cor. 9:1. See Spencer 2005, 133–40.
57. As did Origen (Ropes 1916, 93).
58. E.g., Davids 1982, 12–13.
59. Those who argue for a pseudonymous author are, e.g., Laws 1980, 41; Painter and deSilva 2012, 25; Dibelius 1976, 18–19; Ropes 1916, 47; Eisenman 1997, 10; Hartin 2004, 93; Boring 2012, 438–39.

However, a pseudonymous writer is unlikely to use such a simple self-designation as "James, a slave" for himself.[60] For instance, the Gospel of Thomas (2nd c.) describes the leader who will replace Jesus as "James the righteous, for whose sake heaven and earth came into being" (log. 12). The apostle Paul warned his readers about pseudonymous letters (2 Thess. 2:2–3; 3:17) and exhorted them instead to be truthful (e.g., Eph. 4:15, 25; Col. 3:9). The early church also used authenticity as a criteria for the canon. For instance, the elder in Asia who wrote the fictional Acts of Paul resigned from office after confessing he had "wrongly inscribed" it with Paul's name.[61] Moreover, why should we designate the author of James as pseudonymous or unknown when we have strong evidence for James, the Lord's brother?

The reasons some commentators do not recognize James, Jesus's brother, as the author of the letter may be summarized under four broad concerns.[62]

1. *The letter appears to be disconnected in thought.* Martin Dibelius developed this hypothesis. *Paraenesis* is a series of sayings, or brief moral teachings, without continuity in thought: "*It is not possible to construct a single frame into which [the admonitions] will all fit.*" James has "no theology."[63] James has groups and series of sayings with no continuity between them. The text only has catchwords as mnemonic devices. In addition, the letter has no hint of personal reasons that inspired the author to compose the writing, no specific occasion, no epistolary remarks, and no epistolary ending.[64]

   However, since 1976, contrary to Dibelius, numerous commentators have shown that James is a carefully constructed work, especially Peter Davids.[65] For example, Timothy Cargal cites the dissertation by Manabu Tsuji: "Tsuji's work provides

---

60. See also Vlachos 2013, 4; Davids 1982, 9.
61. *Bapt.* 17; Lea 1991, 538–41.
62. Cf. Painter and deSilva 2012, 22–23.
63. Dibelius 1976, 2, 11, 21.
64. Dibelius 1976, 2–6.
65. E.g., Davids 1982, 25–29. This letter as a "tightly woven composition of several related themes" "amptly refutes the once-common dismissal of James as a jumble of disconnected fragments" (Adam 2013, xx).

clear evidence of both the shifting consensus regarding James and of the emerging direction of scholarly research on the book. There has developed in the past two decades widespread agreement that the letter is not simply a hodgepodge of sayings strung together by catchword links, as Dibelius argued. Moreover, there is general agreement among most researchers regarding the general contours of the book's internal structure."[66] Repetition of words does not necessarily mean that they were added later. In this commentary, I will show how each verse relates to its previous verse. The repetition of words is one way James connects the ideas, as do many other New Testament writers. Jesus's sermons do the same.[67]

James fits in the genre of an encyclical letter, a letter sent to a group of people, common among ancient Jews.[68] The occasion for the letter becomes explicit in the imperatives. James is concerned for the Christianity of these diaspora Jewish Christians, which probably was described to him by messengers. Unlike many Hellenistic letters, James lacks a final greeting. However, David Aune discovered that many Hebrew and Hebrew Hellenistic letters do not have any final greetings, dates, or signatures before the Bar Kosiba period (AD 132–35).[69]

2. *The letter appears to be too extensive in Hellenistic thought and form* for the bishop of Jerusalem. In other words, the Greek is of too good a quality for a son of a Jewish carpenter. Some claim that James uses the diatribe form familiar to Greeks, including dialogue with imaginary persons and rhetorical questions emphasizing points already known. According to Aune, the diatribe reflects the oral public preaching style of wandering Cynic and Stoic philosophers who used the Socratic method of censure and persuasion. Their opponents are imaginary and

---

66. Cargal 1999, 568–69.
67. Dibelius 1976 (8–10) himself illustrates this in, for instance, Matt. 6:34 and 31–33; 10:31 and 28, 26; 37 and 35; 12:36 and 34; 13:12 and 11; 18:12–14 and 10, 6–9.
68. E.g., Acts 15:23–29. See also Bauckham 1999, 13; McCartney 2009, 39, 58.
69. Paul, as he reaches out to the Gentile world, follows the Hellenistic style. Aune 1987, 175–80; also, Francis 1970, 125. On ancient letters, see Bateman 2013, ch. 1.

the objections are hypothetical. Ridicule may be used in these brief questions and answers.[70]

However, James's precedent is not necessarily the Socratic style. Rather, his style is more similar to the prophetic style, especially of Malachi, who uses questions and answers to deal with authentic contemporary issues.[71] Although Malachi addresses the nation of Israel and the temple setting, his concerns are similar to James, such as impartiality (Mal. 2:9–10); humility (4:1); importance of education (2:6–8; 4:4); the second coming (3:2; 4:1, 5); paying the hired worker, care of the widow and orphan (3:5); the need for purity and righteousness (1:11–12; 2:17; 3:3, 18; 4:2); and God as "Father" (1:6; 2:10; 3:17), "one" (2:15), and unchangeable (3:6).[72]

Commentators who disagree that James has too extensive a Hellenistic style and thought will also frequently cite parallel Hebrew writers. Adam explains: now there is no longer a "polar contrast between 'Hebrew' and 'Hellenistic' but rather 'varied degrees of Hellenization within Judaism.'"[73] James was reared in bilingual Galilee. Even Greek was common in Israel.[74] By Isaiah's time, the region was called "Galilee of the Gentiles"

---

70. Aune 1987, 200–201; Ropes 1916, 12–15.
71. E. g., Mal. 1:2, 6–8, 13; 2:10, 14–15, 17; 3:7–8, 13–14. See also chapter 2 tables "Sequence of Questions and Statements" in James 2 and Malachi 1.
72. Both James and Malachi use Elijah as an example (James 5:17–18; Mal. 4:5). Martin (1988) agrees that James stands in the "tradition of the Hebrew prophets" of the eighth to sixth centuries BC (156). James also echoes the prophetic and wisdom concerns (content and images) of Isaiah, Jeremiah, and Proverbs. These books emphasize, as does Malachi, justice for the poor and oppressed, especially orphans and widows; righteous behavior; human humility and mortality; faithfulness to God and to one's spouse; and impending judgment and punishment. However, unlike James, Isaiah and Jeremiah focus on Jerusalem, the temple, and condemnations of the nations. In style, they differ in that their prophetic messages come from visions or oracles that are presented in the narratives. Proverbs too has much concern for the poor including orphans and widows, for justice and righteous behavior, and for humble wisdom expressed in the use of the tongue. But it too is centered on the king and Jerusalem. Proverbs is written in tightly worded proverbs, which James does not use. Amos, Hosea, and Zechariah also discuss similar concerns as those of Isaiah and Jeremiah, but not as extensively.
73. Adam 2013, xviii. See also Laws 1980, 36.
74. See also Robertson 1934, 123; Laws 1980, 40.

(Isa. 9:1). Greek was in everyday use by the second century BC. It was needed for marketplace negotiations. The coastal towns and Decapolis were Greek cities. Galilee had many Gentiles and much commerce and travel. In Herodian Israel, writing in Greek, Aramaic, and Hebrew was widespread at all levels of society.[75] Although James has a fluid Greek style, unlike some Greek rhetoricians, he does not use elaborate periods or studied rhetoric.[76] Some commentators who consider James too Hellenistic even find some Semitisms in his writing.[77] Besides being reared in a bilingual area, the Jewish people were (and still are) renowned in their educational achievements. Josephus claims: "Above all we [Jews] pride ourselves on the education of our children, and regard as the most essential task in life the observance of our laws and of the pious practices, based thereupon, which we have inherited," and the Law "orders that [children] shall be taught to read, and shall learn both the laws and the deeds of their ancestors" (*Ag. Ap.* 1.12.60; 2.25.204). In addition, James as a teacher was remembered for his educational achievements. As a leader in Jerusalem, James would meet many Greek-speaking Jews.[78] James would most likely not need a Greek amanuensis.[79]

3. *The letter has few ideas, interests, and allusions peculiar to any particular phase of early Christianity*, such as the temple, circumcision, validity of the law, death of Christ, justification by faith, resurrection, cultic ritualism, the Holy Spirit, or Eucharist.[80] Bart Ehrman agrees: nowhere does "the author

---

75. Millard 2001, 104, 107, 115, 117, 210; Robertson 1934, 27–29. The rabbis had documents (e.g., bills of divorce) written in Greek and Hebrew (m. Git. 9:6, 8). Greek wisdom was even taught alongside Hebrew Scriptures by Rabbi Simeon (Sot. 49b).
76. Mayor 1913, cclv; Robertson 1934, 123. A "period" in rhetoric is a well-rounded sentence in which one to four clauses or phrases have a circular form (Spencer 1998a, 199–201; Lanham 1991, 112–13). See also "Glossary of Stylistic Terms."
77. E.g., "forgetful hearer" 1:25; "royal law" 2:8; "Lord of Sabbath" 5:4; "he prayed fervently" 5:17 (Dibelius 1976, 36–37; Ropes 1916, 26). See also McCartney 2009, 6. Witherington 2007 adds that only thirteen words in James are not found in the LXX (388).
78. See also Guthrie 1970, 748–49.
79. Cf. Davids 1982, 13; Bateman 2013, 56.
80. E.g., Ropes 1916, 27; Marxsen 1970, 229.

claim to be a member of Jesus's family or to have any first-hand knowledge of his teachings." His examples of ethical behavior are drawn not from the lives of Jesus and his apostles, but from the Jewish Scriptures.[81] Martin Luther introduced the first edition of his German New Testament (1522) with: "In fine, Saint John's gospel and his first epistle, Saint Paul's epistles, especially those to the Romans, Galatians, Ephesians, and St. Peter's first epistle,—these are the books which show thee Christ, and teach thee everything that is needful and blessed for thee to know even though thou never see or hear any other book or doctrine. Therefore is Saint James's epistle a right strawy epistle in comparison with them, for it has no gospel character to it. Therefore I will not have it in my Bible in the number of the proper chief books, but do not intend thereby to forbid anyone to place and exalt it as he pleases, for there is many a good saying in it." Luther put James, Jude, Hebrews, and Revelation at the end of the volume and assigned them no numbers in his table of contents. Tyndale followed Luther's example, but wrote: "Me thynketh [James] ought of ryght to be taken for holye Scripture."[82]

Yet, many of James's ethical injunctions are similar to Jesus's own teachings as preserved in the Gospels, as we shall see in the exposition of the text.[83] There are many affinities to the gospel of Matthew, especially Matthew's Sermon on the Mount. No textual variants eliminate the two clear references to Jesus Christ. The letter presupposes a high Christology, the glorious Lord and judge (1:1; 2:1; 5:8–9). It has eschatology (5:7–9), conversion (1:18, 21; 2:7), and ecclesiology (5:14).[84] Of course his letter will sound different from Paul's letters, since James is early and closely dependent on Jesus's oral teachings. Justification is the first stage of conversion, to which James refers. If Jesus had not been resurrected, how could he be the Lord of glory (2:1)? If his readers were forced to leave the temple in Jerusalem, James should not be expected to refer

---

81. Ehrman 2004, 282.
82. Ropes 1916, 108–9.
83. Even critics of James as the author will agree, e.g., Ehrman 2004, 282. See also Guthrie 1970, 743–44. See also chapter 4 excursus "James Shows Christ."
84. Laws 1980, 2–4, 12, 14, 18–20; Davids 1982, 14–17, 38–41; Dibelius 1976, 23; McCartney 2009, 69–70.

to it. If the questions of Gentiles and circumcision have not come up with these Jews, why would he refer to these issues? Unfortunately, Luther's apprehension of justification by faith through grace was such a moving experience for him that it became his own hermeneutic (or interpreting tool) to create a canon within the canon that limited his appreciation of James's message to Christians who were not living like Christians. John Calvin, who followed, was more balanced in his assessment: "By faith all are justified apart from the works of the law. The same Spirit teaches through James that the faith both of Abraham and of ourselves consists in works, not only in faith. It is sure that the Spirit is not in conflict with himself."[85] He adds that James contends with those who "vainly pretended faith as an excuse for their contempt of good works."[86] In other words, James's letter deals with a different problem than does Paul's letters and thus has different emphases.

4. *The church has always had doubts about the letter of James.* Neither the Muratorian Canon nor Tertullian nor Cyprian mentions it. Marxsen adds that Eusebius "does not accept it as genuine."[87] The Peshitta (5 c.) is the first Syrian witness to include James, 1 Peter, and 1 John.[88]

Nevertheless, I have shown the strong support for James's authorship. Eusebius does not say that James is not genuine. Rather, he simply mentions that some churches had doubts about the letter because few early writers referred to it, but the letter was regularly used in many churches (*Hist. eccl.* 2.23). Sophie Laws concludes that "the epistle was known at an early stage within the Western Church" because the Shepherd of Hermas gives a "strong impression" of familiarity with the letter of James. She adds, Clement of Rome appeals to Rahab and Abraham, as did James.[89] The Muratorian Canon has a

---

85. Calvin 1960, 3.17.11.
86. Calvin 1960, 3.17.12.
87. Marxsen 1970, 231. Laws writes of the "neglect of the epistle in the Western Church from the late second to the mid fourth century" (Laws 1980, 21). In contrast, Mayor finds allusions to James in Tertullian's writings (1913, lxxxi). See "Early Church Traditions about the Letter of James" in this introduction.
88. Dibelius 1976, 51.
89. Laws 1980, 21, 23. *Haer.* 4.13.4; 16.2 also refers to the "friend of God."

corruption at its beginning and end,[90] or it may have omitted James and Hebrews because, as Gentile elements in the church increased, Jewish epistles became less known. Or, possibly, since some second-century Ebionites used James's letter as precedent for a Torah-observant form of Christianity, later Gentiles rejected it.[91] We can be certain that the Alexandrian school, which sought for authenticity, always supported it. Ropes proposes that in the West "it seems to have been men acquainted with the learning and custom of Alexandria who brought the Epistle of James into general use and made it an integral part of the N. T."[92] It is not so much that the church had "doubts" but rather that the church did not always have early extended quotations. But that should be no surprise for a short letter addressed to Jews.

In conclusion, these important questions are ones that might first arise in a simple reading of the letter. However, further prayerful humble study of the letter and the early church can reveal the letter's organic type of structure, its early understanding of Christianity, its acceptance by the church, and the potential bilingual abilities of James. It may appear to differ with some of Paul's understandings, but we will see that, in reality, it complements Paul's views.

STRUCTURE OF THE LETTER OF JAMES

Peter Davids offers an excellent analysis of three themes in the Letter of James.[93] What he is missing is the fourth uniting theme: becoming doers of the word, which is first presented in 1:22–25. The three themes presented earlier in James chapter 1 are summarized in 1:26–27: wisdom about speaking (1:26), wealth and care for the poor (1:27a), and "trials" or control of internal desires (1:27b).[94] James uses a parallel thought structure in 1:2–2:26: trials (1:2–4), wisdom (1:5–8),

---

90. Hennecke 1963, 42. In addition, it is more of an introduction to the NT and pious readings than the definitive listings of NT "Scriptures," as have Origen and Athanasius.
91. Mayor 1913, lxx; Blomberg and Kamell 2008, 28.
92. Ropes 1916, 103.
93. Davids 1982, 25–29; also Francis 1970, 110–26.
94. Francis (1970, 118) calls 1:26–27 "a kind of literary hinge, both recapitulating the preceding introduction of the two main sections and turning the reader to the initial argumentative section of the body of the epistle."

wealth (1:9–11); trials (1:12–18), wisdom (1:19–21), wealth (2:1–17).[95] The chiastic[96] thought structure begins with the last parallel topic: wealth (2:1–26). In his next set he covers the three themes in further detail. The uniting theme (doer of the word) is covered at the conclusion of each topic: wealth (2:1–13) followed by "doer of the word" acts for the poor (2:14–26); wisdom (3:1–12) followed by "doer of the word" reflects wisdom in action (3:13–18); and "trials" from internal desires (4:1–17) followed by "doer of the law" indicates not speaking against another (4:11–12). The terms "doer" (ποιητής) or "action" (ἔργον) occur in each of these four pericopes that present the uniting theme: 1:22–25: ποιητής and ἔργον; 2:14–26: ἔργον; 3:13–18: ἔργον; 4:11–12: ποιητής. The three themes are then reviewed: wealth (5:1–6), persevering in trials (5:7–11), and wisdom about use of the tongue (5:12).[97] The final section explains how to persevere in the midst of trials (5:13–18, 19–20), describing the place of prayer and community to resolve issues of joy, health, and sin.[98] Most commentators are agreed on these subdivisions,[99] but the reappearance of the uniting theme is not always highlighted in studies about the structure of the letter. Becoming doers of the word summarizes chapter 1 (1:22–27) and ends, or is in the middle of each of, the three themes in chapters 2–4 (2:14–26; 3:13–18; 4:11–12). Differences among commentators occur on how to classify 4:1–12: whether this concerns "trials" or "wisdom," and also, whether

---

95. Francis (1970, 111–22) shows how such "double opening statements" were relatively common in Hellenistic letters. They functioned to emphasize the important subject matter of a letter.

96. Chiasm is a reverted type of parallelism, an inversion of the second of two parallel phrases, clauses, etc. It is diagonal arrangement, usually of one to four clauses or phrases in sequences in a well-rounded sentence or period. The first clause corresponds with the last, and the second with the second to last, as in the sequence ABBA, ABCDDCBA, or even ABCBA. A theme may be developed in a chiastic pattern of thought in larger contexts (Spencer 1998a, 189). See "Glossary of Stylistic Terms" in Appendix.

97. Francis (1970, 125) observes that ancient letters may end with an oath formula. Instead, at that point in the letter, James commands the readers not to make oaths.

98. Davids (1982, 25–26) suggests that Christian letters often end with something about prayer and a health wish, e.g., 1 John 5:14–17 (prayer and sin); 2 Cor. 13:5–10 (sin and prayer); Eph. 6:19–20 (prayer); 1 Thess. 5:12–22 (final directions include prayer); Heb. 13:18–19 (prayer). See also Francis 1970, 125–26.

99. Bauckham 1999, 63–64.

to include 4:13–17 with the earlier 4:1–12 or the later 5:1–6.[100] Since James writes concerning internal "desires" as a type of "trial" in 1:2–4, 12–18, and he repeats "desires" again in 4:1–3, then 4:1–12 appears to fit as a further development of the same theme. James 4:13–17 continues the same topic as 4:1–10, addressing one way to handle wrong "desires": to realize one's own mortality. Then, 5:1–6 clearly moves to the theme of wealth. The effect of this overall literary structure is to cause the reader to interrelate the different themes under the broad umbrella of becoming doers of the word, as one should also do in one's structure of life.

The following outline indicates that James 1:21 serves as a helpful thesis sentence: James exhorts the twelve tribes in the dispersion, having laid aside all evil deeds, to receive in humility the implanted word. The positive command to "receive the implanted word" is discussed at the beginning (ch. 1) and end (5:13–20) of the letter, while in the middle of the letter the negative command to "lay aside evil deeds" is covered, including partiality (ch. 2), misuse of the tongue (ch. 3), fighting as the world fights (ch. 4), wealth (5:1–11), and swearing oaths (5:12). Each of these chapters or sections ends (ch. 4 in the middle) with the reason behind the earlier commands, which incorporates the theme of becoming a doer of the word. In effect, the process of receiving the implanted word includes becoming a doer of the word.

As to its genre, the letter of James—a letter written to a group of people—has prophetic and wisdom elements, and hearkens back to the Old Testament law, prophets,[101] and to Jesus's teachings applied to its contemporary first-century situation. However, the letter is always relevant to any situation where Christians are not living out their faith as they should.

What follows is a chart and an outline summarizing my own approach to themes in James.

---

100. Bauckham (1999, 64) keeps 4:13–17 separate from 5:1–6 as summarizing the consensus among commentators. Davids (1982, 28–29), Francis (1970, 121), and McCartney (2009, 67) combine 4:13–5:6 in one larger heading.

101. See "Alternate Theories on Authorship and Sequence of Questions and Statements in James," chapter 2.

Themes in James Become Doers of the Word: Laying Aside All Evil Deeds and Receiving the Implanted Word (1:21–22)		
1. Be wise about unavoidable TRIALS 1:2–4 (A).	2. WISDOM helps you deal with trials 1:5–8. God is generous to give (B).	3. WEALTH: one type of trial is injustice by and for the rich. Have a right attitude to riches 1:9–11 (C).
Inward	**Tongue connects**	**Outward**
4. Avoidable "trials" are sinful internal desires 1:12–18. God, who is good, never gives these trials. **Doer of word keeps spotless 1:27b.**	5. Be slow to speak 1:19–21. **Doer of word hears & acts 1:22–25 & bridles tongue 1:26.**	**Doer of word cares for poor 1:27a.** 6. Do not favor the wealthy over the poor. The rich oppress the poor 2:1–13. **Doer of the word speaks & acts 2:14–26.**
	7. Few should become teachers, because the tongue needs to be tamed 3:1–12. **Doer's wise teaching is reflected in good actions 3:13–18.**	
8. Wrong desires can result in becoming God's enemy. Instead, be humble 4:1–10. **Doer of law does not speak evil against another 4:11–12.** Change wrong desires by realizing one's mortality 4:13–17.		

Themes in James Become Doers of the Word: Laying Aside All Evil Deeds and Receiving the Implanted Word (1:21–22)		
		9. The rich who oppress the poor will be judged 5:1–6.
10. The laborer needs to persevere through trials because the judge is near 5:7–11.	11. Do not swear 5:12.	
12. Use prayer & community to resolve issues of joy, health & sin 5:13–18, 19–20.		

LETTER OUTLINE

James exhorts the twelve tribes in the dispersion, having laid aside all evil deeds, to receive in humility the implanted word.

Greetings: James humbly greets the twelve tribes (1:1). He commands:

I.   Receive the implanted word in the midst of trials (ch. 1).
  A.   Meet trials with joy because of their effects (1:2–4).
  B.   Ask God in faith for wisdom (1:5–8).
  C.   Do not boast in riches because they are perishable (1:9–11).
  D.   Having endured trials, you will be rewarded (1:12–18).
  E.   (thesis paragraph) Receive the implanted word by becoming doers of the word and not hearers only (1:19–27).

II.   Lay aside partiality and faith without actions (ch. 2).
  A.   Show no partiality to the rich (2:1–13).
  B.   (reason) Verbal faith without actions is dead (2:14–26).

III.   Lay aside misuse of the tongue (ch. 3).
  A.   Be careful, because of the misuse of speaking, before becoming a teacher (3:1–12).
  B.   (reason) True wisdom is reflected in a life of good deeds (3:13–18).

IV. Lay aside fighting as the world fights; rather, humble yourself before the Lord and God will exalt you (ch. 4).
   A. Instead of fighting, which makes you God's enemy, humble yourself before the Lord (4:1–10).
   B. Fighting makes you a judge—a person who speaks evil of brothers and sisters; rather, be a doer of the law (4:11–12).
   C. Do not do business as the world does, because such arrogance is inappropriate to humans whose lives are temporary and dependent on God's will (4:13–17).

V. Lay aside wealth (5:1–12).
   A. The rich will be judged (5:1–6).
   B. Therefore, be patient and be ready because the Judge is standing at the doors (5:7–11).
   C. Do not swear oaths (5:12).

VI. Receive the implanted word by being mature in actions (5:13–20).
   A. Deal wisely with suffering, joy, and illness (5:13–18).
   B. Deal wisely with those led astray (5:19–20).

JAMES 1:1–27

TRANSLATION AND GRAMMATICAL ANALYSIS[1]

1:1a James, a slave of God and of the Lord Jesus Christ, to the twelve tribes, the ones in the diaspora, greetings. (initial introductory sentence; main clause; letterhead of letter)

1:2a Consider for yourselves all joy, my brothers and sisters,[2] (initial sentence; main clause)

1:2b whenever you might fall upon various trials, (subordinate adverbial clause; temporal; answers when)

1:3c knowing (subordinate adverbial clause; causal; answers why)

1:3d that the testing of your faith produces endurance. (subordinate noun clause; direct object)

1:4a But let endurance bring about a mature work, (explanatory sentence; main clause)

---

1. See "Definition of Terms in Grammatical Analysis."
2. Ἀδελφός in the plural here is generic (LSJ, 20; BDAG, 18).

1:4b in order that you may be mature and complete in nothing lacking.[3] (subordinate adverbial clause; causal; answers why)

1:5a But if any of you is lacking in wisdom, (initial sentence; subordinate adverbial clause; conditional)

1:5b let him/her ask from the One giving—God—[4]to all generously and without reproaching, (main clause)

1:5c and it will be given to him/her. (main clause)

1:6a But let him/her ask in faith in no way wavering; (explanatory sentence; main clause)

1:6b for the one wavering resembles a wave of the sea being blown by the wind and being tossed here and there. (subordinate adverbial clause; causal; answers why)

1:7a For let not such person suppose for him/herself (explanatory sentence; main clause)

1:7b that he/she will receive anything from the Lord, (subordinate noun clause; answers what)

1:8c [that person is] a two-willed man,[5] restless in all his ways. (subordinate adjectival clause describing the earlier person)

1:9a But let the lowly brother [believer] boast in his high position, (initial sentence; main clause)

1:10b but the rich one in his low position, (main clause)

---

3. Whenever possible, the unusual Greek word order will be retained in the translation. Here the prepositional phrase "in nothing" precedes the participle "lacking," which it modifies.

4. The dashes are not in the Greek text. James has an appositive, not a relative pronoun, such as "who is" God.

5. James uses the sex-specific ἀνήρ when referring to illustrations, the generic ἄνθρωπος (1:7) otherwise, but his intention is for the illustration to represent all believers. The sex-specific term makes the illustration more concrete.

1:10c since as a flower in wild grass he will pass away. (subordinate adverbial clause; causal; answers why)

1:11a For the sun rose[6] with the heat and dried up the grass,[7] (illustrative sentence; main clause)

1:11b and its flower fell off, (main clause)

1:11c and the beauty of its face was ruined; (main clause)

1:11d in the same way also the rich in his/her journey will wither. (subordinate adverbial clause; comparative)

1:12a Blessed is a man[8] [person] (initial sentence; main clause)

1:12b who endures trial, (subordinate adjectival clause; describes "man")

1:12c since having become approved will receive for him/herself the crown of life (subordinate adverbial clause; causal; answers why)

1:12d which is promised to the ones loving him. (subordinate adjectival clause; describing "crown")

1:13a Let no one being tempted say (explanatory sentence; main clause)

1:13b that from God I am being tempted; (subordinate noun clause; direct object)

1:13c for God is untemptable by means of evils, (subordinate adverbial clause; causal; answers why)

1:13d and himself tempts no one. (subordinate adverbial clause; causal)

1:14a But each is tempted by [his/her] own desire dragging away and seducing; (explanatory sentence; main clause)

---

6. James uses the aorist tense for the narrative, whereas we tend to use the present for narrative. See Robertson 1934, 835–36.
7. These are compound verbs since "the sun" is the subject of "rose" and "dried up."
8. See 1:8c.

1:15b then the Desire having conceived bears Sin, (main clause)

1:15c and the Sin having been fully formed gives birth to Death. (main clause)

1:16a Do not deceive yourselves, my beloved brothers and sisters. (additive sentence; main clause)

1:17a Every good gift and every perfect present is from above coming down from the Father of lights, (adversative sentence; main clause)

1:17b from whom there is no change, the one of a turning shadow.[9] (subordinate adjectival clause; describes "Father of lights")

1:18a Having desired he gave birth to us by means of a word of truth (explanatory sentence; main clause)

1:18b in order that we may be a kind of firstfruit of his creations. (subordinate adverbial clause; causal; answers why)

1:19a Understand, my beloved brothers and sisters;[10] (initial sentence; main clause)

1:19a and let every human be quick to hear, slow to speak, slow to anger; (initial sentence; main clause)

---

9. In 1:17, many manuscripts of a variety of text-types support παραλλαγὴ ἢ τροπῆς ἀποσκίασμα ("change of position or turning of a shadow"), but the earliest Greek witnesses are from the fifth century (codexes A and C). I have chosen παραλλαγὴ ἡ τροπῆς ἀποσκίασματος because it is supported by the two earliest and most important fourth-century uncials (codexes Sinaiticus and Vaticanus). The earliest papyri (p²³) from the third century also agrees with τροπῆς ἀποσκίασματος ("change, the one of a turning of a shadow"). The genitive ἀποσκίασματος is also supported in the ninth-century Western translation (it^ff) and some early church fathers (Augustine, Ferrandus, Primasius). Bruce M. Metzger explains that this reading makes sense only if η is read ἡ ("variation which is of [i.e., consists in, or belongs to] the turning of the shadow") (2002, 608).

10. A semicolon is used to indicate a possible end of sentence, which could also be seen as a strong comma, introducing a clause.

1:20a for a man's [person's][11] anger does not work God's righteousness. (explanatory sentence; main clause)

1:21a For this reason having laid aside all filth and abundance of evil in humility receive the implanted word, the one being able to save your lives. (illative sentence; main clause)

1:22a And become doers of [the] word and not only hearers deceiving yourselves, (initial sentence; main clause)

1:23b since, if anyone is a hearer of [the] word and not a doer, (subordinate adverbial clause; conditional)

1:23c that person resembles a man[12] observing well his natural face in a mirror; (subordinate adverbial clause; causal; answers why)

1:24a for he observed himself well (causal sentence; main clause)

1:24b and has gone away (main clause)

1:24c and immediately forgot (main clause)

1:24d of what sort he was. (subordinate noun clause; direct object)

1:25a But the one having stooped to look into the perfect law, the one of freedom, and having remained not having become a forgetful hearer but a doer of action,[13] (adversative sentence; adjectival phrase; describing "this one")[14]

1:25b this one will be blessed in his doing. (main clause)

---

11. In the illustration, James uses ἀνήρ ("man"), but earlier he uses the generic ἄνθρωπος ("human," 1:19b). See 1:8c; 1:12a.

12. See 1:8c. In 1:23, the generic τις ("any") is used in contrast to sex-specific ἀνήρ ("man") in the illustration.

13. Ἔργον is rendered "action" so as not to create confusion with the translation "work," which is used theologically more frequently in English as a contrast with "justification by faith."

14. If "is" is in ellipsis, 1:25a ("the one . . . [is one] not having become a forgetful hearer, but a doer of action") is the main clause while 1:25b is a subordinate adjectival clause, modifying the first "the one."

1:26a If anyone considers [him/herself] to be religious not bridling his/her tongue but deceiving his/her heart, (illative sentence; subordinate adverbial clause; conditional)

1:26b this religious worship is useless. (main clause)

1:27a Pure religious and undefiled worship in the presence of God and Father is this: to visit orphans and widows in their difficulties, to guard oneself spotless from the world. (additive sentence; main clause)

OUTLINE

Greetings: James humbly greets the twelve tribes (1:1).

I. Receive the implanted word in the midst of trials (ch. 1).
   A. Meet trials with joy because of their effects (1:2–4).
   B. Ask God in faith for wisdom (1:5–8).
   C. Do not boast in riches because they are perishable (1:9–11).
   D. Having endured trials, you will be rewarded (1:12–18).
   E. (thesis paragraph) Receive the implanted word by becoming doers of the word and not hearers only (1:19–27).

LITERARY STRUCTURE

In this first chapter, James introduces three themes he will discuss throughout the letter: how to meet trials, how to be wise, and how to view riches. All these themes are undergirded by and interrelated with a fourth uniting theme—becoming doers of the word and not hearers only. Trials affect steadfastness. Wisdom is reflected in a life of action. The unjust use of money will be judged. Every exhortation is followed by an explanation. In 1:2–4, James begins with the setting of the readers. They are Christian Jews dispersed because of persecution, and persecution is their current trial. In 1:5–8, wisdom helps one deal with trials. One type of trial is injustice by and for the rich. The reader should have the right attitude toward riches (1:9–11). Avoidable trials are "temptations"—sinful internal desires (1:12–18). Someone who has received the "implanted word" is a doer of the word and not a hearer only (1:19–27). Those who have received the implanted word must throw off all evil deeds such as lack of endurance, lack of wisdom, being ambivalent, boasting in wealth, blaming God for one's own sinful desires, being deceived, becoming angry quickly, hearing the word but not doing it, allowing oneself to be stained by the world, and ignoring the needy.

Receiving the implanted word, then, includes perseverance, asking for wisdom in faith, being single-minded, viewing wealth as temporary, accepting responsibility for one's own sinful desires, knowing the truth, being quick to hear but slow to express anger, hearing the word and doing it, being separated from the world's evils, and caring for the needy.

EXPOSITION

Receive the Implanted Word in the Midst of Trials (ch. 1)

Letterhead (1:1)

Ancient letters were often written in the following format: the name of the author (in the nominative case): "James . . . slave"; the name(s) of the recipient (in the dative case): "to the twelve tribes, the ones . . . "; and, finally, the greeting (in the infinitive case, functioning as an imperative): "greetings." "Greetings" (χαίρειν) is probably the most common ancient greeting,[15] but it appears in the New Testament as the introduction to a letter only three times, in James 1:1, in the letter directed by James (Acts 15:23), and in the letter written by Claudius Lysias (Acts 23:26). Instead, the apostle Paul uses "grace" and "peace" as his words of greeting.[16] The verb χαίρω has the basic idea of joy or happiness, as, for example, when the magi "rejoiced" when they saw the star had stopped. Basically, "greetings," when used personally, means, "welcome, I am joyful at your coming" (e.g., Matt. 26:49; 28:9; Luke 1:28). In Acts 15:23 "greetings" precedes a letter that indeed brought good news and joy to the church in Antioch (Acts 15:31). In contrast, Claudius Lysias's letter to governor Felix simply explained why Paul was sent to Caesarea (Acts 23:26–35). James's use of χαίρειν confirms the James of the letter is likely the same author as the one in Acts 15:13–21. The word also presages the letter is one to be welcomed by its readers with "joy" (James 1:2).[17]

James describes himself as "**a slave of God and of the Lord Jesus Christ**" (1:1).[18] He emphasizes the extended modifier "of God and Lord

---

15. E.g., *Embassy* 40.315.
16. Except 1 Timothy 1:2 and 2 Timothy 1:2: "grace, mercy, peace."
17. Blomberg and Kamell (2008) see "greetings" and "joy" as examples of linking words that tie together verses 1 and 2, moving the argument forward (48). Davids (1982) adds that James's play on words "allows him to jump from a formal greeting into his subject of concern" (66).
18. James's self-description is similar to his brother Jude ("a slave of Jesus Christ"). See Bateman 2017 for support for "a slave of Jesus, who is the Christ" (102–6).

Jesus Christ" by placing it before the word modified, "slave." Normally, in Greek, the modifier follows the word modified. Thereby, James emphasizes of whom he is a slave.[19] Paul also calls himself a "slave of God" (Titus 1:1) and Peter uses it for all Christian believers (1 Pet. 2:16). Moses is called a "slave of God" in Revelation 15:3 and in the Old Testament.[20] James's namesake "Jacob" is described in several places in the Old Testament as God's "slave."[21] James could be alluding to such passages, but he adds "and Lord Jesus Christ" to emphasize the divinity of the Son. By his use of the metaphor "slave," we can infer that James is obedient to his good Master, God. But, this Master did not force James to be enslaved. James was proud of this Master. D. Edmond Hiebert explains that δοῦλος "aptly sets forth the Christian consciousness that believers are totally dependent upon God, belong wholly to Him, and are convinced that His will is the only true rule for all of His people."[22] This, of course, is the main point that James wants to make to his readers: to be doers of the word (e.g., 1:22).

At the same level of importance as "God" is the "Lord Jesus Christ." God the Father and Jesus the Son are coequal and coeternal, as Jesus said: "I myself and the Father are one" (John 10:30).[23] To describe himself as a "slave" of Jesus is a remarkable statement for James to make of his own earthly brother. Before the resurrection, Jesus's family had thought Jesus was out of his mind (Mark 3:21). Jesus's "brothers and sisters" did not believe in him (John 7:5). However, after Jesus's appearance to James (1 Cor. 15:7), James dramatically changed. Now, Jesus is his "Lord" and "Christ," or Messiah, the Anointed One. In James 2:1, James uses the same phrase ("Jesus Christ") but adds that Jesus is "glorious." What a radical transformation!

James addresses his letter **"to the twelve tribes"** and then clarifies which twelve tribes, "the ones in the diaspora" (1:1). When the phrase "twelve tribes" is used elsewhere in the New Testament, it refers to the twelve tribes of Israel.[24] Matthew 19:28 and Luke 22:30

---

19. See also Hiebert 1979, 59.
20. See also Moses: Rev. 7:3; 2 Kings 18:12; Neh. 10:29; Mal. 4:4; Israel: Isa. 49:3; David: Ezek. 34:23; 37:24–25; 1 Chron. 17:7.
21. Jer. 46:27; Ezek. 28:25; 37:25.
22. Hiebert 1979, 60.
23. Hiebert 1979, 61; Robertson 1933, 10. Other possible renderings are James, "a servant of God, even the Lord Jesus Christ" or "a servant of Jesus Christ, who is God and Lord" (Hiebert 1979, 61; McCartney 2009, 78).
24. Matt. 19:28; Luke 22:30; Rev. 21:12. Acts 26:7 combines the phrase into one word: δωδεκάφυλον ("the twelve tribes"). The phrase is also used in the OT, e.g., Exod. 24:4; 28:21; 39:14; Ezek. 47:13.

suggest the twelve apostles represent the twelve patriarchs of the Old Testament. A φυλή is a "subgroup of a nation characterized by a distinctive bloodline."[25] The twelve tribes refer to the twelve sons of Jacob, originally Reuben, Simeon, Levi, Judah,[26] Zebulun, Isaachar, Dan, Gad, Asher, Naphtali, Joseph, and Benjamin (Gen. 49). Sometimes the two sons of Joseph are counted (Ephraim and Manasseh), omitting Joseph and Levi (e.g., Josh. 13, 15–19). In Revelation 7:5–8 Dan and Ephraim are omitted, replaced by Manasseh and Joseph. Notwithstanding how the tribes are counted, they are a clear reference to the Jewish people. In addition, James refers to "our ancestor Abraham" (2:21), and James and the earliest Christians met in synagogues (2:2). Moreover, probably near this time period, Paul mentions that James, Cephas, and John would emphasize ministry to the "circumcised" (Gal. 2:9).

However, to which "**diaspora**" (1:1) does James refer? The readers were both Christians and Jews, believers in "our glorious Lord Jesus Christ" (2:1) who were undergoing some kind of "trials" (1:2). The word family (διασπορά ["dispersion"], διασπείρω ["scatter"]) comes from the root meaning "to scatter abroad, disperse."[27] In Old Testament times, there were two major dispersions or "scatterings" of the Jews abroad, one by the conquering Assyrians (722–721 BC) and later by the conquering Babylonians (587 BC). Moses had warned the Israelites that, if they did not keep God's covenant, they would be dispersed from Israel to all the kingdoms of the earth (Deut. 28:25; Jer. 15:2; 34:17), and this is what happened.[28] About fifty years after the Babylonian captivity (538 BC), Cyrus allowed Jews to return to rebuild the temple in Jerusalem.[29] Nevertheless, many Jews remained in their homes outside Israel, even through New Testament times. Later, others migrated outside Judea. For instance, the Jewish philosopher Philo, in *The Embassy to Gaius* (AD 39–40), mentions that many Jews lived outside Judea in Egypt, Phoenicia, Syria, Pamphylia, Cilicia, Asia, Bithynia, Pontus, Europe, Thessaly, Boeotia, Macedonia, Aetolia, Attica, Argos, Corinth, Peloponnese, Euboea, Cyprus, Crete, Babylon, and Libya (36.281–83). John 7:35 refers to this larger dispersion of Jews. At Pentecost, Jews came from Parthia, Mede, Elam, Mesopotamia, Judea, Cappadocia, Pontus, Asia, Phrygia, Pamphylia, Egypt, Libya (Cyrene), Rome, Crete, and Arabia

25. BDAG, 1069.
26. Jesus and James were descendants of Judah (Matt. 1:3; Luke 3:33).
27. Thayer, 141.
28. 2 Kings 15:29; 17:6, 23; 18:11–12; 24:14–16; 25:11–12, 18–21; Neh. 1:8.
29. 2 Chron. 36:22–23; Ezra 1:1–5; Neh. 1:9; Isa. 43:5.

(Acts 2:9–11). Peter addresses his first letter to the "elect strangers of the dispersion" in some of the countries mentioned by Philo: Pontus, Galatia, Cappadocia, Asia, and Bithynia (1 Pet. 1:1). The "dispersion" in 1 Peter 1:1 refers to Christian followers of Jesus Christ (1:2), Gentiles (1:14, 18; 2:9–10; 4:3–4) at a later period, probably during Nero's persecution (AD 64–68), a time of a "fiery ordeal" (4:12) when believers throughout the world were undergoing the same sufferings (5:9). They may have left Rome to avoid Nero's persecution.

James refers to Jewish Messianic believers at an earlier period. The verb διασπείρω is most likely used to describe the Jewish Christians who left Jerusalem after the stoning of Stephen to avoid the Jewish persecution (Acts 8:1, 4). At first they left for the provinces of Judea and Samaria. Eventually they traveled as far as Phoenicia, Cyprus, and Antioch, preaching at first only to other Jews (Acts 11:19). These dispersed Jewish believers appear to be James's readership. When the church in Jerusalem (including James) heard of Gentiles becoming Christians, it sent Barnabas to check the situation. He then stayed in Antioch, bringing Paul (Saul) to assist him. Paul and Barnabas stayed there a whole year (Acts 8:22–26). Eventually, after they traveled from Antioch on their first missionary journey to Cyprus, Antioch of Pisidia, Iconium, Lystra, and Derbe, they and other Jewish leaders argued about the necessity of circumcision for Gentile believers, and their disagreement resulted in a council at Jerusalem to decide the matter (Acts 15). James appears to be written before any of these concerns about Gentiles arose (probably between Acts 8:1–14:28, ca. AD 34–48).

The "twelve tribes in the dispersion" (1:1), then, would refer to Jewish Christians dispersed from Jerusalem because of persecution. James as the overseer of the Jerusalem church[30] would be an appropriate Jewish Christian to continue his overseeing of these new Messianic believers, now no longer in his city, Jerusalem. Eusebius agrees that the "whole church" in Jerusalem "at that time consisted of Hebrews who had continued Christian from the Apostles down to the siege" of Hadrian (*Hist. eccl.* 4.5).[31] James's humility is shown because he does not even refer to his role as leader in Jerusalem or as "the

---

30. *Hist. eccl.* 2.1; 3.5, 11; 4.5; 7.19.
31. Ropes 1916 suggests two possible interpretations of the heading: "To the Jews, residing in the dispersion" or "To the dispersed People of God," i.e., the Christian church at large. He supports the latter, interpreting "the twelve tribes" as a metaphor for the church, which is now the new Israel (123–26).

Lord's brother" or as "apostle" (Gal. 1:19), although he presupposes his authority to challenge his readers.[32]

Meet Trials with Joy Because of Their Effects (1:2–4)

James begins right away with one of his three interlocking themes: how to meet **trials** (1:2–4). The readers may have the trial of having left their homes and occupations because of the persecution on account of their faith in the "Lord Jesus Christ" (1:1). They also may have the trial of unjust treatment by the wealthy (2:6–7; 5:1–11).[33] The intense persecution by Saul (Paul) appears to have occurred for about a year (AD 34–35, Acts 8:1–9:31). There was also persecution under Herod Agrippa I (37, 40, 41–44), who killed James, the brother of John (Acts 12:1–2), and intermittent persecution by unbelieving Jews, which Luke documents in describing Paul and Barnabas's first missionary journey (e.g., Pisidian Antioch, Acts 13:45, 50; Iconium, Acts 14:2–6, 19). Persecution by members of the Sanhedrin, temple authorities, and religious leaders was ongoing (e.g., Acts 4:1–6, 15–17, 21; 5:17–40; 6:12), and James himself was eventually killed by some of them. However, meeting trials with joy is one way to receive God's implanted word (1:2, 21). The noun πειρασμός and verb πειράζω come from the root πεῖρα, an attempt, trial, or experiment.[34] For James, it may be something that happens to one (1:2), in the same way as thieves surprise a traveler ("fall upon" one [περιπίπτω] as in Luke 10:30).[35] In that sense, it is a "trial" or difficulty, external to oneself, through which one may have to persevere (1:12).[36] James also uses the word family (πειράζω) as something internal, a passion or desire that entices one. If one succumbs, eventually it leads to sin and spiritual death (1:13–15).

---

32. See also Hiebert 1979, 58.
33. The NT notes other types of external "difficulties" (πειρασμός ["testing"], πειράζω ["to test"]), such as persecution for the faith (1 Pet. 1:6; 4:12; Rev. 2:10; 3:10; Acts 20:19) or physical infirmities (Gal. 4:13–14). Sometimes "difficulties" are wonders accomplished by God to discourage one's enemies (e.g., Deut. 4:34; 7:19).
34. E.g., Heb. 11:29. BDAG, 792. Πειράζω, too, can be used for the simple meaning of "attempt," as in Acts 9:26; 16:7; 24:6. In all these examples, the attempt is disrupted or disrupting, hence πειρατής signifies "brigand," especially "pirate" (LSJ, 1355).
35. Hiebert (1979, 72) explains: "The preposition *peri*, 'around,' pictures the man as being surrounded by the thieves on all sides, with no way of escape, and thus unavoidably 'falling' a victim to their assaults."
36. E.g., Luke 8:13.

This might be called a "temptation."[37] Both are *disrupting experiences*: one unavoidable and external; the other avoidable, internal, harmful. Both, if handled well, may lead to God's approval (1:12). God, though, never intends failure and never creates sinful desires (1:13–15), as opposed to the devil ("the Tempter") or human enemies who may try to cause failure.[38]

However, God may allow difficulties to occur that become occasions for the genuineness of believers' faith to be demonstrated and thereby examined and verified by God. For instance, God "tested" the faith and obedience of Abraham, whether he would trust God to provide the proper animal offering in place of his son Isaac (Gen. 22:1–14).[39] Examining the faith of oneself and others, as God examines our faith, is also good (2 Cor. 13:5; Rev. 2:2). The Old Testament recounts some key events when the Hebrews were exhorted not to "tempt" God by questioning whether the Lord was among them,[40] summarized in the command in Deuteronomy 6:16: "Do not put the Lord your God to the test."[41] In a similar manner, James exhorts his readers not to accuse God of evil because God is completely good (1:13–17).

The surprise in 1:2–3 is that James emphasizes "all joy" (1:2).[42] Not only are these difficulties to be accepted, they are to be welcomed joyfully because of the result: endurance, maturity, and completeness (1:3–4). "**Endurance**" occurs in verses 3 and 4. It concludes verse 3 and begins verse 4 (anadiplosis).[43] The word family (noun ὑπομονή and verb ὑπομένω) is not that frequent in the New Testament (49), but it occurs at least once in eighteen New Testament letters (67 percent), which shows it communicates an important idea. Verse 4 explains further verse 3. Ὑπομονή is "the capacity to hold out or bear up in the face of difficulty,

---

37. Examples in James might be misuse of wealth (2:6, 16; 4:3, 16; 5:1–6), adultery, murder (2:11), envy, selfish ambition (3:14, 16), false judgment (4:11). The same word family is used for misuse of wealth in 1 Timothy 6:9 and lack of self-control in 1 Corinthians 7:5 and Galatians 6:1.
38. E.g., Matt. 4:1; 19:3; 22:17–18, 35; Mark 8:11–12; 10:2; 12:14–15; Luke 4:2, 12–13, 11:16; 1 Thess. 3:5.
39. See also Exod. 16:4; 20:20; Deut. 33:8; John 6:6; Heb. 11:17.
40. E.g., Exod. 17:7; Heb. 3:8–9.
41. See also Num. 14:22. See further on "testing" Spencer and Spencer 1994, ch. 5.
42. He emphasizes the direct object "all joy" by placing it at the beginning of the sentence before the verb "consider for yourselves."
43. Anadiplosis is a rhetorical device, the "repetition of the last word of one line or clause to begin the next" (Lanham 1991, 10).

patience, endurance, fortitude, steadfastness, perseverance."[44] In James
it has more of the idea of "endurance" or "perseverance" than "patience"[45]
because, in the last chapter, James illustrates the concept with the example of Job (5:11). Job voiced plenty of complaining; he was not silent.
But he did persevere, and God rewarded him at the end (Job 42:7–17).
Why bother persevering? James replies, "that you may be mature and
complete" (1:4) and because one has confidence in the nature of God to resolve injustice since God is compassionate and merciful (5:11). Literally,
'υπομονή signifies to remain, to tarry behind, or to stay in a place beyond
an expected point of time,[46] even as the youth Jesus stayed behind in
Jerusalem dialoguing with the teachers, while his parents returned to
Nazareth (Luke 2:44–51). His staying behind was unexpected.[47] Thus,
this word family entails the sense of unexpectedness. James's readers
are in a time of trials, difficult times. By persevering in their faith, they
will become more persevering and, thereby, more mature (1:3–4). James
may be alluding to Jesus's parable of the sower, where the seed in the
good soil has roots to persist in times of testing. It is not choked by cares,
riches, pleasures, but its initial joy persists (Luke 8:13–15). Perseverance
is often mentioned as a key characteristic in the midst of suffering, as
Hebrews so beautifully summarizes: "with perseverance, let us run the
race set before us, fixing our eyes on Jesus" (12:1–2).[48] Perseverance is a
quality of God and of God's writings (Rom. 15:4–5). It is even an aspect
of love (1 Cor. 13:7). It is repeatedly mentioned as a necessary quality
for believers to pursue.[49] Perseverance is an important prerequisite to
gaining life,[50] as Paul summarizes in 2 Timothy 2:12: "If we keep persevering, also we will reign together." Even John Calvin insists that "call
and faith are of little account unless perseverance be added."[51]

James follows with another repetition (anadiplosis): "mature . . .
mature (τέλειος, 1:4). The adjective occurs five times in the letter

---

44. BDAG, 1039.
45. "Constancy" in faith is a "virtue highly prized by the Jews and frequently
exemplified by cases from their history" (Ropes 1916, 136).
46. Thayer, 644; BDAG, 1039.
47. In Acts 17:14 Paul had to leave Thessalonica quickly for Athens, while
his coworkers Silas and Timothy stayed behind in Berea.
48. See also Rom. 12:12; 2 Cor. 1:6; 2 Thess. 1:4; Heb. 10:32; 12:2–3, 7; 1 Pet.
2:20; Rev. 1:9; 2:2–3; 3:10; 13:10; 14:12.
49. E.g., Rom. 5:3–4; 2 Cor. 6:4; 12:12; Col. 1:11; 2 Thess. 3:5; 1 Tim. 6:11; 2
Tim. 2:10; 3:10; Titus 2:2; 2 Pet. 1:5–7; Rev. 2:19.
50. E.g., Matt. 10:22; 24:13; Mark 13:13; Luke 21:19; Rom. 2:7; 8:25; Heb.
10:36.
51. Calvin 1960, 3.6.

(26 percent of its NT uses),[52] and indeed it introduces another important theme for James. The letter is written to believers. God has "implanted" the word in their lives (1:21), but now that seed or little seedling needs to mature. How does it mature? By perseverance and by actions (1:4; 2:22). The word family (adjective τέλειος and verb τελειόω, etc.) comes from τέλος, "end," "conclusion," or "consummation," and it can be rendered as "perfect" or "mature."[53] Jesus commands his listeners to "therefore, be perfect as your Father, the One in heaven, is perfect" (Matt. 5:48). Looking at this verse out of its context is an intimidating experience. If all humans are sinful, how can we be "perfect," without any flaws? And, indeed, "perfect" is an apt description of God's gifts, God's law, God's will (James 1:17, 25; Rom. 12:2). It is the opposite of making many mistakes (James 3:2). Hebrews teaches that perfection is achievable through Jesus's perfect sacrifice (Heb. 10:14; 11:40; 12:23). But this perfection is due to God looking to our representative, Jesus, who is perfect (2 Cor. 5:21). The literal use of these words reminds one of the root τέλος: to complete work or complete days, to finish.[54] In the same way that a child may physically become a mature adult, a young believer may spiritually become a mature believer. The spiritual end may be perfection and unattainable in this life, but moving toward that end is what God expects.[55] Hebrews describes the process of education as moving from milk to solid food (5:12–14). Paul describes the process as developing from children who are tossed about by false doctrine to adults who have grown into the Head, Christ (Eph. 4:13–16).[56] Enduring sufferings through persecution is one way to become more mature (Heb. 2:10; 5:8–9; 7:28),

In other words, James exhorts his readers to allow perseverance to develop into maturity (1:4). He adds two explanatory synonyms: "complete" (ὁλόκληρος) and "in nothing, lacking" (1:4). Ὁλόκληρος refers to "complete in all its parts, in no part wanting or unsound,"[57] as stones

---

52. James has five of nineteen occurrences in the NT. The verb τελειόω ("make perfect") is most frequent in Hebrews: 39 percent of NT uses, nine of twenty-three.
53. LSJ, 1769, 1772; BDAG, 995.
54. E.g., Luke 2:43; 13:32; John 4:34; 5:36; 17:4; 19:28.
55. The present tense ("produces" and "bring about" [James 1:3, 4]) pictures a continuing process (Hiebert 1979, 75, 77). Blomberg and Kamell 2008 explain: "We can aspire to maturing in this lifetime, but we will ultimately attain perfection in the eschaton" (50).
56. See also 1 Cor. 2:6; 14:20; Phil. 3:15; Col. 1:28; 4:12.
57. Thayer, 443.

untouched by a tool (Deut. 27:5–6; 1 Macc. 4:47), or as a crippled man who is now completely healed (Acts 3:16). Believers should be mature and spiritually healthy, not deficient in anything.[58] The repetition (pleonasm)[59] of these three words and phrases (1:4b) emphasizes one basic idea: the believer should aim to be completely mature.

Ask God in Faith for Wisdom (1:5–8)

James now gives an example of a deficiency, lack of wisdom, and uses repetition to connect this verse with the earlier one (anadiplosis: "lacking . . . lacking" [λείπω]).[60] James began with trials, the setting of the readers. **Wisdom** helps them deal with adversities. He begins with the subordinate clause, the protasis or condition: "if any of you is lacking in wisdom" (1:5). If someone already has wisdom, this verse is not pertinent, but as a first class condition (present indicative), referring to a present or alleged reality and stated as if a fact,[61] this condition is likely representative of the readers. Hiebert explains that the first step in gaining wisdom is consciousness of need.[62] And, outside of God, who can say one has reached perfection in wisdom?

James then commands the reader to **"ask"** (1:5), and even "keep on asking" (present tense)[63] throughout one's life. The readers do not ask just anyone for wisdom, but are to ask the source of all wisdom, God. God is not miserly, but extremely generous. Again, James uses a three-part repetition (pleonasm), two positive attributes and one negative in 1:5: "the One giving" (δίδωμι) "to all generously" (ἁπλῶς) "without reproaching" (ὀνειδίω) (1:5). The character of the source of wisdom is accentuated.

To have a smoother translation, many versions translate **"giving"** as a finite verb, for example, "God, who gives" (NRSV, NIV), but "give" is a participle, emphasized by preceding its noun: "the One giving—God" is a more literal translation that brings out the durative or ongoing action of God's giving. The CEB communicates this ongoing nature with

---

58. Hiebert 1979 complains that, "unfortunately, many believers succumb to spiritual infantile paralysis" (77).
59. Pleonasm is the doubling and repetition of words of similar meaning and of thoughts of similar content, as well as of all forms of rhetorical devices that add words to the basic sentence (Spencer 1998a, 203).
60. Hiebert 1979 agrees that repetition of the idea of "lacking" provides a link of thought between verse 5 and verse 4 (78–79).
61. A first class condition is "assumed as true" (Robertson 1933, 13; Hiebert 1979, 79; Blomberg and Kamell 2008, 50).
62. Hiebert 1979, 79.
63. See also Robertson 1933, 13; Hiebert 1979, 80.

the translation: "God, whose very nature is to give to everyone without a second thought."[64] The giving of wisdom is not restricted to the already wise person but "to all." This giving is generously done (ἁπλῶς). Ἁπλῶς comes from ἁπλόος, which literally refers to something single-folded or simple, in contrast to "two-folded" or compounded or mixed.[65] Thus, it is a type of giving that is not hidden but openhearted, without secret requirements. It emphasizes the great generosity of God, after whose model the Macedonians gave (2 Cor. 8:2). God's generosity does not make the receiver feel inadequate or reprimanded. "Reproach" (ὀνειδίζω, ὀνειδισμός, ὄνειδος) is often used as an aspect of persecution, specifically the insult or slander that may accompany it.[66] God will never reproach any believer who asks for wisdom. With such a God, the final result is assured: "it will be given" (1:5). God is the "giving" God who "gives" (δίδωμι is repeated for emphasis).

The character of the One who is asked for wisdom is described in 1:5; the character of the one requesting, or the way to **ask**, is described in 1:6–8. The requester is to have complete confidence that God will answer positively ("in faith, in no way wavering," 1:6). Then James describes the negative way to ask in a comparison (simile):[67] as "a wave of the sea, being blown by the wind and being tossed here and there" (1:6).

James further describes asking in 4:2–3. He repeats the need for asking (αἰτέω), as opposed to coveting and killing to reach one's desires, and explains what not to ask to spend on pleasures that keep one from maturing as a believer (cf. Luke 8:14). The contrast between 4:2–3 and 1:5 is that in 1:5 the object asked for is one approved by God—in other words, wisdom. For example, God affirms Solomon for asking for wisdom, not long life or riches or the life of his enemies (1 Kings 3:9–12).[68] When Jesus taught, he also mentioned other actions or qualities worth asking God for in the Lord's Prayer: God's will to be done, daily bread, forgiveness of debts, and rescue from evil (Matt. 6:8–13). James

---

64. See also REB: "God is a generous giver" or NLT: "our generous God."
65. LSJ, 190–91.
66. E.g., Matt. 5:11; 27:44; Mark 15:32; Luke 1:25; 6:22; Rom. 15:3; Heb. 10:33; 11:26; 13:13; 1 Pet. 4:4. Ὀνειδίζω in these passages means "to find fault in a way that demeans the other" as opposed to Matthew 11:20, wherein it refers "to find justifiable fault with someone" (BDAG, 710).
67. A simile is an explicit comparison using a word such as "like" or "as" between two things of unlike nature that yet have something in common, so that one or more properties of the first are attributed to the second (Spencer 1998a, 207).
68. Solomon's wise teachings are recorded in Proverbs.

echoes Jesus's teachings on the importance of asking (Matt. 7:7–11; Luke 11:9–13), on asking in faith (Matt. 21:22; Mark 11:24), and on the Father in heaven's good gifts to be bestowed on those asking (Matt. 7:11; Luke 11:13). Asking in Jesus's name by active participants in the new covenant is also crucial.[69] The apostle John summarizes the importance of obedience: we receive from God "whatever we ask [αἰτέω], because we obey his commandments and do what pleases him" (1 John 3:22 NRSV). No wonder Paul and Timothy keep praying for the Colossians: "and asking [αἰτέω] God to fill" them "with the knowledge of his will through all spiritual wisdom and understanding" (Col. 1:9 NIV).[70]

Wisdom (1:5) certainly is a part of maturity, a characteristic of God, which will assist in trials.[71] As a teacher himself, James is interested in wisdom (James 3:1; 1 Cor. 12:8). Later in his letter he describes the characteristics of wise people who have received their wisdom from God. Their wisdom is demonstrated by their good actions (3:13). He characterizes wise people (σοφός) as pure, peaceable, reasonable, compliant, full of mercy and good fruits, impartial, without hypocrisy, and righteous (3:17–18). Wise people will not further evil (3:14–16).[72] Jesus himself is described in his incarnate state as growing in wisdom.[73] As the incarnate Son, like the Father, he possessed wisdom, greater than the wisdom of Solomon.[74] God is the "only wise God" with profound depths of wisdom (Rom. 11:33; 16:27). In his prayer, Daniel blessed God for his wisdom (Dan. 2:20–23). Consequently, God is the One most appropriate as a source of wisdom. During times of persecution, wisdom is essential to correct opponents (e.g., Luke 21:15; Col. 4:5–6). For instance, opponents of Stephen could not oppose his wisdom (Acts 6:3–5, 9–10). Wisdom is also necessary to teach others to be mature (Col. 1:28; 3:16; cf. James 1:4). Thus, the wisdom one should request is a characteristic of God, an aspect of maturity, demonstrated in godly actions.

---

69. John 14:13–14; 15:7, 16; 16:23–27. See also Spencer and Spencer 1990, 98–100, 115–16.
70. See also Eph. 1:17.
71. Wisdom is "that moral discernment that enables the believer to meet life and its trials with decisions and actions consistent with God's will" (Hiebert 1979, 79–80) and "the ability to discern *how* [God] would have us live" (Blomberg and Kamell 2008, 52).
72. Human wisdom is not necessarily the same as God's wisdom, e.g., Rom. 1:21–23; 1 Cor. 1:17–20; 2:6–7, 13; 3:18–20; 2 Cor. 1:12; Col. 2:23.
73. Luke 2:40, 52.
74. Jesus: Matt. 11:19; Mark 6:2; Luke 11:31; 1 Cor. 1:24; Col. 2:2–3; Rev. 5:12; Father: Luke 11:49; Eph. 1:8–9; 3:10; Rev. 7:12.

James describes who to ask in 1:5 and how to ask in 1:6. He repeats "ask" (αἰτέω) in verse 6, connecting the two main clauses. Then he employs repetition (anadiplosis) in verse 6 to conclude the first main clause and begin the second subordinate clause (διακρίνω, "waver," is repeated). Διακρίνω and διάκρισις are composed of κρίνω plus the prefix δία. The root idea of δία is "two," "by twos" or "between."[75] If κρίνω has basically the idea of **choose**, separate, select, judge,[76] διακρίνω in James accentuates the idea of choosing between two options. In James it is a negative concept. In 1:6 someone "**wavers**," not being sure whether God will answer his/her prayer for wisdom, or whether God is truly generous,[77] or whether he or she wants God's wisdom. The individual's "uttered request has not terminated the inner indecision" between the competing desires of "God and the world (James 4:3–4)."[78] In 2:4 Christians are differentiating between the rich and poor, favoring the rich over the poor. In 1:6 the person cannot come to a decision between two options; in 2:4 the person comes to a wrong decision between two options. In 1:6 the right decision is faith or trust in God's character. Jesus uses διακρίνω similarly, for example: "If you may have faith and do not waver, . . . you might say to this mountain, 'Be lifted up and thrown into the sea' . . . and whatever you might ask in prayer believing, you will receive" (Matt. 21:21–22).[79] In 2:4 the right decision is a righteous one, treating the poor person and the rich equally.

James uses an analogy from the sea. Every simile or metaphor[80] has two parts: the image and the concept to which the image alludes. **Doubt** or lack of faith is the concept in 1:6. "A wave of the sea, being blown by the wind and being tossed here and there" is the extended image. What can we learn about the image that is analogous to the concept?

James was reared in Nazareth, about fifteen miles from the Sea of Galilee and less than thirty miles from the Mediterranean Sea.[81] Jerusalem is about forty miles from the Mediterranean. James lived

---

75. Robertson 1934, 580.
76. Thayer, 360–61.
77. Blomberg and Kamell 2008, 52; McCartney 2009, 89.
78. Hiebert 1979, 84.
79. See also Mark 11:23; Acts 10:20; 11:12; Rom. 4:20; 14:23; Jude 22. This meaning appears first in the NT in Jesus's teachings (e.g., Matt. 21:21) (BDAG, 231).
80. A metaphor is an implied or implicit comparison between two things of unlike nature that yet have something in common so that one or more properties of the first are attributed to the second (Spencer 1998a, 196).
81. Harrison 1985, 171.

close enough to have observed the seas. Κλύδων refers to *"rough water."*[82] Ordinary **waves** are the result of wind blowing unevenly on the surface of the ocean. As the wind increases, the waves grow higher. In the open sea, wave crests may reach heights of about one hundred feet above their troughs. The power of the wind to control might be seen in a great storm such as a tsunami, which may advance over the ocean depths at a speed of approximately 450 to 500 miles per hour and inundate the land as much as one hundred feet above normal sea level.[83] Luke uses κλύδων to describe the waves that rattled the boat at the Sea of Galilee (Luke 8:23). Sudden squalls would come down from the summit of Mount Hermon to the Sea of Galilee with "terrific force (*seismos megas*) like an earthquake."[84] Mark 4:37 and Luke 8:23 term the wind a "whirlwind (*lailaps*) in furious gusts."[85] Josephus, the historian, uses κλύδων to describe the great storm that almost sank Jonah's ship in the Mediterranean (*Ant.* 9.10.210), and the author of 4 Maccabees uses it to describe the waves in the "world-filling flood" that Noah's ark endured (15:31).

Thus, lack of faith in God's character and ability creates rough waters. The wave, like doubt, is passive. It cannot control where it goes[86] and, as a result, it becomes tossed "here and there" (1:6). Rough waves can batter a boat and cause it to sink[87] or keep a boat from going forward as planned (e.g., Acts 27:4, 7). The boat can be propelled forcefully to where it should not go, becoming out of control, no longer able to hold cargo (e.g., Acts 27:14–20). In contrast, large ships guided by rudders can be driven by these same strong winds (ἄνεμος) to their destination (James 3:4). Lack of faith in God is not an unimportant and insignificant private matter. It has extreme repercussions.

James goes on to explain further the nature of a **doubter** in 1:7–8 and adds some descriptive metaphors. He introduces the illustration using the more abstract and inclusive term "person" or "human" (ἄνθρωπος) in 1:7; then, to be more concrete in the illustration and metaphor, he uses "man" (ἀνὴρ) in 1:8. Women, of course, also can be

---

82. BDAG, 550. Κλύδων refers to "a dashing or surging wave in contrast with *kuma* (successive waves)" (Robertson 1933, 14); Ropes 1916, 141.
83. Shepard 1987, 59–60.
84. Matt. 8:24; Robertson 1930a, 69.
85. Robertson 1930a, 69.
86. Ἀνεμίζω ("be driven by wind") and ῥιπίζω ("be tossed about") are passive words (BDAG, 77, 906). This is the "earliest known example" of ἀνεμίζω, probably coined by James from ἄνεμος ("wind") (Robertson 1933, 14). See also "Unusual Words and Phrases in James" in the Appendix.
87. E.g., Matt. 14:24; Mark 4:37; Luke 8:23.

"two-willed," "restless" in all their "ways" (1:9). The illustration represents any believer.

The Lord does not respond favorably to **"double-willed"** or "two-willed" people.[88] "Double-willed" (δίψυχος) is a unique word first found in James 1:8 and 4:8,[89] being composed of two Greek words (δίς or "twice" and ψυχή).[90] Ψυχή comes from ψύχω, "to breathe, blow."[91] Thus, a crucial meaning in the New Testament for ψυχή is a life. For example, an angel told Joseph to return to Israel because the ones seeking the "child's *life* are dead" (Matt. 2:20). James uses ψυχή for "life" in the Jerusalem council's letter (Acts 15:26). Paul notes that Eutychus still had his "breath" or "life" in him when he fell (Acts 20:10). A second use of ψυχή refers to a self, a person, or a human being, for example, "Those who find their *life* will lose it, and those who lose their *life* for my sake will find it" (Matt. 10:39 NRSV). Jesus is not promising that his disciples will never die, but he is asking them to give themselves over to obey his will.[92] Sometimes ψυχή may simply refer to persons[93] or to people from a spiritual perspective (Heb. 13:17; 1 Pet. 2:11, 25). A third use of ψυχή is the inner being of a living person, as when Jesus tells his disciples: "My *soul* is overwhelmed with sorrow to the point of death" (Matt. 26:38 NIV). His inner being is grieved as he contemplates his future death. The inner being may refer to people's will (e.g., Acts 14:22), effort (Col. 3:23), or whole self, including love (1 Thess. 2:8). A group with one ψυχή is completely united in will (Phil. 1:27). James uses ψυχή in a similar manner in the Jerusalem council's letter to describe the mind or emotions of the Gentiles: the circumcised party had said words troubling their "minds" (Acts 15:24). This latter use is similar to his use in the letter.

James 1:8 does not refer to two living lives, but rather to two selves or two inner beings within one person because this person is undecided. His or her will, mind, emotions, and effort are inclined in two

---

88. I chose "two-willed" or "double-willed" as opposed to "double-minded" as a translation because "mind" suggests abstract thought open to suggestions, while "will" is more concrete, related to decisions that then will affect actions. "Two-selves" is another possible translation.
89. See also Robertson 1933, 15; BDAG, 253; Hiebert 1979, 87; Blomberg and Kamell 2008, 53. See also "Unusual Words and Phrases in James" in the Appendix.
90. Thayer, 153.
91. Thayer, 677.
92. See also Mark 8:34–35.
93. E.g., Acts 2:43; 3:23; 4:32; 7:14; 2 Pet. 2:14.

different directions: the one desires God's wisdom; the other does not. If God is "generous" or "single-folded" (ἁπλῶς, 1:5), this person in contrast is "double-folded." In James 4:8 δίψυχος parallels "sinners" and opposes a pure heart, someone submitted to God, resisting the devil. Possibly, then, δίψυχος hearkens back to the Old Testament "double-hearted" (בְּלֵב וָלֵב) as in Psalm 12:2 (MT 12:3): "They utter lies to each other; with flattering lips and a double heart they speak" (NRSV). In contrast, the tribe of Zebulun sought to help King David "whole-heart-edly" or with their whole heart (1 Chron. 12:33 [MT 12:3]).[94] God, too, wants believers who love and obey him with their whole hearts (e.g., Deut. 6:5; 26:16; 2 Chron. 6:14).

Being δίψυχος is then further described in 1:8 as "**restless** in all his ways." Ἀκατάστατος, "restless," is repeated in James 3:8. There it describes the untamed tongue, which is full of deadly poison, as a venomous animal (3:7–8). The noun form "restlessness" (ἀκαταστασία) is used of society upheavals (Luke 21:9; 2 Cor. 6:5) and fighting (James 3:16; 2 Cor. 12:20). In effect, the two-willed person becomes like a wild beast, a snake slithering in many different directions, not going toward the clear goal of mature godly wisdom but instead wreaking havoc wherever it goes.

Do Not Boast in Riches Because They Are Perishable (1:9–11)

Verse 9 appears to introduce an unrelated topic. **But**, like 1:5, δέ introduces a transition.[95] Verses 9–11 return to the initial theme in 1:2, trials,[96] and to the overall theme of the letter: having thrown off all evil deeds, in humility receive the implanted word. One type of trial and evil deed is injustice by and for the rich. Therefore, James's readers need to have the right attitude to riches. Such an attitude will assist in the reception of the implanted word. James uses the singular "**brother**" to represent the Christian believer (1:9). "Brother" is concrete language in this extended illustration. If a "two-willed" believer is uncertain in his

---

94. See also Hiebert 1979, 87; Ropes 1916, 143–44; Davids 1982, 74.

95. Δέ ("but") "marks a transition between subsections within the two parts of chap. 1 . . . the mild adversative has just the proper force to make the transition between sections while at the same time signaling that they must be held apart" (Davids 1982, 75). Robertson (1934, 1184) considers the narrative and transitional use of δέ as primary, signifying "in the next place." "A new topic may be introduced by δέ in entire harmony with the preceding discussion." See also Wallace 1996, 674; Hiebert 1979, 88.

96. See also Robertson 1933, 15; Ropes 1916, 144; McCartney 2009, 95; Barnes 1949, 21.

attitude toward receiving God's wisdom (1:5–8), this worldly perspective is reflected in prejudicial attitude and action toward the poor and rich. This theme will be developed in 2:1–9. But, here in 1:9–11, James turns the worldly view upside down. The poor "brother" who is contrasted with the "rich one"[97] is described as "lowly," yet having a "high position" (1:9). The rich is described as "lowly," while appearing to have a beautiful "face" (1:10–11). The poor person needs to remind himself of his high view before God, while the rich needs to remind her/himself that she or he is not as impressive as the world might think because riches are temporary. By faith in Christ, the poor and the rich are equals.[98]

Ταπείνωσις (noun), ταπεινόω (verb), ταπεινός (adj.) (1:9) literally refer to "not rising far from the ground," to being low of stature or size, as a mountain or hill "made low" (Luke 3:5). The word family may be used metaphorically to refer to a person who appears unimpressive, not someone prominent, as a mountain might be prominent, or to an attitude wherein one assigns oneself or another to "a lower rank or place."[99] For James, and others, "**lowly**" may describe the poor Christian (1:9), but also the humble person (1:10; 4:6, 10).[100] Jesus uses this word family to describe himself, a gentle person (Matt. 11:29; Isa. 53:7–8 LXX). Jesus's coming from heaven to become human and die on the cross is called becoming "lowly" (Phil. 2:8). Mary uses this word family to describe the poor and hungry, those not powerful but humble in attitude as opposed to the wealthy, powerful, and haughty.[101] It is the attitude of children (Matt. 18:4) and the repentant, humble person (Luke 18:10–14). Paul also uses it to describe his own leadership style, unimpressive to the Corinthians (2 Cor. 10:1; 11:7–8). In itself it is not an impressive glory (Phil. 3:21). But current lowliness masks a future heir to God's glorious kingdom (James 1:12; 2:5).[102]

---

97. "Rich one" is in antithesis to "the brother, the lowly one" (1:9–10). Scholars differ over whether the rich person is a Christian or not. In chapter 5, the rich are negatively judged. In 1:10, if the rich were to boast in their lowly state, they would not rely on wealth (cf. 1 Tim 6:17–19). In that case, "brother" refers to both Christians, and "lowly one" is contrasted with "rich one" (Hiebert 1979, 92). "Let the brother boast" is in ellipsis (implied) in the second clause in 1:10.

98. "As the poor brother forgets all his earthly poverty, so the rich brother forgets all his earthly riches. The two are equals by faith in Christ" (Lenski 1946, 535).

99. Thayer, 614; LSJ, 1757.

100. See also 1 Pet. 5:5–6.

101. Luke 1:48, 51–53. See also Matt. 23:6, 12; Luke 14:10–11; Phil. 4:12.

102. See also Hiebert 1979, 90; Painter and deSilva 2012, 70.

James, like his Lord Jesus[103] and his mother Mary (Luke 1:46–55), includes a number of passages on **reversal of positions** brought about by Jesus and his incarnation. The oppressed are liberated by Jesus's teachings and life. God is the Savior who favors the humble, especially the "slave," the hungry, and the poor. Life is therefore ironic because God reverses positions and joy is the result.[104] Position reversal is cited in James 1:9–10; 2:1–5; and 4:6, 10. The position of the rich is reversed with the poor, while the position of the poor is reversed with the rich. Ultimately, the manner in which God chose a poor, humble, but devout woman, Mary, as the means for God's incarnation is a synecdoche[105] of Jesus's ministry which was presaged in Isaiah 52–53: Jesus "was despised and rejected by others; a man of suffering and acquainted with infirmity; and as one from whom others hide their faces he was despised, and we held him of no account" (53:3 NRSV). Jesus himself lived out the dramatic irony of position reversal.

James goes on to describe why the beautiful face of the rich is deceptive in an extended simile: "as a flower in wild grass [ἄνθος χόρτου] he will pass away. For the sun rose with the heat and dried up the grass [χόρτος], and its flower [ἄνθος] fell off, and the beauty of its face was ruined" (1:10–11).[106] He uses an image (metaphor) in the final clause: the rich "will wither" (μαραίνω) (1:11).

"Flower" (ἄνθος, 1:10) occurs only three times in the New Testament. From 1:10–11 we learn that this is a flower found among wild grass (χόρτος) or a **"wildflower"** destroyed by the heat. The heat[107] dries up the grass (or stalk), which in turn causes the flower to fall off its stem

103. E.g., Matt. 20:25–28; Mark 10:45; Luke 22:25–30; John 12:24–26.
104. See Spencer 2014a, 97–105.
105. Synecdoche is "substitution of part for whole, genus for species, or vice versa," such as "All hands on deck!" (Lanham 1991, 148).
106. James uses polysyndeton in 1:11 to highlight each of the four steps of the process: (1) the sun rose with the heat, (2) the sun dried up the grass, (3) its flower fell off, (4) the beauty of its face was ruined. In polysyndeton the same or even different conjunctions or connecting particles are deliberately used a number of times in close succession between each clause, word, or phrase (Spencer 1998a, 204). See also Vlachos 2013, 35.
107. Καύσων may refer to "the sirocco, the dry east wind from the desert (Job 1:19)" (Robertson 1933, 16). But since the rising sun is accompanied by heat, James seems to refer to heat caused by the sun, not the scorching wind (Vlachos 2013, 35). Moreover, the sirocco "blows constantly day and night" for a three- or four-day period (Davids 1982, 78). Jesus refers to the south wind; when it blows, it would be hot (Luke 12:55).

with the result that the beauty of that flower is ruined. 1 Peter 1:24 clearly refers to Isaiah 40:6–8: "All flesh is grass [χόρτος], and all the glory of a human is as the flower of grass [ἄνθος χόρτου]. The grass withers [ξηραίνω], and the flower fades [ἐκπίπτω]" (LXX). James, Peter, and Isaiah use the image of a wildflower that withers to refer to temporary human glory, but in Isaiah and 1 Peter, the flower is contrasted to God's word, which endures forever (1 Pet. 1:23, 25). James compares the flower to the wealthy, who look impressive and powerful, but these attributes are temporary.[108] The Old Testament also uses the flower as a synecdoche for human mortality, contrasted in Psalm 103:15–17 to the Lord's everlasting mercy.

Χόρτος (1:10) may refer to the green grass of a meadow[109] (but then usually the adjective "green" is added) or to wild grass in contrast to cultivated plants,[110] or to the stalk, the first part of a plant's growth.[111] Thus, ἄνθος χόρτου refers either to a "wildflower," or "a flower in wild grass," or "a flower on a stalk." The concept is similar to Jesus's analogy of "grass in the field" or "lilies," which, alive today and tomorrow, are thrown into the oven (Matt. 6:28–30; Luke 12:27–28). But, in Jesus's instance, it is a positive image and model for human reliance on God.

This flower is beautiful, personified as having a "face" (1:11). Michael Zohary considers that the poppy (*Papaver rhoeas*), common in the fields of Israel, might fit the wildflower that James has in mind. It has beautiful red flowers that last only two to three days. Each plant has several long stems terminating with flowers.[112]

Different verbs are used to describe what eventually happens to this flower: "pass away" (παρέρχομαι), "dry up" (ξηραίνω), "fall off" (ἐκπίπτω), "ruin" (ἀπόλλυμι), and "wither" (μαραίνω, 1:10–11). James will develop his view of the unjust rich later in more negative terms (5:1–6). Psalm 37 has a similar message: Do not be envious of the wicked because "they will soon fade like the grass, and wither like the green herb" (37:1–2 NRSV).

---

108. See also Job 15:30.
109. E.g., Mark 6:39; John 6:10; Rev. 8:7; BDAG, 1087.
110. E.g., Matt. 6:30; BDAG, 1087.
111. E.g., Mark 4:28; Rev. 9:4; BDAG, 1087.
112. Zohary 1982, 172.

Having Endured Trials, You Will Be Rewarded (1:12–18)

James 1:12 is a summary of this first section[113] and a bridge to the second type of "trials": internal sinful desires (1:13–18).[114] As a summary, 1:12 reminds readers that, having endured trials, they will be rewarded. The poor should not have to endure the "trial" of being insufficiently valued by the world and the church (1:9–11). But, if they persevere, they will be rewarded. So will the "rich" if they learn to exalt in their humble status.

A number of words occur in 1:12 that have appeared previously: "endurance" (ὑπομονή, ὑπομένω, 1:3–4), "man" (ἀνήρ, 1:8), "trial" (πειρασμός, 1:2), "testing" (δόκιμος, δοκίμιος, 1:3), and "receive" (λαμβάνω, 1:7). One rhetorical technique that James uses is repetition of words (pleonasm) to connect his topics. By repeating these words, he connects 1:12 with the earlier section. In 1:3–4, James explains what endurance does (it produces maturity) and why it is worthwhile (one may become mature and complete, lacking nothing). Now, he gives a further benefit: the nature of the reward that person will receive, "the crown of life" (1:12).[115] The crown of life is not given to everyone, but only to the "man who endures trial." Again, James uses the sex-specific singular term ἀνήρ because he uses sex-specific terms in his illustrations (e.g., 1:8),[116] but then at the end of the sentence he uses the generic plural term "to the ones loving him."

In 1:2 "trials" is in the plural, referring to external unavoidable events that happen to one, such as persecution for the faith. Persevering faithfully (not double-willed) to God the Trinity is lauded in 1:12, but here the singular is used for **"trial"** and "man." Possibly, in this summary illustration, James wants to encourage every (singular) believer as he or she has surmounted each trying event.[117] The believer seeks to pass each "trial" and to be affirmed ("approved"). The gift of the "crown

---

113. That James 1:12 is a conclusion to 1:2–11 is affirmed by Hiebert 1979, 97; Vlachos 2013, 39; Davids 1982, 78–79; McKnight 2011, 105–6. Cf. Dibelius 1976, 88–89.

114. See also Laws 1980, 69; McCartney 2009, 104.

115. As opposed to the doubting "two-willed" person who does not receive (λαμβάνω) anything from the Lord (1:7).

116. In the Old Testament, "blessed is the man" (μακάριος ἀνήρ) repeatedly occurs, as in Psalm 1:1, where "man" (ἀνήρ) renders the Hebrew אִישׁ "man" or "mortal," "each," "every," "one" (BDB, 35–36; Kistemaker 1986, 46; Ropes 1916, 150; Poythress and Grudem 2000, 329).

117. Hiebert (1979, 98) suggests the singular is collective, "pointing to trial as the characteristic feature of present human experience."

of life" only comes after these two stages: (1) persevering in a trial, (2) becoming approved. What is the point of "testing" after God's word has been implanted in one? Testing helps God's seed to grow and demonstrates its genuineness. And what is being tested, according to the New Testament? Faith (1 Pet. 1:7; 2 Cor. 13:5), obedience (2 Cor. 2:9; 9:13), genuineness of apostleship (2 Cor. 13:3), ministry (1 Cor. 3:13; Gal 6:4), love (2 Cor. 8:8), and the spirits (1 John 4:1). Some examples of tested and approved people are Apelles (Rom. 16:10) and Timothy (Phil. 2:22). Δόκιμος suggests one is "genuine on the basis of testing."[118] Approval may be demonstrated by seeing a sign and coming to an accurate conclusion, such as predicting that when the south wind blows it is going to be hot, and it becomes hot (Luke 12:55–56).

The extended metaphor in James 1:12, the testing that results in a **crown** (στέφανος), probably alludes to athletics. Norman Gardiner explains that "the most coveted prize in the Greek world was the wreath of wild olive which was the only prize at the Olympic Games." The highest ancient honors were bestowed by the emperor.[119] Instead of olive branches, which are perishable and become brittle, God's crown partakes of the same nature as the ruler who bestows it. James's crown bestows eternal life because it comes from the eternal living God.[120] Other New Testament writers describe other qualities of the crown, which all flow from the nature of God: righteousness (2 Tim. 4:8), imperishability (1 Cor. 9:25), glory (1 Pet. 5:4), and becoming people-centered (1 Thess. 2:19–20; Phil. 4:1). In the Old Testament, crowns of gold were given to rulers[121] and thus were a symbol of glory (Job 19:9), but in James 1:12 the glory of the crown is not accentuated but rather its life-giving attribute. It is similar to the "crown of life" promised to believers in Smyrna who would die for their faith but yet live on (Rev. 2:10).[122] In an athletic contest, only one winner receives a crown. But from God there is no limit of crowns, and each persevering believer receives one crown. James Adamson explains: "Whereas the athletes have human competitors, the Christian's adversaries are the powers of darkness, trying to drive him out of the course and prevent his ever finishing it."[123] James

---

118. BDAG, 256.
119. Gardiner 1930, 2, 35–36, 47–48.
120. "Life" as an adjective characterizes the crown as consisting in life. See also Spencer 2014b, 141; Blomberg and Kamell 2008, 69; Mayor 1913, 49.
121. E.g., Ps. 21:3; 1 Macc. 10:20; 13:37; 2 Macc. 14:4. The Son of Man will have a crown of gold (Rev. 14:14).
122. See also Luke 6:22–23; 21:19; Matt. 24:13.
123. Adamson 1976, 68.

himself received God's crown of life when he was martyred for his proclamation of his faith before the crowd.

Another description of persevering believers is that they **love** the Lord (1:12). James uses a present participle (ἀγαπῶσιν) to describe such ongoing love of God in action. And its promised rewards are the crown of life (1:12), wealth in faith and inheritance (2:5), revelation about Jesus Christ crucified (1 Cor. 2:9), all things working for good (Rom. 8:28), and the triune God coming to them (John 14:23).[124] Leslie Mitton summarizes: "Those who love God are those who respond in obedience to the word of Christ."[125] What is the end result? Such a person is "happy" or "blessed" (μακάριος).[126]

Now James repeats **"trials"** (1:12–14, πειρασμός [noun], πειράζω [verb]) to bridge his discussion to another type of trials: "temptations" or internal sinful desires.[127] These "trials" are avoidable. They are described further in 1:14–15. James emphasizes the phrases "being tempted" and "from God" in 1:13a, thereby beginning and ending the first two clauses with the concept of "being tempted": "let no one, being tempted, say that from God I am being tempted" (1:13a). "To tempt" (πειράζω) and its opposite, "not to tempt" (ἀπείραστος), occur four times in just this one sentence.[128]

James begins with his usual command ("let no one say"), presenting the state of the reader who is in a "trial" (1:13–14). However, this trial is caused by the reader's own desire (ἐπιθυμία). "Own" is emphasized by being placed before the word modified ("desire," 1:14). One's own desire is contrasted with God's actions. The tempted person is quoted as saying: "from God I am being tempted" (1:13). This very wrong and blasphemous thought is answered in the following clauses: (1) God is untemptable[129] from evils; (2) and God tempts no one (1:13); (3) each human is tempted by his/her own desire (1:14); (4) rather, every good gift comes from God (1:17); (5) God has no evil side; and (6) one example of God's good gifts is human rebirth (1:18). This wrong thought (1:13a) is one example of the

---

124. See also Exod. 20:6; Deut. 5:10; 7:9; 30:19–20.
125. Mitton 1966, 46.
126. "Happy because of circumstances" (the circumstance of receiving such a crown) and "favored" (only the Lord is able to give such a crown) (BDAG, 610–11).
127. See earlier exposition on 1:2–4.
128. "No one" (μηδείς) and "no one" (οὐδένα) begin and end 1:13 for emphasis (Vlachos 2013, 44).
129. "Unable to be tempted" (Vlachos 2013, 43–44). See also Robertson 1933, 18; Mitton 1966, 47; McKnight 2011, 114–18.

evil deeds that must be thrown off or ended. Genuine humility includes accepting one's own responsibility for actions.

Chapter 1, verse 13 is an apt summary of the nature of **God**. In contrast to humans, God cannot be tempted by "evils."[130] Dan McCartney explains: "God does not tempt to evil, because to do so would be contrary to his character."[131] God may test people's obedience or love,[132] as Jesus tested the disciples' faith (John 6:6), but God never causes or encourages evil thoughts or actions.[133] John has a similar point to James's in 1 John: "The love of the Father is not in those who love the world; for all that is in the world—the desire of the flesh, the desire of the eyes, the pride in riches—comes not from the Father but from the world" (2:15b–16 NRSV).[134] Some evil deeds mentioned in James are anger (1:19–20), not bridling the tongue (1:26; 3:5–12), favoritism to the rich and depreciation of the poor (2:1–6, 9; 4:11; 5:1–4), envy, selfish ambition, coveting, fraud (3:14, 16; 4:2; 5:4), friendship with the world (4:4), false boasting (4:16), and swearing oaths (5:12).

In contrast to God, any human evil desire is self-initiated.[135] James clearly uses "**desire**" (1:14) (ἐπιθυμία [noun], ἐπιθυμέω [verb]) in a negative way.[136] "Desire" precedes action, is individual, and leads to sin and death (1:14–15). It can be so strong that it could lead to murder (4:2). The root idea is θυμός ("passion" or "strong feeling") from θύω: "to rush along or on, be in a heat, breathe violently."[137] Thus, ἐπιθυμέω means "to keep the θυμός turned upon a thing," hence, "to have a desire for."[138] Passions and desires can be neutral or positive as well as negative. For instance,

---

130. "Evils" [κακῶν] is a genitive of origin or reference signifying "by means of" or "with reference to."
131. McCartney 2009, 105.
132. E.g., Abraham, Gen. 22:1–16; Exod. 16:4; 20:20.
133. The plural κακός probably refers to the variety of "evil deeds" as opposed to "evil" in the singular as a general concept or a specific case, as in James 3:8, which refers to the tongue. See also BDAG, 501.
134. See also Sir. 15:11–13. In contrast, the pagan deities are liable to temptation (e.g., Spencer, Hailson, Kroeger, and Spencer 1995, ch. 3).
135. James repeats πειράζω ("to test") in 1:14 to show continuation of topic.
136. Stoic philosophers also tend to view "desire" as negative. Zeno includes under "desire or craving" "irrational appetency" such as want, hatred, contentiousness, anger, attraction, wrath, and resentment (*Lives* 7.111, 113). The difference though, according to Friedrich Büchsel (1965), is that "in Greek philosophy ἐπιθυμία" is "in conflict with" "rationality. It is estimated ethically rather than religiously" (169).
137. Thayer, 293; LSJ, 810.
138. Thayer, 238.

the prodigal son and destitute Lazarus desired to eat because they were hungry (Luke 15:16; 16:21). Jesus desired to be with his disciples (Luke 22:15). The righteous might desire to see the fulfillment of prophecies or the return of Jesus[139] or to see other believers (1 Thess. 2:17) or to be an overseer (1 Tim. 3:1) or to persevere (Heb. 6:11). In contrast, the New Testament has many examples where "desire" (or "passion") leads to sinful behavior, for instance, looking the wrong way at a woman (Matt. 5:28), coveting another's possessions,[140] committing idolatry or sexual immorality, testing and lack of trusting the Lord (1 Cor. 10:6–10).[141] Paul summarizes desires of the "flesh" as "sexual immorality, impurity and debauchery; idolatry and witchcraft; hatred, discord, jealousy, fits of rage, selfish ambition, dissensions, factions and envy; drunkenness, orgies, and the like" (Gal. 5:19–21a NIV).[142]

James then begins an extensive metaphor, a personification,[143] where "desire" is personified as a woman[144] who conceives and bears children (1:14–15). The process of temptation takes several stages: (1) Desire drags away (ἐξέλκω), (2) deceives (δελεάζω, 1:14), (3) conceives (συλλαμβάνω, 1:15), (4) bears (τίκτω) Sin, and then, when (5) Sin is fully formed (ἀποτελέω), (6) Sin[145] brings forth (ἀποκυέω) the child Death.[146]

Temptation begins with "**dragging away**" (ἐξέλκω, 1:14) and seducing by deception (δελεάζω). Ἐξέλκω is a composite of "draw" or "drag" (ἕλκω or ἑλκύω) intensified by the preposition "out of" (ἐκ),[147] signifying "drag out."[148] It could be used literally of drawing someone out

---

139. Matt. 13:17; Luke 17:22; 1 Pet. 1:12.
140. Acts 20:33; Rom. 7:7–8; 13:9; 1 Tim. 6:9.
141. See also Rom. 1:24; 1 Thess. 4:5. "Desire" (ἐπιθυμία, ἐπιθυμέω) is an important concept for Paul: 46 percent of the NT usages are by Paul (twenty-five of fifty-four).
142. See also Mark 7:21–23.
143. Personification invests abstractions (qualities, ideas, or general terms), inanimate objects, or nonhuman living things with human qualities or abilities, especially with human feelings (Spencer 1998a, 202).
144. "Desire" (ἐπιθυμία) in Greek is feminine in grammatical form.
145. James uses anadiplosis to show the successive or progressive nature of sin. "Sin" (ἁμαρτία) ends the first clause and begins the second clause in 1:15. See also Vlachos 2013, 46.
146. Verses 1:14–15 are similar to Proverbs 7:4–27 in that someone is being seduced away from Wisdom toward death. However, for James the seducer is "desire" within oneself.
147. Or "from within" (Robertson 1934, 596). The form ἐξέλκω is not found elsewhere in the NT, but it is found in the LXX.
148. LSJ, 534, 590.

of a pit (e.g., Joseph, Jeremiah),[149] or out of water (2 Sam. 22:17) or hauling out fish with a net.[150] Thereupon, it could be used of forcing (or dragging) someone to the authorities, or to be killed, as the crowd that seized Paul then dragged him outside the temple to kill him.[151] James uses the verb (ἕλκω) in 2:6 to refer to the rich "dragging" the poor to court. The verb can also be used in a more neutral way to describe the maidens wanting to be "drawn" after the king (Song 1:4), or a fighter drawing a sword out before using it[152] or a human drawing out breath.[153] In effect, the object is helpless as it or he is hauled out, in some cases, to health (as were Joseph and Jeremiah) or to potential death (as the fish or Paul). In James 1:14 ἐξέλκω is clearly negative.

Δελεάζω (1:14) signifies to "**entice**," possibly "catch by a bait." The "bait" is the δόλος or δέλεαρ.[154] In the New Testament and the Septuagint, δόλος always signifies "deceit." For example, "deceit" (the noun δόλος) is one of the negative characteristics that comes from within humans (Mark 7:22) but was not found in Jesus (1 Pet. 2:22). The chief priests and the elders sought to arrest Jesus in some deceitful way so that they could kill him without interference from the supportive crowds (Matt. 26:4). Peter uses the verb δελεάζω in a context of sexual immorality to describe the "seducing" or deceiving of unstable people (2 Pet. 2:14). One would have expected James to reverse the sequence in 1:14 to begin with δελεάζω. First, a victim such as a fish is caught, then it is hauled up and away in a net. But in James 1:14, by beginning with "drag away out" (ἐξέλκω), James communicates the overwhelming power that desire has in tempting a person. First, the desire drags one away before it seduces by deceit. The metaphor of sexual seducement begins in 1:14 and continues through 1:15. Since 1:15 clearly uses a sexual metaphor, 1:14 likely is the same,[155] so James warns in 1:16: "Do not deceive yourselves."

In contrast, some scholars see two metaphors, one in 1:14 relating to fishing and hunting and another in 1:15 relating to sexual

---

149. Gen. 37:28 (ἐξέλκω); Jer. 38:13.
150. John 21:6, 11. Oppian describes the strife between the fisher and the fish, "the one eager to rush away, the other eager to pull [ἕλκω] him in" (*Hal.* 3.322).
151. Acts 21:30; Job 20:28; 3 Macc. 4:7.
152. John 18:10; Judg. 20:2, 46.
153. Ps. 119:131; Jer. 14:6. It can also be used in a positive way: John 6:44; 12:32.
154. LSJ, 377; Thayer, 128, 155.
155. The development of a metaphor is the extent to which the author develops the ramifications of a certain comparison (Spencer 1998a, 197).

immorality.[156] Thayer mentions that ἐξέλκω is a "hunting and fishing" metaphor, but then he adds that "the language of hunting seems to be transferred" in James 1:14 to the "seductions of a harlot, personated by ἐπιθυμία."[157] In the ancient fishing manual *Halieutica* by Oppian, δόλος always relates to some action to deceive and ensnare. For example, the ox-ray fish "by might . . . could not overpower anything, but *by craft he ensnares* and overcomes even cunning men" (2.147), and, "as when men *devising a trick* of war against their foes . . . arm themselves" with armor from the slain so as to be able to enter the enemy's city (3.560). Sometimes a female fish is used to ensnare grey mullets:

> [They] are beguiled by a female *trailed* [ἕλκω] in the waves. . . . When they behold her, they gather around in countless numbers and wondrously overcome by her beauty they will not leave her but everywhere the spells of desire lead them charmed, yea even wert thou to draw forth the female *snare* [δόλος] from the water and lead them to the unfriendly dry land: they follow in a body, and heed neither *fraud* [δόλος] nor fishermen. But even as youths when they remark the face of a woman exceeding fair first gaze at her from afar, admiring her lovely form, and thereafter they draw near and, forgetting all, walk no more in their former ways but follow her with delight, beguiled by the sweet spells of Aphrodite: even so shalt thou behold the humid crowd of the Mullets passionately thronging. But swiftly with them love turns to hate; for speedily the fisher lifts the well-wrought net and spreads its lap and takes spoil unspeakable, easily enveloping the fishes in the embrace of the meshes. (4.127–46; see also 4.93–110)

In this illustration "to drag or trail" (ἕλκω) precedes "to deceive or ensnare" (δόλος). Oppian uses the example of a female as the one who deceives. However, Oppian also uses another example where females pursue male fishes, "drawn by [ἕλκω] the passion of desire the females hast after the males with rush incontinent. . . . There is much Passion among fishes and Desire and Jealousy" (1.492–500). Such a feminine metaphor also begins in James 1:14. But the difference between Oppian and James is that in James the female snare is within, not without, the

---

156. E.g., Davids 1982, 84; Ropes 1916, 156–57; McCartney 2009, 106. Danker's *Lexicon* points out that a "fishing metaphor is probable" with δελεάζω (BDAG, 217).

157. Thayer, 222.

person. The "desire" (ἐπιθυμία) is what drags away and, if allowed, results in one being ensnared by deception.

After seduction (δελεάζω, 1:14), **conception** (συλλαμβάνω) is next, and after nine months the child is born (τίκτω, 1:15). The angel Gabriel's message to Mary shows the sequence: "And behold *you will conceive* [συλλαμβάνω] in your womb and *you will bear* [τίκτω] a son" (Luke 1:31). Conception occurs before the nine months of pregnancy (Luke 1:24, 36, 57). Τίκτω refers not to the process of becoming pregnant, conception, or to the process of being in labor (e.g., John 16:21), but rather to the birth of the child, the time the child comes out of the birth canal (e.g., Luke 2:6–7). Usually in the New Testament it is used literally, for example, when an angel communicates to Joseph in a dream that Mary "will give birth to a son, and you will call his name Jesus" (Matt. 1:21).[158] The birth of a child should be a happy event, as when Eve and Adam bore Cain and Abel (Gen. 4:1–2), or Sarah bore Isaac (Gen. 17:17–19), but, in James's case, the child that is born is called "Sin" and when that child is fully formed,[159] it is recognized as "Death."

James uses the less common word ἀποκυέω to describe what has been delivered of this pregnancy,[160] the ghastly **Death** (1:15). No mother wants to deliver a child that is already dead, but this child is Death itself! Desire looked good before the child came. This birth is a parthenogenesis birth, a virgin birth. Since desire is inside a human, God cannot be blamed for having created this child. This birth is in contrast to the birth in James 1:18 created by the Creator of lights by means of a word of truth. James's metaphor in 1:15 is similar to Paul's in Romans 5:12–14, but James speaks not of the past (death through Adam's choice) but of the present and individual responsibility. Death is again mentioned at the end of James's letter: "The one having turned back a sinner from his erroneous wandering will save his life from death" (5:20). What is Death? Death is the result of continued sin, sin come to fruition (1:15), by those who do not love God in their actions (1:12), who will be condemned by the Judge (5:3, 9). Death characterizes not only the child but also the parent. Demonic characteristics will typify the parent's actions (e.g., 4:1–4). Edmond Hiebert explains: "Sin, having been born, has its own life and development."[161] Death begins now and continues forever, even as eternal life begins now and

---

158. See also Matt. 1:23; 2:2; Luke 2:11.
159. BDAG, 123: ἀποτελέω signifies to finish or be fully formed.
160. BDAG, 114: ἀποκυέω refers to "delivery of that with which one has been pregnant," with ἀπό retaining its perfective force.
161. Hiebert 1979, 108.

continues forever (1:12).[162] Eternal death is "the loss of that life of fellowship with God."[163]

James then commands his summarizing point: "Do not **deceive** yourselves" (1:16). Πλανάω literally means "to cause to stray, to lead astray, lead aside from the right way."[164] Following the wrong desire can indeed lead the reader astray. Πλανάω may refer to an animal or human who wanders off from the straight, correct, and safe path into a dangerous desert, mountain, cave, hole, or a wrong path.[165] In 1:16 the verb is present tense, indicating this is a current problem. The passive or middle voice can be translated "be deceived" or "deceive yourselves." Since the earlier verses (1:13–15) concern an internal human desire, the middle voice ("deceive yourself") seems more applicable. In contrast, in 5:19–20 the passive voice is used, indicating that there James refers to someone "led astray" by someone else from the path of truth to a false path. Thus, in 1:16 the "beloved brothers and sisters" deceive themselves. They cause themselves to be led astray by misunderstanding who God is in contrast to who they are.

James refers to **"brother"** in the plural (1:16) to indicate "brothers and sisters" twenty times in this letter.[166] "Brother" is a metaphor for equality. For example, Emperor Gaius (Caligula), according to Josephus, had the "audacity" to address the pagan deity Jupiter as "brother," making himself equal to a god (*Ant.* 19.1.1.4). "My beloved brothers and sisters" occurs three times in the letter (1:16, 19; 2:5),[167] each of those times intensifying James's expression of love for his fellow Christians. The readers are his "siblings" and "beloved." By this phrase, he tries to encourage his readers toward a positive decision.

He then returns with a beautiful image to the topic of God's nature (1:13, 17–18), in contrast (implied) to human nature (1:14–16). The subject has parallel terms[168] ("every good gift and every perfect

---

162. Perkins (1995, 101) states that "those who persist in sin receive the antithesis of the crown of life. They experience death." See also Mitton 1966, 50.

163. Hiebert 1979, 109.

164. Thayer, 514.

165. Heb. 11:38; Matt. 18:12–13; 1 Pet. 2:25.

166. See excursus on "Significance of Gender Language in James," in chapter 1.

167. "My beloved brothers and sisters" also occurs in 1 Corinthians 15:58 and Philippians 4:1. "Our beloved brother" is used in 2 Peter 3:15 about Paul. James's letter refers to Barnabas and Paul as "our beloved" (Acts 15:25).

168. Parallelism is the repetition of a syntactic or structural pattern. Demetrius (*Eloc.* 23) says like corresponds with like throughout: article opposed to article, "connective to connective, like to like," everything is parallel,

present") emphasizing the type of **gifts** that should more than satisfy every healthy human desire. These gifts are not from within (1:14) but "from above" (ἄνωθεν, 1:17).[169] James repeats (pleonasm) synonyms for "gifts" (δόσις, δώρημα), "perfect" (ἀγαθός, τέλειος), and "every" (πᾶς). In this sentence, the reader first dwells on the nature of what is from God ("every good gift and every perfect present is from above") as a way to tell us about God. God is explicitly mentioned later in the sentence ("the Father of lights"). The whole sentence alludes to a sun-shower. Rain falls down from above, but at the same time the sun or moon is shining. Normally the sun or moon causes shadows, but not in this case. The image continues in 1:18 where the rain has caused earth to produce "a firstfruit." James has used an image to communicate an analogy. Like the sun and rain, God causes physical and spiritual life and growth and nutrition, but unlike the sun and moon, God's "light" creates no shadow. God has no dark side. Israel is an arid land, where the early and late rains are eagerly awaited (5:7). Having both light *and* rain is unusual and in itself a great gift. The gift of rain is a harvest (5:18, καρπός), which provides nutrition and a reason for thanking God (1:18, "firstfruit," ἀπαρχή).

In James the two words for "gift" allude back to wisdom given from "the One *giving*, namely, God, to all generously and without reproaching" (1:5). The two nouns James uses in 1:17, one feminine (δόσις) and one neuter (δώρημα), both come from the same verb, δίδωμι. Both begin with the same Greek letter.[170] Neither is common in the New Testament. Δώρημα is rare in prose.[171] Paul uses δόσις to refer to financial gifts (Phil. 4:15)[172] and δώρημα to refer to the gifts of reconciliation, justification, righteousness, and salvation obtained when Christ died for human sinners (Rom. 5:9–17). The related δωρεά is also used of gifts from God, such as living water, the Holy Spirit, and grace.[173]

---

from the beginning to the end (Spencer 1998a, 198). This sentence is not "parallelism," but the subject does have "parallel terms" or pleonasm.
169. "From above" (an adverb) is emphasized by being placed before the verb "is."
170. Thus, some versions repeat "gift" as in the ESV ("every good gift and every perfect gift"), but that rendering does not bring out the two different words for "gift."
171. LSJ, 464.
172. Robertson (1933, 19) and others think that "*dosis* is the act of giving" (progression) while *dōrēma* is "the gift itself" (result) (Hiebert 1979, 110–11; Kistemaker 1986, 55).
173. John 4:10; Acts 2:38; 8:20; 10:45; 11:17; 2 Cor. 9:15; Eph. 3:7; 4:7; Heb. 6:4.

The adverb can be used of life, finances, or God's grace.[174] Aspects of the meaning of δίδωμι are covered in both nouns. In the image, the gifts are a "natural product," such as a crop or harvest. Δόσις and δώρημα can refer to a gift given as an "expression of generosity" or a gift from a "financial transaction."[175]

The gifts are modified by two different synonyms: "good" (ἀγαθός) and "perfect" (τέλειος). "Good" (ἀγαθός) is used both here and in 3:17 to describe what comes "from above" (ἄνωθεν) and not from the world or from evil (3:15). "Above" (ἄνωθεν from ἄνω) is a synecdoche used elsewhere of God's presence. For example, Jesus said, "I am from above" (John 8:23), and John comments, he is "the One coming from above" who is "above all" (John 3:31). Since God is "Spirit" (John 4:24), one would imagine that God is all around (e.g., Eph. 4:6 "over all and through all and in all").[176] However, the heavens, which God created, are also a symbol of God's presence (e.g., John 11:41).

Goodness is an aspect of God's character (1:17), the One who gives "good gifts to the ones asking" (Matt. 7:11). Jesus said: "No one is good except one—God" (Mark 10:18; Luke 18:19). The opposite of goodness is deception (John 7:12). Thayer's definition of "good" as "benevolent, kind, generous" certainly fits.[177] Psalm 118 is a helpful passage to define "goodness" since it begins and ends on that topic: "Give thanks to the Lord, for he is good, for his mercy endures forever" (vv. 1, 29). God's goodness is exemplified in this psalm by God's relational mercy and his answering prayer, helping people, being faithful and powerful, and providing salvation, life, and righteousness. The temple praise team would sing: "O give thanks to the Lord, for he is good; for his steadfast love endures forever" (1 Chron. 16:34; 2 Chron. 5:13). The rabbis agreed. For example, Rabbi Judah taught that for rain and good tidings one should say: "Blessed is he, the good and the doer of good" (m. Ber. 9:2).

The synonym τέλειος (1:17) is used several times in James: as a goal for the believer (1:4; 3:2; 2:22 [verb]) and description of God's law (1:25). Τέλειος can signify maturity or perfection.[178] In 1:17 "**perfection**" is an apt understanding since the gift comes from God. God's gift is perfectly fit for its purpose. It is not deficient or harmful in any way.

---

174. Rom. 3:24; Gal. 2:21; 2 Cor. 11:7; 2 Thess. 3:8; Rev. 21:6; 22:17.
175. Δίδωμι: BDAG, 242.
176. The One "in whom we live and move and have our being" (Acts 17:26). See Spencer, Hailson, Kroeger, and Spencer 1995, 137–39.
177. Thayer, 3.
178. See 1:4 exposition.

God's "perfect present" will help the believer to become perfect or mature. Receiving God's wisdom is one way to become mature.

Now James tells us from whom (and from where) these gifts come: "coming down from the Father of lights" (1:17). He continues the imagery "from above" by now adding "**coming down**" (καταβαίνω, 1:17). βαίνω refers to motion ("come" or "go") and κατά indicates the direction is "downwards" ("come or go down").[179] While the New Testament often uses καταβαίνω literally, such as the "rain came down" (Matt. 7:25, 27) or a windstorm came down from the mountain to the lake (Luke 8:23), it also uses the word to describe the presence of the Trinity— the Father, the Son, or the Spirit,[180] as the Son of Man *came down* from heaven. Angels also come down from heaven,[181] as does the New Jerusalem.[182] The Son will return to earth from heaven (1 Thess. 4:16). Thus, James's image continues the idea that the gifts "come down" from God, who is "above." The participle ("coming down") also indicates James does not refer to a one-time event of generosity.[183]

Finally, James indicates who sends these gifts ("the **Father of lights**") and in an adjectival clause describes him as "from whom there is no change, the one [meaning the change] of a turning shadow" (1:17).[184] The plural "lights" most likely refers to Genesis 1:16: "God made the two great lights—the greater light to rule the day and the lesser light to rule the night—and the stars" (NRSV). Φωστήρ is used in Genesis (LXX), but φῶς is used in Psalm 136:7–9: give thanks to the Lord of lords "who made the great lights, for his steadfast love endures forever; the sun to rule over the day, . . . the moon and stars to rule over the night" and in Psalm 56:13, the "land of lights." In Psalm 148:3 φῶς seems to summarize sun, moon, and stars. Isaiah 30:26 uses φῶς to refer to "light" of the moon and "light" of the sun.[185] James's use of plural "lights" is different from use in the rest of the New Testament, which tends to use φῶς in the singular literally to refer to, for instance,

---

179. LSJ, 302, 882, 884.
180. Acts 7:34; Son: John 3:13; 6:33, 38, 41–42, 50–51, 58; Spirit: Matt. 3:16; Mark 1:10; Luke 3:22; John 1:32–33.
181. Matt. 28:2; John 1:51; Rev. 10:1; 18:1; 20:1.
182. Rev. 3:12; 21:2, 10.
183. See also Blomberg and Kamell 2008, 73.
184. See translation for discussion of variant. I have concluded that the best attested reading is παραλλαγὴ ἤ τροπῆς ἀποσκίασματος.
185. Wisdom 13:2 uses φωστήρας οὐρανοῦ ("lights of heaven") to refer to what became misunderstood as pagan gods.

a "light from heaven" which blinded Saul,[186] or the light(s) of a torch (Acts 16:29) or a lamp (Luke 8:16; 11:33), but mainly in metaphorical uses, as in "God is light" (1 John 1:5, 7) and dwells in "unapproachable light" (1 Tim. 6:16), and Jesus is "the light of the world" (John 9:5). Christians in a derivative way are "now light in the Lord" (Eph. 5:8). But the context of James's use is creation and rebirth (1:17–18), in contrast to creation of sin (1:14–15).

"Father" (πατήρ, 1:17) is a common metaphor for God in the New Testament, especially in John's writings. "Father" is the most frequent term for God in the New Testament because of its frequent use in the gospels of John and Matthew, but, outside of these gospels, "Lord" is the most frequent metaphor for God and Jesus.[187] The biblical metaphor of God as "Father" presents a paradoxical picture of a very powerful "father" who is also very tender. "Father" is also a synonym for "Ruler" or "Judge." "Father" for God is used three times in James. In 1:17 "Father" alludes to God's capacity to create,[188] in 1:27 to God's concern for humans who can be easily oppressed (orphans and widows), and in 3:7–9 to the creator of animals. "Lord" signifies a relationship of obedience and submission because humans are not equal to the God of the Bible.

Titles Used for the Trinity in James							
Title:	Lord	Father	Name	Above	Judge	Lawgiver	One
Number of references:	14	3	3	3	2	1	1
References:	1:1, 7; 2:1; 3:9; 4:10, 15; 5:4, 7, 8, 10, 11, 14, 15	1:17, 27; 3:9	2:7; 5:10, 14	1:17; 3:15, 17	4:12; 5:9	4:12	2:19

---

186. Acts 9:3; 22:6, 9, 11; 26:13.
187. "Father" for God occurs 258 times in the NT. If the uses in the Gospels of John and Matthew are removed, only ninety-nine references remain in the NT. "Lord" occurs 252 times in the NT, 236 outside of the gospels of John and Matthew. See further on "father" in Spencer, Hailson, Kroeger, and Spencer 1995, 113–20, 211–15.
188. Therefore, CEB translates the phrase "the creator of the heavenly lights." Similarly, Philo calls God "the Father and Maker of the world" and "its Lawgiver" (*Moses* 2.8.487).

Like the rest of the New Testament, James uses "Lord" most frequently as a metaphor for the First and Second Persons of the Trinity. "Name" is the third most frequent synecdoche for God in the New Testament and one of the more frequent terms in James.[189] Judgment is one aspect of an ancient "father" of a nation. In effect, the "Father of lights" is the "Creator of lights," but the term "Father" connotes more intimacy and personal care than "Creator." A caring "father" would want to give his children good gifts, rewards, wisdom, and truth (1:5, 12, 17–18).

The end of 1:17 may be translated "the Father of lights, from whom there is no": (1) "**change** or **shadow** *of* turning" (or, "change or shadow that is cast by turning"; "shadow" or ἀποσκίασμα is in the nominative case)[190] or (2) "change, *the one* of a turning *shadow*" (or "the turning of a shadow"; ἀποσκίασματος is in the genitive case). The older Greek manuscripts support the latter rendering, which I have used for this commentary.[191]

Παραλλαγή (1:17) refers to change of position, movement, or variation.[192] It is used in 2 Kings 9:20 regarding Jehu son of Nimshi for the way he rode his horse with furious haste, referring specifically to the rapid movement of his horse. Τροπή refers to turn, turning, change,[193] as in Deuteronomy 33:14 for the changes of the sun, which causes different fruits to grow in different seasons (ἡλίου τροπῶν).[194] Ἀποσκίασμα, "shadow," also may refer to the measures of time by the shadow on the sundial.[195] Thus, the phrase may be rendered "the Father of lights, from whom there is no movement, the one of a turning shadow."

A shadow is a dark figure or image cast on the ground by a body intercepting light.[196] The sun and moon cast shadows as the light is blocked by a body. As the earth rotates, the shadow moves. God's literal "lights" (the sun and moon) cast shadows, but God's metaphorical lights do not cast shadows. This does not mean that God is impassive, unresponsive to pleas for mercy or requests for wisdom. Rather, it

---

189. "Name" (ὄνομα) refers to the First and Second Persons of the Trinity 117 times in the NT.
190. E.g., NRSV, NTME, ESV.
191. See also Ropes 1916, 162–64. The entire phrase is unique in the Bible.
192. LSJ, 1316. BDAG, 768, says it rarely refers to astronomy.
193. LSJ, 1826.
194. LXX. See also Job 38:33. Τροπή may also be used of the turns in a battle, e.g., 1 Macc. 4:35; 5:61; 2 Macc. 12:27, 37.
195. LSJ, 217.
196. *Random House Webster's* 2001, 1756.

means that there is no evil of any kind, only good, in God's character.[197] This is an image that further describes God as "untemptable by means of evils, and himself tempts no one" (1:13) and the giver of only good gifts (1:17). Every metaphor is like and unlike its concept. In this one, God's gifts come down from the sky like rain in a sun-shower, but, unlike the sun, God's lights do not create any shadows.

This "sun-shower" results in the earth producing a wholly good harvest, symbolizing human **rebirth** (1:18). The delivery in verse 18 contrasts with the delivery (ἀποκύεω) in verse 15: one impelled by God's desire (βούλομαι) versus another by human desire (ἐπιθυμία), one by means of a word of truth versus another by an internal deceit and temptation, one regarding truth versus another sin, one resulting in firstfruits[198] versus another in the child Death. The same main verb is used (ἀποκύεω) in both verses, but in verse 18 the aorist denotes a one-time event, the rebirth,[199] whereas in verse 15 the participles ("dragging away and seducing," "having conceived," "having been fully formed") and present indicative ("gives birth") denote more of a process.

The means of rebirth ("a **word of truth**," 1:18) will again be alluded to later in verse 21 ("the implanted word"). What is the "word of truth"? Commentators have answered this question in various ways, centering on how the phrase fits in the context of the letter or the rest of the New Testament, who is acting, and allusions outside the letter. If God is doing the birthing, then God is the one using a "word" to bring birth. The God who by means of a word created the lights in the sky and created humanity (Gen. 1:14, 26; 2 Pet. 3:5) can recreate humanity.[200] Since James writes to believers ("brothers and sisters" who share his faith, e.g., 1:2–3), "birth" here refers to spiritual rebirth, not to the birth of all humans. Both here and in 1:21 he appears to allude to Jesus's parable of the sowing of the seeds (Luke 8:1–15).[201] Jesus explains that "the seed is the word of God" (Luke 8:11). Some seed "fell into the good soil and, having grown, it produced a harvest [καρπός][202] a hundred times greater" (Luke 8:8). "The word of God" in Luke 8:11

---

197. Thus, CEB translates the phrase "in whose character there is no change at all." Laws (1980, 73) agrees that James insists in "the consistency of God as only and always the giver of good."
198. Hiebert (1979, 118) notes the emphatic location of "his," thereby emphasizing the difference of God's creation from human creation.
199. See also Hiebert 1979, 116.
200. See also Laws 1980, 75–78.
201. See also McCartney 2009, 110.
202. This same word is used in James 3:17–18; 5:7, 18.

may have a dual reference. God is the One behind the process,[203] and God is the content of the message.[204] The human "sower" distributes the seed. Thus, in James 1:18, "a word of truth" indicates the way the Father gives birth, 1:21 is the result of 1:18, the word or message is implanted, and in 1:22–23 James urges obedience to that message.[205] Verse 18 looks at the process from God's perspective. This verse is key for observing the initial stage of rebirth and justification, on which Paul elaborates in his own letter to the Romans. Verse 21 then looks at the process from a human perspective, the human response after the word has been planted.

Many commentators conclude that in using "a word of truth," James refers to the preaching of the word by humans.[206] In other words, God brings rebirth by humans preaching the gospel message. The phrase "word of truth" (λόγος, ἀλήθεια) occurs five times in the New Testament, four times by Paul.[207] It refers to the message of good news that was heard (Eph. 1:13; Col. 1:5), to a type of ministry describing a genuine servant of God (2 Cor. 6:7), and to the oral or written gospel message (2 Tim. 2:15). The main impetus for this interpretation is outside James, as J. B. Mayor writes: the "word" is "explained in the parallel passage, 1 Pet. i.25," as in Romans 10:8, 17: "God's instrument for communicating the new life."[208] However, the context of James should take priority over Paul's use of the term. In James 1:18, God is the active agent, and the immediate context refers to God as the creator (1:17–18).[209] "Word of truth" may refer to the human transmission of the good news, but here it refers to God's transmission of the good news.

A further allusion of James may relate to his use of ἀπαρχή in 1:18. Continuing the metaphor of birth and new life, the "child" is not Death, but instead it is "a kind of **firstfruit**" of God's "creations" (1:18). The birth is a singular collective (ἀπαρχή, "firstfruit"). The Old Testament process of offering the firstfruit(s) also provides a helpful background

---

203. "God" is in the subjective genitive; thus, God produces the word.
204. "God" is in the objective genitive; thus, the word is about God.
205. The verb "say" (λέγω) is used in James to introduce quotations: 1:13; 2:3, 11, 14, 16, 18, 23; 4:6, 13, 15.
206. E.g., Robertson 1933, 21 as in 2 Cor. 6:7; Ropes 1916, 166; Hiebert 1979, 116; Vlachos 2013, 49; Blomberg and Kamell 2008, 75; Dibelius 1976, 105; Davids 1982, 89; Mayor 1913, 63.
207. Kohlenberger, Goodrick, and Swanson 1995, 598.
208. Mayor 1913, 63. Ironically, in these passages ῥῆμα is used, not λόγος. But Mayor also refers to Eph. 1:13; 2 Cor. 6:7; 2 Tim. 2:15; and Col. 1:5.
209. See also Laws 1980, 77–78.

to verse 18. The Hebrews were exhorted to offer some of the first of all the "fruit" (harvest), and take it to the tabernacle (temple), and bring it to the priest (Deut. 26:1–3).[210] At this point, the person offering the firstfruits of the harvest was to recite the "avowal," Deuteronomy 26:5–10, which is a recital of God's work among the Israelites. According to the Mishnah, if this avowal was not recited before the eating of the firstfruits, the person was liable to the "Forty Stripes," forty less one lashes between the shoulders (m. Mak. 3:3, 10). Reciting the avowal was that important! At the end of this recitation, the worshiper bowed before the Lord (Deut. 26:10), then the worshiper, Levite, and immigrant celebrated (Deut. 26:11). The passage then describes who should be included in the third-year (year of the tithe) celebration: the Levites, the aliens, the orphans, and the widows (Deut. 26:12–13). The event is summarized by an exhortation to walk in the ways of the Lord and keep his commandments (Deut. 26:17–18), closing with a promise that the Lord's people are honored people (Deut. 26:19). Giving of the firstfruits was extremely important both in Old Testament times and in James's time as well. One of the tractates in the Mishnah is even called "Firstfruits" (m. Bik.). The metaphorical meaning of ἀπαρχή was used elsewhere in the New Testament to refer to the resurrected Christ (1 Cor. 15:20) as the first of many to be resurrected; to the Holy Spirit (Rom. 8:23) as the down payment of future glory; and to converts such as Epaenetus and Stephana's household (Rom. 16:5; 1 Cor. 16:5; 2 Thess. 2:13) as the first of many converts in Asia and Achaia.

James refers to believers as "firstfruit,"[211] analogous to the first of the harvest and thereby dedicated to God, set apart as holy, and a witness to God's goodness and blessings. The declaration of the avowal may be compared to a "word of truth," the good news of God's work in their lives. Verse 18 sets up the future beneficiaries, when those who do God's word (James 1:22) provide for the needy, the orphans, and the widows (1:27) and honor the poor (2:5). Is the word of truth said by the Father of lights or by the human worshiper? In James, the Father of lights speaks a word of truth causing the act of rebirth that produces

---

210. In Exodus 22:29–30 animals and children were included, but firstborn sons were redeemed. See also Exod. 23:16, 19 (which is cited in m. Bik. 1:9); Lev. 23:10; Num. 18:12–19; Deut. 18:4. The time for the offering is mentioned in Exod. 34:22; Lev. 23:15–22; Num. 28:26; Deut. 16:9–12; m. Ma῾as. S. 5:6.
211. A few commentators think "firstfruit" refers specifically to Jewish Christian believers, as opposed to Gentiles (Hiebert 1979, 117–18; McKnight 2011, 131).

the firstfruit (1:18). Moreover, even the avowal in the Old Testament is a human recitation of *God*'s work among Israel. So, everything God creates is good (Gen. 1:31; 1 Tim. 4:4), including this gift of rebirth.

Receive the Implanted Word by Becoming Doers of the Word and Not Hearers Only (1:19–27)

Suddenly, with another verb of command (**"understand"**),[212] James begins his thesis paragraph (1:19–27), repeating again his endearing phrase "my beloved brothers and sisters" (1:16, 19). He wants his readers to receive the implanted word by becoming doers of the word and not hearers only. In the earlier subdivisions of chapter 1, all the sections had related to the context of trials, the subdivisions connecting further with each other stylistically by repetition (anadiplosis) (1:4–5), use of δέ for a transition (1:8–9), a summary, and repetition (pleonasm) (1:11–12). In 1:19, James connects with the earlier verses by repeating "my beloved brothers and sisters." But the abrupt sentence with two imperatives (ἴστε, ἔστω) makes this sentence stand out as it introduces this next section of the chapter (1:19–27), which summarizes his main message and ties together his three themes relating to trials, wisdom, and wealth.[213]

James wants his Christian family "to grasp the meaning," "understand, recognize, come to know, [and] experience"[214] what he has been saying (earlier in 1:18 and following 1:19a). He does not want the believers to be like Jesus's disciples who heard the parable of the sower but did not understand it so as to apply it to their lives (Mark 4:13). The second half of James 1:19, in an abrupt sentence (asyndeton),[215] develops one application of understanding by doing: "and let every human be quick to hear, slow to speak, slow to anger" (1:19b). The asyndeton, which omits the final "and," gives a staccato effect, making each phrase equal in importance. The first two phrases are clearly antithetic (and

---

212. A command also begins the earlier sections: 1:2, 5, 9. Verse 1:12 does not have a command, but 1:13 does.
213. Instead of considering 1:19 to be an unrelated saying, as one might expect, Dibelius insists it introduces 1:19–27 (1976, 108–9). McCartney (2009, 115) considers 1:19 to be "a bridge verse." Blomberg and Kamell (2008, 81) suggest "all of vv. 19–27 can be seen as explaining how to avoid turning trials into temptations, as in vv. 13–18."
214. Οἶδα, BDAG, 694.
215. Asyndeton is the deliberate omission of conjunctions between a series of related words, phrases, or clauses separated by commas (Spencer 1998a, 188).

parallel):[216] "**quick to hear**, slow to speak." Now James uses the generic "human" (ἄνθρωπος) in the singular to signal for each reader to ponder. "Quick to hear" is an important theme for Jesus, as well as Proverbs. James's exhortation may be understood at the literal level: use your faculty of hearing before you use the faculty of speaking. For example, Solomon teaches, "One who spares words is knowledgeable; one who is cool in spirit has understanding. Even fools who keep silent are considered wise; when they close their lips, they are deemed intelligent" (Prov. 17:27–28 NRSV).[217] Ἀκούω also has to do with a deeper level of understanding that will result in repentant action. For instance, in James 2:5 James exhorts his readers to understand his message about the poor and to stop discriminating against them because God has chosen them. The parable of the sower has to do with the capacity of the different "soils" to hear and understand (e.g., ἀκούω is repeated fifteen times in Matt. 13:9–23). The parable ends "the one having ears, let him/her hear" (Matt. 13:9). Jesus tells his disciples that their ears are blessed, "for they hear" (Matt. 13:16). And, finally, the one who receives the seed that falls on good soil is the one who hears and understands the word (Matt. 13:23). In a similar way, if another believer "sins against you," Jesus teaches, show him/her the fault. If he "listens" to you, it means that he agrees with your assessment and is willing to change (Matt. 18:15–16). At this deeper level, in 1:19 James is exhorting his readers to hear his message and the message God reveals by understanding and agreeing, and then changing their actions appropriately. In 1:22 genuine hearing should result in doing (or action).

Why then does James move at the end of 1:19 to "**anger**"? In Proverbs, wisdom and anger are closely tied to speaking, for example: "A soft answer turns away wrath, but a harsh word stirs up *anger*. The tongue of the *wise* dispenses knowledge, but the mouths of fools pour out folly" (15:1–2 NRSV); "A fool gives full vent to anger, but the wise quietly holds it back" (29:11 NRSV); "Whoever is slow to anger has great understanding, but one who has a hasty temper exalts folly" (14:29 NRSV).[218] Solomon rephrases these ideas: "The patient in spirit are better than the proud in spirit. Do not be quick to anger, for anger lodges in the bosom of fools" (Eccl. 7:8b–9 NRSV). Jesus son of Sirach takes these Old Testament teachings and adds: "Be quick to listen, but over your answer

---

216. The first two phrases are parallel, but the parallelism is broken by the last phrase, which lacks an article.
217. Herman 2017 develops the importance of listening in postmodern evangelism (41).
218. See also Prov. 10:13, 19; 13:3; 16:32; 18:4, 6–7; 29:20, 22; Eccl. 5:1–2.

take time," and "If you are content to listen, you will learn; if you are attentive, you will grow wise" (Sir. 5:11; 6:33 REB). The rabbis agreed: the disciple who is "swift to hear and slow to lose" (what he has learned) has a happy lot (m. 'Abot 5:12). Rabbi Shammai advises: "Say little and do much" (m. 'Abot 1:15).[219] Anger may cause even a devout person to disrespect God. Moses's anger at the rebellious Israelites impelled him to strike the rock twice, not simply command the rock, with the result that Moses could not enter the promised land.[220] Anger affects others and oneself. Jesus also taught his disciples to guard against anger. Anger can be destructive: "You have heard that it was said to the people long ago, 'You shall not murder, and anyone who murders will be subject to judgment.' But I tell you that anyone who is angry with a brother or sister will be subject to judgment" (Matt. 5:21–22 NIV).

In other words, James tells his readers to ask for genuine wisdom that encourages one to hear, understand, and eventually speak in a healing and knowledgeable manner. Later in the letter James will return to the nature of godly speaking (1:26; 3:1–12) and godly wisdom (3:13–18; 5:7) in contrast to demonic strife (4:1–5, 11–12) and negative actions (e.g., 4:13–16; 5:12). Wisdom affects one's listening and one's acting. Being careful to listen *before* speaking will result in less ungodly anger. Anger may involve punishing words and actions. God's "anger," unlike human anger, is never rash or unjust. God's anger eventually comes on those who are disobedient (Eph. 5:6). The Lord does not want any to perish, but wants all to come to repentance (2 Pet. 3:9). In contrast, human anger is often unduly impatient and does not result in God's righteousness (James 1:20).[221] Verse 20 is an explanation and illustration of 1:19.[222] "Righteousness" here is one of God's characteristics, mentioned even in Deuteronomy 32:4 as a synonym of holiness. The opposite is "all filth" and "abundance of evil" (1:21). Righteousness is a quality obtained by Abraham and Rahab by their faithful actions (2:21–25).

"For this reason" (inferential conjunction διο[223]) begins 1:21, summarizing the chapter and explicitly stating the thesis of the letter. The

---

219. The rabbinic and Old Testament encouragement of silence as a background to 1 Timothy 2:12 may be found in Spencer 1985, 74–81; 2013, 58–63.
220. Num. 20:1–13; 27:13–14; Deut. 1:37; 3:25–27; Ps. 106:32–33; 1 Cor. 10:4 (Kistemaker 1986, 57).
221. Paul has a similar concern about human anger in Eph. 4:26, 31–32; Col. 3:8; 1 Tim. 2:8.
222. The end of 1:19 and start of 1:20 are also connected by anadiplosis, the repetition of ὀργή. See also Vlachos 2013, 53.
223. See also Wallace 1996, 673, 761.

participial phrase ("having laid aside all filth and abundance of evil") precedes the main verb ("receive") because this action is indispensable before the "implanted word" may be fully received. Ἀποτίθημι may literally refer to taking off clothes and **laying them down**,[224] as when the witnesses to Stephen's stoning took off and laid down their robes at Saul's feet (Acts 7:58), or when Nicanor took off and laid down his "glorious apparel" before he escaped (2 Macc. 8:35). In a similar fashion, the believer needs to take off and lay down "all filth and abundance of evil" (1:21). James repeats two negatives (pleonasm). The first negative, **"filth"** (ῥυπαρία), comes from ῥύπος, which signifies "dirt," "dirt as refuse differentiated from soil."[225] For example, Job says: "If I wash myself with soap and cleanse my hands with lye, yet you will plunge me into *filth*, and my own clothes will abhor me" (9:30–31 NRSV). The adjective ῥυπαρός is used in James 2:2 to describe the clothes of the poor. "Dirt" (ῥύπος) may be used as a synonym for "sin," as when the high priest Joshua is described as dressed with "filthy clothes" (Zech. 3:3–4), or as in Isaiah where the Hebrews left in Jerusalem would be called "holy" once the Lord had washed away the "filth" of Zion (4:3–4).

The synonym for "all filth" is **"abundance of evil"** (κακία, 1:21). The adjective κακός was used already in this letter to describe what cannot tempt God (1:13). In 3:8 κακός describes the untamed tongue. Thus, verbal sins such as anger and undue haste to speak are included in "evil" (1:19).[226] However, "abundance" certainly implies that much quantity and every kind of evil can be included in this list, as Paul describes: "They were filled with every kind of wickedness, *evil*, covetousness, malice. Full of envy, murder, strife, deceit, craftiness, they are gossips, slanderers, God-haters, insolent, haughty, boastful, inventors of evil, rebellious toward parents, foolish, faithless, heartless, ruthless" (Rom. 1:29–31 NRSV). Other New Testament authors have used similar imagery: once one takes off the rags of evil or the former way of life, anger, or sin,[227] then new "clothes" of the new self may be put on,[228] or the person may remain naked (to run, in Hebrews 12:1, or to live as a newborn child, in 1 Peter 2:1).[229] If refuse is piled over the soil, how can the seed reach the good soil?

---

224. BDAG, 123.
225. BDAG, 908.
226. See also McKnight 2011, 141–42; Mitton 1966, 63.
227. Rom. 13:12; Eph. 4:22; Col. 3:8; Heb. 12:1; 1 Pet. 2:1.
228. Eph. 4:22; Col. 3:8; Rom. 13:12.
229. Ἀποτίθημι ("throw off") and κακία ("evil") both may be found in James 1:21; Col. 3:8; 1 Pet. 2:1.

Then James emphasizes "in **humility**" by placing it before the main verb "receive" (1:21).[230] "Humility" or "gentleness" (noun: πραΰτης; adjective: πραΰς) is not from a frequent biblical word family, but it is from a significant one. In James 1:21, it describes the way to receive the implanted word, and in 3:13 it describes the type of wisdom a truly learned person should have. It is "tamed" (3:7–8). Πραΰς may refer to "mild, soft, gentle," as opposed to angry (1:19).[231] Jesus said that he is *gentle* and humble in heart" and gives rest to those with heavy burdens (Matt. 11:28–30). Therefore, compassion and kindness are aspects of πραΰτης. Paul appeals to this characteristic of Jesus when he exhorts the Corinthians (2 Cor. 10:1). No wonder those with a similar quality will inherit the earth (Matt. 5:5; Ps. 37:11; 76:9). Jesus combines πραΰτης (humility and appearing unimpressive) with great power (Zech. 9:9 [vv. 8, 10] cited in Matt. 21:5). Moses was characterized by great humility (Num. 12:3),[232] as was David when in God's presence (Ps. 132 [131]:1 LXX). David teaches his listeners that, to be taught by the Lord, one must be humble (Ps. 25:9). Humility is then an important aspect of the Christian life, exemplified by James himself when he begins his letter by describing himself simply as a "slave of God" (1:1).

The **"implanted word"** (1:21) is not planted by oneself (cf. 1:14–15), but it is planted by another.[233] That one is the Father of lights (1:17–18). Jesus communicates similar principles when he prays to the Father about his disciples: "The words which you gave to me, I gave to them, and they themselves received them and know truthfully that from you I came and they believed that you sent me" (John 17:8). The word of truth is given by the Father, but still it must be received or welcomed. "Implanted" (ἔμφυτος) is a combination of "in" (ἐν) and "to plant" or "grow" (φύω): to plant in. "To plant or grow" (φύω) is used in the parable

---

230. See also Hiebert 1979, 130.
231. LSJ, 1459.
232. Mitton 1966 describes Moses as having "heroic courage and indomitable purpose." In general, πραΰτης refers to "a full consecration to an unselfish purpose to the complete exclusion of self-seeking and self-assertion, and of any spirit of resentment and retaliation" (65).
233. Barnabas, who probably lived between AD 70–132, alludes to James 1:21: "The one who placed within us the implanted (ἔμφυτος) gift of his covenant understands" (9:9; see also 1:2). The word ἔμφυτος does not occur in the rest of the NT or LXX. Although ἔμφυτος ("implanted") occurs earlier than in James's letter, James is the first recorded author to relate the adjective to λόγος ("word"), according to the TLG, accessed August 29, 2017, by James Darlack, head librarian, Gordon-Conwell Theological Seminary, Hamilton, MA. See also "Unusual Words and Phrases in James" in Appendix.

of the sower: some seed *grew* on the rock while other seed *grew* in the good earth (Luke 8:6, 8). Only the latter yielded plants that matured to harvesttime. Strabo uses "implanted" literally to refer to products produced from farming (*Geogr.* 3.3.5, C154). The word planted by God and received in humility is the only one able to save sinners (1:21).[234]

This verse (1:21) may be used as an orientation point into this letter because the letter discusses various evils that must be laid aside, such as partiality (ch. 2), misuse of the tongue (ch. 3), fighting as the world fights (ch. 4), and wealth (5:1–11). As well, the reader needs to receive God's implanted word by growing in mature actions. Laying aside evil and allowing God's implanted word to grow are human actions done in cooperation with the sovereign Lord. The last section of chapter 1 (1:22–27) on becoming doers of the word undergirds and unites the earlier three themes: how to meet trials (1:2–4, 12–18), how to be wise (1:5–8), and how to view riches (1:9–11). Doing God's word has inward and outward components (overcoming trials and wealth, respectively). The tongue, a component of wisdom, is the medium between the inward and outward expressions of one's personality (1:19–20).

"Word" (λόγος) is repeated four times between 1:18 and 1:23. The "word" is planted by God (1:18) and heard (1:19, 23), but then must be followed (1:22–23). To **"hear" the word** is good, but it is not sufficient. Verse 1:22 introduces verses 22–27, but it also rephrases 1:21 in different words. To "receive the implanted word" (1:21) includes hearing and doing God's word (1:22). The verb for "hear" in James 1:19 (ἀκούω) is different from the root verb for "hearer" in 1:22: ἀκροάομαι. Ἀκροάομαι is a more narrow word signifying to listen, especially "of those who hear lectures." Consequently, ἀκροατής is a *"hearer*, of persons who come to hear a public speaker."[235] In Isaiah, a "learned hearer" is parallel to a warrior, judge, prophet, counselor, elder, and captain (3:2–3). The comparable ἀκροατήριον refers to an "auditorium," a place of assemblage for hearing, such as a lecture room.[236] In Acts 25:23, the ἀκροατήριον was the place set aside for hearing and deciding cases where Agrippa, Bernice, Festus, the military tribunes, and prominent citizens of Caesarea met to hear Paul's case.[237] Thus, a "hearer of the

---

234. See also 1 Thess. 1:6; 2:13; Acts 8:14; 11:1; 17:11; Adamson 1976, 81. Whitlark (2010) agrees: the "implanted word" expresses "a motif of enablement grounded in inward transformation experienced through the gospel proclamation" (146).
235. LSJ, 56.
236. LSJ, 56; Thayer, 24.
237. Robertson 1930b, 438.

word" connotes someone who may listen in order to judge and may feel distant from the speaker, not experientially involved. These elements of judgment will be developed later in James (2:4, 12–13; 4:11–12). The "hearer-only" is opposite from the "hearer-and-doer" (1:22–23).[238]

Paul has a similar thought in Romans 2:13; however, there the object of "hearer" is the "law" (νόμος), not "word" (λόγος): "For not the hearers of the law are righteous before God, but the doers of the law will be righteous." Paul's audience is comprised of Jews who claim to be righteous but do not obey old covenant laws. They need God's justification (Rom. 2:1–24; 3:21–26). James's audience are Jews who claim to be Christian but do not obey God's new covenant laws ("word"). God has given them rebirth (including "justification"), but they are not maturing. What then is a **"doer of the word"**? "Doer" (ποιητής) comes from the verb ποιέω. In James, ποιέω often has to do with action, behavior, practice, and production. For example, James commands: *act* in obedience to Scripture (2:8), "speak and in the same way *act*" (2:12), *do* mercy (2:13). He warns that fig trees do not *produce* olives (3:12), but commands them to *do* peace (3:18) and *practice* a job, such as a business (4:13, 15). But he also writes about those who *do* sins (5:15). Sometimes thought is included in ποιέω: to believe God is "one" is a true thought (2:19). A synonym for "doer," one who acts, is ἔργον, a "doer" who "works" (e.g., 2:14). As we shall see in chapter 2, "action" is a clearer translation than "works," since "works" can become confused with Paul's use of these words in a different, more pejorative context.

James returns to the topic of deception in 1:22. He has used three different verbs for **"deception"** so far in chapter 1: δελεάζω (v. 14), πλανάω (v. 16), and παραλογίζομαι (v. 22).[239] Παραλογίζομαι is used by Paul to describe how false reasoning or arguments can deceive the listener (Col. 2:4).[240] (Δελεάζω connotes deception by trickery; while πλανάω connotes deception by straying off the right path.) The deception in James 1:22 is the idea that only hearing God's word is sufficient for reception of God's implanted word to grow.

James now explains why hearers and not doers of the word deceive themselves (1:23–24) and then, in contrast, describes a hearer *and* doer (1:25). James repeats **"word"** (λόγος) in 1:23. In 1:22 λόγος is

---

238. See also Matt. 7:24–27; Luke 11:28; 1 John 4:20; Ezek. 33:31.
239. See also James 1:26 (ἀπατάω).
240. See also Thayer, 484. Λογίζομαι may denote to calculate, to give careful thought to a matter (BDAG, 597–98). Addition of the preposition παρά implies that the thought is "beside" or "alongside" or "beyond," not in the truth (Robertson 1934, 613, 616).

the implied object of "hearer" (ἀκροατής), but in 1:23, λόγος is explicitly stated because James will develop the meaning of the phrase ("hearer of [the] word"). The "word" of truth is the means by which a believer receives rebirth (v. 18), and that word is implanted in the believer. That inward word must be followed (vv. 22–23). But then in verses 23–25, that word is outside of the believer, serving as a mirror that reflects one's genuine inward self (v. 23). In 1:25 the "word" is now disclosed to be the "perfect law, the one of liberty." God is behind the process of rebirth and is the content of the message (1:18). Thus James in 1:23–25 transitions to the content of the message. The message is both placed within the believer and is exterior to the believer.

What is that "word" in 1:23–24? It is a judge of humans, perfect, freeing, and instructing in laws. Thus it refers to the Old Testament as seen through the eyes of the new covenant. If James's letter were written after the persecution mentioned in Acts 8:1–4 but before the Jerusalem council in Acts 15, the "word" to which James refers would include Jesus's teachings, as the numerous allusions in the letter indicate, and the early church's preaching as well. It might also refer to Matthew's gospel, which could have been written by then.[241] The "royal law" is described as a writing illustrated by quotations from the Pentateuch: Leviticus 19:18 (James 2:8); Exodus 20:13–14 and Deuteronomy 5:17–18 (James 2:11). Genesis 15:6 is cited in James 2:23, and Proverbs 3:34 in James 4:6.[242] And so far we have noticed allusions to Jesus's teachings on humility, such as the use of "slave" as a positive self-identification; asking in faith without wavering; the importance of perseverance, wisdom, maturity; the reversal of positions; readiness to hear and to act; and the danger of

---

241. According to the early church, Matthew was the first gospel written, followed by Mark (*Haer.* 3.1; *Hist. eccl.* 5:8; 6:14, 25). Mark's gospel was written after Peter came to Rome but before Paul left Rome (AD 62). Mark's gospel was probably consulted by Luke. Galatians, even if addressed to the south Galatian cities (Acts 13:13–14:24), was probably written after James's letter (ca. AD 49) (Guthrie 1970, 458). Mark could have been written during Claudius's reign (AD 41–54), as early as AD 44, but more likely later, during Nero's reign after Peter's visit to Corinth (1 Cor. 1:12; 3:22; 9:5), between AD 54–57 (*Hist. eccl.* 2.14–16). Luke's gospel may have been researched while Paul was in prison in Caesarea (AD 57–59). It is cited in 1 Timothy 5:18 as Scripture. Acts appears to have been completed before Paul was released from prison. See Spencer 2007, 276–77.

242. The "law" is the "authoritative body of truth that is the foundation of the Christian faith. It is the message contained in the apostolic preaching and now embodied in the New Testament" (Hiebert 1979, 136). See also McKnight 2011, 157–58.

anger and internal desires. Both Jesus and James used many images of nature (including the temporary quality of wildflowers), and James alludes to the virgin birth. The parable of the sower with the word given by the Father is a recurring allusion by James. James appears to have listened to many of his brother's teachings, rather than copied word for word from a written source.

As before (e.g., 1:8, 12, 20), James uses "a man" (ἀνήρ, 1:23) to make his illustration concrete, but he introduces the simile with gender inclusive words: "anyone" (τις), "that person" (οὗτος), "hearer" (ἀκροατής), and "doer" (ποιητής) (1:22–23). Often today we stereotype women as always looking at themselves in **mirrors**, but James uses a man for the illustration. Paul too includes everyone in his mirror illustrations: "now we see in a mirror dimly" and "all of us" see the "glory of the Lord as though reflected in a mirror" (1 Cor. 13:12; 2 Cor. 3:18 NRSV). Many ancient hand mirrors of polished bronze and silver have been found. Often a servant might hold a mirror before her mistress so she could see herself.[243] Tertullian, after condemning women's hairdos, also condemns men over attention to their looks. He writes that men seek to deceive by cutting the beard "too sharply," plucking it out here and there, shaving round about the mouth, arranging the hair and disguising its hoariness by dyes, removing "incipient down all over the body," fixing each hair in place with a pigment, smoothing "all the rest of the body by the aid of some rough powder," and, further, taking "every opportunity for consulting the mirror; to gaze anxiously into it" (*Cult. Fem.* 2.8).

The man in James's illustration also **observes** well (κατανοέω, 1:23–24) his natural face—it is not a fleeting glance. The preposition κατά intensifies νοέω,[244] which by itself means to grasp or comprehend something on the basis of careful thought.[245] Κατανοέω then signifies "to look at in a reflective manner" or "to think about carefully."[246] For example, when Moses saw the burning bush, he was amazed; thus he approached closer *to observe more closely* what was happening (Acts 7:30–31). In a similar fashion, when Peter saw the sheet come down from heaven, *he observed it more closely* and then saw what kind of animals were gathered there (Acts 11:6).[247] What did the man in James see? He saw "his **natural face**," "the way he really looks," or his birth

---

243. Stephens 1987, 363, 365–66, 376.
244. In composition, κατά ("down") often has a perfective force, as in κατανοέω (Robertson 1934, 606).
245. BDAG, 674–75.
246. BDAG, 522.
247. Also see Matt. 7:3; Luke 20:23; Acts 27:39; Rom. 4:19.

face (1:23).[248] Γένεσις is used in the New Testament for "birth" (e.g.,
Matt. 1:18; Luke 1:14) and the related γενέσια signifies "birthday"
(e.g., Herod: Matt. 14:6). The man sees his face as it looks naturally
before he works to improve it or mask it.

James repeats κατανοέω in 1:24, using the aorist tense as a way to
summarize the completion of the process[249] (1:24 vs. present participle
in 1:23). The man then leaves the mirror and immediately forgets "of
what sort he was" (1:24).[250] He forgets what kind of person the mirror
showed him to be.[251] The mirror served as a judge reflecting his true
character and, by implication, what he should do (e.g., 1 Cor. 3:13).
Afterward, the man lives in a totally different world than the world
of the mirror. In contrast to the next person (1:25), he does not look at
the mirror in humility, remaining at the mirror until its impact affects
him; instead he forgets, not forming what he has heard into action,
and, thereby, not being blessed.

The first action of the second person is to **stoop to look** (1:25).
Παρακύπτω signifies to bend oneself down (κύπτω);[252] to be alongside
(παρά);[253] "to bend over for the purpose of looking"; to crouch over to
see something better; "to look at with head bowed forwards; to look
into with the body bent; to stoop and look into."[254] For example, Peter
stooped to look into the tomb, and there he saw linen wrappings (Luke
24:12). (Even in Israel today, some ancient tombs are carved in the side
of a hill, below ground level.) In contrast, an ancient hand mirror can
be brought and held at any level. Therefore, the focus here is how one
holds the "mirror": the process should include humbling oneself.

And what does each see? They do not simply see their own reflection; they see "the **perfect law, the one of freedom**" (1:25). The adjective τέλειος has already been used in 1:17 to describe the nature of
God's gifts. One such gift is God's word of truth (1:18), which here is
called the "perfect law" (1:25). There are no flaws in God's law or God's
will (Rom. 12:2) or God's person (Matt. 5:48) or God's love (1 John 2:5;
4:12, 17). By the law being further described as "the one of freedom,"
James alludes to the new covenant, or the transformed old covenant.

---

248. BDAG, 192; Thayer, 112; Robertson 1933, 23.
249. I.e., seeing the event of observation as a whole (Robertson 1934, 832–35).
250. He uses polysyndeton, repeating "and" twice, thereby giving equal weight
    to each action: observe and go away and forget.
251. God, in contrast, never forgets (Luke 12:6; Heb. 6:10).
252. BDAG, 575.
253. Robertson 1934, 613.
254. BDAG, 767; Thayer, 484.

The new covenant is the completion[255] of the old. James repeats the phrase "the law of freedom" in 2:12, in that context alluding to its synonym "mercy" (2:13). One startling teaching that Jesus shared had to do with freedom: "the truth will set you free" (John 8:32). Literally, "freedom" was often used to refer to one's political or legal state.[256] One interpretation of "slavery" is not being able to stop sinning (John 8:34). Instead, "if the Son sets you free, you will be free indeed" (John 8:36 NIV). Paul also taught this concept to the Galatians: "For you were called to freedom, brothers and sisters, only do not use your freedom to indulge the flesh, rather through love become slaves to one another" (Gal. 5:13). In his letter, James presupposes he is free politically, but is now Christ's slave (1:1; cf. 1 Cor. 7:22). He writes as a reborn follower of his Lord, Jesus Christ (1:1,18, 21; 2:1). "Faith" (πίστις) is an important theme for James (the noun occurs sixteen times and the verb three times). Therefore, "freedom" is an allusion to Jesus's teachings and his present empowering presence.

Next, the person described in 1:25 **"remains"** (παραμένω).[257] Παραμένω, "to remain beside," usually has a more intensive sense than simply "remain" (μένω).[258] For instance, the wild man of Luke 8:27 could not live in a house (μένω), in contrast to Paul who might remain "beside" the Corinthians for the winter or who planned to stay alive to be present with the Philippians (1 Cor. 16:6; Phil. 1:25). In the same way, the person of 1:25 remains in the presence of the perfect, freeing law,[259] thereby not forgetting what they hear,[260] but rather acting on it.[261]

James ends the sentence with the clause that further describes what will happen to the person of 1:25: "This one will be **blessed** in his doing." In the process of obedience comes a blessing. This is the second blessing mentioned in James's letter. Both blessings are future ones. The earlier blessing for the person who perseveres under trial will be receiving the crown of life (1:12). This second blessing

---

255. "Perfect" (τέλειος) also has to do with "completion" or "finishing," as in, e.g., Luke 2:43; 13:32; John 4:34; 5:36; 17:4; 19:28.
256. E.g., John 8:33; 1 Cor. 7:21; 12:13; Gal. 3:28; 4:22–23; Eph. 6:8; Col. 3:11; 1 Pet. 2:16.
257. James repeats the same prefix as a play on words: παρακύπτω (stoop to look) and παραμένω (remain).
258. See also Robertson 1933, 24.
259. The participle reinforces the idea of continuing to look and remain.
260. Even reading by oneself was done aloud in ancient times.
261. A "doer of action" is a pleonasm, repeating two synonyms for action: ποιητής ἔργου.

comes in the very actions of obedience. Doing good is its own reward and brings happiness to the doer. For example, helping widows and orphans (1:27) brings happiness to the giver as well as the receiver. Enumerating who will be blessed was an important aspect of Jesus's teaching. Those blessed include the poor in spirit, those who mourn, the humble (meek), those who hunger and thirst for righteousness, the merciful, the pure in heart, the peacemakers, and those who are persecuted for righteousness' sake (Matt. 5:3–11).[262] James may have heard the woman who blessed Mary, to whom Jesus replied in response: "Blessed are the ones hearing God's word and obeying it" (Luke 11:27–28).[263] In addition, the person obeying God will be blessed at Jesus's return.[264]

James now moves to a concrete summary and application in 1:26–27. The doer of the word (1:22–25) is wise in the midst of trials (1:2–4, 12–18), has wisdom and is slow to speak (1:5–8, 19–21), and has a right attitude to riches (1:9–11). In these next verses, James combines attention to the inward and outward person with a concrete illustration. James begins with attention to the tongue, the connection between the inward and outward person. The person, from an inward perspective, should not have a deceived heart. Then, the person, from an outward perspective, should care for those most easily oppressed: the orphan and widow. James concludes with a warning to give inward attention to the effect or influence of the outside world.

He begins with a conditional clause: "if anyone considers [him/herself] to be religious" (1:26). A first class condition assumes its present reality. The indicative mode states the condition as a fact.[265] A first class condition was also used in 1:5 and 23. Why would James write about those who need wisdom and need to act on their faith if the lack of these attributes were not present in some of the readers of this letter?

---

262. See also Luke 6:20–22.
263. See also John 13:17; Acts 20:35. The person will be blessed in what he does: "the blessing that comes to one who lives in harmony with the will and purpose of God and knows the blessing of friendship with God" (Painter and deSilva 2012, 80). Blessing may be "in the process of the doing" or "as a product of the doing" (McKnight 2011, 161).
264. See also James 5:8–9; Luke 12:43; 14:13–14: "Blessed *for* what he does" (Laws 1980, 87).
265. First class condition assumes the actual existence of such an individual, but the identity is indefinite (Hiebert 1979, 139).

James defines a **"religious"** (θρησκός)[266] person in modifying present participles: someone bridling his tongue and not deceiving his heart (1:26). The corresponding noun (θρησκεία) further defines "religious" in a positive way: "to care for orphans and widows in their difficulties, to guard oneself spotless from the world" (1:27). Θρησκεία refers to religious worship, especially "external, that which consists in ceremonies" or "cultic rites."[267] Θρησκεία is a general neutral term describing religious observance, including that of the Jewish religion, as when Paul told King Agrippa that he belonged to the Pharisees, the "strictest sect of our *religion*" (Acts 26:5).[268] Josephus uses θρησκεία to describe worship at the temple in Jerusalem as one without statues of any kind, certainly not of the Emperor Gaius Caligula, who promoted himself equal to the gods (*Ant.* 18.8.6.287). Emperor Augustus also used θρησκεία to describe the accustomed religious worship of the Jews (*Ant.* 19.2.283–84). Antiochus used θρησκεία to describe Jewish worship, which did not include eating pork and food offered to idols (4 Macc. 5:2, 6, 13). When he invited the elderly Eleazar to eat such "unclean" food, Eleazar responded that the Jewish "philosophy" "instructs us in temperance, so that we are superior to all pleasures and lusts [ἐπιθυμία]; and it exercises us in manliness, so that we cheerfully undergo every grievance. And it instructs us in justice, so that in all our dealings we render what is due; and it teaches us piety, so that we worship the one only God becomingly. Wherefore it is that we eat not the unclean" (4 Macc. 5:23–24). Thus, for a pious ancient Jew, genuine worship acceptable to God included not worshiping idols or eating unclean food. But for James, genuine worship was keeping oneself "clean" from the world, watching what one said, and taking care of those easily oppressed (1:26–27). James, of course, would agree that only one God is to be worshiped (2:19).

To "bridle" the **tongue** will be further developed in 3:2–3, where bridling a horse with a bit (χαλινός) is compared to bridling or leading by a bridle[269] one's own tongue. The tongue is important to James as a teacher (3:1–2).[270] Wisdom and the tongue are related in the Old Testament. The right use of the tongue is an important theme in

---

266. Θρησκός in adjective form first occurs in James 1:26 (*TLNT* 2, 200).
267. Thayer, 292; BDAG, 459.
268. Θρησκεία can also be used to describe worship of idols or angels (Col. 2:18; Wis. 14:18, 27; [verb: 11:15; 14:16], *Ant.* 18.9.5.344, 348–49; *Ag. Ap.* 2.35.254). See also *TLNT* 2, 200–204.
269. Thayer, 664. See also James 1:19.
270. See also 1 Cor. 14:19.

Psalms and Proverbs. Wisdom herself declares that "all the words of my mouth are righteous; there is nothing twisted or crooked in them" (Prov. 8:8 NRSV; 3:16 LXX). David teaches, "The mouths of the righteous utter wisdom, and their tongues speak justice" (Ps. 37:30 NRSV). His son Solomon agrees: "The tongue of the wise dispenses knowledge, but the mouths of fools pour out folly"; "A gentle tongue is a tree of life"; and the capable wife "opens her mouth with wisdom, and the teaching of kindness is on her tongue" (Prov. 15:2, 4a; 31:26 NRSV). Peter also insists on guarding one's tongue from evil as an aspect of living in harmony with other Christians (1 Pet. 3:8, 10). He cites Psalm 34: "Which of you desires life, and covets many days to enjoy good? Keep your tongue from evil, and your lips from speaking deceit" (34:12–13 NRSV). The two-willed person, instead, flatters or speaks falsehood (Ps. 12:2). James would heartily agree with Proverbs 18:21: "Death and life are in the power of the tongue, and those who control it will eat its fruits."

The tongue is the outward manifestation of what's inside a person, the "heart." The heart is deceived or misled (ἀπατάω, 1:26) if the person is only a hearer but not a doer of the word (1:25). Such a person is misled by a half-truth. For example, the serpent misled Eve by confusing her by asking if God had ordered her not to eat from *any* tree in the garden and assuring her if she ate she would not die (Gen. 3:1, 4; 1 Tim. 2:14).[271] The half-truth described in James's letter is to think that hearing the word is enough. But it is not enough if it is not obeyed. If hearing God's word does not affect one's speech, then this so-called "religious worship" (θρησκεία) is "useless" or "a waste of time" (μάταιος).[272] God tells Judah through Isaiah that bringing offerings to the temple is a *waste of time, of no effect,*[273] if it is not accompanied by ceasing to do evil and learning to do good, seeking justice, rescuing the oppressed, defending the orphan, and pleading for the widow (Isa. 1:13–17). James likewise exhorts his listeners to remove all filth and evil, act on God's word, and control their speech (1:21, 25–26) if they want their worship to have any effect or truth.

Genuine worship is shown in action toward others and oneself. In 1:26 James explains what *not* to do, but in 1:27 he explains what to

---

271. See also Eph. 5:6; Spencer 2013, 70–72.
272. Μάταιος is emphasized by James placing it before the subject ἡ θρησκεία.
273. Μάταιος may refer to spending one's time in a practice that has no value and is a waste of time, such as engaging in battles about genealogies and contentions and battles pertaining to the law (Titus 3:9), worshiping false gods (Acts 14:15; 1 Pet. 1:18; Isa. 44:9), or believing one's sins have been forgiven if Christ is not raised from death (1 Cor. 15:17).

do.[274] He repeats θρησκεία, at the beginning of 1:27 and the end of 1:26 (anadiplosis). This style, thereby, emphasizes what he defines: "worship." This noun is followed by repetition (pleonasm) of two synonyms: **"pure"** (καθαρός) and "undefiled" (ἀμίαντος). These words are common in the Old Testament for the laws of cleanliness. The Lord commands Aaron to "distinguish between the holy and the common, and between the unclean [ἀκάθαρτος] and the *clean*" (καθαρός, Lev. 10:10 NRSV). This basic principle affected food;[275] humans;[276] items, such as vessels, cloths, and houses;[277] and offerings;[278] as well as other actions. The basic principle remains in the new covenant, but Jesus's blood sacrifice has eliminated the need for any such ceremonial cleansing or sacrifice.[279] Purity is now demonstrated, according to James, in worship that is outwardly and inwardly active (James 1:27).

The Israelites were to learn that the Lord is holy. The adjective **"undefiled"** (ἀμίαντος, 1:27) does not occur in the Old Testament, but the verb "to defile" (μιαίνω) is very frequent. For instance, the Lord teaches Moses that the people "shall not defile" themselves with unclean animals "and so become unclean. For I am the Lord your God; sanctify yourselves therefore, and be holy, for I am holy" (Lev. 11:43–44 NRSV). Consequently, the Jewish religious leaders did not enter Pilate's palace at Passover in order to avoid "ceremonial uncleanness" (John 18:28, μιαίνω). Priests prayed that Nicanor would not defile the temple in Jerusalem by building at its spot a temple to Dionysus: "Holy Lord from whom all holiness comes, keep this house, so recently purified, *free from defilement* forever" (2 Macc. 14:36 REB, ἀμίαντος).

Παρά is frequently used with the dative to refer to persons in the sense of "among,"[280] or in God's presence; thus, we may render the opening words of 1:27: "pure and undefiled worship *in the presence of God and Father*." If "God and Father" is a hendiadys,[281] "Father" may

---

274. "The two points are not exhaustive but representative" (Hiebert 1979, 142).
275. E.g., Lev. 11:47; 20:25; Mark 7:14–19; Acts 10:15; 11:9; Rom. 14:20.
276. E.g., leprosy: Lev. 13:6, 13, 17, 34, 37, 39–41, 58; 14:7–9; Matt. 8:2–3; 10:8; 11:5; Mark 1:40–42; Luke 4:27; 5:12–13; 7:22; 17:12–14, 17.
277. E.g., Lev. 14:49, 53; 15:12; Matt. 23:25–28; Luke 11:39–41.
278. E.g., Lev. 14:49.
279. E.g., Titus 2:14; Heb. 9:22–23, 28; 10:2; 1 John 1:7, 9.
280. Robertson 1934, 614.
281. Hendiadys is the "expression of an idea by two nouns connected by 'and' instead of a noun and its qualifier" (Lanham 1991, 82).

modify "God" to signify "Father God."[282] **"Father"** in 1:17 connotes God as creator, the creator of lights, as also in 1 Corinthians 8:6: "one God, the Father, from whom are all things." In James 1:27 "Father" connotes the loving care that God has for the needy: "orphans and widows in their difficulties." If God is someone's "Father," then as a Father he should be loved, trusted, and obeyed. Jesus told the unbelieving Jews that "if God were your Father, you would love me, for I myself came from God" (John 8:42). In a similar fashion, if God is the "Father" of the readers, they too should care for orphans and widows in trouble and keep themselves spotless from the world. So far in chapter 1 James has communicated that God gives wisdom to those who ask, has no evil, is totally good, is righteous, and is caring.

Ἐπισκέπτομαι may simply refer to one person **"visiting"** others (1:27), as Paul said to Barnabas: "Come, let us return and *visit* the believers in every city where we proclaimed the word of the Lord and see how they are doing" (Acts 15:36 NRSV). "Visit" implies to stay and look at or after someone (σκοπέω, "to observe" or "look," and ἐπί, "at," "upon," or "after"), to "examine with the eyes" to see how someone is doing.[283] At the judgment, Jesus will see if his followers took care of ("visited") the sick and the inmates in his name (Matt. 25:36, 43). Many times the Lord is described in the Old Testament as "visiting" people to help them; for instance, to help Sarah conceive (Gen. 21:1–2), to lead them to Canaan (Gen. 50:24–25), to provide food (Ruth 1:6), to care for the earth (Ps. 65:9), and to save (Ps. 106:4). When the Lord informs Moses that the Israelites would be delivered from the Egyptians, the people perceived that the Lord had "visited" them and saw their "affliction" (θλίψις, Exod. 4:31). Thus, ἐπισκέπτομαι connotes visiting, observation, and remedial action.

---

282. One article refers to one Person. Mitton 1966, 77, suggests, "God, who is the One we know as Father." The same phrase "God and Father" also occurs in 1 Cor. 15:24; Eph. 5:20. "God Father" may be found in Gal. 1:1; Eph. 6:23; Phil. 2:11; Col. 3:17; 1 Thess. 1:1; 2 Thess. 1:2; 1 Tim. 1:2; 2 Tim. 1:2; Titus 1:4; 2 Pet. 1:17; 2 John 3; Jude 1; "God and Father of our Lord Jesus Christ": Rom. 15:6; 2 Cor. 1:3; 11:3; Eph. 1:3; 1 Pet. 1:3; "God our Father and Lord Jesus Christ": Rom. 1:7; 1 Cor. 1:3; 2 Cor. 1:2; Gal. 1:3; Eph. 1:2; Phil. 1:2; 2 Thess. 1:1; Philem. 3; "God and our Father": Gal. 1:4; 1 Thess. 1:3; 3:11, 13; "one God and Father of all": Eph. 4:6; "God our Father": Col. 1:2; 2 Thess. 2:16; "God and our Father": Phil. 4:20; "God Father of our Lord Jesus Christ": Col. 1:3; "God and his Father": Rev. 1:6.
283. Thayer, 242, 579. E.g., a priest would visit and look at or examine former lepers to see if they were clean (Lev. 13:36).

In what kind of situation are the widows and orphans? Θλίψις denotes "trouble that inflicts distress, oppression, affliction, tribulation."[284] Their **"trouble"** includes difficulties from their state as orphans or widows, from the outside (1:2). Θλίψις (noun) and θλίβω (verb) literally refer to pressure,[285] such as the pressure of a crowd (Mark 3:9) or the pressure from labor pains (John 16:21). In the New Testament the word family refers to serious difficulties such as persecution[286] resulting in beatings, imprisonments,[287] hunger, famine, and poverty;[288] Christ's sufferings (Col. 1:24); disputes (2 Cor. 7:5); end-time troubles (Matt. 24:29; Mark 13:19, 24); and even suffering due to one's own sin (Rom. 2:9; Rev. 2:22). Thus, these orphans and widows are not having simple troubles; rather, their "difficulties"[289] are serious.

Why has God chosen someone who cares for **orphans and widows** (1:27) as an illustration of one who hears and does God's word? The letter itself provides some suggestions. Some of the dispersed Christians may themselves have been orphans and widows, children who lost their parents or wives who lost their husbands as a result of Saul's persecution. Saul dragged off men and women and put them in prison (Acts 8:3). They may then have become some of the poor discriminated against in the diaspora synagogues (James 1:2–4, 9–10; 2:4–6). The rabbinical laws exhorted the husband's family to take care of the widow (m. Ketub. 4:12; 12:3), but that did not always happen. Sometimes religious leaders stole the property of widows and orphans (Mark 12:40; Luke 20:47). James's own mother, Mary, may have been a widow since Joseph, her husband, is not mentioned after Jesus's early ministry. In addition, at his death, Jesus asked John to take care of her.[290]

James uses the imagery of "firstfruit" for reborn believers (1:18), which is a reminder of the third-year celebration of the harvest, which benefitted the feeding of orphans and widows (Deut. 26:12–13; 14:29).[291] This festival is a reminder of the many Old Testament laws protecting orphans and widows; for example: "You shall not abuse any widow or orphan. If you do abuse them, when they cry out to me, I will surely

---

284. BDAG, 457.
285. BDAG, 457; Thayer, 291.
286. Matt. 13:21; 24:9; Mark 4:17; Acts 11:19; 14:22; 20:23; 1 Thess. 1:6; 3:3–4, 7; 2 Thess. 1:4; Heb. 10:33; 11:37; Rev. 1:9; 2:9–10; 7:14.
287. 2 Cor. 6:4–5; Eph. 3:13; Phil. 1:17; 4:14.
288. Acts 7:11; Rom. 8:35; 2 Cor. 8:2.
289. See also CEB.
290. Matt. 13:55; Luke 2:43–51; 4:22; John 6:42; 19:26–27.
291. See exposition of James 1:18.

heed their cry" (Exod. 22:22–23 NRSV).[292] God shows great concern for innocent people who have difficulties, having lost parents or husbands. When Moses summarizes God's self-revelation, he includes God's concern for the orphan and widow: "For the Lord your God, the One who is God of the gods and Lord of the lords, the Mighty, the Great, the Strong, and the Wonderful, who is not partial and does not take bribes executing justice for the orphan and widow and loves a stranger to give to him food and clothing" (Deut. 10:17–18). God's great power is not used to be overbearing but to help the defenseless. The psalmist calls God "Father of orphans and protector of widows" (Ps. 68:5 NRSV).[293] One of the measures of Job's virtue was his treatment of orphans and widows (Job 22:9; 31:16–23). One reason the Jews were exiled was their unjust treatment of orphans and widows. Orphans' property was not protected (Prov. 23:10; Mic. 2:2).[294] Even after the exile, landowners oppressed their hired workers, widows, and orphans (Mal. 3:5). Money was collected by the Jewish religious leaders in Jerusalem for the relief of widows and orphans, but it was sometimes stolen or diverted (2 Macc. 3:10–13; 8:28). The early church had its own collection for widows (Acts 6:1) and eventually its own order of prayer for widows not helped by family (1 Tim. 5:4–16).[295]

James returns to the theme of "pure" and "undefiled" by emphasizing "**spotless**" (ἄσπιλος)[296] in the second part of the description of genuine worship (1:27b).[297] This second action is directed toward oneself. The concept ("spotless") is also descriptive of Old Testament ceremonial law, although the word ἄσπιλος itself does not occur in the Septuagint. For instance, Peter explains that believers were redeemed by the "precious blood of Christ, a lamb without blemish or *defect*" (1 Pet. 1:19 NIV). The tongue, in contrast, can cause defects to the whole body (James 3:6 σπιλόω). Peter uses the same adjective for exhortation to encourage his readers: "strive to be found *spotless* and without blemish" (2 Pet. 3:14). James uses a strong verb, τηρέω, which literally signifies "keep watch over, guard,"[298] such as to guard a prisoner (e.g., Matt. 27:36, 54; Acts 16:23). With the same diligence as a guard might keep an eye on preventing a prisoner from escaping or from

---

292. See also Deut. 24:17–21; 27:19; Ps. 82:3.
293. See also Ps. 146:9.
294. Also, Isa. 1:16–17, 23; 10:1–2; Jer. 5:28; 7:5–6; 22:3; Ezek. 22:7.
295. See also Barn. 20:2; 1 Clem. 8:4.
296. Ἄσπιλος is emphasized by preceding its verb "to guard," τηρέω.
297. Stated in an asyndeton.
298. BDAG, 1002.

being freed, the readers are to keep an eye on themselves, preventing invasive thoughts and negative actions from entering their lives. The believer is not to become a friend to the world of iniquity (James 3:6; 4:4).

THEOLOGICAL AND HOMILETICAL
TOPICS IN CHAPTER 1

The first chapter of James answers a number of theological questions. What do we learn about God? How might one respond to times of persecution? How may one mature as a Christian? What different types of trials are there? What rewards does God provide for the mature Christian? How can we work with God to see that God's "implanted" word grows into beautiful fruit in our lives?

When preaching or teaching, many topics and images may be used to communicate to others the content of James chapter 1. This chapter offers lessons on theology (God's nature) and soteriology (the process of human salvation). Sharing a description of James's own life may serve as an example of a marvelously transformed life. James's four interrelated themes should be covered: (1) trials, (2) wisdom, and (3) wealth, as they relate to becoming (4) doers of the word. Sermons may be given on 1:5–8: Trial or Temptation, Why Persevere, How to Become Mature, How to Gain Wisdom, and How to Ask While Not "Drowning." God's character can be taught as Our Generous God and Our Wise God. In 1:9–11, pictures from Israel such as the wildflower and the Sea of Galilee can illustrate the text. Topics might be How to Have High Rank in God's Kingdom; and, in 1:12–18, What Is God's Crown? (compared to Olympic crowns): How to Get It and Why. Sermons can describe God's character: Our Good God; or, in 1:19–27, Our Impartial God or God Our Protector. Two types of birth can be compared, the Virgin Birth of Death versus the Birth of Life. A "word of truth" can be interpreted by means of Luke 8:1–15. The Father of lights as a sun-shower can even offer opportunity for children to draw. The relation between speaking and anger in 1:19–27 may be helpful to one's listeners, or a sermon on What Clothes Should We Discard and Which Ones Should We Receive? Other key topics are Who Is a Doer of the Word, How to Grow God's Implanted Word, Let Your Mirror Be Your Master, and What Is Real Worship?

James offers many vivid and concrete illustrations that should interest today's visual postmodern.

SIGNIFICANCE OF GENDER LANGUAGE IN JAMES

	Gender Language in James Chapter 1				
Verse	Masculine (pro)noun intended to be generic	Masculine noun intended to be illustrative	Feminine noun/verb intended to be illustrative	Generic/feminine (pro)noun intended to be generic	Neuter (pro)noun intended to be illustrative
2	ἀδελφοί μου "my brothers"			ταῖς δώδεκα φυλαῖς *** "the twelve tribes"	
5	(τοῦ διδόντος) "the One giving"			Τις "any"	
6	ὁ διακρινόμενος* "the one wavering"				κλύδωνι *** "wave" (simile)
7	(κυρίου) "Lord"			ὁ ἄνθρωπος *** "person/human"	
8		ἀνὴρ "man"			
9	ὁ ἀδελφὸς "brother" . . . ὁ ταπεινὸς** "lowly"				
10	ὁ πλούσιος ** "the rich"				ἄνθος "flower" (simile)
11	ὁ πλούσιος** "the rich"				ἄνθος "flower" . . . ἡ εὐπρέπεια*** "the beauty" (simile)
12	τοῖς ἀγαπῶσιν* "the ones loving"	ἀνὴρ "man"			
14	ἕκαστος** "each"		τῆς ἐπιθυμίας "desire"		

Gender Language in James Chapter 1					
15			ἡ ἐπιθυμία "desire"		
16	ἀδελφοί μου ἀγαπητοί "my beloved brothers"				
17	(πατρὸς) "Father"				
18			(ἀπεκύησεν) "gave birth"		ἀπαρχήν*** "firstfruit" . . . κτισμάτων "creations"
19	ἀδελφοί μου ἀγαπητοί "my beloved brothers"			ἄνθρωπος*** "human/ person"	
20		ἀνδρὸς "man"			
22				ποιηταὶ*** "doers" . . . ἀκροαταὶ*** "hearers"	
23	οὗτος "that person"	ἀνδρὶ "man" (simile)		τις "anyone" . . . ἀκροατὴς*** "hearer" . . . ποιητής*** "doer"	
24	ὁποῖος "what sort"				
25	ὁ παρακύψας* "the one having stooped to look" . . . οὗτος "this one"			ἀκροατὴς*** "hearer" . . . ποιητὴς*** "doer"	
26				τις "anyone"	
27	(πατρὶ) "Father"				

Key: *verb used as a noun; **adjective used as a noun; ***noun is grammatically masculine or feminine in form, which is not relevant to natural gender; pronouns that modify a noun or serve as object are omitted from analysis; language about God is in parentheses.

When we translate, we need to differentiate between grammatical gender and natural gender. Grammatical gender from the Latin *genus* refers to "class" or "kind," a form of classification of categories that has nothing to do with sex. Natural gender refers to sexual categories. In Greek the generic form or prior gender will sometimes later become the masculine form when a second category, the feminine, is developed. For example, διάκονος, "minister," is a masculine or omicron (o) stem noun that is used of men and women (e.g., Ephesians 3:7 of Paul; 1 Timothy 4:6 of Timothy; Romans 16:1 of Phoebe). However, with the passage of time, διάκονος was given first a feminine as well as a masculine article and then a feminine (διακόνισσα or "deaconess") as well as a masculine ending (διάκονος). Words such as ἄνθρωπος ("person/human"), ἐπιθυμία ("desire"), ἀπαρχή ("firstfruit")—although masculine, feminine, and neuter in form—do not have anything necessarily to do with sex.[299] In addition, Greek words can be generic or nongeneric in meaning but inclusive or exclusive in form. Almost all commentators agree that when James uses ἀνὴρ ("man") in chapter 1, he intends it to be generic in meaning. Thus, the translator needs to decide if the form or the sense or intention of the original should be translated. If only the form is rendered in translation, such as "man," a reader may conclude that the word refers only to men.[300] But if only the sense is rendered in translation, such as rendering ἀνὴρ as "person," then the reader may miss the changes in form that the writer uses. Do we focus on the original text or the contemporary listener?

᾽Αδελφός in the singular is clearly a term used for a "brother," in contrast to ἀδελφή, "sister." However, the plural ἀδελφοί can be used for an audience that includes men and women. Thus, if today we render it as "brothers," many will conclude that the women are not really included or addressed. James likes to use such a term, I think, not because he is excluding women but because he likes to bring out the idea that his readers are his equals, and part of Christ's family of siblings.[301] The above chart indicates that James does use the masculine article as

---

299. See further Spencer, Hailson, Kroeger, and Spencer 1995, 121–25; Spencer 1998b.
300. For example, Strauss (1998, 142) concludes from studies today that when "man" is used as a generic term, it is often misunderstood to refer only to males. Carson (1998, 124, 126) notes that the plural of ἀνὴρ ("fellows") clearly includes a woman in Acts 17:34 and the default meaning of ἄνθρωπος is generic, a human being.
301. Johnson (2004, 233) also concludes that "James is egalitarian rather than authoritarian."

a generic term, which is common practice in the Greek language. It also shows his creativity and flexibility. The four times that he uses ἀνήρ, he combines it with a generic term. For instance, in 1:7–8 and 1:19–20 he introduces the illustration with the more generic ἄνθρωπος ("human/person") before he moves to the more concrete ἀνήρ. Not as immediately noticeable but also true is that in 1:12 he begins with ἀνὴρ but then ends the sentence with the more generic τοῖς ἀγαπῶσιν ("the ones loving"), while 1:23 begins with the generic τις ("anyone"), ἀκροατὴς ("hearer"), ποιητής ("doer"), and οὗτος ("that person") before the use of ἀνήρ ("man") in the simile. The masculine term πατρὸς ("Father") for God is then described with a feminine term ἀπεκύησεν ("gave birth"), but then the product is a neutral term: ἀπαρχή ("firstfruit"), which shows that the God of the Bible is neither masculine nor feminine, unlike the pagan gods of James's time. We also learn from this chart that James balances masculine, feminine, and neuter illustrations: a wave (1:6), a double-willed man (1:8), a flower (1:11), a man (1:12), desire bearing a child (1:14–15), giving birth and a harvest (1:18), a man's anger (1:20), a man looking in the mirror (1:23–24), a person stooping (1:25). These are not all the metaphors that he uses, but they indicate his variety. He does not always confine himself to the masculine form, or the feminine, or the neuter. He exemplifies for speakers today the necessity to be creative in using illustrations but also to use a variety of illustrations that appeal to one's whole audience of men and women.

JAMES 2:1–26

TRANSLATION AND GRAMMATICAL ANALYSIS[1]

2:1a My brothers and sisters, not in partiality have faith in our glorious Lord Jesus Christ. (initial sentence; main clause)

2:2a For if a man[2] with a gold ring in splendid clothing might enter into a synagogue, (illustrative sentence; subordinate adverbial clause; conditional; third class)

2:2b and also a poor [person] in dirty clothing might enter, (subordinate adverbial clause; conditional; third class)

2:3c but you might show more respect to the one wearing the splendid clothing (subordinate adverbial clause; conditional)

2:3d and you might say: (subordinate adverbial clause; conditional)

2:3e "You stay seated there in a good place," (subordinate noun clause; direct object)

2:3f and to the poor [person] you might say: (subordinate adverbial clause; conditional)

2:3g "You stand there (subordinate noun clause; direct object)

---

1. See "Definition of Terms in Grammatical Analysis."
2. See 1:8c.

2:3h or stay seated under my footstool," (subordinate noun clause; direct object)

2:4i and have you not differentiated among yourselves (main clause)

2:4j and become judges with evil thoughts? (main clause)

2:5a Listen, my beloved brothers and sisters; (additive sentence; main clause)

2:5a has not God selected the poor of the world [to be] rich in faith and heirs of the reign (explanatory sentence; main clause)

2:5b which he promised to the ones loving him? (subordinate adjectival clause; modifies "reign")

2:6a But you have insulted the poor! (adversative sentence; main clause)

2:6a Do not the rich oppress you (illustrative sentence; main clause)

2:6b and they themselves drag you into court? (main clause)

2:7a Do not they themselves slander the good name, the one being called upon you? (illustrative sentence; main clause)

2:8a If indeed you perform [the] royal law according to the writing, (explanatory sentence; subordinate adverbial clause; conditional)

2:8b "Love your neighbor as yourself," (subordinate adjectival clause; describes "writing")

2:8c you do well; (main clause)

2:9a but if you act with partiality, (adversative sentence; subordinate adverbial clause; conditional)

2:9b you act sinfully being convicted by the law as a transgressor. (main clause)

2:10a For whoever might guard all the law, (causal sentence; subordinate noun clause; subject)

2:10b but might stumble in one, (subordinate noun clause; subject)

2:10c has become guilty of all. (main clause)

2:11a For the One saying, (illustrative sentence; main clause)

2:11b Do not commit adultery, (subordinate adjectival clause; answers which one)

2:11c said also, (main clause; continued)

2:11d Do not murder; (subordinate noun clause; direct object)

2:11a but, if you do not commit adultery, (adversative sentence; subordinate adverbial clause; conditional; first class)

2:11b but you murder, (subordinate adverbial clause; conditional; first class)

2:11c you have become a transgressor of [the] law. (main clause)

2:12a In the same way speak (explanatory sentence; main clause)

2:12b and in the same way act as coming to be judged by [the] law of freedom. (main clause)

2:13a For the judgment without mercy [comes] to the one not having done mercy; (causal sentence; main clause)

2:13a mercy triumphs over judgment. (adversative sentence; main clause)

2:14a What is the benefit, my brothers and sisters, (initial sentence; main clause)

2:14b if someone may say to have faith, (subordinate adverbial clause; conditional; third class)

2:14c but he/she may not have actions; (subordinate adverbial clause; conditional; third class)

2:14a faith is not able to save him, is it? (illative sentence; main clause)

2:15a If a brother or sister may exist naked (illustrative sentence; subordinate adverbial clause; conditional)

2:15b and may be lacking daily nourishment, (subordinate adverbial clause; conditional)

2:16c but someone might say to them from among you, (subordinate adverbial clause; conditional)

2:16d "Go in peace, (subordinate noun clause; direct object)

2:16e warm yourselves, (subordinate noun clause; direct object)

2:16f and be satisfied," (subordinate noun clause; direct object)

2:16g but you might not give to them the necessary things of the body, (subordinate adverbial clause; conditional)

2:16h what is the benefit? (main clause)

2:17a In the same way also the faith, (explanatory sentence; main clause)

2:17b if it may not have actions, (subordinate adverbial clause; conditional; third class)

2:17c is dead with respect to itself. (main clause continued)

2:18a But someone will say: (illustrative sentence; main clause)

2:18b "You have faith, (subordinate noun clause; direct object)

2:18c I also have actions. (subordinate noun clause; direct object)

2:18d Show to me your faith apart from the actions, (subordinate noun clause; direct object)

2:18e I also will show to you from my actions the faith." (subordinate noun clause; direct object)

2:19a You believe (illustrative sentence; main clause)

2:19b that God is one, (subordinate noun clause; direct object)

2:19c you do well; (explanatory sentence; main clause)

2:19a even the demons believe and shudder. (illustrative sentence; main clause)

2:20a But you wish to know, o empty-headed human, (additive sentence; main clause)

2:20b that faith apart from actions is inactive? (subordinate noun clause; direct object)

2:21a Was not Abraham our father proved righteous from actions having offered Isaac his son upon the altar? (illustrative sentence; main clause)

2:22a You see (explanatory sentence; main clause)

2:22b that faith works together with his actions (subordinate noun clause; direct object)

2:22c and from the actions faith was perfected, (subordinate noun clause; direct object)

2:23a and the writing was fulfilled, the one saying: (illustrative sentence; main clause)

2:23b "And Abraham believed God, (subordinate adjectival clause; describing which "writing")

2:23c and it was reckoned to him for righteousness," (subordinate adjectival clause)

2:23d and he was called "a friend" of God. (subordinate adjectival clause)

2:24a You see (illative sentence; main clause)

2:24b that from actions a person is proved righteous and not from faith alone. (subordinate noun clause; direct object)[3]

---

3. These are compound verbs. The elliptical verb "is made righteous" is dependent on one subject "person."

2:25a And likewise also Rahab the prostitute, was she not from actions demonstrated as righteous, having welcomed for herself the messengers and having sent away by another road? (illustrative sentence; main clause)

2:26a For as the body apart from spirit is dead, (explanatory sentence; adverbial subordinate clause; comparative)

2:26b likewise also the faith apart from actions is dead. (main clause)

OUTLINE

II. Lay aside partiality and faith without actions (ch. 2).
   A. Show no partiality to the rich (2:1–13).
   B. (reason) Verbal faith without actions is dead (2:14–26).

LITERARY STRUCTURE

James's parallel thought structure of three reoccurring themes which began in chapter 1 (trials [1:2–4], wisdom [1:5–8], wealth [1:9–11]; trials [1:12–18], wisdom [1:19–21]) is now completed in chapter 2 with a discussion of wealth (2:1–17). The fourth uniting theme (doer of the word) is covered at the conclusion of chapter 2, as the doer of the word speaks and acts (2:14–26). The synonymous terms "doer" (ποιητής) and "action" (ἔργον) occur in 1:22–25 and 2:14–26. The negative aspect of the thesis sentence (1:21) (having laid aside all evil deeds) is covered in this chapter's discussion against partiality to the wealthy. The reason behind the command (show no partiality to the rich), presented in the first half of the chapter, is developed in the second half of the chapter (verbal faith without actions is dead). The process of receiving the implanted word in humility includes becoming a doer of the word by becoming impartial to wealth and the wealthy.

Thus, the theme of partiality versus impartiality underlies the first set of illustrations (2:1–16) in the chapter, while courageous actions underlie the second set of illustrations (2:21–25), but all the illustrations flesh out what genuine faith looks like. Partiality should certainly not be part of faith in Jesus Christ (2:1). The first illustration (2:2–7) is set in a synagogue. The attractive "face" of a flower (1:11) is now developed, as a man with "splendid" attire entering a place of worship is treated in a different way from the unattractive poor. James then defends the place of the poor as special to those with faith and disparages the rich as oppressive (2:5–7). Why is that? When the rich oppress the poor, they slander the good name that was given to the heirs of God's reign. Being partial also breaks the Old Testament law to love one's neighbor. To disobey even one Old Testament commandment is to become guilty of violating the whole law. People who are not merciful, acting like the oppressing rich and the prejudiced greeter, will be treated themselves without mercy by God.

James, then, in a more abstract manner, relates this illustration of an "evil deed" to the meaning of genuine faith (2:14–26). A faith not illustrated in action cannot save.

He returns to the example of the treatment of the poor. In the first illustration, the poor are treated partially or unjustly, without the dignity they deserve. In this next illustration, the poor person's physical needs are not helped with action (2:15–16). Analogously, faith to be alive must have action that flows from it (2:17). James illustrates this idea with two people conversing with each other: one with only verbal faith, the other with verbal faith that is demonstrated by action (2:18). James then moves to a theological illustration. Saying God is "one" is good but insufficient if it does not flow into obedient fear (2:19). James follows this with two Old Testament illustrations: Abraham's offering of his son Isaac, and Rahab's welcoming of the Hebrew messengers (2:21–25). He concludes with a principle that actions indicate a living faith even as the spirit indicates a living body (2:26). In chapter 1, James has dealt with believers who think they have faith because they have *heard* God's word (1:22); in chapter 2, he deals with believers who think they have faith because they *say* they have faith (2:14). Neither hearing nor speaking is sufficient by itself to demonstrate live, genuine, saving faith. An "implanted" faith has action that works together with faith and completes it.

EXPOSITION

Lay Aside Partiality and Faith without Actions (ch. 2)

Show No Partiality to the Rich (2:1–13)
James develops further consideration of the poor (1:27) in chapter 2. He uses "my brothers and sisters" (ἀδελφοί μου) as a term of endearment to soften the command that follows: "not in **partiality**[4] have faith in[5] our glorious[6] Lord Jesus Christ" (2:1). He emphasizes

---

4.   Or, "acts of favoritism" (NRSV).
5.   Objective genitive signifies "faith in" (e.g., Mark 11:22; Robertson 1933, 27; Painter and deSilva 2012, 91; Vlachos 2013, 68).
6.   Genitive of quality or character. The genitive functions most likely as an adjective modifying "Jesus Christ," e.g., Ropes 1916, 187.

"not in partiality" by placing the phrase before the verb "have." This sentence governs the topic of the treatment of the wealthy and the poor through verse 17. The verb προσωπολημπτέω (2:9) has its first appearance in James.[7] Although this word family is not frequent in the New Testament (six references), the concept is an important one. Προσωπολημψία is a combination of two words (πρόσωπον ["face"] and λαμβάνω ["receive"]),[8] literally, "to receive a face." The "face" is an important synecdoche in the New Testament. It can refer to a literal face or visage (e.g., James 1:23), or it can represent a person's or group's will, personal attention, presence, favor, or whole being, as when Peter and the apostles "left rejoicing from the *face* of the Sanhedrin" (Acts 5:41), or as when Paul describes the churches as having one "face" (2 Cor. 8:24).[9] "Face" may also stand for superficial characteristics such as nationality, power, wealth, and legalism (e.g., Matt. 22:16; Deut. 10:17–18).

Eduard Lohse suggests that the phrase "to receive a person" may have come from "the respectful oriental greeting in which one humbly turns one's face to the ground or sinks to the earth. If the person greeted thus raises the face of the man, this is a sign of recognition and esteem."[10] James wants the poor to be recognized and treated with the same esteem as received by the wealthy.

God is always described as impartial in the Old and New Testaments, going back to Moses's summary of God's character: "The Lord your God is God of gods and Lord of lords, the great God, the mighty One, and the awesome One, who will not be partial ['lift up the face(s)' to people] and takes no bribe, executing justice for the orphan and the widow, and loving the stranger, providing to him food and clothing" (Deut. 10:17–18). God is not affected by any external pressure to be unjust. Moreover, God is especially attentive to those who may be easily oppressed: the orphan and the widow and the stranger.

---

7. BDAG, 887. The noun προσωπολημψία ("partiality," 2:1) also occurs in Romans 2:11; Ephesians 6:9; and Colossians 3:25; but these NT letters were most likely written after James. Peter first uses the adjective προσωπολήμπτης ("one who is partial") in Acts 10:34. See in Appendix "Unusual Words and Phrases in James."
8. E.g., Luke 20:21; Gal. 2:6; Lev. 19:15.
9. See also the will of a person or group: Luke 9:51; 2 Cor. 1:11; personal attention, favor, or presence: Matt. 18:10; 1 Cor. 13:12; 2 Cor. 2:10; 4:6; Col. 2:1; 1 Thess. 2:17; 3:10; 2 Thess. 1:9; Heb. 9:24; 1 Pet. 3:12; Jude 16; Rev. 22:4.
10. Lohse 1968, 779.

Thus, when human judges are appointed, they also must not prefer the "small" or the "great" (Deut. 1:17; 16:19). This law is first stated in Leviticus to judge one's neighbor justly: "You shall not be partial to the face of the poor and not honor the face of the great" (19:15). (This is probably the law to which James refers in 2:9.) The New Testament reiterates these ideas. God is described as impartial when it comes to economic status (Eph. 6:9; Col. 3:25), as in James 2:1, 9, and to ethnic background or power (Jew and Gentile, as in Acts 10:34; Rom. 2:11; Gal. 2:6). God is the impartial judge (1 Pet. 1:17). Jesus, as God incarnate, is known even among his enemies as truthful to all, no matter their background (Luke 20:21). Therefore, since God the Trinity is impartial, it should be impossible to maintain a faith in Jesus that is partial to the wealthy (2:1).

James clearly writes to fellow believers because he mentions "*our Lord Jesus Christ*" (2:1). What is the significance of his describing Jesus as "**glorious**"? In this context, if Jesus is "glorious," so too are his heirs glorious (2:5), and thus the poor are more than competitors with the temporary glory of the wealthy (1:11; 2:2).[11] Humans may have glory, such as the wealthy Solomon (Matt. 6:29; Luke 12:27). Light has "glory" (Acts 22:11). But Jesus's glory did not come from shiny, expensive clothes. Rather, his glory is the same Shekinah glory as the Father's, whose glory is so great that even a devout human like Moses could not enter into the tabernacle when it was filled with the glory of the Lord (Exod. 40:34–35).[12] James and Jesus's other disciples saw Jesus's glory, "the glory as of the only begotten from the Father" (John 1:14).[13] Jesus demonstrated some of his preexistent glory to Peter, John, and James at the transfiguration when his clothes became dazzling white (Luke 9:29, 32). This "glorious" Lord is Jesus Christ who need not be partial to the powerful because he is already victorious, nor will he be partial to the oppressive wealthy at the final judgment (James 5:1–9).

James begins a series of questions, followed by statements summarizing the truths he intends to teach, in a similar style as the prophet Malachi's.

---

11. The later Ebionites, in contrast with James, thought that Jesus was not the Lord of glory but "plain and ordinary," righteous only through growth of character (*Hist. eccl.* 3.27).
12. See also Robertson 1933, 27.
13. See also John 12:41; 17:5, 24; Titus 2:13; Heb. 1:3.

Sequence of Questions and Statements in James Chapter 2[14]

Question	Statement
2:2–4[15]; 2:5; 2:6b; 2:7	2:6a; 2:8–9; 2:10*; 2:11; 2:12; 2:13
2:14a*; 2:14b; 2:15–16*	2:17*; 2:18; 2:19a; 2:19b
2:20; 2:21	2:22–23; 2:24
2:25	2:26

Sequence of Questions and Statements in Malachi Chapter 1[16]

Question	Statement
1:2b; 1:2c	1:2a; 1:2d–3; 1:4; 1:5
1:6a; 1:6b; 1:6d; 1:7b	1:6c; 1:7a; 1:7c

---

14. James chapter 1 has no questions.
15. This reference and every one with an asterisk in this chart has a subjunctive verb.
16. The analysis of Malachi is based on the translation of the Masoretic Text by the Jewish Publication Society 1955. The analysis of James is based on the translation of the Greek text by the author.

Sequence of Questions and Statements in Malachi Chapter 1[16]	
Question	Statement
1:8c; 1:8d; 1:8e; 1:9c	1:8a; 1:8b; 1:9a; 1:9b; 1:10a; 1:10b; 1:11; 1:12
1:13b	1:13a; 1:14

Like the Socratic diatribe style, the questions and answers used by James are teaching methods intended to censure and persuade. The Greek diatribe had questions and objections representing students' viewpoints. Unlike the Socratic style, James has not created imaginary characters and opponents with theoretical points of view. James deals with real concerns, as did Malachi.[17]

James uses the aorist subjunctive tense ("might enter," "might show," "might say," 2:2–3) in four conditional clauses to create a scenario for the readers to visualize.[18] The subjunctive here is the mode of proposal and expectation.[19] James is recalling to their attention an event that has occurred and will occur, probably repeatedly, but it is also archetypal of one common practice of partiality: preference to the impressive wealthy. The concluding indicative mode (2:4) ("have you not differentiated among yourselves and become judges with evil thoughts?") indicates a real problem in the diaspora to which James wants a transformed response from the audience.[20]

The setting is a **synagogue** (2:2), where these Messianic Jews attend for teaching and worship. They no longer attend temple services

---

17. Malachi tends to move from statements to questions, whereas James moves from questions to statements. See also Aune 1987, 200–201.
18. A similar technique is used in the illustration of 2:15–16.
19. Here instead of doubt, hesitation, prohibition, anticipation, hope, or will (Robertson 1934, 928).
20. Mongstad-Kvammen (2013, 144) agrees that the account is "probable and likely to occur."

since they have fled Jerusalem. Synagogues were found in every city that had at least ten "men of leisure" (m. Sanh. 1:6; m. Meg. 1:3; 4:3).[21] They served as centers for worship and study, community activities, and places of justice. Synagogues were lay run. Worship was held at noon on the Sabbath. Abbreviated services were held Mondays, Thursdays, Sabbath afternoons, and feast days. Benches for the congregation would line the walls. Elders would face the people. More distinguished senior worshipers would occupy the front steps with the younger ones behind. Men and women were probably segregated. The Seat of Moses was a stone chair for the especially honorable person (e.g., Matt. 23:1–6). Others might sit on mats on the floor or stand.[22]

Local synagogues would have a receiver of alms in charge of the weekly money chest, from which the local poor were supported and the plate from which any needy person could obtain a daily portion.[23] James's first concern is dignity afforded the poor in this religious setting, not simply physical need. Physical needs will be addressed later in 2:15–16.

As in the other illustrations (e.g., 1:8), the concrete "man," not the abstract generic, is used (2:2). Two different people enter: one with a "gold ring in **splendid** clothing" and another who is poor with "dirty clothing." The "poor" person is described in the abstract, not by gender. Gold might have been used in ancient times for valuable currency, or to decorate pagan deities or even the temple,[24] but this man simply used it to decorate himself.[25] Mongstad-Kvammen makes an excellent case for the gold ring and clothing symbolizing a man in the equestrian rank, a rank second to the senatorial order.[26] His "splendid clothing" adds to the "gold ring" his high position (2:2–3). "Splendid"[27] signifies "luminous" or "bright" because the word family is also used to describe the light given in the sky by lightning or by the morning star or by the sun.[28] It is a symbol of royalty and wealth (Luke 16:19; 23:11). At the transfiguration, Jesus's face "shown" like the sun (Matt. 17:2). Angels, having come from

---

21. Schürer 1973–79, 2:438–39.
22. Sukenik 1934, 47, 58–61, plates IX, XV; Runesson, Binder, and Olsson 2010, 133; Schürer 1973–79, 2:424–54.
23. Schürer 1973–79, 2:437.
24. E.g., Matt. 10:9; 23:17; Acts 17:29.
25. Later, the philosopher Epictetus (c. AD 50–120) describes a "white-haired old man with many a gold ring on his fingers" (χρυσοῦς δακτυλίος) (*Disc.* 1:22, 18).
26. Mongstad-Kvammen 2013, 100, 127, 144, 203–4. See also Laws 1980, 98.
27. Λαμπρός (adj.), λάμπω (verb), λαμρότης (noun), λαμπρῶς (adv.).
28. Luke 17:24; Acts 26:13; Rev. 22:16.

God's presence in heaven, have this kind of brightness,[29] as does the river in the new Jerusalem (Rev. 22:1). By the entrance of this "luminously" dressed man, the attenders might have great hope for contributions to their building fund and synagogue projects, as well as for connections to influential and powerful people, and maybe even for contributions to the alms money chest. Voluntary associations were important places to receive benefactions from wealthy members of the city. In return, by honoring their patrons, members could increase or maintain their status and rank in the city.[30] In contrast, the poor person would probably not contribute anything, but would rather deplete the money chest and even antagonize the wealthy by their smell. The poor clothing, instead of bright and luminous, is "dirty" or "filthy" (2:2). Although ῥυπαρός often symbolizes sin (e.g., 1:21), it does not in 2:2.

The **poor** person may be the unpaid harvester (5:4) who has no water to clean his clothes and no other outfit to use for the synagogue meeting. The poor could include the disabled, the sick, the hungry, the orphan, and the widow.[31] The "poor" are often grouped together with the blind, lame, leprous, deaf, hungry, mournful, captive, and oppressed in the Gospels.[32] They could be starving as a result of famine (Acts 11:28–30). Several famines did occur in Claudius's reign (AD 41–54).[33] The "poor" may be persons deprived of inherited status through debt, sickness, or becoming a widow or orphan.[34] Their clothing was filthy, so how could they be harmed by sitting on the filthy floor?

The response of the congregation could have been to welcome both the poor *and* wealthy persons. However, instead, they "look upon with care" or "show more respect" (ἐπιβλέπω) to the exterior aspects of the visitors, their clothing (what they were "wearing," 2:3). Ἐπιβλέπω implies an extensive look (e.g., Gen. 19:26, 28). The Lord promises to the Hebrews who are obedient to his covenant: "*I will look* upon you and I will increase you and I will multiply you and I will maintain my covenant with you" (Lev. 26:9). Because of their exterior attire, the rich man is blessed, but not the poor. The congregation has not remembered that Jesus was known for evaluating people from their inside personality, not from their external appearance (Luke 20:21; John 7:24). This was a message God taught the Israelites many years earlier

---

29. Acts 10:30; 12:7; Rev. 15:6.
30. Mongstad-Kvammen 2013, 96.
31. James 1:27; 2:15; 5:13–14; Acts 3:2; 6:1; 8:7; 9:39.
32. Matt. 11:5; Luke 4:18; 6:20–21; 7:22; 14:13, 21.
33. Bruce 1990, 276.
34. Mongstad-Kvammen 2013, 130–31.

at the election of David: humans "look on the outward appearance, but the Lord looks on the heart" (1 Sam. 16:7 NRSV). Instead, they command the rich man, "You stay seated there," and command the poor, "You stand there." To get any seat was to be in a good place, but this particularly wealthy man is to sit in a "good place" (καλῶς), either on the front bench or even on the most distinguished Seat of Moses. The poor person could be a man or a woman, young or elderly. They have a choice to stand or sit, but neither has any dignity. The sitting is specified as "under my **footstool**" (ὑποπόδιον), a place of great indignity. This is a place for one's enemies (Luke 20:43, citing Ps. 110:1). God is so great that the whole earth is like a "footstool" to his "throne" (Matt. 5:35, citing Isa. 66:1). Moreover, humans are exhorted to "worship at his footstool. Holy is he!" (Ps. 99:5 NRSV). The poor are being treated as enemies who should be debased, while the speaker ("my footstool") is in the place of God! Is this what God wants? James answers, "No!" followed by three immediate explanations in 2:4–6.

In the first-century Roman and Jewish context, the preference given to the wealthy man is understandable. "Partiality was a given" aspect of proper Roman and Jewish etiquette. "It was both the normative and the normal behaviour,"[35] Ingeborg Mongstad-Kvammen explains. Clothing and seating were significant for establishing rank. For instance, citizens were recognized by their *toga pura*, equestrians by their gold ring and *angustus clavus* on their tunics, and senators by their *latus clavus* on their tunics and a special *toga*. Senators and equestrians had special seating privileges at the theater, circus, and probably the public games and banquets.[36] Jewish religious leaders also sought special seating in synagogues and banquets.[37] These signs indicated the different value of different persons. In contrast, the poor represented one of the lowest ranks in society. Only women, gladiators, and slaves were lower in rank. Thus, James's exhortation to be impartial in seating was most countercultural to the first-century Roman and Jewish society.[38]

James's perspective is given in the form of three rhetorical questions.[39] First, "Have you not **differentiated** [διακρίνω] among yourselves and become judges with evil thoughts?" (2:4). Διακρίνω has the basic idea of choosing between two options. In 1:6, the person cannot

---

35. Mongstad-Kvammen 2013, 99, 134.
36. Mongstad-Kvammen 2013, 100, 132.
37. E.g., Mark 12:39; Luke 11:43; 14:7–14; 20:46.
38. Mongstad-Kvammen 2013, 100, 128, 132, 134–35.
39. The negative οὐ expects an affirmative reply: "not so?" (BDAG, 734; Robertson 1934, 917).

come to a decision; in 2:4 the person comes to a wrong decision, which is to show more care, respect, and value to the wealthy than to the poor believer. All probably claim to be believers since James writes "among *yourselves*" (2:4).[40] If they are all "brothers and sisters" (2:1, 5), the wealthy and powerful have no more value than the poor and powerless. They are in the same family. Judging in itself is not wrong. Every human must come to judgments, evaluations, or decisions from observations; as Jesus explains, "When evening comes, you say, 'It will be fair weather, for the sky is red,' and in the morning, 'Today it will be stormy, for the sky is red and overcast'" (Matt. 16:2–3 NIV). Moreover, in James's letter, God as judge is highly esteemed.[41] But the judgments James criticizes in 2:4 are ones that rank believers based on economic status. As a result, these "differentiating" believers become "judges with evil thoughts" (2:4). Certainly it is possible, then, that they seated the wealthy man in a place of honor with the expectation of benefit to themselves, while placing the poor person in a place of dishonor so as to hide him or her because he or she offered no benefit. The assembly has "wavered" (1:6) between God's standards and the world's standards but has put its trust in the wealthy person, not in God.[42]

The second response is even stronger. The **poor** are not simply to be treated equally to the rich; they may even be greater. James calls the readers to "hear," and augments his terms of endearment to encourage their positive response: "*Listen*, my *beloved* brothers and sisters" (2:5). He explains: "Has not God selected the poor of the world to be rich in faith and heirs of the reign which he promised to the ones loving him?" (2:5).[43] This statement (in the form of a question to elicit a response) may hearken back to the Magnificat, the praise poem of Mary, James's mother: God my Savior "has looked with favor [ἐπιβλέπω, used also in James 2:3] on the humble state [ταπείνωσις, used also in James 1:10] of his slave [δοῦλος, used also in James 1:1]" (Luke 1:47–48). Mary notes from God's election of her as the mother of the Lord that, as a result, the "Mighty One has done great things for me. . . . He has brought down the powerful from their thrones and lifted up the humble, filled up the hungry with good things, and sent the rich away empty" (Luke 1:49, 52–53). God selected Mary, who was poor.

At first glance one might think that James writes, "God has selected the poor *and only the poor* to be rich in faith and heirs." In that

---

40. See also McCartney 2009, 140.
41. James 3:1; 4:12; 5:9, 12.
42. See also Mongstad-Kvammen 2013, 147, 161.
43. Οὐ again expects an affirmative reply.

case, God has completely reversed the prejudices of the time. However, that reading would omit the second half of the sentence. The poor are selected "to be rich in faith and heirs of the reign which [God] promised" (2:5). Thus, James has not stated anything about the spiritual state of those who are wealthy in this verse.

James himself was most likely not reared in a wealthy home (see the introduction). And, if Joseph did die before Jesus's resurrection, that would place additional financial strain on the family of at least eight (mother, five boys and two or more sisters, e.g., Matt. 13:55–56; Mark 6:3). Consequently, James is very empathetic with the poor. He affirms Paul and Barnabas on their ministry to the Gentiles but asks "only one thing": that they "remember the poor" (Gal. 2:10). Jesus's own calling was one to "proclaim good news to the poor" (Luke 4:18). The Beatitudes begin: "Blessed are the poor, for yours is God's reign" (Luke 6:20) and "Blessed are the poor in spirit for theirs is heaven's reign" (Matt. 5:3). Both on the plain (Luke 6:20) and on the mountain (Matt. 5:3), Jesus highlights the poor, referring to both the literal poor and the metaphorical "poor." James further defines the "poor" in his letter as "the ones loving" God (2:5). Not all poor love God and are not greedy. But these "poor" are also in the active process of loving God.[44] In James 1:12, God promises the crown of life to this same group: "the ones loving him."[45] Wealth is often an impediment to giving one's life over to worship and obedience of God.[46] For instance, the wealthy young man who wanted to receive eternal life was willing to obey all the commandments, but not willing to sell his possessions and give to the poor (Matt. 19:16–22). In contrast, the poor widow contributed all she owned to the temple treasury, not simply her surplus money (Mark 12:41–44).

If the poor might lack money and an inheritance, God would give them "wealth" in faith and an inheritance in God's reign or kingdom (2:5). Thus, to the discerning observer, the poor believers are in reality "wealthy." Moreover, they do have an inheritance. God's "reign" or "kingdom" (βασιλεία) is an important New Testament theme. It

---

44. Ἀγαπῶσιν ("loving") is a present participle, which implies duration. McCartney (2009, 142) agrees: it "is a progressive participle, implying a continuous, ongoing love for God." God's love (Hebrew, *hesed*) will be shown to those who "love" God and "keep" his commandments (Exod. 20:6) (McKnight 2011, 196).
45. See also Rom. 8:28; 1 Cor. 2:9. In contrast, Mary declares that God's mercy is for those "fearing him" (Luke 1:50).
46. E.g., Matt. 19:23–24; Mark 10:23–26; Luke 18:24–25. However, compare to Joseph of Arimathea (Mark 15:43; Luke 23:50–53).

encompasses Jesus's message, model, and person.[47] Like the poor, it may not begin in an impressive manner, but it is important.[48] It belongs to the childlike[49] and is global in scope.[50] It requires obedience and priority.[51] It is offered to all but is not given to those who disobey its covenant of righteousness.[52] It is both now and not yet, present and in the future.[53]

All this the poor have inherited, nevertheless, those who act with partiality have "**insulted**," not honored, the poor by their treatment of them (2:6). James emphasizes "you" by placing the plural pronoun at the beginning of the sentence,[54] highlighting the irony of the situation. "Insult" (ἀτιμάζω) is a strong verb. It is close to killing someone. For example, in Jesus's parable, the tenant farmers who did not want to pay the vineyard owner his share of the produce, beat the head of and "insulted" the second messenger. The third messenger was killed (Mark 12:4–5). When the Jewish leaders accused Jesus of being a Samaritan and demon-possessed, they "insulted" him (John 8:49). Flogging was part of the way the Sanhedrin dishonored Peter and the other apostles (Acts 5:40–41). When David's envoys had half their beards shaved off and their garments cut off in the middle by Hanun the Ammonite, they were ashamed and insulted (2 Sam. 10:5). As a result, their nations went to war (2 Sam. 10:6–8). Solomon cautions: "The one dishonoring [insulting] the needy sins, but the one showing mercy to the poor [πτωχός] is most blessed" (Prov. 14:21 LXX). Thus, ἀτιμάζω (ἀτιμία [noun], ἄτιμος [adj.]) can range from extreme malice to deep insult. Some treated Jesus the Messiah this way.[55] James is outraged that this behavior was exhibited in a worship setting by Christian against Christian. Moreover, Mongstad-Kvammen explains that to dishonor the poor is equivalent to dishonoring God because the poor are God's elect.[56]

---

47. Matt. 4:17; Mark 1:15; 9:1–3; Luke 4:43; 8:1; 9:11; 17:20–21; Acts 28:31.
48. Matt. 13:3–46; Mark 4:30–32; Luke 13:18–21.
49. Matt. 18:1–5; 19:14–15; Mark 10:14–16; Luke 18:16–17.
50. Matt. 8:11; Luke 13:29.
51. Matt. 5:10, 20; 7:21–23; 19:11–12; 21:23–43; 25:1–13; Mark 9:47; Luke 9:60–62; 14:15–27; 18:29–30; Acts 14:22; 2 Thess. 1:5.
52. Matt. 6:33; 18:23–35; 20:1–16; 22:1–14; 1 Cor. 6:9–10; Gal. 5:19–21; Eph. 5:5.
53. Matt. 13:24–30, 47–50; Luke 22:18; 1 Cor. 15:50–54; Rev. 11:15; 12:10–11.
54. See also Vlachos 2013, 73; Blomberg and Kamell 2008, 114.
55. See also Isa. 53:3; Matt. 13:57; Mark 6:4.
56. Mongstad-Kvammen 2013, 166.

James then gives his third response, his strongest, which is to complain of the treatment by the rich of the poor, again in the form of rhetorical questions: "Do not the rich **oppress** you and themselves drag you into court? Do not they themselves slander the good name, the one being called upon you?" (2:6–7). The answer is "Yes, they do!" James is outraged that the rich would be given preferential treatment in light of their oppression of the poor in court and slandering of their name (James 2:6–7). The second half of the first sentence develops the first half. In other words, dragging believers into court is one way the wealthy oppress James's readers (2:6). "Oppress" (καταδυναστεύω) may be defined as "to exercise harsh control over one, to use one's power against one."[57] Frequently, it is the widow and orphan who are oppressed because they have little power.[58] Their inheritances and properties can be stolen (Mic. 2:2). Workers' wages and pledges from debtors can be withheld.[59] In the Old Testament, καταδυναστεύω is also used for conquering cities and stealing and enslaving people.[60] Oppression of the poor is repeatedly denounced in the Old Testament (e.g., Amos 4:1–3; 8:4–8).[61] Micah proclaimed: "The rich men of the city are steeped in violence; her citizens are all liars, their tongues utter deceit" (6:12 REB). The practice of oppression of the poor continued in New Testament times. Jesus denounced the teachers of the law who gave a show of piety but meanwhile sought the best seats in the synagogues and "devoured" the houses of widows.[62]

The rich "themselves **drag** [ἕλκω] you" (2:6). A similar verb (ἐξέλκω) is used in 1:14. The poor, as victims, are helpless to stop the rich drawing them toward potential death, even as desire "drags" a person away to spiritual death (1:14–15). The same verb (ἕλκω) is used to describe the way Paul and Silas were forced to go to the magistrates in Philippi (Acts 16:19).[63] This is no conference of equals to resolve a concern of mutual interest. The poor are then brought to a place of judgment (κριτήριον). For the Jews, this might be a synagogue, a group of judges, a lesser Sanhedrin, or the greater Sanhedrin,[64] or for the

---

57. Thayer, 331.
58. James 1:27; Jer. 7:6; 22:3; Ezek. 22:7; Mal. 3:5.
59. James 5:4; Ezek. 18:12, 16; 22:29; Mal. 3:5.
60. Exod. 21:(16)17; 2 Chron. 21:17; Neh. 5:5; Hos. 5:11.
61. See also 1 Cor. 11:20–22.
62. Mark 12:38–40; Luke 20:45–47. See Spencer and Spencer 1990, 40–64.
63. See also Acts 21:30–31.
64. See summary of procedure in Schürer 1973–79, 2:226.

Romans, the praetor or chief magistrate, such as Pontius Pilate, Gallio, Felix, or Festus.[65]

Moreover, the rich **slander** (βλασφημέω) the "good name" of the poor (2:7). Often a good name may be all the poor may have. James repeats "themselves" (αὐτοί, 2:6, 7) for the oppressors to emphasize that these wealthy folks are the very ones who drag them into court and slander their names.

Βλασφημέω (βλασφημία) is often associated with disrespectful speech toward God, alluding to the second of the Ten Commandments: "You shall not make wrongful use of the name of the LORD your God, for the Lord will not acquit anyone who misuses his name" (Exod. 20:7 NRSV). Thus, if Jesus were not God incarnate, it would be "blasphemy" for him, "being a human being," to make himself God (John 10:33). But "blasphemy" may also be used of humans to humans, where one human speaks in "a disrespectful way that demeans, denigrates, maligns" another.[66] One person may misrepresent another's good actions as evil.[67] Slander is a false witness which intends to be harmful.[68] For example, Paul's enemies intended to harm him in their disrespectful speeches at Pisidian Antioch and at Corinth (Acts 13:45; 18:6). The evil actions of the Israelites, which resulted in their exile, were grounds for God's name to be slandered among the Gentiles. They did not "know" God's name, in other words, how wonderful God is (Isa. 52:5–7). In a similar manner, the "good name" of the poor, who were elected by God to be "wealthy in faith and heirs of [God's] reign" (2:5), was being treated disrespectfully, speech being used to demean them. The actions of the wealthy were oppressive (2:6) and their speech deprecating (2:7).

"**Name**" (ὄνομα) is a synecdoche for the person (2:7). In James chapter 5 it represents the Lord (5:10, 14). In 2:7, it represents the poor person. The name of those who are poor is "good" (καλός): noble, praiseworthy,[69] and pleasing to God. In Acts, several times a person is described with two names, for example, Joseph was renamed

---

65. John 18:28–31; Acts 18:12–16; 23:26–26:32. According to the Mishnah, smaller cases, such as those involving property, were decided by three judges (m. Sanh. 1:1; 3:1). The high priest could make judgments (m. Sanh. 2:1; John 18:12–14).

66. BDAG, 178.

67. E.g., Rom. 3:8; 14:16; 1 Cor. 10:30; 2 Pet. 2:12.

68. Spencer 2013, 45, about 1 Tim. 1:20.

69. BDAG, 504.

"Barnabas" by the other apostles because he was so encouraging.[70] So too the poor have been renamed. James uses a similar phrase in 2:7 as he did in his speech in Jerusalem (Acts 15:17). There he cites Amos 9:11–12, the Gentiles "over whom my name has been called," but in this letter the poor are those "over whom [God's] name has been called" (2:7). In other words, the poor, like the Gentiles, have been affirmed as full members of God's reign. Their "good name" is "Heir of God."[71] However, in their context, false and demeaning words were said about them at court by the rich.

James now returns to a summary of the Ten Commandments: **"Love your neighbor** as yourself" (2:8, citing Lev. 19:18 and Jesus[72] [Matt. 22:39]). By disrespecting the poor, they have not loved them as they would themselves want to be loved. Chapter 2 verses 8–9 is one extended thought teaching that acting in partiality (προσωπολημπτέω,[73] 2:9) is the opposite of loving one's neighbor. The context of Leviticus 19 is significant. In that passage, the congregation is exhorted not to steal, deal falsely, lie, defraud a neighbor, render an unjust judgment, be partial to the poor, defer to the great, slander, or profit by the blood of a neighbor (Lev. 19:11–18).[74] Instead, they should leave a harvest for the poor and judge with justice (Lev. 19:9–10, 15).[75] Michael Fiorello clarifies that Leviticus 19 implies that "communal holiness is defined as love expressed in displays of integrity and guardianship for one's neighbor."[76] Mongstad-Kvammen summarizes: "The love command represents both the fulfillment of the Law *and* the quintessence of the

---

70. Acts 4:36. See also Acts 1:23; 10:5, 18, 32; 11:13; 12:12, 25.
71. "God" is the closest antecedent (2:5). Other commentators think the "good name" was that of "Jesus, pronounced over them in baptism" (e.g., Painter and deSilva 2012, 95; Laws 1980, 105–6; Dibelius 1976, 141; McCartney 2009, 143). Adam 2013 comments that, if the letter is early, probably "it is that James here refers to God" (42). I think that the earlier context of 2:5 is crucial in defining the "good name." Since the rich man has visited the synagogue where Christians are welcomed, he is not likely a persecutor of their faith. The wealthy have picked on the poor to oppress, not the Christians as a group.
72. The Greek is word for word the LXX but also an exact translation of the Hebrew. James's words are also exactly the same Greek words Jesus used. See also Laws 1980, 109–10.
73. See exposition James 2:1.
74. See also McCartney 2009, 44–45.
75. Lev. 19:12–13 warns not to swear falsely nor withhold wages of a laborer, which are discussed in James 5:4, 12.
76. Fiorello 2012, 560.

Law."[77] James's description in 2:6–7 implies the rich could have committed these wrong actions.

The law of Leviticus 19:18 is a "royal" one, given by the greatest king: God (2:8). **"Royal"** (βασιλικός, adj.) is the same word family as "reign" (βασιλεία, noun, 2:5). The adjective is also used of human "kings" or "rulers," such as Herod (Acts 12:20–21).[78] Thus, the "royal law" is the one given by royalty, God, for all the members of his reign or kingdom.[79] When a congregation defers to the great while debasing the poor, they sin in not living according to the rules of God's reign and therefore become a gathering of transgressors (παραβάτης), according to Leviticus 19:18 and in particular 19:15 (James 2:9).[80] Scot McKnight summarizes James's focus: "The act of partiality leads to a status: 'transgressors.'"[81] Thus, Edmond Hiebert adds: "Their partiality is not a trivial fault, to be dismissed lightly as of no consequence." The law "is personified and pictured as a witness whose testimony exposes them each time they practice partiality."[82] The wealthy, whom they favored, did steal, bear false witness, and covet their neighbor's houses (Exod. 20:15–17). As Jesus taught, to do to others as one wants done to oneself summarizes all the Law and the Prophets (Matt. 7:12). Sin leads to conviction by the law as transgressors (James 2:9).

Verses 9–11 mutually define each other. How is someone convicted by the law? Disobedience of any part of the law results in conviction as a sinner. One example James has been emphasizing is discrimination, preferring the rich over the poor Christian (2:9). Another illustration is committing murder but not adultery (2:11). The principle is stated in verses 10–11: disobeying even one law makes one a transgressor. The same God has stated all the laws.

"Guard" (τηρέω, 2:10) has been used already in the letter (1:27) in regard to oneself. In verse 10, it is used for the law. Τηρέω was used literally of the actions of guards describing the process of guarding a prisoner, such as guarding Jesus on the cross,[83] Peter in prison (Acts 12:5–6), Paul and Silas in Philippi (Acts 16:23), and Paul in

---

77. Mongstad-Kvammen 2013, 185.
78. See also 2 Macc. 3:13.
79. See also BDAG, 170; LSJ, 309. The Latin *lex regia* is a law "which came from the king" (Robertson 1933, 31).
80. See also Deut. 1:17; 16:19.
81. McKnight 2011, 210. See also Spencer on "transgressor" (2013, 72).
82. Hiebert 1979, 165.
83. Matt. 27:36, 54.

Caesarea.[84] The first-century prisoners were not held in automated, closed prisons as today, but in temporary places in buildings, caves, and pits where constant surveillance for each prisoner was needed. The personification of Wisdom metaphorically brings out the process entailed in guarding: "Happy is the human who guards [φυλάσσω] my ways; watching daily at my doors, *guarding* [τηρέω] at the posts of my entrances" (Prov. 8:32, 34).[85] This process is evident in the earlier use: "*to guard oneself* spotless from the world" (1:27). This guarding is clearly an ongoing process.[86] In 2:10, James employs a more common concept of the verb, to "guard" the law, as in Acts 15:5, where the Pharisee Christians demand that the Gentiles must "guard [obey] the law of Moses." Their focus was circumcision, while James focused on obeying the Ten Commandments. The New Testament also uses as a synonym for "law" "commandments" (ἐντολάς, Luke 18:20). The connotation in τηρέω is vigilance, as well as obedience and protection of the commandments. The person James describes guards "all the law" but fails at "one" law[87] (2:10). The subjunctive is again used to describe the situation (see also 2:2–3). This person might be similar to the rich ruler who claimed to obey all the commandments yet who was not willing to give generously to the poor (Luke 18:18–23).[88] The law the person has not obeyed is the law to love one's neighbor as oneself (2:8).

Disobedience is described as "stumble, trip, fall" (πταίω, 2:10; 3:2).[89] **"Stumble"** is an appropriate translation (NIV, NTME), but "fall" may be more exact. Πταίω is used literally in the Old Testament to describe complete defeat by an army, as when the Israelites "fell before the Philistines" and four thousand men were killed.[90] A person might stumble or trip, but not necessarily fall, but the Old Testament uses describe persons who fall and are killed by an enemy ("defeated" NRSV, REB). Thus, "guard" (τηρέω) and "fall" (πταίω) are military images. A

---

84. Acts 24:23; 25:4, 21.
85. Φυλάσσω is a synonym of τηρέω. See also Acts 12:4–6.
86. "To guard" is also in the present tense, which "can be assumed to be durative" (Robertson 1934, 890).
87. "One" (ἑνί) is masculine singular to match "law" (νόμος). Adam adds that James used νόμος to refer to the single love commandment in 2:8 (2013, 45–46).
88. See also Matt. 19:16–22; Mark 10:17–22.
89. LSJ, 1546.
90. 1 Sam. 4:2. See also 1 Sam. 4:3; 2 Sam. 2:17; 10:15, 19; 18:7; 1 Chron. 19:19.

battle is being fought—to guard all the law—but that battle is lost if one law is not "protected."

"Guilty" (ἔνοχος, 2:10) is a law term.[91] It refers not to the punishment itself, but to the decision that one indeed is guilty of a crime. For example, the high priest decided Jesus had blasphemed by comparing himself to God. The Sanhedrin then decided he was liable (ἔνοχος) to death as an appropriate punishment for this crime.[92] James says in 2:10 that failure of one of God's commandments leaves one in a state of guilt.[93] Some rabbis agreed with James. Rabbi Hanina ben Gamaliel (AD c. 80–120) concluded: "He that commits one transgression thereby forfeits his soul" (m. Mak. 3:15). Rabbi Judah the Patriarch (c. AD 165–200) said: "Be heedful of a light precept as of a weighty one" (m. 'Abot 2:1). Another tractate concludes: he that "neglects a single commandment" shall not "inherit the land" (m. Qidd. 1:10).[94] Philo explains that failure to submit to even the smallest ancestral tradition affects all of them, "because as with buildings if a single piece is taken from the base, the parts that up to then seemed firm are loosened and slip away and collapse into the void thus made" (*Embassy* 16.117). Paul states a similar thought from the other perspective: if a man is circumcised, "he is obligated to obey the whole law" (Gal. 5:3). In contrast, Rabbi Akiba (c. AD 50–135) said, although the world is judged by grace, "yet all is according to the excess of works [that be good or evil]" (m. 'Abot 3:16). In other words, obedience and disobedience were to be compared at the judgment to see which was greater.

James agrees with the former. He illustrates his point (2:11) by referring to the first two commandments mentioned by Jesus in Luke 18:20. This verse appears to be a direct quotation from Jesus, as cited in Luke 18:20. These commandments (sixth and seventh) are originally described in Exodus 20:13–14 and are repeated by Moses in Deuteronomy 5:17–18. The Hebrew uses the *qal* imperfect tense, which can be translated in Greek as a future or subjunctive tense. The Septuagint translates it as a future active indicative.

---

91. LSJ, 572.
92. Matt. 26:65–66. See also *Ant.* 17.5.127.
93. He uses the perfect tense for "become" (γίνομαι). See also Adam 2013, 46–47.
94. See also Gal. 3:10, citing Deut. 27:26; Gal. 5:3.

James 2:11 Compared to Similar Biblical References			
Bible Text	Sequence of commandments	Tense of verbs	Translation
Exod. 20:13–14; Deut. 5:17–18[95] Hebrew	Murder precedes adultery	Qal imperfect	"Do not murder. Do not commit adultery. Do not steal."
Exod. 20:13–14 LXX	Adultery precedes murder	Future indicative	"Do not commit adultery. Do not steal. Do not murder."
Deut. 5:17–18 LXX	Murder precedes adultery	Future indicative	"Do not murder. Do not commit adultery. Do not steal."
Matt. 19:18	Murder precedes adultery	Future indicative	"Do not murder. Do not commit adultery. Do not steal."
Mark 10:19	Murder precedes adultery	Aorist subjunctive	"Do not murder. Do not commit adultery. Do not steal."
Luke 18:20	Adultery precedes murder	Aorist subjunctive	"Do not commit adultery. Do not murder. Do not steal."
Rom. 13:9	Adultery precedes murder	Future indicative	"Do not commit adultery. Do not murder. Do not steal."
James 2:11	Adultery precedes murder	Aorist subjunctive	"Do not commit adultery. Do not murder."

In contrast, James uses the aorist subjunctive in the exact same sequence as does Luke 18:20, not the sequence nor the tense of the Old Testament references. Thus, it appears that "the One saying . . . said also" would refer to Jesus, who was cited earlier in 1:1 and 2:1.[96] The aorist subjunctive is a more classical way to cite a prohibition, although the future volitive (command) is frequent in the Septuagint.[97] In the Old Testament the punishment for both is death.[98]

---

95. Agrees with Greek Codex A.
96. Cf. "God": Blomberg and Kamell 2008, 118; Vlachos 2013, 81; Laws 1980, 114; Witherington 2007, 461.
97. Robertson 1934, 851–52, 874.
98. Lev. 20:10; Num. 35:30.

Adultery may be defined as having freely chosen sexual relations with someone who is not one's spouse, but it also includes the internal lust that precedes action.[99] The Old Testament uses "adultery" as a metaphor for idolatry.[100] James does the same in 4:4, where he describes those who are friends with the world as "adulterers." **Murder** is intentional killing with a desire to hurt, as opposed to unintentional killing.[101] Jesus further defines "murder" as anger without cause, which flows from the heart.[102] James also comments that murder comes from internal desires (4:1–2) and that the landowners have murdered innocent laborers (5:4–6). Humans must not be murdered because they were created in God's image (Gen. 9:6). For the same reason they must not be cursed (James 3:9). Paul also summarizes the Ten Commandments as "love your neighbor as yourself" because love does no wrong to a neighbor (Rom. 13:9–10; cf. James 2:8). Adultery and murder harm the neighbor. Therefore, no one can be acceptable if they murder but do not commit adultery (James 2:11).

James then makes an analogy to his overall theme of being doers of the word who hear and act in a consistent manner (1:22–25): "In the same way, speak and, in the same way, act" (2:12). A doer of the word does all that the law requires consistently because he or she will be judged by the **"law of freedom"** (2:12). The perfect law of freedom has already been mentioned (1:25). "Freedom" alludes to the new covenant, the transformed old covenant. This law is the same as the "word" (1:23), the Old Testament as seen through the eyes of the new covenant, including Jesus's freeing teachings[103] and his present empowering presence. As we will see, James is not saying that being a doer of the law justifies one; rather, he is saying that the new covenant expects a genuine believer to speak and act consistently and not to discriminate.

This law is a **merciful law** (2:13), especially merciful to the powerless, such as the poor. James alludes to Jesus's teaching: "For with the judgment you judge you will be judged" and "Blessed are the merciful, for they themselves will receive mercy" (Matt. 7:2; 5:7).[104] James thus warns his readers that if they do not exercise mercy, they will

---

99. Matt. 5:27–28; 15:19; Mark 7:22; Luke 16:18; Rom. 7:3.
100. E.g., Jer. 3:9; Ezek. 23:43–45; Hos. 4:12–14.
101. Num. 35:15; Deut. 4:42; 19:4–6.
102. Matt. 5:21–22; 15:19; Mark 7:21.
103. Jesus's voice has been evident in this paragraph several times, in James's citations of Jesus, as recorded by Matthew 22:39 (Lev. 19:18) and Luke 18:20 (Exod. 20:13–14). Painter and deSilva 2012 summarize: the "law of liberty" is "the Jewish law as interpreted by Jesus" (97).
104. See also Matt. 6:12, 14–15; 18:33; Obad. 15.

be judged without mercy because they are not living according to the covenant of mercy, to which they claim to belong. Mercy (ἔλεος) is a key quality of God, who provides the wisdom from above (3:17). God's mercy was revealed early to Moses: God bestows mercy on those who love him and keep his commandments.[105] Bestowing mercy does not contradict justice. God does not dismiss guilt (ἔνοχος, Exod. 34:7, the same word as in James 2:10), but God forgives and "saves" repentant sinners.[106] What does "mercy" look like? When Jesus ate with tax collectors and sinners in order to save them, he was merciful (Matt. 9:10–13; 12:7). When the Samaritan saw the half-dead man by the road from Jerusalem to Jericho and bandaged his wounds, poured oil and wine on them, put him on his own animal, brought him to an inn, took care of him, and paid his stay, he was merciful (Luke 10:30–37). Thus, Jesus's practice of and teachings in favor of healing, exorcism, and forgiveness are further examples of mercy.[107] As Thayer explains, ἔλεος is "kindness or good will toward the miserable and afflicted, joined with a desire to relieve them."[108] A symbol of mercy is the early and late rain when it came to the land of Israel (Hos. 6:3; James 5:7). Mary, James's mother, was cognizant of the importance of God's mercy (Luke 1:50, 54).

One would expect that judgment should triumph over mercy, but not when the all-powerful God is characterized as merciful (2:13). **"Triumph over"** (κατακαυχάομαι) can be a negative action, as when the wisdom from below "boasts" or "exults over"[109] truth (James 3:14) or when some Roman Gentiles were "exulting over" some Jews (Rom. 11:17–18). Plunderers who win might "boast over" their plunder as "calves in the grass and push with the horn as bulls" (Jer. 50:11). But κατακαυχάομαι can also be a positive action. When the Lord strengthens a people, then "they shall boast in" the Lord's "name" (Zech. 10:12 LXX). In James 2:13, κατακαυχάομαι has positive connotations because indeed mercy is superior and more powerful than judgment. Mercy belongs to God: "God, being rich in *mercy*, because of his great love with which he loved us, despite we being dead through trespasses, made us alive together with Christ . . . and raised us up with him and seated us with him in the heavenly places in Christ Jesus, so that in the ages to come he might show the immeasurable riches of his grace in

---

105. Exod. 20:6; 34:7; Deut. 5:10; 7:9.
106. Rom. 11:30–32; Eph. 2:4–5; Titus 3:5; 1 Pet. 1:3; 2:10; Jude 21.
107. Healing and exorcism: Matt. 9:27; 15:22; 17:15; 20:30–34; Mark 5:18–19; 10:46–48; Luke 17:12–13; 18:35–39; forgiveness: Matt. 18:26–33; 1 Tim. 1:13–16.
108. Thayer, 203.
109. BDAG, 517.

kindness toward us in Christ Jesus" (Eph. 2:4–7). Mercy, working through the "implanted word," can indeed save us (James 1:21).

Verbal Faith without Actions Is Dead (2:14–26)
James continues in 2:14–26 to explain why the readers should be "doers of the word, and not merely hearers" (1:22),[110] beginning and ending the next section with the same question: "What is the benefit?" (2:14, 16).[111] He repeats again his endearing term, "my brothers and sisters" (2:14),[112] before he exhorts the readers to be doers of the word who act for the poor (2:14–16). He employs the subjunctive tense, again, to visualize the situation. The principle in 2:14 is illustrated by the scenario in 2:15–16. The principle is then repeated and rephrased in 2:17. The two "if" adverbial clauses in the present subjunctive tense portray expectation and possibility ("if someone may say to have faith, but he or she may not have actions"), but the conclusion is "What is the benefit?" and "Faith is not able to save him, is it?" (2:14).[113] James reiterates his main topic: verbal espousing of faith not demonstrated in action is not a saving faith. He previously explained how hearing about the faith but not acting on it is self-deceiving (1:22–26). These persons have not truly received the "implanted" saving word (1:21). James 2:14 is a reflection of 1:21. Both verses include the verbs "able" (δύναμαι) and "save" (σῴζω). Δύναμαι signifies "to possess capability (whether because of personal or external factors) for experiencing or doing someth[ing]."[114] From a positive perspective, the "implanted word" has the capability to save people (1:21). From a negative perspective, the un-implanted word, or verbal faith not demonstrated in actions, has no capability to save (2:14).[115] Later, James will describe this type of faith as "dead" and "inactive," not demonstrating justification (2:17, 20, 24–26).

110. This is a similar message to Jesus's in Matthew 7:21–23; John the Baptist's in Luke 3:8; and Paul's in Romans 1:5; 6:17–18.
111. The same phrase occurs in 1 Corinthians 15:32. Epictetus uses it without the article (τί ὄφελος, *Disc.* 3.24, 51).
112. See also 1:2; 2:1; 3:1, 10, 12; 5:12, 19. See excursus at the end of chapter 1 on "Significance of Gender Language in James."
113. The final conclusion in 2:14 is stated in the present tense. Robertson 1934 explains: "A maxim often has the pres[ent] ind[icative] in the apodosis" (1019).
114. BDAG, 261–62.
115. McKnight 2011 clarifies that "save" refers both to moral transformation and the final judgment, as in 5:20 (229).

He again uses an example of the poor. The first developed illustration concerns actions disrespectful of the poor (2:2–7), while this illustration concerns actions unhelpful for the poor (2:15–16). This is the only place where James uses both the singular "**brother**"[116] and "**sister**." In previous illustrations he has used "man" (ἀνήρ)[117] and the generic "poor" (πτωχός, 2:2) or "rich" (πλούσιος, 1:11). The familial sibling terms clearly indicate believers in the Lord Jesus Christ (2:1, 15). The plural (ἀδελφοί) is employed in 2:14 to address the readers, and then the singular is employed in the illustration (2:15).[118] This makes the illustration more concrete. James wants poor women to be included, but he does not want poor men to be excluded. He mentions "widows" earlier (1:27). "Orphans" could be male or female. But the illustration is not limited to widows and orphans, but refers to any poor believer in need of clothing and food.[119]

He continues use of the subjunctive tense as he did in the previous illustrations. The poor brother or sister is described as in a state (ὑπάρχω)[120] of nakedness and lacking daily nourishment (2:15). This is not a one-time need. "**Naked**" (γυμνός) may be literal, as a baby at birth,[121] similar to those who see their "birth-face" in the mirror (James 1:23), or it may be a hyperbole signifying inadequate clothing, as the apostles, who were "hungry and thirsty," "*poorly clothed* and beaten and homeless."[122] Probably the poor lacked the warm exterior garments needed in cold weather, or their garments were in poor condition; they certainly lacked the attractive clothing of the wealthy (James 2:2). Greek and Roman clothing included a brassiere or corset, tunic covered by a cloak (outer garment), a cape, a cap or shawl, and footwear.[123] In Jerusalem in January, the temperature averages 45° Fahrenheit (7° Celsius), and throughout the winter the temperature frequently falls to or below the freezing point.[124] Taking care to clothe

---

116. The singular "brother" is used in 1:9.
117. The singular "man" is used in illustrations in 1:8, 12, 23.
118. In the same way, plural terms are used in 5:16a, while the singular is used in the illustration in 5:16b–18.
119. See also Gal. 6:10.
120. Ὑπάρχω is a synonym for εἰμί, which here indicates "to be in a state or circumstance," "be inherently (so)" or "be really" (BDAG, 1029).
121. E.g., Job 1:21; Eccl. 5:14; Hos. 2:3.
122. 1 Cor. 4:11 (NRSV); verb: γυμνιτεύω.
123. Stephens 1987, 334–37.
124. Finegan and Melamid 1987, 542. Peter warmed himself (θερμαίνω) at a fire during Jesus's arrest (Mark 14:54, 67; John 18:18, 25). When I visited Jerusalem in January, I wore a sweater, pants, scarf, raincoat, *and* hat during the daytime. Galilee was warmer.

the poor has a rich biblical tradition, including Jesus's admonition: "I was naked and you gave me clothing" (Matt. 25:36). If you clothe "one of the least of these my brothers and sisters, you have done so to me," he says (Matt. 25:40). The Lord tells Ezekiel that the just person does not oppress anyone and gives bread to the hungry and clothing to the naked (18:7, 16).[125] For James, clothing the needy means clothing heirs of God's kingdom (James 2:5; Matt. 25:34).

"**Nourishment**" (τροφή, 2:15)[126] is a general term that may include food and drink (Matt. 6:25–26; 24:45). Laborers deserve to receive sufficient means for such nourishment according to Jesus (Matt. 10:10), but some harvesters were not receiving such, while their landowners were fattening themselves (James 5:4–5). While some needs are simple, like John the Baptist's "nourishment" being simply locusts and wild honey (Matt. 3:4), food and clothing are still basic necessities (ἐπιτήδειος). Employers should ensure their workers are amply provided for, since the body's wellbeing concerns God the Father (James 2:16; Luke 12:22–23, 31). As Jesus specified in his model prayers, so too James specifies that nourishment is a *daily* affair, "food for the day."[127] Each Christian brother or sister genuinely has needs for the day. They are not running a scam or misusing their income. James gives an example of how a richer Christian brother or sister might respond in a spiritual-sounding manner but not alleviate any literal needs, making three unhelpful commands: "Go in peace, warm yourselves, and be satisfied" (2:16).

"**Go in peace**" is a traditional Jewish salutation.[128] When Jesus encountered the woman with the twelve-year hemorrhage, "go in peace" signified his healing her disease and accepting her for making him unclean by touching him (Mark 5:34). "Peace" is an important aspect of God's wisdom (James 3:18). "Peace" (εἰρήνη) signifies "harmony" and "well-being,"[129] neither of which have been disbursed when the poor Christian in James's illustration was sent away empty-handed. No good was accomplished. Their clothing needs were not resolved, so they are still cold; their nourishment needs were not satisfied, so they are still hungry.

In 2:17, James makes the point that declaring "peace" when there is no action to ensure peace is analogous to declaring "faith" when

125. See also Job 22:6; 24:7, 10; 31:19; Isa. 58:7; 1 John 3:17–18.
126. BDAG, 1017.
127. Matt. 6:11; Luke 11:3. Jesus uses a different phrase: "daily bread" (ἐπιούσον ἄρτον) but refers to the same concept.
128. E.g., Judg. 18:6; 1 Sam. 1:17; 20:42; 2 Sam. 15:9; Luke 7:50.
129. BDAG, 287.

there is no action to demonstrate it. Such faith has no benefit or good. In reality, such "faith" is "dead." It has no life. It is a seed that has no growth or a soil without a seed (1:21).

James begins 2:18 with an adversative (ἀλλά) signifying "but, nevertheless, yea moreover," serving as a climax to his previous argument.[130] James's persona argues against someone ("one of you," v. 16, person 1) who says, "Go in peace," while not feeding and clothing the poor person (2:15–16). The other generic "someone" (τις) is "I" (person 2), representing James's own perspective, the doer of the word (2:18). Person 1 ("you") has the same perspective as the illustration in 2:15–16. James writes as himself in 2:19.

Person 2 Describing Persons 1 and 2 (2:18–20)[131]	
Person	Quotation
1	"You have 'faith'"
2	"I also have actions"
1	"Show to me your faith apart from the actions"

---

130. Thayer, 27. Ἀλλά originally was the neuter plural of ἄλλος, "otherwise," "indicating a difference with or contrast to what precedes" (BDAG, 44). In reality, it is "this other matter" (Robertson 1934, 1185–86).

131. Commentators differ over (a) who is the speaker of "someone will say"—is this James's or the opponent's viewpoint?, (b) does this speaker say the first noun clause ("you have faith") or both initial noun clauses?, and (c) who is "you" and "I"? (Hiebert 1979, 182). The rationale for my own view follows: 2:18 has four noun clauses. Most commentators agree that the last noun clause ("I also will show—from my actions—the faith") represents James's perspective. Then the earlier noun clause ("show to me your faith apart from the actions") easily is in contrast to James: they have contrasting prepositions (χωρίς vs. ἐκ) and the second prepositional phrase is emphasized as a contrast to the regular order of the first prepositional phrase ("apart from the actions"). Κἀγώ signifies "I *also*," showing that the same speaker (person 2) claims to have the same "faith" as the other speaker. Then, who is the "someone" who introduces the half-dialogue? If ἀλλά is treated more as an addition or climax to 2:17, then it can easily represent James's viewpoint. It is an addition to 2:17 but a contrast to 2:15–16. James simply chose to develop his argument in this indirect manner ("someone") rather than begin with the more direct "I will say." James does not use the first person singular ("I") for himself anywhere else in the letter. Mayor says the writer, "with his usual modesty, puts himself in the background" (1913, 99). Paul uses a similar technique in 2 Corinthians 12:2–5.

Person 2 Describing Persons 1 and 2 (2:18–20)[131]	
Person	Quotation
2	"I also will show to you from my actions the faith."
1	"You believe that God is one . . . " (even demons believe that)
1	"O empty-headed human . . . [with] faith apart from actions"

What James previously accomplished by using the subjunctive tense, he now does with this one-sided conversation, which the reader should visualize as two people dialoging, with person 2 providing the content of the dialogue (like captions in a silent movie). James's audience is composed of believers who, because they have heard God's word and say they have faith, thereby think they really have faith (James 1:25; 2:14). They have orthodoxy but not orthopraxy. Person 2 does not have only actions, but has faith *and [with]* actions. If faith is the "implanted word" (1:21), then it cannot be seen apart from growth. Faith implanted by God's word of truth grows actions that can be seen. These faithful actions illustrate or prove one's faith (2:18). The preposition **"from"** (ἐκ, 2:18) is significant, basically signifying "out of" or "from within."[132] It is used in 2:18 and again in 2:22, 24, 25, and climaxing in 3:13. What has been "within" (faith) has come outside in actions. James contrasts the statement of person 1, "apart from [χωρίς][133] the actions," with the statement of person 2, "from [ἐκ] my actions." The latter is emphasized (as the correct answer) by placing the prepositional phrase "from my actions" *before* the object "the faith" (2:18). People's own actions are the evidence of their faith.

By translating ἔργον as **"action(s),"** we differentiate James's letter from Paul's letters. The difference in translation indicates the difference in concept. Actions (or works) are a result of genuine faith, but they do not justify someone.[134] Paul writes about "works" of the *law* (νόμος), whereas James writes about "works" of the *word*. James writes about a saving faith (2:14). Paul agrees with James that repentant believers who turn to God should do *deeds* consistent with repentance (Acts 26:20). He explains, we have been created in Christ Jesus "for good *works* [actions] which God prepared beforehand that in them we might walk" (Eph. 2:10). Paul prays so that the Colossians "may

---

132. Robertson 1934, 596; "source" (Wallace 1996, 371).
133. Occurring separately or independently (BDAG, 1095).
134. See also discussion of 2:23.

lead lives worthy of the Lord, fully pleasing to him," as they "bear fruit in every good *work*" and as they "grow in the knowledge of God" (1:10 NRSV). Paul emphasizes, especially in Romans and Galatians, the initial stage of repentance, which leads to God's approval and acceptance or justification. One would need to demonstrate perfect obedience to God's Old Testament covenant laws to accomplish that goal, but perfection is impossible.[135] James states this stage in 1:18 and 21 but then moves on to discuss in more detail the later stage of demonstrating that regeneration in action obedient to God's new covenant word. Jesus also admonishes his disciples to "practice what they preach" (Matt. 23:3 NIV). They should let their "light shine before others, so that they may see your good *works* and give glory to your Father in heaven" (Matt. 5:16 NRSV). He defines the wise person in the Sermon on the Mount as the one who hears his words *and* does them (Matt. 7:24). Moreover, only the person who does the will of the Father will enter the kingdom of heaven (Matt. 7:21). However, they are *not* to do good deeds simply to be seen by others (Matt. 23:5).

James goes on to cite an important doctrine of the Jews: "God is **one**" (2:19). He emphasizes "you" by adding the pronoun at the beginning of the sentence ("*you* believe").[136] He also emphasizes the predicate adjective ("one") by placing it before the verb "is" ($\epsilon\math{i}\mu\acute{\iota}$) and subject ("God"):[137] "that—*one*—is God." James alludes to Deuteronomy 6:4, the beginning of the *Shema* ("hear"). Devout, free adult male Jews were required to recite Deuteronomy 6:4–9; 11:13–21; and Numbers 15:37–41 twice a day in the early morning and evening to coincide with the temple services.[138] The *Shema* also began the synagogue service. Jesus cites Deuteronomy 6:4–5 in answer to the question, Which is the most important commandment? (Mark 12:28–29). Jesus followed the Septuagint order: "Hear, Israel, Lord our God, Lord—*one*— is," emphasizing "one."[139] Paul also emphasizes "one" in Romans 3:30, "one is God" ($\epsilon\hat{\iota}\varsigma$ $\acute{o}$ $\theta\epsilon\acute{o}\varsigma$), and in 1 Corinthians 8:6, "for us there is one

---

135. E.g., Rom. 3:20, 27–28; 4:2, 6–8; 9:30–33; Gal. 2:16; 3:2, 5, 10.
136. See also Hiebert 1979, 186; Adam 2013, 54.
137. All the earliest Greek manuscripts (fourth-century codices Sinaiticus and Vaticanus and the earliest Western text [sixth-century italic[s]] as well as a variety of other text types) support "one" ($\epsilon\hat{\iota}\varsigma$) preceding the subject "God" in James 2:19. The later Greek codices K[c] and L follow the LXX order: subject, predicate object, verb. But all the Greek texts emphasize "one" by having it precede the verb or subject.
138. M. Ber. 1:1–4; 2:1–4; 3:3; m. Tamid 5:1; m. Meg. 4:3.
139. The Hebrew implies but does not insert the verb "is."

God [ε̂ἰς θεὸς], the Father, from whom are all things and for whom we exist" (NRSV).[140] James follows this pattern.

Jews were renowned for being monotheistic in ancient times. The ancient philosopher Philo points out that only Jews "acknowledge one God who is the Father and Maker of the world." Only "the nation of the Jews" considered deification of a human "the most grievous impiety" (*Embassy* 16.115, 117–18). The historian Josephus adds that Moses represented God as "One, uncreated and immutable to all eternity" (*Ag. Ap.* 2.167).[141] That the God of Israel is the only true God worthy of all devotion is a major Old Testament theme (Mark 12:30; Deut. 6:4–5). For instance, the prophet Malachi asks: "Have we not all one father? Has not one God created us? . . . Judah has been faithless . . . and has married the daughter of a foreign god" (Mal. 2:10–11 NRSV). James says the readers do well to hold onto this doctrine.

But then he adds that the "demons" also "believe" (πιστεύω, 2:19)— and, as a consequence, they "**shudder**" (φρίσσω). "Believe" (πιστεύω) will be further defined in 2:21–25. Genuine saving faith has no doubts, is focused on the "Lord Jesus Christ," and is acted upon or shown by actions (1:6; 2:1, 14, 17–18, 20, 26). The demons know that God is unique and are also fearful of God's power (e.g., Matt. 8:29), an idea affirmed also by later Jewish writers (T. Sol. 2.1). Even God's commander-in-chief of the powers above causes *shuddering* and trembling and fear (T. Ab. A 9.5–6). Φρίσσω may signify the effect of cold to give a feeling of chill, shiver, shudder, chatter, or the effect of fear (e.g., Dan. 7:15). It can also refer to hair that stands on end (e.g., Job 4:15) or the noise in the throat of one just dying, the death rattle.[142] Thus, the demons have a truthful knowledge of God, yet they do not see God as worthy of their trust and devotion, since they will not give either. Therefore, for James's readers to say they have "faith" but not to act on it is to him just as bad as demons who know God and are terrified. Such knowledge is not salvific (Rev. 20:10).

James now rebukes the reader with the earlier perspective (2:15–19): "O **empty-headed** human," leaving no doubt as to his low opinion of this view (2:20). He uses the generic (and more abstract) ἄνθρωπος ("human") since this is not an illustration. Note, James does not use the term μωρός ("fool"), which Jesus says not to use in Matthew 5:22, but rather κενός, which basically has the meaning of "empty." For example, in the parable of the tenants, the owner wanted to receive

---

140. See also Eph. 4:6; 1 Tim. 2:5.
141. See also *Ant.* 3.5.91.
142. LSJ, 1955.

his share of the produce of the vineyard. Instead, the tenants seized the owner's messenger, beat him, and sent him back "empty-handed" (κενός, Mark 12:3). The messenger returned without any produce. Paul explains to the Corinthians that if Christ has not been raised, their preaching is "empty," in other words, devoid of any truth and to no purpose (1 Cor. 15:14). "Empty" words can deceive, such as words claiming that immoral persons can have an inheritance in Christ's reign (Eph. 5:5–6). According to James, persons who take the viewpoint that faith can exist apart from actions are "empty-headed."[143] Their views have no truth in them, serve no purpose, and even deceive.

James previously stated that faith without actions is "dead" (2:17). Now he adds that that kind of faith is "**inactive**" (ἀργός, 2:20). Jesus uses the same word literally in the parable about laborers in the vineyard. The landowner found laborers "standing in the marketplace *idle*" or "unemployed" (Matt. 20:3). They were inactive, without work to do. Ἀργός is properly "not working the ground." The opposite is an active worker.[144] A synonym is "unfruitful" (2 Pet. 1:8), "of things from which no profit is derived, although they can and ought to be productive; as of fields, trees."[145] The "empty" human has "empty" actions. Such faith is "unemployed."[146] Or we can say the word is implanted in fallow or untilled soil.

James now goes on further to prove his point with two illustrations, one from Abraham's life and one from Rahab's (2:21–25). James in 2:23 cites Genesis 15:6, as does Paul in Romans 4:3,[147] but they appear to draw out two contradictory interpretations. James concludes Abraham was "justified from works" (ἐξ ἔργων, 2:21): "faith works together with [Abraham's] works/actions and from the works/actions

---

143. Or "senseless" (JB). Blomberg and Kamell (2008, 135) and Adam (2013, 55) also translate this phrase "O empty person" and "empty-headed person," respectively.
144. LSJ, 236. Ἀργός comes from ἀ + ἔργον ("without work") (Thayer, 72). Vlachos (2013) (and others) states the wordplay: "A faith without works *does not work*" (95).
145. Thayer, 72.
146. Inactivity can lead to falsehood, as in 1 Timothy 5:13 (Spencer 2013, 131–32).
147. James's and Paul's quotations are identical. Paul also cites Genesis 15:6 in Romans 4:9, 22, and Galatians 3:6. The Septuagint, though, uses "Abram" (Ἀβραμ), while James and Paul use "Abraham" (Ἀβραάμ), the later name (Gen. 17:5) that indicates the sign of the covenant and Abraham as the father of many nations. The Hebrew does not cite "Abram" in Genesis 15:6 (it is earlier in 15:1) and also uses the Tetragrammaton, which normally is translated "LORD."

faith was perfected," and "from works/actions a person is proved righteous and not from faith alone" (2:22, 24). Paul, in contrast, concludes
Abraham was *not* "justified by works" (ἐξ ἔργων, Rom. 4:2, 4, 5–6). He
was reckoned as righteous before he was circumcised, not after (Rom.
4:10–11). His righteousness did not come through the law (Rom. 4:13).
Other direct references to Genesis 15:6 may be found. Phinehas's zeal
to obey God "was counted to him as righteousness" (Ps. 106:30–31, referring to Num. 25:7–13). The author of 1 Maccabees also cites Genesis
15:6: Mattathias, before he died, told his sons to be "zealous for the law,
and give" their "lives for the covenant" of their "fathers" (2:50 REB). He
then cites numerous acts of the ancestors to encourage them, including
Abraham's: "Was not Abraham found faithful [πιστός] in temptation,
and it was reckoned to him for righteousness?" (2:52).

James and Paul agree that it is Abraham's faith that God reckons
or counts as righteousness. To **"reckon"** (λογίζομαι) properly is
used of "numerical calculation."[148] Abraham's faith was "counted" or
"calculated"[149] as righteousness. Jesus was *numbered with* the transgressors" (Luke 22:37; Isa. 53:12) when he was crucified between two
criminals (Luke 23:32). The calculating is what is similar. Abraham's
faith was "set down" to his "account"[150] as "righteousness." What is
faith? James defines "faith" as belief demonstrated by actions, while
Paul defines "faith" as a gift from God, eliminating the accusation of
sin, and *not* work done for wages (Rom. 4:3–9; Ps. 32:1–2).

Even though James and Paul refer to the same Scripture, because
of their different audiences, they accentuate two different, but complementary, applications. The context of each letter is essential to understand their interpretations. James discusses what is a saving, live faith:
it is a faith that acts. He compares two kinds of faith, one apart from
actions (a fallow faith) versus one that is a part of actions (an implanted
or tilled faith). An implanted faith has actions that work together and
complete faith. His readers are Jewish believers who have heard God's
word and say they have faith and therefore think they really have it.
However, faith is not hearing or declaring by itself. Faith in action precedes the reckoning of righteousness. A fallow faith is an empty shell.

Paul, in contrast, writes to Jewish and Gentile believers who lack
unity because they each consider themselves superior to the other (Rom.
3:9–18; 11:17–24; 12:3). He wants to prove that Gentiles and Jews have
the same basis for faith and righteousness. He compares two kinds of

148. LSJ, 1055.
149. LSJ, 1055.
150. LSJ, 1055.

righteousness: one from faith, which is perfect and open to everyone; and one from the law, which can never be perfect and is distinct to Jews and a cause for boasting (Rom. 3:20, 27–30). Faith as a gift precedes the reckoning of righteousness. James mentions Paul's emphasis as a first stage in chapter 1: the implanted word of truth is a gift from the Creator of lights (1:17–21). Paul mentions James's emphasis as a last stage: obedience is a sign of spiritual worship (Rom. 12:1–2).[151] Using the parable of the seed (Luke 8:5, 8, 11, 15) as an analogy, Paul emphasizes whose seed it is—God's—while James emphasizes the receiving soil, which should be "a good soil." For both, faith is salvific.

Although both James and Paul refer to "**works**" (ἔργων), James's "works" are works or actions from the "word" (λόγος, 1:21, 22), while Paul's "works" are works from the "law" (νόμος, e.g., Rom. 4:13–16; Gal. 2:16). James uses λόγος ("**word**") to refer to rebirth by the Father of lights (1:17–21). A "doer of the word" then acts on that transforming rebirth given by God (1:22–23). As Jesus taught, his genuine family hears *and does* God's word (Luke 8:21; 11:28). Paul can use "God's word" in a similar manner,[152] but he does not refer to λόγος in this way in the context of Romans 4:3. God's re-creating word is the basic foundation for James's message. When James uses νόμος ("law"),[153] it refers to the Old Testament as seen through the eyes of the new covenant.[154] Moreover, he does not write that the doing of the law justifies. Νόμος ("law") in Paul refers to the Old Testament as seen through the eyes of Jews who have not been reborn through Jesus. The law is good because it shows sin, but it does not give one a state of righteousness that guarantees approval by God. Jews claim to follow the law, but they do not succeed completely. They still need the perfect sin offering, Christ Jesus.[155]

Both James and Paul cite Genesis 15:6; however, each relates this verse to a different later incident: Genesis 17 or Genesis 22.[156] Circumcision (discussed in Genesis 17) is important to Paul because it was a key sign of being Jewish[157] and a member of the covenant, and he

---

151. See also Rom. 6:1–2; 8:3–9; 10:3; 11:22; 13:9–14.
152. E.g., Rom. 9:6; 2 Cor. 4:2; Col. 1:25–27; 1 Thess. 2:13; 2 Tim. 2:9.
153. James 1:25; 2:8, 9, 10, 11, 12; 4:11.
154. See James 1:23–25.
155. E.g., Rom. 2:17–24; 3:19–22, 27–30; 4:7–8, 11; 5:1–2, 6–10, 13, 20; 7:5, 7–12; 8:2–3; 10:4–10.
156. By using the title "Abraham," both writers connect the "Abram" of Genesis 15 to the "Abraham" who will be later cited.
157. "The circumcised" was a synecdoche for the Jews, e.g., Rom. 4:9; Col. 4:11.

wants to make sure Gentiles are included in the new covenant. James writes at an earlier period when his readers appear to be only Jewish believers in Jesus as the Messiah. James cites the action of Abraham's willingness to offer his son Isaac upon the altar (2:21) because in this incident God is testing Abraham's faith or trust in and love of God. God "knows" Abraham loves God if he demonstrates that love in action (Gen. 22:12). God wanted to observe Abraham's act of obedience. God did not order Abraham to kill Isaac; rather, he commanded Abraham to "**lead**" Isaac up to the land of Moriah (Gen. 22:2).[158] James uses the verb ἀναφέρω, which literally signifies to "carry or bring up, to lead up" or "to cause to move from a lower position to a higher, take, lead, bring up."[159] It is used in this sense when Jesus "leads up" a mountain Peter, James, and John so they can witness Jesus's transfiguration (Matt. 17:1; Mark 9:2). Abraham too led Isaac up the mountain to the wooden altar (θυσιαστήριον, James 2:21; Gen. 22:3, 6–8). Abraham learned that the Lord would provide an offering (Gen. 22:8–9, 14); in addition, Abraham was given an opportunity to identify with God the Father, who offered his only son for the sake of others.[160] The "work" or "action" to which James refers is the action of loving obedience to be willing to lead with the intention of offering an only son to God. Faith in action is the sign of God's righteousness. The "work" or "action" to which Paul refers is the action of obedience distinguishing membership in the covenant (Gen. 17:10–14). This physical sign, circumcision, signified that Abraham was to be the father of a multitude of nations, which Paul interprets as Jew and Gentile (Gen. 17:4; Rom. 4:12–17).

James then further explains that the example of Abraham's willingness to offer his son Isaac back to God shows faith **working together** (συνεργέω) with actions and faith maturing (or being "perfected," τελειόω, 2:22). Συνεργέω (2:22) is a composite of σύν ("with") and ἔργω/ ἔρδω ("do work"), signifying to "work together with, help in work, cooperate"[161] in contrast to ἀργός ("inactive," 2:20). Actions by themselves do not make one righteous; rather, actions "cooperate" with faith. Paul expresses a similar idea when he exhorts the Corinthians: "And *working together with* [God], we also exhort [you] not in vain [κενός] to receive God's grace" (2 Cor. 6:1). Paul, like James, uses "empty" (κενός, James 2:20) to describe grace or faith received but which is not acted

---

158. The author of Hebrews posits that Abraham relied on God to raise the dead (11:19).
159. Thayer, 43; BDAG, 75.
160. See Spencer and Spencer 1994, 95–96.
161. Thayer, 603; LSJ, 683, 1711.

upon. In Paul's example, Paul and Timothy work together with God. The cognate noun συνεργός refers to coworkers. Coworking with colleagues is an important theme for Paul (e.g., 1 Cor. 3:9; 16:16). James personifies "faith" and "actions" as coworkers who together make faith alive (James 2:22).

Furthermore, faith should develop and grow from the implanted seed to a fully grown harvest (2:22). The word family τέλειος (adj.) and τελειόω (verb) has occurred already.[162] Faith does not "perfect" actions, but actions perfect faith because actions help faith mature. One can see this maturity in Abram's own life. The Lord promises Abram that he would give the land of the Canaanites to his "seed" (Gen. 12:7), but Abram despairs because he thinks the slave Eliezer will be his heir (Gen. 15:2–3). Then he and Sarai take matters into their own hands and Abram conceives Ishmael through the concubine Hagar (Gen. 16:1–4). But God wants Abram's son to be conceived by Abram *and* Sarai, even though Abraham was now a hundred years old (Gen. 18:9–15; 21:1–7). It took Abram many years for his faith or trust in God to mature, although the initial belief and "reckoning of righteousness" was much earlier.

James now combines two scriptural passages (Gen. 15:6; Isa. 41:8) to establish a principle (2:23). Hillel summarized this type of proof as "a main proposition from two scriptural passages" (*binyan ab mishene kethubim*).[163] The principle can then be applied to other passages. Being called a "**friend of God**" (φίλος) indicates the maturity of Abraham's faith. James 2:23 is a precise translation of the Hebrew of Genesis 15:6 and Isaiah 41:8. In Isaiah, God says: "You Israel are my servant Jacob, whom I have chosen, the seed of Abraham, my friend."[164] In Isaiah, God calls Abraham "*my* friend" (Hebrew). In addition, Jehoshaphat prayed to God, reminding him that the land was given forever to the "seed of Abraham, your friend"[165] (2 Chron. 20:7). A "friend" is someone loved (ἀγαπάω), but even more, someone who is rewarded by receiving special favors: "I am with you," God promises Israel; "I will strengthen you, I will help you, I will uphold you with my victorious right hand" (Isa. 41:10 NRSV).

"Friend" of God refers to more than someone loved or an equal. Rather, the "friend" of God is akin to the ancient "friend" of the king,

---

162. James 1:4, 17, 25; 3:2. See exposition of James 1:4.
163. T. Sanh. 7:11; Schürer 1973–79, 2:344.
164. The Hebrew reads "my friend," while the LXX has "Abraham [Ἀβραάμ], whom I have loved" (ἀγαπάω).
165. LXX has "Abraham, the one being loved by you."

an official title conferred by a ruler on powerful and distinguished persons. Such a friend would obey the ruler and help the ruler in the time of need and in return receive high honors, financial gifts, power, protection, and other benefits. For example, Antiochus tried to entice Mattathias to carry out his decrees by offering that he and his sons "will be enrolled among the king's Friends; you will all receive high honours, rich rewards of silver and gold, and many further benefits" (1 Macc. 2:18 REB). The position was tied to a specific ruler. The relationship implies access for communication. It would be comparable in the United States to "ministers" (such as members of the cabinet) appointed by the president or in Roman times to "friends of Caesar" (John 19:12). God conferred this honorary title on Abraham because of his actions, an honor to Abraham demonstrating access to God yet still not a relationship of equals. Using the same analogy, Jesus tells his disciples they are his "friends" if they do what Jesus commands them: "I have called you friends, because I have disclosed to you everything that I heard from my Father. You did not choose me: I chose you" (John 15:15–16 REB).

This imagery is one appealing to ancient Jews. Moses spoke to God "face to face," as a "friend" (φίλος) (Exod. 33:11). The Book of Jubilees (c. 161–140 BC) describes Abraham as recorded on the heavenly tablets as "a friend of God" (Jub. 19:9). Philo (20 BC–AD 40) says that God gave Abraham the gift of friendship: "Abraham my friend" (referring to Gen. 18:17) (Sobr. 11.55–57).[166] Rabbi Meir (c. AD 140–65) describes the person who studies the law as a "friend, beloved of God" who is clothed regally and given kingship (m. 'Abot 6:1). Abraham as a "friend of God," a positive illustration for his Jewish readers, contrasts with what they were in reality, "friends of the world" (4:4).

James reiterates the main principle he wants to propose from these two passages (2:23) in 2:24: "You see that from actions[167] a person[168] is made righteous and not from faith alone." James uses the word family "**made righteous**" (δικαιόω [verb], δικαιοσύνη [noun], δίκαιος [adj.]) several times in his letter. These words all come from the root δίκη ("right, justice").[169] Some lexicons emphasize

---

166. The LXX has "servant" or "child" (παῖς) (BDAG, 750). The Hebrew has no equivalent term.
167. He emphasizes "from actions" by placing the phrase before the verb.
168. Again, James uses the generic ἄνθρωπος ("human," 2:20, 24).
169. Thayer, 151.

the definition "righteous,"[170] while others "justice,"[171] because the word includes both concepts. Approval by God when it refers to the individual may be called "righteousness"; when it extends to the individual in relationship to others it may be called "justice" or "righteousness." James writes that anger does *not* produce "righteous" or "just" behavior toward others (1:20–21). This would include moral virtue.[172] When the righteous laborer is oppressed, this is not "just" (5:6). Peace resulting in a "harvest of righteousness" (3:18) would include both holy and just behavior (qualities described in 3:17). The examples of Abraham, Rahab, and Elijah are examples of courageous and faith-demonstrating actions pleasing to God, holy and righteous actions, such as fully trusting God to keep his promise although one's only son might appear to be required as a sacrifice, trusting God by welcoming enemy soldiers, or trusting God to have power over the weather (2:21–25; 5:16–18). These actions by themselves alone do not make one acceptable to God, but neither does verbal faith without demonstration in action.[173]

---

170. Thayer, 148–50.
171. BDAG, 246–47.
172. Cf. N. T. Wright (2009), who emphasizes "righteousness" as "acquittal" or change of status as a result of a judge's pronouncement within the law court context, not morally uprightness and virtue. He infuses one first-century definition ("justice, the business of a judge" [LSJ, 429; *TLNT* 1, 319–20, 337] into all NT uses (90–91, 206, 213). In contrast, Ceslas Spicq explains that the OT and NT link God's justice with goodness (referring to, e.g., Ps. 116:5), taking the meaning beyond the realm of the legal (*TLNT* 1, 322, 324). Thus, both Paul and James can write, it is not the hearers of God's law or word who are righteous but the doers of it (Rom. 2:13; James 1:22). Δικαιόω in James refers to the demonstration of faith in moral and just action and action trusting God's good and sovereign nature.
173. McCartney 2009 renders 2:23 "to *prove* or *demonstrate* that someone is righteous or in the right." Abraham's obedience "manifested his righteousness and thus brought to fruition God's declaration of Abraham's righteousness that occurred several years earlier" (162–64). John Calvin (1960) agrees: James "is speaking of the declaration, not the imputation, of righteousness." Abraham proves his righteousness "by obedience and good works, not by a bare and imaginary mask of faith." James demands of "believers a righteousness fruitful in good works[;] . . . an empty show of faith does not justify" (3.17.12). He adds: the word "justified" has a "twofold meaning. . . . Paul means by it the gratuitous imputation of righteousness before the tribunal of God; and James, the manifestation of righteousness by the conduct, and that before men" (Calvin, n.d., 2568).

Summary of James's and Paul's Use of Abraham in Genesis 15:6							
Writer	Audience	Type of "works"	Stage	Kind of faith	Sequence & definition of righteousness	Gen. 15:6 compared to other OT reference(s)	Analogy: parable of seeds
James	Jewish Christians, not obedient	Word (λόγος) loving obedience	Later	Faith in action	Initial faith as sign precedes demonstration of righteousness before God = trust of God expressed in moral & courageous action	Gen. 22 mature faith shown by offering of Isaac + Isa. 41:8	Good soil (Luke 8:8, 15)
Paul	Jewish & Gentile Christians, not united	law (νόμος) perfect obedience	Initial	Faith as gift	Faith precedes reckoning of righteousness by God = acceptance by God as having fulfilled God's law, sins are forgiven, results in sign of circumcision	Gen. 17 circumcision + Ps. 32:1–2	Owner of soil = God (Luke 8:5, 11)

"**Abraham**" is frequently referenced in the New and Old Testaments.[174] Repeatedly Abraham is grouped with his progeny Isaac and Jacob as representative members of God's covenant with Israel.[175] Sometimes only Abraham is mentioned.[176] Abraham is a crucial synecdoche for Jews,[177] but John the Baptist and Jesus challenged that by warning that claiming Abraham as one's ancestor was not enough; instead they should "be *doing* what Abraham *did*" (NRSV).[178]

In contrast to Abraham, "**Rahab**" has only three New Testament references (Matt. 1:5; James 2:25; Heb. 11:31)[179] and five Old Testament references.[180] Nevertheless, James uses her actions also as an explanation of Genesis 15:6. Hebrews (written after James's letter) cites both Abraham and Rahab as exemplary people of faith (11:8–19, 31). Hebrews, like James, includes references to Abraham offering Isaac, his only son (11:17–19), and Rahab welcoming the spies in peace (11:31). In Hebrews, faith is defined as "the assurance of things hoped for, the conviction of things not seen" (11:1 NRSV).

Josephus calls Rahab an "innkeeper,"[181] which she was, but, according to the Bible, she was also a "**prostitute**" or "harlot,"[182] someone "engaged in sexual relations for hire," or "one who practices sexual

---

174. "Abraham/Abram" has seventy-three references in the New Testament (Kohlenberger, Goodrick, and Swanson 1995, 1–2); 191 in Genesis, and forty-eight in the rest of the Old Testament (LXX).
175. E.g., Exod. 2:24; 3:6, 15–16; 4:5; 6:3, 8; 32:13; 33:1; Lev. 26:42; Num. 32:11; Deut. 1:8; 6:10; 9:5, 27; 29:13; 30:20; 34:4; 2 Kings 13:23; 1 Chron. 16:16–17; 29:18; 2 Chron. 30:6; Ps. 105:9; Matt. 8:11; 22:32; Mark 12:26; Luke 13:28; 20:37; Acts 3:13; 7:32.
176. Ps. 47:9; 105:6, 42; Isa. 51:2; Luke 1:55, 73; 16:22–31.
177. E.g., John 8:53; Acts 13:26; Rom. 11:1; 2 Cor. 11:22; Gal. 3:29.
178. John 8:39. See also Matt. 3:9; Luke 3:8.
179. Ῥαάβ in James 2:25 and Joshua 2:1 (LXX) is likely the same woman as Ῥαχάβ, the ancestor of "Boaz" (Matt. 1:5). Rahab is dated after ca. 1406 BC, the traditional date for Joshua's invasion (Barker 2006, Old Testament Chronology, 297). Matthew (Ῥαχάβ) uses the Greek χ, which sometimes is used for the Hebrew ח (BDF, 21–22). Josephus uses the form Ῥαάβη (Ant. 5.2.8, 9, 11, 15, 7.30, while the NT and LXX use Ῥαάβ.
180. Josh. 2:1, 3; 6:17, 23, 25.
181. Ant. 5.1.2.7–8, 10, 5.26, 7.30.
182. See also, for other references to πόρνη/πορνεία: Ezek. 16:32–33; Matt. 21:31–32; Luke 15:30; 1 Cor. 6:15–16. Πόρνη ("prostitute") is the same cognate family as πορνεία "sexual immorality."

immorality."[183] Inns were often immoral places.[184] Rahab may have been involved in prostitution as part of the worship of pagan Canaanite gods or goddesses.[185] In that case, her conversion was all the more impressive. Nevertheless, her actions demonstrating her faith showed her righteousness before God. She made an effort to welcome as guests the two enemy spies sent out to Jericho, the first city Joshua and the Israelites would reach when they crossed the Jordan River to win over the land given them by the Lord. This initial war effort would set for Israel a decisive model for the cities to follow. God promised Abraham the land of Canaan,[186] and Rahab helped make that promise a reality.[187] The spies came at night and were staying at Rahab's house, but their presence was discovered by the king of Jericho. Rahab's "**welcome**" of the spies was not simply giving them a place to eat and rest; it was also hiding them on the roof, misleading the king of Jericho's messengers, and sending the spies out through a window in the city wall in the opposite direction from the pursuers (Josh. 2:1–7, 16, 21–22). James leaves out the amazing testimony that she gives that "the Lord your God, he is God in the heaven above and upon the earth below" (Josh. 2:11) and the negotiation she does to save herself and her extended family on the basis of having "hid the messengers" (Josh. 2:12–14; 6:17, 22–25). James assumes her statement of faith. He focuses on her courageous actions, which demonstrated her faith. As a result of her actions, Rahab married into the Hebrew family and became a foremother of the Messiah Jesus (Matt. 1:5).[188]

James concludes this section with a simile: faith apart from actions[189] is similar to the body apart from the spirit. They are both "dead" (2:26). "Body" is parallel to "faith," "spirit" to "actions."[190] It is the same thought as 2:17 and an apt conclusion to this section (2:14–26). How is

---

183. BDAG, 854: πόρνη, זֹנָה.

184. Wiseman 1964, 9.

185. E.g., Exod. 34:15–16; Lev. 20:2–5. Wiseman (1964, 10) thinks Rahab is not a cult prostitute.

186. Gen. 12:7; 15:7; 17:8; 1 Chron. 16:18–20; 2 Chron. 20:7; Ps. 104:9–12.

187. Nolland (2005, 74) agrees: Rahab's "inclusion makes possible the evocation of the [exodus from Egypt and] entry into the Promised Land—a key phase of salvation history which otherwise goes unmarked."

188. Carter 2002, 119. According to the *Babylonian Talmud*, Joshua married her. Eight prophets who were also priests descended from her, including Jeremiah and Huldah (b. Meg. 14b).

189. See exposition of James 2:18.

190. Verse 26 is a perfect parallelism: the first clause, article to article, like to like, is parallel to the second clause. See "Glossary of Stylistic Terms."

the "body" like "faith"[191]? The body is like an empty crafted pot, without life, if it has no faith. Chapter 2 verse 26 is reminiscent of Genesis 2:7: "God formed the human of fine soil from the earth; and breathed into his face the breath [πνοή] of life, and the human became a living life" (LXX). Πνοή ("breath" or "wind") and πνεῦμα ("breath," "blowing," "spirit/Spirit") are cognates of the verb πνέω ("blow," "breathe out").[192] Without the "spirit" or "breath of life" the body is dead, as happened to the widow of Zarephath's son when he fell sick. His death was indicated by his not having the "breath of life" (1 Kings 17:17). Only the human, unlike the animals,[193] receives the breath of life directly and personally from God.[194] James will develop the significance of being created in God's likeness in the next chapter (3:7–10).

Thus, from 2:14–26 we have learned that James is advocating for a saving, active, live, beneficial, righteous, fully grown, demonstrating faith—as opposed to a dead one, which does not save, is inactive, dead, without benefit, deceptive, and fallow or untilled.

THEOLOGICAL AND HOMILETICAL
TOPICS IN CHAPTER 2

The second chapter of James answers a number of theological questions. What is impartiality? How important is being impartial? How does it relate to God's character? How does James want the poor to be treated and why? How does treatment of the poor relate to love and mercy? How do actions relate to faith, according to James? What do Abraham and Rahab illustrate? What is salvific faith and what is its opposite? How does righteousness relate to faith? Why do they differ? How are they similar? Why does friendship with God include obedience?

When preaching a series on James, you could do one sermon on the need to be impartial (2:1–13) and another on the nature of live faith (2:14–26). Follow James's example and treat your listeners as dear friends, not as enemies. He uses many illustrations that can be described in their first-century setting and lend themselves to an

---

191. One might have expected that the "body" would be synonymous to "actions," while the "spirit" to "faith." But James is not focusing on those who do good deeds but have no faith, as in "the body apart from the spirit" or "actions apart from faith"; rather, he is focused on the problem of faith without actions.

192. BDAG, 832–38.

193. Gen. 7:21–22.

194. Gen. 2:7. Keil and Delitzsch 1973, 78–80.

analogous contemporary example. This chapter also illustrates how one verse (Gen. 15:6) can be applied differently in various contexts. Faith in action could be compared to faith as a gift, using Jesus's parable in Luke 8:5–15.

You might begin your sermon with a contemporary example or skit of how someone might be encouraged to favor the wealthy, a certain ethnic group, the powerful, the higher ranked, or the externally impressive. Then you can describe James's point that the poor Christian must be treated with dignity and respect and give the reasons why: they are glorious and full heirs of God, and God wants us to love our neighbors, who include the poor, so that we too can be treated with mercy. In addition, material wealth is temporary. The action of impartiality is modeled on God's character as impartial and merciful, on God the Trinity as one God, and on Jesus's incarnation model. Lack of respect for the poor reflects disrespect for God. Believers should also care for genuine physical needs. All are valuable before God and in the church. Impartiality is evil and not part of living according to God's reign. But to be able to live impartially, one must trust God to bless us and not merely try to curry favors from externally impressive humans. One must be countercultural—friends of God, not friends of the world.

You could also begin with a contemporary example of someone who says one thing and then acts differently. Or you could begin by describing a man and a woman who each represent a larger principle. He or she is a "synecdoche," a part that represents a whole. Your goal would be to inspire listeners to speak and act consistently. Then you can describe Abraham and Rahab, how they each exhibited saving faiths which were alive and active, full-grown, and "implanted" and "tilled." They demonstrated actions as evidence of verbal faith.

The letter of James is especially appropriate for audiences who have heard God's word and say they have faith, thereby thinking they really have faith but in reality do not.

WHO ARE THE POOR TODAY?

James's letter refers to the poor as widows, orphans, the hungry, unpaid harvesters, and probably the disabled and sick. They are men and women, adults and children. Some studies of ancient Greco-Roman times estimate that 25–28 percent of the population were "truly poor" and 30–40 percent were subsistence-level, unskilled workers, which means that 55–68 percent of first-century society struggled in poverty.[195] Today the "poor" is a relative term. In 2015, in the United States,

---

195. Spencer 2017, 30.

the Census Bureau considered as "poor" a single individual who earned yearly under $12,331 (over 65 it was only $11,367), a single parent with one child earning $16,337 or less, and a family of two adults and two children with an income of $24,339 or less. Thirty-three percent of the poor are children. The United States Census Bureau considered 13.5 percent "poor" in 2015.[196] Many of these poor are minorities: 26.6 percent Hispanics, 27.4 percent blacks, 12.1 percent Asians, and 9.9 percent non-Hispanic whites.[197] Thus, a single "poor" individual in the United States earned $34 or less per day and $1,028 or less per month. However, if we were to take a plane to the Dominican Republic, the land of my birth, the "poor"—more than a third of the island—earn less than $1.25 a day, especially those who live in rural areas. As a matter of fact, almost one half of the world's population live on less than $2.50 a day and 80 percent live on less than $10 a day.[198] The poor in the United States living on $34 a day have a better income than 80 percent of the rest of the world's "poor." In other words, the poor are not a minority in today's world but a majority. We should ask: Are they a part of our own church? How many churches in the United States (and elsewhere) have rich and poor worshiping together? In 2009, my own denomination, the Presbyterian Church (U.S.A.), had 5.2 percent of members who earned less than $10,000 and 11.8 percent of members who earned between $10,000 and $24,999 a year (total 17 percent).[199]

196. United States Census Bureau, "Poverty," https://www.census.gov/topics/income-poverty/poverty.html; see also University of Michigan Poverty Solutions, "Poverty Facts," https://poverty.umich.edu/about/poverty-facts, accessed August 22, 2017.
197. University of Michigan Poverty Solutions, "Poverty Facts," http://npc.umich.edu/poverty, accessed July 14, 2016. Moreover, in the United States financial abuse and fraud costs older Americans, many of whom are widows, up to $36.5 billion per year (National Council on Aging, "Elder Abuse Facts," https://www.ncoa.org/public-policy-action/elder-justice/elder-abuse-facts, cited by Tuoti 2017, A1).
198. DoSomething.org, "Eleven Facts about Global Poverty," https://www.dosomething.org/us/facts/11-facts-about-global-poverty, accessed August 8, 2011; Stephanie Lamm, "Poverty in the Dominican Republic," The Borgen Project, February 10, 2014, https://borgenproject.org/poverty-dominican-republic, accessed August 22, 2017; Anup Shah, "Poverty Facts and Stats," http://www.globalissues.org/article/26/poverty-facts-and-stats, accessed January 8, 2020.
199. Deborah Coe, Coordinator of Research Services for the Presbyterian Mission, accessed this information on August 25, 2017, from "U.S. Congregational Life Survey, Wave 2, 2008/2009, Presbyterian Church (U.S.A.)

The church growth movement originally discouraged Christians from including people of a variety of economic classes and ethnicities in new church plants because that would slow church growth. For instance, Donald McGavran explains: "People like to become Christians without crossing racial, linguistic, or class barriers." Unbelievers prefer to join churches whose members have the same "color, stature, income, cleanliness, and education." Thus, new churches should normally be "homogeneous units of a society."[200] These probably do achieve rapid growth, but what are the ramifications for such a strategy? In James 2:2–4, the congregants are encouraged not to give special seating to the rich and inferior seating to the poor. But in such a church growth strategy, which mirrors the economic and racial divisions of the church, the poor will not even be included in the local middle-class church. As I heard one white lay leader ask a visiting black family in a New Jersey church many years ago, "Wouldn't you feel more comfortable in one of your own churches?" Today, we might say or imply the same thing to the poor in a middle- or upper-class church.

Despite the pressure by advocates of the homogeneous church growth movement to plant only a homogeneous church, our new church fellowship insisted on creating a congregation where the middle class and poor could worship together. Although very difficult to integrate our diverse perspectives, we ended up with a group of people where almost half earned less than $10,000 a year and 64 percent earned less than $24,999 a year.[201] While we may not have grown quickly, Christians of different economic, educational, and ethnic backgrounds learned to worship God together.

So who are the poor in our church? They are not a faceless class, an "issue" for the wealthy to discuss, but individual, unique people with self-respect and dignity. Most are a great encouragement to the rest of us. Rosa[202] is the daughter of a married Latin American ambassador and his mistress. Rosa is a woman of no country because her United States passport was taken from her, even though she never lived in the land of her father. But when she worships, she enlivens the congregation with her tambourine and shouts of enthusiasm. Sheila, a widow, is a deacon of the church who sleeps overnight with children who have

Attender Survey," Association of Religion Data Archives (ARDA) http://thearda.com/archive/files/analysis/PC08ATT/PC08ATT_Var102_1.asp.
200. McGavran 1990, 163, 167, 177.
201. Triennial visit January 8, 2012. No one earned $100,000 or more. Thirty-seven percent have parents born outside of the United States.
202. All names have been changed for privacy.

been removed from their homes for overactive behavior. She saves her money, assisted by the deacon's fund, to be able to feed the whole church once a month. Harry is another deacon who goes out into the marshes to pick up decorative flowers for florists to make Christmas wreaths, deeply scratching his hands and arms in the process. He, along with his wife, directs our prayer outreach. Beverly works as a nurse's aide. When we did not have enough food for a church meal, she went home and gathered her own donations given to her from the local food bank and cooked so much food that we had lots to give away to another church meeting in our building. Bob is a man who had never been allowed to go outside without an escort because of mental issues. Now he is so happy to come by himself that he claps at the end of almost every praise and worship session in appreciation. One of our pastors brings a carload of low-income children to the church. Carla stays on the street because she insists on bringing her alcoholic male friend into the Young Women's Christian Association housing, even though that is not allowed. She also has mental health and possibly substance-abuse issues herself. Some of our "poor" are temporarily so because they study at local colleges and seminaries.

What is my point? Some of the poor Christians who attend our church are indeed "rich in faith and heirs" of God's reign. We need them. They contribute much to the life and ministry of our church. Thus, when we pray for church growth, we need to separate people from finances. We should pray for the finances we need and pray separately for the people to come. God has answered these two distinct prayer requests for my church by giving us a free three-story building and the equivalent of one full-time pastoral salary. The homeless poor in our city include those who use their money in substance abuse, but poor Christians are not people we should try to avoid; rather, they are wonderful people who can enrich the church by their faith-full actions.

JAMES 3:1–18

TRANSLATION AND GRAMMATICAL ANALYSIS[1]

3:1a Let not many become teachers, my brothers and sisters, (initial sentence; main clause)

3:1b knowing (subordinate adverbial clause; causal; answers why)

3:1c that we will receive greater judgment. (subordinate noun clause; direct object)

3:2a For all we stumble much. (causal sentence; main clause)

3:2a If any in word does not stumble, (explanatory sentence; subordinate adverbial clause; conditional)

3:2b that one is a mature man [person] able to bridle even all the body. (main clause)

3:3a But if into the mouths of the horses we place the bits (illustrative sentence; subordinate adverbial clause; conditional)

3:3b in order that they obey us, (subordinate adverbial clause; final; purpose)

3:3c also all their body we can guide. (main clause)

---

1. See "Definition of Terms in Grammatical Analysis."

3:4a Behold[2] also (illustrative sentence; main clause)

3:4b the sailing vessels, being so great and by means of strong winds being driven, is guided by a very small rudder (subordinate noun clause; direct object or main clause)

3:4c wherever the desire of the one guiding wills. (subordinate adverbial clause; local)

3:5a Likewise also the tongue is a small member and greatly boasts. (illustrative sentence; main clause)

3:5a Behold (explanatory sentence; main clause)

3:5b how small a fire how great a forest kindles! (subordinate noun clause; direct object or main clause)

3:6a Also the tongue [is] fire. (illustrative sentence; main clause)

3:6a The tongue, the world of unrighteousness, is constituted among our members, the one defiling all the body and setting on fire the wheel of life and being set on fire by hell. (explanatory sentence; main clause)

3:7a For every species of wild animals and also birds, creeping animals and also sea creatures are [being] tamed and have been tamed[3] by the human species, (illustrative sentence; main clause)

3:8b but the tongue of humans no one is able to tame, a restless evil, full of deadly poison. (main clause)

3:9a With it we bless the Lord and Father (illustrative sentence; main clause)

3:9b and with it we curse humans, the ones according to the likeness of God having been made; (main clause)

---

2. "Behold" is a finite verb or demonstrative particle functioning as an adverb (BDAG, 468; Robertson 1934, 302). See also 3:5; 5:4, 7, 9, 11.
3. These are compound verbs, both of which depend on the same extended subject.

3:10a out of the same mouth comes out blessing and curse. (alternative sentence; main clause)

3:10a It is not appropriate, my brothers and sisters, these such to be. (illative sentence; main clause)

3:11a The spring from the same opening does not pour forth sweet and bitter water, does it? (illustrative sentence; main clause)

3:12a A fig tree is not able, my brothers and sisters, to make olives (illustrative sentence; main clause)

3:12b or a grapevine [is not able to make] figs, can they? (main clause)

3:12a Neither salt [is able] to make sweet water. (illustrative sentence; main clause)

3:13a Who is wise and learned among you? (initial sentence; main clause)

3:13a Let him/her show out of good conduct his /her actions characterized by gentle wisdom. (explanatory sentence; main clause)

3:14a But, if you have bitter jealousy and self-centeredness in your heart, (adversative sentence; subordinate conditional clause)

3:14b do not boast against and lie against the truth.[4] (main clause)

3:15a That wisdom is not the one from above coming down (explanatory sentence; main clause)

3:15b but [that wisdom is] earthly, worldly, demonic.[5] (main clause)

3:16a For where [there is] jealousy and self-centeredness, (explanatory sentence; subordinate adverbial clause; locative)

3:16b there [is] restlessness and every evil deed. (main clause)

---

4. These are compound verbs, both modified by "against the truth."
5. Ἀλλά tends to separate identical grammatical clauses. Therefore, "that wisdom is" is implied.

3:17a But the from-above wisdom on the one hand first is pure, (adversative sentence; main clause)

3:17b then [is] peaceable, reasonable, persuadable, full of mercy and good fruits, not partial, not hypocritical. (main clause)

3:18a Then[6] a fruit of righteousness in peace is sown by the ones doing peace. (explanatory sentence; main clause)

OUTLINE

III. Lay aside misuse of the tongue (ch. 3).
   A. Be careful, because of the misuse of speaking, before becoming a teacher (3:1–12).
   B. (reason) True wisdom is reflected in a life of good deeds (3:13–18).

LITERARY STRUCTURE

In chapter 3 James returns to the theme of wisdom (1:5–8, 19–26). Being doers of the word, or receiving the implanted word, is demonstrated in speech (3:1–12). The tongue needs to be tamed (3:1–12), and wise teaching is reflected in good actions (3:13–18).

EXPOSITION

Lay Aside Misuse of the Tongue (ch. 3)

Be Careful, Because of the Misuse of Speaking, before Becoming a Teacher (3:1–12)

James surprises his readers, "my brothers and sisters,"[7] with a command not to become teachers (3:1): "Let not many become teachers." The immediate reason is expressed in the subordinate clause: "knowing that we will receive greater judgment" (3:1).

What is a **teacher** (διδάσκαλος)? Verse 3:1 is the only time the word family for διδάσκαλος occurs in the letter. The word family is not used elsewhere in the New Testament of James, but in 3:1–2 James

---

6. Μέν . . . δέ can be used in a series to separate thoughts, but not necessarily in contrast (BDAG, 630). Verse 3:18a is closely tied to 3:17 and could also be seen as part of the same sentence.
7. Ἀδελφοί in the plural refers to men and women: "brother and sister" (LSJ, 20). See discussion in "Gender Language in James," in chapter 1.

includes himself as a teacher with the first person plural: "we will receive . . . we stumble." He considers himself a teacher *and* also considers that he, like other Christian teachers, errs "much" (3:2). The verb "to teach" (διδάσκω) is the reduplicated causal form of δάω (to cause to learn).[8] Thus, a teacher is someone qualified to cause others to learn. The primary effect is on the intellect (vs. "exhort" [νουθετέω], "put [τίθημι] in mind [νοῦς]," which refers more to affecting behavior).[9] If an evangelist is a messenger of God's good news of salvation who preaches, baptizes, and instructs people in the basics of faith,[10] a "teacher" continues instruction with more advanced knowledge. Jesus, when on earth, taught, preached, and healed (e.g., Matt. 4:23). Thus, teaching was one of the ways in which God's reign is furthered. The evangelist and the teacher are especially included in Jesus's Great Commission to "make disciples of all nations, baptizing them" and "teaching them to obey everything" Jesus commanded (Matt. 28:19–20). It is one of the spiritual gifts (χάρισμα) included in the lists of 1 Corinthians 12:28–30, Romans 12:6–8, and Ephesians 4:11. Peter divides gifts into two broad categories of speaking and serving (1 Pet. 4:10–11). Teaching is a gift that entails primarily speaking and, as such, is a ministry of the word as opposed to a ministry of service (Acts 6:2–4; Rom. 12:8). A spiritual gift is a gift of God's grace and proof of God's joy. God gives joy (χάρις) to people by strengthening them, so that they can in return strengthen others, and all can thank God. Teaching, as also serving as an apostle, prophet, evangelist, and pastor, equips other Christians for the work of service and builds up the body of Christ so all can mature in Christ (Eph. 4:12–13).

Teachers are word merchants. They love to lecture. Every spiritual gift can be properly or improperly used. Teachers must be careful, as their content can be wrong and the way they use their gift can be wrong. They are limited by faith. None of the gifts are a guarantee or sign of salvation.[11] The only sign of salvation is whether we obey God (Matt. 7:21–23). Also, gifts need to be cultivated.[12]

---

8. LSJ, 371, 421.
9. BDAG, 679; Thayer, 429. Νουθετέω might describe the encouraging manner one talks to a child or sibling (1 Cor. 4:14; 2 Thess. 3:15). Both actions (teaching and admonishing) are needed to help people mature (Col. 1:28).
10. E.g., Philip: Acts 8:4–12; 21:8; Timothy: 2 Tim. 4:5. See also Spencer 1985, 108.
11. E.g., Luke 6:46–47; Rom. 12:3, 6–7.
12. E.g., 1 Tim. 4:14; 2 Tim. 1:6.

James is concerned about the ways gifts are used. Even though teachers must speak, James wants them to be *"slow* to speak" and "quick to *hear"* (1:19). He will now develop what he mentioned earlier: they must "bridle their tongues" (1:26; 3:2). Even though they may not have been given the ministry of service, they must develop the practice "to visit orphans and widows in their difficulties" and, like all other Christians, keep themselves "spotless from the world" (1:27).

Many of James's readers might want to become teachers. Paul and Timothy later had the same problem: many at Ephesus desired to be "teachers of the law, perceiving neither what they say nor concerning what they assert" (1 Tim. 1:7). The problem at Ephesus was more the content of the teaching, but for James's readers the issue was more the manner of teaching, the divorce of teaching from ethics. As Paul complained to the Galatians: Peter and Barnabas and others "were not acting in line with the truth of the gospel" (Gal. 2:14 NIV). They at that time had orthodoxy (right doctrine) but not orthopraxy (right practice).

But why will teachers receive greater judgment in the future (3:1)? First of all, James is following Jesus's teachings. Jesus told his disciples that the teachers of the law would "receive greater condemnation" (see the similar phrases in Luke 20:47 and James 3:1). A teacher could demand greater respect and privilege while, behind the scenes, "devour widows' houses" (Luke 20:47). They could sit in the most honored Seat of Moses in the synagogues (Matt. 23:2–3).[13] Fellow Jews would rise when a scribe passed by. Scribes[14] had to undergo a course of study for several years. According to Joachim Jeremias, "The scribes were venerated, like the prophets of old, with unbounded respect and reverential awe." He adds, "From all corners of the world young Jews streamed to Jerusalem to sit at the feet of the masters whose teaching resounded throughout Jewry." For example, Hillel came from Babylonia, Hanan ben Abishalom from Egypt, Nahum from Media, and Paul from Tarsus in Cilicia. The Pharisaic communities especially gave scribes unconditional obedience.[15] According to the *Mishnah*, the teacher had priority over the father when a son sought to retrieve lost property because "his father did but bring him into this world, but his teacher that taught him wisdom brings him into the world to come." The son was also obligated to help carry a burden or ransom for his teacher over his father (m. B. Mes. 2:11).

---

13. See also Painter and deSilva 2012, 113–14.
14. The terms "scribe," "teacher," and "rabbi" are synonyms (Jeremias 1969, 236). E.g., John 1:38.
15. Jeremias 1969, 242–44.

A "**judgment**" (κρίμα, 3:1) is the decision following legal action against someone, the legal decision rendered by a judge.[16] One of the criminals who hung at Jesus's side at the cross stated that all three of them were under "the same sentence of condemnation" (Luke 23:40; 24:20). Teachers are constantly making judgments or decisions as a result of deliberation. And Jewish religious leaders, such as scribes and rabbis, could make decisions about interpretations of the Bible. Jesus taught that "with the judgment you make you will be judged" (Matt. 7:2 NRSV). James also has described in 2:13 that one will be judged in the same manner as one has already judged. Consequently, a teacher as a judge would receive the corresponding judgment that he or she has given. Judgment can come in this life or at death or at Jesus's second return.[17]

Teachers not only may sin themselves, but by teaching they may cause many others to sin. And, if later they are judged for their sin, all their students are left dismayed and confused. Hiebert summarizes: "Increased influence means increased responsibility; the greater the impact upon others, the greater the accountability."[18] Moo explains that "greater knowledge brings with it a greater responsibility to live according to that knowledge." Moreover, the tongue is "the main tool" of a teacher's ministry.[19]

James goes on to explain the cause for the greater judgment: "**for all we stumble much**" (3:2). He will go on to illustrate with several analogies how the tongue is hard to control (3:3–12).[20] Teachers must speak constantly, but James wants their words and actions to please God (2:12). All humans, likewise, must communicate with others, and therefore all the following exhortations apply to all people. Words are one fruit of the inner person (Matt. 12:33–37). Jesus warns that what we say is important: "on the day of judgment you will have to give an account for every careless word you utter; for by your words you will be justified, and by your words you will be condemned" (Matt. 12:36–37 NRSV). Proverbs warns: "When there is too much talk, offence is never far away; the prudent hold their tongues" (10:19 REB). To "stumble"

---

16. BDAG, 567.
17. On the final judgment, see Acts 24:25; Rom. 14:10–12; 1 Cor. 3:13–15; 2 Cor. 5:10; Heb. 9:27–28; Rev. 20:11–15.
18. Hiebert 1979, 206. See also Matt. 18:6; Luke 12:48; McCartney 2009, 179. Ropes says that James's warning in 3:11 has no similar earlier or Jewish parallel (1916, 228).
19. Moo 2015, 155.
20. See also Adamson 1976, 140.

(James 3:2–3) signifies to "fall" (see 2:10). James already mentioned that one becomes a "transgressor" simply by failing to do *one* law (2:9–10). In 3:2 he adds that teachers fail not infrequently, but a "great number" or a "large" quantity of times.[21] "Many" teachers are falling "many" times! On the one hand, this fact may be greatly discouraging; on the other hand, it is encouraging because it means that all of us teaching are in the same condition as even the most righteous James.

What then is the goal? The goal is to control the words we say—not to "stumble" (repeated twice—a pleonasm) but rather to become mature, which is defined as "able to bridle even all the body" (3:2b). James uses the generic **"any"** (τις) in the subordinate clause ("If any in word does not stumble"), followed by the masculine noun "man" ("that one is a mature man able to bridle even all the body," 3:2b). The generic "any" indicates he writes to men and women teachers,[22] while the sex-specific term "man" gives specificity to his illustration (as he did previously in 1:7–8, 19–20, 23; 2:2). Jesus used this same literary technique to end the Sermon on the Mount: "Therefore everyone [πᾶς ὅστις] who hears these words of mine and puts them into practice is like a wise man [ἀνήρ]. . . . But everyone [πᾶς] who hears these words of mine and does not put them into practice is like a foolish man [ἀνήρ]" (Matt. 7:24, 26 NIV). "Man" (ἀνήρ) is sex-specific, but its use in an illustration is to communicate a specific, concrete image, not to refer only to men. Using the translation "man" renders the form of the original Greek,[23] while the translation "person" renders the author's meaning or intention, to be specific in the illustration but inclusive in the application.[24] James does not intend only for men to "bridle" their tongues. Both translations lack some precision.

The "mature man" begins extended illustrations of a small item that controls a large powerful item (a "bridle" for a horse, 3:2–3; then intensified with a "rudder" for a sailing ship, 3:4). These are positive images, followed by destructive negative images (fire from hell defiling the body, 3:5–6; and wild untamed animals, 3:7–8), and ending with contradictory images (fresh water and salt water; olives from a fig tree or figs from a grapevine, 3:10–12). The use of "bridle" in 3:2 foreshadows the first positive image (bridling a horse, 3:3) and "all the body" foreshadows the first negative image (defiling all the body, 3:5–6).

21. BDAG, 847–48.
22. E.g., Prisca and Aquila (Acts 18:26).
23. E.g., KJV, HCSB, ESV, REB.
24. Examples of inclusive translations: NIV 2011, NRSV, NLT, TEV, CEB, CEV.

James uses "**bridle**" (χαλιναγωγέω) as a metaphor in 3:2 and 1:26. The object in 1:26 is "tongue," while in 3:2 it is the whole body, indicating that James refers to an individual's control of oneself. The "**bit**" (χαλινός, 3:3) refers to the bit and bridle. A "bridle" is part of the tack or harness of a horse, consisting usually of a headstall or headpiece, a bit that goes in the mouth, and reins attached to the bit; it can be a strap or thong. The bit rests in the corner of the horse's mouth. Since the bit rests in the mouth, it can control the mouth or tongue (1:26), but then with the entire bridle, the rider can control the whole body of the horse (3:2–3). Josephus tells us that Asinaeus was warned about approaching Parthian enemies by the neighing of horses, "not like that of horses grazing but like that of horses with riders, for I also catch the jingling of bridles" (*Ant.* 18, 9.2.320). The bridles restrain and compel. They are individually fitted to a horse. Poor-fitting bridles may leave a horse uncomfortable, may result in the rider's lack of control while riding, or may cause unclear communication between rider and horse.

Likewise, the mature (τέλειος) person not only uses a "bridle" but individualizes the bridle for comfort and effectiveness and becomes skillful in using it. One way to become mature is to become an integrated personality where the unrighteous thought from the inner person is not allowed to escape as an unrighteous word to harm others (see 1:4, 17).

The first extended illustration (a metaphor) begins with the subordinate conditional clause ("if into the mouths of the horses we place the bits," 3:3). This condition is a prerequisite. The horse will not **obey** and its body will not be guided if the bit is not placed in the mouth. This condition places the responsibility for control on the teacher, no one else. The second subordinate clause is a purpose clause ("in order that they obey us"). The bit is not placed in the mouth to torture the horse but to persuade it to obey the rider. James employs "obey" (πείθω) only once in his letter, but it is used frequently elsewhere in the New Testament. It can signify "persuade" in an active or causative sense, to cause others to do or to believe as one wants, or, in a passive sense, to oneself, to agree to believe or do (follow) as another wants. For example Paul, by explaining and testifying to the kingdom of God, tried to *persuade* the Jewish leaders in Rome about Jesus. Some were *persuaded* by what Paul said, while others did not believe (Acts 28:23–24). Similarly, the bit in the horse's mouth works to cause the horse to agree to follow the rider's guidance. The horse then "obeys."[25]

---

25. A person can "obey" the truth (Gal. 5:7) or "obey" leaders and submit to their authority (Heb. 13:17).

The final goal is for the rider to "guide" the whole body of this giant animal (3:3). According to Everett Olson, the domesticated horse has "outstanding importance for its use in transportation." It weighs more than two thousand pounds (900 kg) and is characterized by strength, speed, and a high degree of intelligence.[26] **"Guide"** (μετάγω) is used twice in James: in 3:3 referring to riding a horse and in 3:4 to steering a ship (pleonasm). The verb has a causative sense, literally to lead (ἄγω) over (μετά).[27] In the Septuagint, μετάγω basically signifies to carry from one land to another, as God who *led* or *carried* the Hebrew captives or as Pharaoh Necho *brought* King Jehoahaz son of Josiah to Egypt.[28] One being caused another being(s) to be led over, transferred, or directed to another place.[29]

Thus, the sequence of 3:3 is as follows: (1) the rider places a bit in the mouth of the horse, (2) the horse obeys the rider, (3) the whole body of the horse can be led to where the rider wants. The human is analogous to the rider, the bit, and the horse. The rider is the human will that desires to become a wise person. That person has inner desires (1:14–15, 20–21; 4:1). However, evil desires need to be tamed (3:7) (that is the role of the bit), so that the tongue voices words that lead to wise actions[30] (the horse) (2:12, 14, 18; 3:2). Proper guidance leads to "from above wisdom" (3:17–18). In contrast, human lack of control of one's words can lead to "earthly" wisdom, including jealousy and self-centeredness (3:14). The "natural" person uses no bit or control on speech and thus gives no guidance to actions.

The horse, like the ship, is a means of transportation, in the same way as actions lead people to consequences. The horse can accomplish much by its strength, speed, and intelligence. The question is, is it being led to do good actions? Or is it not at all domesticated and instead running wild, leading the rider where it feels like going?

How does someone "bridle" the tongue? James has already made some suggestions: ask God for wisdom (1:5–8, 17–18), be slow to speak, quick to hear (1:19), receive the implanted word (1:21), and study the

---

26. Olson 1987, 255.
27. Thayer, 404.
28. 1 Kings 8:47; 2 Chron. 6:37; 36:3. See also 1 Esd. 1:45; 5:69; Sir. 10:8; 2 Macc. 1:33.
29. See also LSJ, 1111; BDAG, 638.
30. The "body" appears to signify actions, which is the topic of the context (2:8–26; 3:2, 13). Some commentators conclude the "body" refers to the church. See summary of arguments in McCartney 2009, 181–83.

perfect law (1:25). In addition, he will suggest, submit to God (4:7–10), confess sins to one another, and pray for one another (5:16).

The sailing **ship** is an inanimate but even larger item of transportation, intensified by strong winds (3:4). "Behold" (ἰδού) "draws attention to what follows." Thus, James calls the reader "to closer consideration and contemplation" of this second illustration.[31] "Also" reinforces the similarity of the second illustration (3:4) with the first (3:3).[32] As with the earlier illustration of a horse (3:3), 3:4 compares a "small member" with its great effect (3:5). The "ship" (πλοῖον) especially refers to a "merchant ship," either a "rather large sea-faring ship" or a "small fishing vessel."[33] In this context, πλοῖον refers to a large seafaring vessel because James's first adjectival phrase describes the ship as "being so great" (3:4). James was reared in Nazareth, about fifteen miles from the Sea of Galilee and not far from the Mediterranean Sea;[34] thus, he would be acquainted with ships. Acts refers to a number of larger ships that went from port to port on the Aegean and Mediterranean seas.[35] In the first and second centuries AD, Rome was famous for its sea transport. According to Lionel Casson: "Rome's merchant marine had more and bigger ships than any had ever had before or were to have afterward for the next fifteen hundred years."[36] The average sailing ship could carry 100–500 tons and was 100–150 feet long and 30–40 feet wide. The large government ships could carry 350–500 tons, and grain ships could carry 1200 tons of grain and were as large as 180 feet long, forty-five feet wide, and forty-four feet deep. A large grain ship could feed everyone in Athens for a year. The biggest ancient merchant ships carried 1700–1900 tons and as many as 600–1000 passengers on long voyages. Paul and 275 others were shipwrecked on such a large merchant ship.[37] Thus, the ship was much bigger and more powerful than the horse.

James secondly describes a ship that "by means of strong winds" is "being driven" (3:4). **"Wind"** (ἄνεμος) in the New Testament is always a strong wind. Whenever a boat is overcome by a wind, ἄνεμος

---

31. BDAG, 468.
32. See also Hiebert 1979, 210.
33. BDAG, 830–31. E.g., John 21:3–6.
34. Harrison 1985, 170–71.
35. E.g., Acts 20:3–16, 38; 21:1–8; 27:2–37; 28:3–13.
36. Casson 1964, 49, 56.
37. Sea vessels were primarily to transport cargo (e.g., Acts 21:2–3). Casson 1971, 171–73; Casson 1994, 153, 156, 158–59; Villiers 1963, 29; *Life* 15.

is used.[38] It is contrasted with a gentle south wind in Acts 27:13–15. In addition, James heightens the power of the winds by modifying it with the adjective "strong" (σκληρός) (a pleonasm). "Strong" ("hard") contrasts with "soft" (μαλακός).[39] Such strong winds could easily lead to a ship becoming out of control. For example, the violent wind (ἄνεμος) that rushed down the mountains in Crete[40] drove off course the large Alexandrian ship bound for Italy, eventually causing the ship owners to lose all their cargo, the ship, and almost all the lives on board (Acts 27:6–44). But James writes of strong winds that could be harnessed for good and used to guide a ship (μετάγω) by a small **"rudder"** or steering oar (πηδάλιον). A large ship would have two rudders connected by a crossbar operated by one person.[41] Smaller ships would have one rudder at the side rear, like a pole with a paddle; most of it would be under water, with the top guided by a steersman or pilot.[42]

Operating the rudder of a sailing ship took skill and strength.[43] The rudder would guide the ship "wherever the desire of the one guiding wills" (3:4). Similarly, King Jehoash had a **"desire"** or "inclination" (ὁρμή) to repair the temple. Therefore, he raised money and hired workers for its repair (*Ant.* 9.8.2.161). In the same way, people who control their tongues (rudder) can guide their own actions (ship) to do great things. Skill is needed and focus. Winds that can lead to disaster can be otherwise channeled for good ends. As Proverbs teaches: "How good is a timely word!" (15:23); "A gentle answer turns away wrath, but a harsh word stirs up anger" (15:1); "The hearts of the wise make their mouths prudent, and their lips promote instruction. Gracious words are a honeycomb, sweet to the soul and healing to the bones" (16:23–24 TNIV). In contrast, "The words of the wicked lie in wait for blood, but the speech of the upright rescues them" (12:6 TNIV).

James reiterates his main point: "Likewise also the tongue is a small member" (3:5). It can "bridle even all the body" (3:2), even as a bit controls a horse and a rudder controls a sailing ship. James now transitions to negative powers of the tongue: it "greatly boasts." (3:5). Josephus uses the same verb **"boast"** (αὐχέω) to describe the Arcadians who "boast" of their antiquity even though at a later date they had hardly learned

---

38. E.g., Matt. 8:26–27; 14:24; Mark 4:36–39; 6:48–51; Luke 8:22–24; John 6:18; Acts 27:4–8, 14–15.
39. LSJ, 1076, 1612.
40. Ramsay 2001, 263.
41. Casson 1971, 224; BDAG, 811; LSJ, 1400.
42. Casson 1994, 157.
43. Casson 1971, 226, 228–29.

the alphabet (*Ag. Ap.* 1.4.22). Liddell and Scott's *Lexicon* defines αὐχέω as "plume oneself" and the noun (αὐχήεις) as "braggart."[44] Literally, these related words refer to "lift up the neck" (αὐχήν); hence "to boast."[45] One revolt against God is described by the chronicler as "lifting up of the necks against" the Lord (2 Chron. 29:6). Αὐχήν can also refer to the "handle of the steering-paddle in a ship,"[46] which implies that the tongue can be used for good (to steer) or for evil (to boast).

James calls his readers to think further ("behold") on his next illustration: "How **small** a fire how great a forest kindles" (3:5). Normally ἡλίκος, an interrogative pronoun, signifies "how big, how great," frequently as an expression of wonder, referring to size or age.[47] However, because earlier James contrasts the "small" tongue that "greatly boasts" (3:5), most interpreters would conclude that "ἡλίκον refers to smallness and ἡλίκην greatness of the size."[48] Many of us may remember the public park ranger Smokey the Bear's warning about the danger of a flame to cause a forest fire: "Only *you* can prevent wildfires!" The same is true in the ethical and spiritual realm.[49] "Fire" in 3:5 has a literal meaning, such as a fire that can be kindled in winter in order to warm those around it.[50] The Bible describes fires as consuming, intense, and unquenchable, producing smoke and roaring across mountains.[51] In this context, James reminds the readers of the great havoc words can create.

In 3:6, James adds a further, more intensive point: not only can the tongue create forest fires, it *is* a **fire**: "Also the tongue is fire. The tongue, the world of unrighteousness, is constituted among our members, the one defiling all the body and setting on fire the wheel of life and being set on fire by hell" (3:6). He repeats "fire," now as a metaphor (3:5, 6, pleonasm). Outside of its literal use, "fire" (πῦρ) is frequently used to signify judgment or purity or passion.[52] For example, Jesus warns: "If you say, 'You fool,' you will be in danger of the fire of

---

44. LSJ, 285.
45. Thayer, 87. See also Ps. 12:3.
46. LSJ, 285.
47. LSJ, 768–69; Thayer, 277.
48. Robertson 1934, 734; LSJ, 769; Thayer, 277; BDAG, 436. See also Luke 19:3.
49. See also Prov. 26:21; 16:27; Ps. 120:3–4.
50. E.g., Luke 22:55; Acts 28:2–5.
51. Anderson 1979, 196–97, referring to Deut. 4:24; 32:22; Obad. 1:18; Jer. 7:20; Ps. 68:2; 83:14 (forest).
52. E.g., passion, 1 Cor. 7:9 (πυρόω).

hell" (Matt. 5:22, γέενναν τοῦ πυρός).[53] Jesus and others taught about a place called "hell," which is eternal with an unquenchable fire, where there is "weeping and gnashing of teeth."[54] To this place, at the end, the devil and his angels will be sent.[55] In James 5:3, "fire" symbolizes this final judgment. But, in addition, hell itself uses fire to destroy, as Paul warns the Ephesians to "take up the shield of faith, with which you can extinguish all the *flaming* [πυρόω] arrows of the evil one" (Eph. 6:16 NIV). The evil one, whose presence is "hell," causes fires. Similarly, false wisdom comes from *below*, not above, and is "earthly, worldly, *demonic*" (3:15).

"Fire" can also be a symbol of God's presence because "fire" purifies, as well as destroys, for example, when fire purifies impurities in gold (e.g., Rev. 3:18). God may thus be described as a "consuming fire" of impurities, a judge.[56] But in James 3:5, the tongue's fire is "the world of unrighteousness," which defiles the rest of the body and others ("the wheel of life").[57] The tongue is defiled by the evil within a person[58] and defiles that person's actions. Its ultimate source is *not* God's wisdom but the fire from hell, a euphemism for the evil one.[59] This fire destroys; it does not purify.

The phrase setting on fire "the **wheel of life**" (τροχὸν τῆς γενέσεως, 3:6) is variously interpreted by different commentators. Within its context, it is part of a description of "the tongue is fire." Three present participles connected by "and" (polysyndeton) further describe this world: "the one defiling all the body" and "setting on fire the wheel of life" and "being set on fire by hell." All phrases are clearly negative. The middle phrase ("setting on fire," φλογίζω) is the active counterpart to the passive final phrase: "being set on fire" (φλογίζω). Some have suggested that the middle phrase ("setting on fire the wheel of life") comes from

53. See also on judgment, Matt. 13:40, 42; 18:9; 23:15; Mark 9:43, 48; Luke 3:17.
54. Matt. 13:42, 50; 18:8.
55. Matt. 25:41; Rev. 20:10.
56. E.g., Exod. 3:2; Deut. 4:23–24; Heb. 12:29. Friedrich Lang (1968) observes that "in almost all the OT theophanies fire appears as a way of representing the unapproachable sanctity and overpowering glory of Yahweh" (935). Also, "the destruction of Sodom and Gomorrah by fire and brimstone (Gn. 19:24) exerted a strong influence on subsequent ideas of divine judgment" (936).
57. For a summary of different interpretations of "world of unrighteousness," see McCartney 2009, 185–88.
58. James 1:14–15; Matt. 12:34–35; 15:16–20.
59. See also McCartney 2009, 190–91.

the Orphic mysteries, the wheel of human origin, a circle of "blessing," birth, death, reincarnation, over and over again.[60] This image from a pagan source in no way fits in this context. Τροχός or "wheel," in contrast, is a common word in the Greek Old Testament, although it occurs only in James in the New Testament. It can refer to the literal wheels of a chariot or a wagon or an oxcart.[61] It can also refer to an instrument of torture (e.g., "the wheel and the fires," 4 Macc. 15:22). As part of a chariot, wheels could also refer as a synecdoche to the destruction of an enemy. For example, the wise king crushes the ungodly, and "brings a wheel upon them" (Prov. 20:26). "Fire" and "wheel" are both used in Psalm 82 (83):13–14: "Make them as a wheel; as stubble before the face of the wind. As fire which shall burn up a wood, as the flame may consume the mountains" (LXX). These Old Testament passages illustrate the negative image of a "wheel." In that case, James may be saying that, as the tongue defiles one's actions, the tongue, as a "wheel," *destroys* one's own life (existence or experience, γένεσις).[62] Such a person is made to be "as a wheel" set on fire that consumes oneself and others.[63] This fire connects with the fire of hell, which ultimately causes fires of unrighteousness.[64]

Since accents on Greek words came much later in the transmission process, τροχός can also be accented τρόχος, which signifies "course of life, a circular race, a race-course."[65] The footrace was mostly a race between two poles (the imagery used by Paul in 1 Corinthians 9:24–27, τρέχω), but chariots would run in a circle. In this case, James would

---

60. BDAG, 192; Ropes (1916, 239) writes that such a view is "nonsense"; "nothing could be more opposed to James's robust doctrine of moral responsibility than the idea of a fatalistic circle." Dibelius points out that normally "circle" (κύκλος) is used in Orphic writings, not "wheel." Nevertheless, he "assumes" "cycle" or "wheel of becoming" became an alternate expression for "circle of becoming," which was adapted by Jewish authors (1976, 196, 198). Davids (1982, 143) and others (e.g., Painter and deSilva 2012, 120) suggest that the "wheel of becoming" is a nontechnical term dependent upon "an original Orphic formulation."

61. E.g., 2 Sam. 24:22 LXX; 1 Kings 7:30; Isa. 5:28; 29:5 LXX; 41:15 LXX.

62. BDAG, 192. See also James 1:23.

63. "Life's varied relationships" are "set ablaze by an uncontrolled tongue" (Hiebert 1979, 218).

64. Τροχός can also refer to the circular "ring playing on the bit of a bridle" and the "ring for passing a rope through" on a "ship" (LSJ, 1829). In this meaning, then, the "ring of life" would be set on fire.

65. LSJ, 1829. See McCartney 2009, 190.

describe "setting on fire the course of life," as it were, going in a circle spreading the fire around to oneself and others.

Both of these negative options are possible in this context. "The wheel of destruction" has an Old Testament background, the "course of life" is more related to contemporary illustrations. Both are strongly negative and destructive.

James goes on to give further illustrations (metaphors) of the danger of uncontrolled speech. The tongue is now described as a variety of **wild animals** (3:7–8). Four different categories are presented in two pairs:[66] (a) "every species of wild animals [θηρίον] and also birds [πετεινόν]," and (b) "creeping animals [ἑρπετόν] and also sea creatures [ἐνάλιος]" (3:7). Three of these terms[67] occur in Genesis 1:20–30 and in the summary in 9:2–3a: "on all the wild animals [θηρίον] of the earth, on all the birds [πετεινόν] of the sky, and on all things moving upon the earth, and upon all the fishes of the sea. . . . And every creeping animal [ἑρπετόν] which is living shall be to you for meat." Instead of "fish" (ἰχθύς), James uses "sea creatures" (ἐνάλιος, "of the sea").[68] "Wild animals" basically live on the earth, as opposed to "creeping animals" or "reptiles,"[69] who may move between habitation in water or on the ground.[70] Thus, they are related to but different than "sea creatures,"[71] which remain in the sea. "Wild animals" on the earth are related to but different than "birds," which fly above the earth in the "firmament of heaven" (Gen. 1:20).[72] The "sea creatures" include "fish" (ἰχθύς) and the "great whales" (κήτη) (Gen. 1:21, 26). Θηρίον is a general term for "wild animals" in the New Testament, such as those who live in the wilderness (Mark 1:13). They can include serpents (Acts 28:3–5). Sometimes they are a means of death, sometimes synonymous with evil.[73] "Birds" (πετεινόν) may symbolize a wild animal that is carefree (Matt. 6:26;

---

66. The two pairs are connected by "and also" (τέ—καί), which has an "inner bond" (Robertson 1934, 1178–79; Robertson 1933, 43).
67. See also these terms in Acts 11:6 (Θηρίον, ἑρπετόν, πετεινόν); Rom. 1:23 (ἑρπετόν, πετεινόν).
68. LSJ, 553.
69. BDAG, 393. Ἑρπετόν comes from ἕρπω "to creep, crawl," hence "serpent" or "reptile" but "chiefly of serpents" (Thayer, 250). See also Robertson 1933, 43.
70. Genesis 1:24 appears to contrast reptiles with the wild animals of the earth.
71. BDAG, 330; "marine," Thayer, 213.
72. Πετεινός are "flying or winged animals," hence "birds" (Thayer, 507).
73. E.g., Ezek. 14:21; Rev. 6:8. See also Spencer 2014, 25–26.

Luke 12:24), but birds may also symbolize evil, specifically birds that eat seeds thrown on paths.[74]

All these wild animals "are being **tamed**" (present tense) and "have been tamed" (perfect tense, δαμάζω, 3:7). This is God's mandate to humanity ("the human species") that they have "dominion over" all these other living creatures (the animal "species," Gen. 1:26, 28; Ps. 8:6–8; James 3:7).[75] James defines "dominion" as "taming" or "subduing." The same verb is used of Legion in Gerasenes, who could not be *restrained* by chains, but whom Jesus made peaceful by commanding the evil spirits to depart (Mark 5:3–4, 8, 15).[76] Thus δαμάζω is a strong verb that signifies "subdue," but the earlier illustration clarifies that the goal of subduing is to be able to guide the animals or ships to accomplish one's will (3:3).

The tongue is then compared to such wild or undomesticated animals: "But the tongue [γλῶσσαν] of humans no one is able to tame, a restless evil, full of deadly poison" (3:8). James repeats the same verb (δαμάζω) to connect verse 8 with verse 7. The tongue cannot be subdued. What is it like? "Restless evil, full of deadly poison [ἰός]." "**Restless**" and "restlessness" (ἀκατάστατος, ἀκαταστασία) are used three times in James[77] of the two-willed person (1:8), the tongue (3:8), and the wisdom from below, which is full of evil deeds (3:16). In 3:8, this evil is described as "full of **deadly poison**." Θανατηφόρος combines θάνατος ("death") and φέρω ("bringing").[78] For example, one noble Jewish mother, because of her faith in God and zeal to obey God's commandments, did not prevent her seven children from being killed but "voted" for resisting their adversary "bringing" the children "death" (4 Macc. 15:26).

James alludes in 3:8 to the poison of a snake, such as attacked Paul (Acts 28:3–6). The unsubdued tongue is like a snake poisoning itself and thus causing death to itself and to others, the death caused

---

74. Matt. 13:4, 19; Mark 4:4, 15; Luke 8:5, 12.
75. Dibelius (1976, 199) and Martin (1988, 116–17) cite contemporaries of James who also mention how humans tame animals. Philo also refers to how a bit controls a spirited horse. For Philo, this is an example of human sovereignty over animals (*Creation* 28.84–87). For James, this is an example of what humans need to do to themselves: control their speech.
76. Δαμάζω is used of "iron" which is strong and subdues in Daniel 2:40 LXX. See also McCartney 2009, 191.
77. Three of its seven uses in the New Testament, or 43 percent, occur in James's letter.
78. "Death-bringing" or "deadly," Thayer, 282.

by jealousy and self-centeredness.[79] David uses similar imagery in his psalms: regarding those who live as if God does not exist, their "throat is an open sepulcher; with their tongues [γλῶσσαν] they have used deceit; the poison [ἰός] of asps is under their lips: whose mouth is full of cursing and bitterness; their feet are swift to shed blood; destruction and misery are in their ways; and the way of peace they have not known; there is no fear of God before their eyes" (Ps. 13[14]:3 LXX). David also pleads delivery from the evil persons who have "sharpened their tongue [γλῶσσαν] as the tongue of a serpent; the poison [ἰός] of asps is under their lips" (Ps. 140:3).[80] James uses similar imagery for his readers who claim to be Christians, but are not acting like Christ. What a terrifying image that one's own tongue is a poisonous snake that cannot be subdued!

James gives an example[81] of what an untamed tongue will do: "With it we bless the Lord and Father[82] and with it we curse humans, the ones according to the likeness of God having been made; out of the same mouth comes out blessing and curse. It is not appropriate, my brothers and sisters, these such to be" (3:9–10). If one can ask in a "wavering" manner, with two contradictory wills (1:5–8), one can also speak in a "wavering" manner, with two contradictory statements. James's readers are Jewish Christians who have been taught to **bless** the Lord throughout the day: in the morning, afternoon, and evening in conjunction with the temple sacrifices in Jerusalem, before and after meals (e.g., "Blessed art thou the Lord our God, King of the world, who brings forth bread from the earth"), when traveling, and when seeing a wonder created by God.[83]

To "bless" (εὐλογέω [verb], εὐλογία [noun], 3:9) is to give a good word (literally) or to celebrate with praises.[84] Jesus follows in the Jewish traditions, blessing God for food,[85] but he also blesses people. He blesses his disciples before he is carried up to heaven and blesses even children brought to him.[86] He blesses and is worthy of blessing. The many

---

79. James 3:14, 16; synonym of fighting in Luke 21:9 and 2 Corinthians 6:5; 12:20. Of the more than thirty-five species of snakes in Israel, only seven are poisonous, such as the viper (Alon 1969, 195, 202–3, 205–6, 209).
80. See also Rom. 3:13; Gen. 3:1–7.
81. See also Laws 1980, 154.
82. Synonym is "Creator." See also Isa. 63:16; Mal. 2:10; Laws 1980, 155.
83. M. Ber. 1:1; 6:1–8; 7:3; 9:1–2, 4; Schürer 1973–79, 2:457; Spencer 1990, 127.
84. Thayer, 259; Robertson 1933, 44.
85. E.g., Matt. 14:19; 15:36; 26:26; Mark 6:41; 8:7; 14:22; Luke 9:16; 24:30.
86. Luke 24:50–51; Mark 10:13–16.

angels encircling God's throne agree: "Worthy is the Lamb that was slaughtered to receive power and wealth and wisdom and might and honor and glory and blessing!" (εὐλογία, Rev. 5:12 NRSV). Paul agrees: "Blessed [εὐλογητός] be the God and Father of our Lord Jesus Christ, who *has blessed* [εὐλογέω] us in Christ with every spiritual *blessing*" (εὐλογία, Eph. 1:3a). This blessing of God is as it ought to be because God is worthy of celebration with praises. However, those created in God's image should be similarly treated. Humans, of course, must not receive the worship due to God (Rom. 1:21–23), but having been created in God's likeness affects the way they are treated. They too should be blessed as images of God.

In the earlier verses (3:3–8), James alludes to God's mandate to humans to subdue the earth. James now directly (3:9) refers to Genesis 1:26–27: "And God said, 'Let us make Adam in our image, according to our *resemblance* [ὁμοίωσις] and they will rule over the fish of the sea and over the birds of the sky and over the animals and over all the earth and over all the moving things which move upon the earth.' And God created the Adam in his image in the image of God he created him, a male and a female he created them."[87] There is a similarity between God and the humans God created and, thus, humans are special because God is special. After the flood, Noah and his family are allowed to kill animals for food, as well as to harvest and eat vegetables (Gen. 9:2–3), but they are not allowed to kill humans: "The one shedding human blood, instead his blood will be shed, since in God's image, I made the human" (Gen. 9:6, author's trans. of LXX). Humans are distinct in God's creation because they are similar to their Creator. They must not be murdered (Exod. 20:13). In human rebirth, humans as well should reflect God's righteousness and holiness (Eph. 4:24). **Cursing** of humans, in effect, curses God in whose image they were created; while blessing a human, in effect, blesses God (Matt. 25:40, 45). The poor are special not only because they are heirs of God's reign (James 2:5) but also because they are created in God's likeness, as are the rich. When the rich slander the poor (2:6–7), they are, in effect, "cursing" (καταράομαι, 3:9) them. "Disputes and conflicts" (4:2), speaking evil against another (4:11), condemning the righteous (5:6), and grumbling against another (5:9) are ways one's opponents are "cursed."

To "curse" (κατάρα) is the opposite of to "bless" (εὐλογία).[88] Those that are condemned to the eternal fire along with the devil are "cursed"

---

87. Repeated in Gen. 5:1–2.
88. Thayer, 335; e.g., Gen. 12:3.

(Matt. 25:41). They do not inherit God's kingdom (Matt. 25:34). To command a tree no longer to bear fruit is to "curse" it (Mark 11:14, 21). To be cursed by God because one has rejected the promise to obey God means that one is in want and difficulties (Deut. 27:12–28:68). Thus, to "curse" other humans is to cause them to be in want and difficulties. In James 3:8–9, James writes about what is done with the "tongue," or words. What is done with words will often then result in harmful action (e.g., 2:1–7).

James creates a partial parallelism emphasizing the initial phrase "with it":

With it we bless the Lord . . .
with it we curse the humans. (3:9)

In doing so, he draws attention to the funnel ("it"—"the tongue" in the "mouth," 3:8–10) from which come two contradictory actions: blessing and cursing. The curses have made the whole mouth unclean and thus affect the very blessings uttered, in the same way as a corpse causes uncleanness to those who touch it and, if they are not purified, they eventually defile even the Lord's tabernacle (Num. 19:11–13). These actions do not accomplish James's overall goal for his readers to have integrated personalities.

Verses 11–12 all illustrate verse 10. So far, James has used illustrations of transportation (animate: a horse, and inanimate: a ship [intensified by winds], 3:2–4), fire that destroys (3:5–6), wild animals that need to be subdued (3:7–8), and now images of inanimate, contradictory, and impossible situations involving different waters, fruits, and vegetables (3:11–12). All these images depend on the sense of taste, which of course is located in the mouth.

The **"spring"** (πηγή, 3:11) is a symbol for the "mouth" (στόμα, 3:10). The mouth that is the source for blessings and curses is compared to a spring that spews out both fresh and bitter water. James uses μήτι, which invites a negative answer:[89] "The spring from the same opening does not pour forth sweet and bitter water, does it?" (3:11). The answer is "no"! A spring (πηγή) is a "flow or seep of ground water escaping at the earth's surface."[90] Ground water is contained in water-saturated rocks. Springs come from hilltops, higher layers, limestone, or lava.[91] Springs are important everywhere as sources of water, but especially in

---

89. Μήτι is more emphatic than μή (BDAG, 649).
90. Wilson 1987, 461.
91. Wilson 1987, 461–62.

Israel, which is very dry. God created the springs of water (Ps. 17[18]:15 LXX; Rev. 14:7). Before the earth had rain, it would be watered by water rising up from a fountain in the ground (Gen. 2:6; Prov. 8:24, 28). Springs of water are symbols of blessing,[92] of righteous people,[93] and of God.[94] Normally, in the land, "sweet"[95] (or "fresh"[96] or "clean,"[97] γλυκύς) water is found, which is drinkable, but the sea too may have its own springs (Job 38:16) that provide salt water. The same spring water cannot be drinkable ("sweet") *and* undrinkable[98] ("bitter"[99] or "salty"[100]) at the same time.

James uses the adjective "**bitter**" (πικρός), which is always negative in the New Testament.[101] It describes a type of jealousy in verse 14. Water that is "bitter" or "brackish" can cause death (e.g., Rev. 8:11). After Peter realized he had denied his Lord, when Jesus looked at him in the courtyard after he was arrested, in shame, Peter "wept *bitterly*" (Luke 22:61–62). It is a synonym for evil, anger, jealousy, and cursing.[102] In James 3:11, πικρός stands for "cursing," while γλυκύς for "blessing" (3:10). If this is impossible in nature, how then can it be possible in humans? It is a physical impossibility, unnatural, for "sweet" and "bitter" to "pour forth" or gush out, and certainly not *abundantly*.[103]

James repeats again his term of endearment, "my brothers and sisters" (3:10, 12), as he continues to illustrate how one's words should be positive ones that bring peace (3:18; Rom. 3:14–15; Ps. 10:7–9): "A fig tree is not able, my brothers and sisters, to make olives or a grapevine is not able to make figs, can they? Neither salt is able to make sweet water" (3:12). These images continue the theme of impossible actions in nature, which should be the same for the tongue. A fig is sweet, while an olive is bitter. James places the two words being compared next to each other, in this way heightening the contrast: "*a fig tree* [συκῆ]

---

92. E.g., Prov. 6:11 LXX; Isa. 35:7; 41:18; 49:10.
93. Prov. 10:11; 13:14; 16:22; 18:4.
94. Jer. 2:13; 17:13; Ps. 36:9; Isa. 12:3; John 4:14; Rev. 7:17; 21:6.
95. Γλυκύς is compared to honey in Revelation 10:9–10. See KJV, NTME, TEV, HCSB; BDAG, 201.
96. NRSV, NIV, REB, NLT, CEB, ESV.
97. CEV.
98. "Brackish": NRSV, REB; "dirty": CEV.
99. KJV, NTME, NLT, TEV, HCSB; BDAG, 813.
100. NIV, CEB, ESV.
101. Also, the cognates: πικραίνω ("make bitter"), πικρία ("bitterness"), πικρῶς ("bitterly").
102. Acts 8:23; Rom. 3:14, citing Ps. 10:7; Eph. 4:31; Heb. 12:15.
103. Βρύω, LSJ, 332; Thayer, 106; BDAG, 184.

olives [ἐλαία] to make or *a grapevine* [ἄμπελος] *figs* [σῦκον]? Neither *salt* [ἀλυκός] *sweet* [γλυκύς] water to make." A reference to "figs" begins and ends 3:12, while a reference to water ("spring," "water," 3:11, 12) begins and ends these images, tying them together as a unit (3:11–12).

The **fig tree** is frequently mentioned in Scripture.[104] It is native to warm climates and probably the most cultivated tree in the world. There are more than one thousand species.[105] When the leaves come out, summer is near[106] and winter is past: "The fig-tree has put forth its young figs, the vines put forth the tender grape" (Song of Sol. 2:13). Figs, olives, grapes, and water are frequently mentioned together in the Old Testament as signs of blessing. The Lord promised the Israelites to bring them to a good land: "a land with flowing streams, with springs and underground waters welling up in valleys and hills, a land of wheat and barley, of vines and fig trees and pomegranates, a land of olive trees and honey . . . where you will lack nothing. . . . You shall eat your fill and bless the LORD your God for the good land that he has given you" (Deut. 8:7–10 NRSV). In days to come: "They shall all sit under their own vines and under their own fig trees" (Mic. 4:4 NRSV).[107] Jotham developed a parable to sway the people by using the imagery of olive, fig, and vine trees (Judg. 9:7–14). In it, the olive was cited for its rich oil (9:9), the fig for its sweetness and delicious fruit (9:11), and the vine for its wine that cheers people (9:13). Therefore, James has used illustrations of botany common and important to his listeners.

The **olive tree**, of which there are four hundred species,[108] is abundant in the East and naturalized in other warm countries.[109] The olive and fig may have originated in Israel.[110] When my husband and I traveled to southern Spain, we saw thousands of cultivated olive trees flourishing in 100-plus-degree weather. Jesus and his disciples often gathered on the Mount of Olives outside of Jerusalem.[111]

---

104. Greek OT and NT has 56 references to συκῆ ("fig tree") and σῦκον ("fig").
105. Stapleton 1885, 19; Zohary 1982, 59.
106. Matt. 24:32; Mark 13:28; Luke 21:29–30.
107. See also Num. 20:5; 2 Kings 18:31; Ps. 105:33; Isa. 36:16; Jer. 8:13; Neh. 13:15; Hos. 2:12; 9:10; Hag. 2:19; 1 Macc. 14:12.
108. Zohary 1982, 57.
109. Stapleton 1885, 30. The Greek OT and NT have fifty-five references to ἐλαία ("olive oil") and ἐλαίων ("olive orchard"), but some of them refer to the oil made from olives (e.g., Exod. 27:20; 30:24).
110. Alon 1969, 19.
111. Matt. 24:3; 26:30; Mark 14:26; Luke 21:37; 22:39; Acts 1:12.

The **grapevine**, one of fifty species, is a climbing shrub. Of the three, it is the one most frequently mentioned in Scripture.[112] It is also found in mild climates. There are more than fifteen hundred varieties of grape.[113] Jesus often used vineyards in his parables.[114] The wine made from grapes is a symbol of the blood of the covenant of forgiveness.[115] Jesus even described himself as the true vine (John 15:1, 4–5).

A wild olive shoot might be grafted onto a cultivated olive tree (Rom. 11:17, 24), but there is no natural way olives will grow from a fig tree, nor figs from a grapevine. Indirectly, James implies that if one finds olives on a tree it is not a fig tree; and if one finds figs on a tree, that tree is not a grapevine. Rather, "each tree is known by its own fruit. Figs are not gathered from thorns, nor are grapes picked from a bramble bush." Jesus explains the analogy: "The good person out of the good treasure of the heart produces good, and the evil person out of evil treasure produces evil; for it is out of the abundance of the heart that the mouth speaks" (Luke 6:44–45 NRSV).[116] The nature of good and bad "fruits" will be described in the verses that follow (3:13–18), ending by referring to the imagery of fruits again at the end of the chapter: the wisdom from above has "good *fruits*. . . . Then a *fruit* of righteousness in peace is *sown* by the ones doing peace" (3:17–18).

James closes this section by referring again to "sweet water" (3:11, 12). Before he was exhorting that the mouth should not gush out blessings (sweet) and curses (bitter); now he adds that salt water cannot produce "sweet water" (3:12). Unlike "bitter" (πικρός), "**salt**" (ἁλυκός) is a more positive or neutral term, in the same way as figs, olives, and grapes are all positive or neutral terms. The Dead Sea has salt springs on its shore.[117] Hiebert explains: "Neither a salt spring or the Sea of Salt could be expected to produce sweet water."[118] Jesus had challenged his disciples to be "the salt [ἅλς] of the earth" (Matt. 5:13; Luke 14:34–35) and to have "salt among yourselves, and be at peace among one another" (Mark 9:50). Speech "seasoned with salt" is gracious and causes peace between people (Col. 4:6). But James's last illustration raises

---

112. The Greek OT and NT have 177 references to ἄμπελος ("grapevine") and ἀμπελῶν ("vineyard").
113. Stapleton 1885, 23.
114. Matt. 20:1–8; 21:28, 33, 39–41; Mark 12:1–2, 8–9; Luke 13:6; 20:9–16.
115. Matt. 26:29; Mark 14:25; Luke 22:18.
116. See also Matt. 7:16–18.
117. Ropes 1916, 243; Gen. 14:3; Num. 34:3, 12; Deut. 3:17; Josh. 15:2, 5.
118. Hiebert 1979, 225. But in Ezekiel's vision, sweet water from the temple transforms the Dead Sea into fresh water (Ezek. 47:8–10).

the question pointedly: what kind of water are we? Or, what kind of wisdom do we demonstrate in our actions?

True Wisdom Is Reflected in a Life of Good Deeds (3:13–18)

James now raises the key question for his many want-to-be teachers: "Who is wise and learned among you?" The question applies to all who seek wisdom (1:5–8) and all who claim to have knowledge. James then answers his own question: "Let him/her show out of good conduct his/her actions characterized by gentle wisdom" (3:13). What is God's understanding of learning or learning's true measure? "Let [the truly wise and learned] show out of good conduct his/her actions characterized by gentle wisdom" (3:13).

"**Wise**" and "learned" often appear together as a pleonasm, two ideas that are synonyms,[119] yet their meanings are not identical. Both terms indicate experts who are learned, but "wise" emphasizes the practical effect of the knowledge.[120]

James began his letter with the topic of wisdom (1:5). The wise and generous God can give it to the person who asks with confidence that God can provide it. Such wise people are quick to hear and slow to speak. They act on God's word (1:19–25) and control what they say (1:26), so that their resultant actions lead to God-pleasing actions (3:2–12). Such wisdom is "gentle" or humble (πραΰτης, 3:13), coming down from God who is "above," not from below, where the evil one dwells (3:15). James characterizes the wise as pure, peaceable, reasonable, persuadable, full of mercy and good fruits, not partial, not hypocritical, and righteous (3:17–18). They do not have bitter jealousy and self-centeredness in their hearts; they do not boast against and lie against the truth; they are not earthly, worldly, nor demonic (3:14–15). In the New Testament, the wise are contrasted with infants and the foolish.[121] They are comparable with scribes, debaters, the powerful, those of noble birth, and judges.[122] They use their time well, doing God's will (Eph. 5:15–17).

Jesus was called "master" (ἐπιστάτης), as was Apollos, David, and the leaders of the Hebrew tribes.[123] "**Learned**" (ἐπιστήμων

---

119. E.g., Deut. 1:13, 15; Isa. 5:21; Sir. 21:15.
120. Hiebert defines the Jewish wise person as someone "who possessed moral insight and skill in deciding practical issues of conduct" (1979, 227).
121. Matt. 11:25; Luke 10:21; Rom. 1:14, 22.
122. 1 Cor. 1:20, 26–27; 3:18; 6:5.
123. Luke 5:5; 8:24, 45; 9:33, 49; 17:13.

[noun], ἐπίσταμαι [verb]) emphasizes "experts" in a field[124] who use their minds to understand facts. For example, Apollos had been instructed in Christianity and had taught accurately, but he was not fully "learned" since he *knew* only about John's baptism. Priscilla and Aquila had to teach him more information about baptism by the Holy Spirit (Acts 18:25–26). The merchant who made business plans was limited (ἐπίσταμαι) because he did not have the facts about what would happen tomorrow (James 4:14). Many facts are mentioned using the verb (ἐπίσταμαι), for example: Cornelius knew that Jews could not visit Gentiles (Acts 10:28), silversmiths knew they got their wealth from selling Artemis's trinkets (Acts 19:25), the Ephesians knew how Paul lived among them (Acts 20:18), Jews knew that Paul used to imprison Christians (Acts 22:19), and Paul knew Governor Felix had been a judge (Acts 24:10).

We often trust what people say about their own and others' character and accomplishments. However, wise and learned people do not demonstrate their wisdom and knowledge by speaking about themselves, according to James, but rather by their behavior (3:13). They exhibit or show something that can be apprehended by one or more of the senses.[125] For example, earlier James explained that genuine faith is demonstrated by actions (2:18). He repeats the same principle, but now it is knowledge and wisdom that are exhibited by actions (3:13). The word order in 3:13b emphasizes the origin of the action: "Let show *out of* good conduct actions" (ἀναστροφή). Normally, the sentence would read: "Let show [his] actions out of good conduct in gentle wisdom." Two prepositional phrases modify the verb "let show" (δείκνυμι), "out of [ἐκ] good conduct," contrasting with "in [ἐν] gentle wisdom." Ἐκ indicates "from within," the origin, while ἐν indicates the present sphere or accompanying circumstance.[126]

"**Conduct**" (ἀναστροφή, 3:13) is one's mode of life or behavior or "walk."[127] It can be good or bad.[128] Paul describes his previous *way of life* in Judaism: "I was violently persecuting the church of God and was trying to destroy it" (Gal. 1:13 NRSV). "Conduct" is not normally speech, but accompanying action: "Set the believers an example in speech, in *conduct*, in love, in faith, in purity" (1 Tim. 4:12). Peter warns Christian wives to win over their non-Christian husbands "without a

---

124. BDAG, 381; Thayer, 248. They "stand" (ἵστημι) "above" (ἐπί) others.
125. Δείκνυμι, BDAG, 214.
126. Robertson 1934, 596, 588–89; Hiebert 1979, 227.
127. Thayer, 42.
128. E.g., Eph. 2:3 (ἀναστρέφω); 4:22; 1 Pet. 1:18.

word," but instead with pure and reverent "conduct" or behavior alone (1 Pet. 3:1–2). "Actions" (ἔργον) are synonymous with "conduct" (e.g., 1 Pet. 1:17). "Actions" (ἔργον) may be a broader term than "conduct" (ἀναστροφή), since ἔργον may include speech (James 1:4; 2:17–25), but ἀναστροφή does not normally. In 3:13, James says that actions (ἔργον) come from the basis of a good way of life (ἀναστροφή).

The second modifying prepositional phrase of "let show" (δείκνυμι) is "characterized by gentle wisdom" (3:13).[129] Any wisdom from God would be **"gentle"** since God is gentle (πραΰτης). Jesus is "gentle," as were Moses and David.[130] Πραΰτης (πραότης)[131] describes the way to receive the implanted word (1:21). If the word is planted by the Father of lights, then believers must be humble because their new life is not due to their own efforts. The adjective (πραΰς [πρᾶος]) may refer to a soft sound as opposed to an angry response. It also may refer to a bridle that tames or makes a horse mild or to taming wild animals.[132] It is an apt word to allude to James's earlier discussion. Here wisdom is "tamed." It can describe a certain type of wisdom, a tamed one (genitive of description), or what wisdom should produce, gentleness (subjective genitive).[133] If in 1:21 James describes the way to receive God's implanted word—in humility—now, in 3:13, he describes the way to do wisdom: in humility. This foreshadows the end of the chapter: "taming" people by making peace between them (3:17–18). When one "tames" oneself, only then can one "tame" others. In contrast, many Hellenistic writers saw meekness and humility as vices.[134] The church James speaks to sometimes seems to be taking their advice, seeking pugnacious leaders,[135] not humble ones who seek peace and resist being "overly impressed" by a sense of their own "self-importance."[136]

The importance of actions as a reflection of genuine wisdom is described by other (later) Jewish leaders. For example, Rabbi Hanina ben Dosa (active c. AD 80–120) said: "He whose works exceed his wisdom,

---

129. McCartney (2009, 198–99) suggests that "gentle" should modify "wisdom."
130. Num. 12:3; Ps. 131:1.
131. LSJ, 1461.
132. LSJ, 1459.
133. Moo (2015, 168) takes "wisdom" as a genitive of source: deeds "that demonstrate wisdom are to be *done in the humility that comes from wisdom.*" Adam agrees: "gentleness that comes from wisdom" (2013, 71).
134. Laws 1980, 160; Davids 1982, 150.
135. Cf. 1 Tim. 3:2–71.
136. BDAG, 861.

his wisdom endures; but he whose wisdom exceeds his works, his wisdom does not endure" (m. 'Abot 3:10). Rabbi Eleazar ben Azariah (c. AD 50–120), reflecting on Jeremiah 17:7–8, commented: "He whose works are more abundant than his wisdom" is like "a tree whose branches are few but whose roots are many; so that even if all the winds in the world come and blow against it, it cannot be stirred from its place" (m.' Abot 3:18). These rabbis have contrasted wisdom with works, as opposed to James who says wisdom should be accompanied by actions. James hearkens back to the true teacher who walked with the Lord "in integrity and uprightness, and he turned many from iniquity" (Mal. 2:6 NRSV).

In 3:14–16, James mentions the opposite of genuine wisdom: "But, if you have bitter jealousy and self-centeredness in your heart, do not boast against and lie against the truth. That wisdom is not the one from above coming down but that wisdom is earthly, worldly, demonic. For where there is jealousy and self-centeredness, there is restlessness and every evil deed." James's technique throughout the letter is regularly to contrast positive and negative illustrations and commands.

What to Do versus What Not to Do	
Positive	Negative
1:2–5	1:6–11
1:12	1:13–15
1:16–18	1:19–24
1:25	1:26
1:27	2:1–20
2:21–3:4	3:5–12
3:13	3:14–16
3:17–18	

James emphasizes the direct object ("bitter jealousy") by placing it before the verb ("you have," 3:14).[137] As well, he emphasizes the entire conditional clause ("if you have bitter jealousy and self-centeredness in your heart") by placing it before the main clause ("do not boast against and lie against the truth," 3:14). Thus, the readers, as they listen to the

---

137. See also Hiebert 1979, 229.

letter, must first include (or not include) themselves in the "if" clause,[138] asking, Do I have "bitter jealousy"? Do I have "self-centeredness" in my heart? "Heart" is singular, while "your" is plural, implying that these negative traits are both individual and relational.

"**Jealousy** and self-centeredness" (3:14), a pair of synonyms (pleonasm), contrasts with "wise and learned" (another parallel pair of synonyms, 3:13). "Jealousy and self-centeredness" will be repeated again in 3:16, further defined by the following pair of synonyms, "restlessness and every evil deed" (3:16). Ζῆλος, its literal base being "to be heated or to boil,"[139] can be good or bad. It always includes intense feelings.[140] In that sense, ζῆλος hearkens back to the tongue as "fire" (3:5–6). Zeal can be good if it is zeal to do good and to be pure.[141] God is a zealous or "jealous" God because God accepts worship only to himself. God is not syncretistic. God is holy and thus a "consuming fire."[142] But this same "heat," zeal, or ardor can be directed not to pursue good but to pursue evil. God wants what belongs to him (2 Cor. 11:2). When people want what belongs to others, that becomes "envy" or covetousness.[143] The last of the Ten Commandments, not to covet what belongs to our neighbor, is a counterpart to the first two commandments, to worship only the one true God (Exod. 20:2–6, 17). In the same way, adultery and stealing are wanting and acquiring what is not ours (Exod. 20:14–15). In the New Testament, much "jealousy" or "envy" was directed at the apostles for attracting large followings (e.g., Acts 5:16–18; 13:44–45; 17:4–5). Those who are envious then seek to harm those they envy. The patriarchs also were jealous of Jacob's praise of Joseph and, therefore, sought to kill him (Acts 7:9). The apostle Paul had a similar problem at the church in Corinth as James had with his readers. At Corinth, jealousy resulted in the believers pitting one leader against another, rather than seeing them all as cooperating in different ways in the same venture (1 Cor. 3:3–13). Jealousy was occurring among the dispersed "twelve tribes," but James's letter does not mention leadership competition. Paul

---

138. The subordinate clause is a first-class condition, assuming the reality of the condition.
139. Ζῆλος ("zeal"), ζηλόω ("be zealous"), ζηλωτής ("one who is zealous")—Thayer, 271; Ropes 1916, 245.
140. BDAG, 427.
141. E.g., 2 Cor. 9:2; Titus 2:14; 1 Pet. 3:13.
142. Exod. 20:5; Deut. 4:24; 5:9; 6:15; Josh. 24:19; Ps. 69:9; John 2:17.
143. See also m. 'Abot 5:10.

also called envy a worldly action, in the same category as fighting, boasting, and arrogance.[144]

James modifies "jealousy" with the adjective "bitter" (3:14), the same adjective used in 3:11. In 3:11, πικρός, which symbolizes "cursing" as opposed to "blessing," contrasts with "sweet" water that is healthy. Thus, this type of jealousy induces harm (death and illness) to those imbibing it. It is not God's pure "jealousy."

Ἐριθεία may signify "strife," "contentiousness," "**selfishness**," or "selfish ambition" (3:14). For Aristotle, ἐριθεία was the self-seeking pursuit of political office by unfair means.[145] It often appears in the New Testament in the same category as jealousy, anger, and fighting.[146] It is synonymous with causing trouble, rejecting the truth, and following evil (Rom. 2:8; Phil. 1:17). Paul defines the opposite as love, humility, and not considering oneself and one's own interests as more important than the interests of others (Phil. 2:3–4). In James 3:14, self-centeredness, selfish ambition, and self-seeking would fit the meaning well since those feelings begin in the "heart," the inner part of oneself,[147] and then erupt out into negative words and actions.

When "envy" (ζῆλος) combines with "self-centeredness" (ἐριθεία), boasting against (or exulting over) and lying against the truth is the result (3:14). Mercy is superior and more powerful than ("triumphs over") judgment (2:13), but people who are jealous and self-seeking must not triumph over or exult over (κατακαυχάομαι) the truth. What is the "truth" here? If what they are doing does not please God, then the truth is that their actions are *not* from above, but rather are from below (3:15). This "truth" represents the "facts of the case" (e.g., Mark 5:33).[148] These facts are that genuine wisdom is displayed by good conduct accompanied by gentle wisdom (3:13),[149] the kind of wisdom that grows from the Father's implanted "word of truth" (1:18).

James adds a beautiful image that God's wisdom comes down "**from above**" (3:17–18) in contrast to another source of wisdom that does *not* come down from above (3:15). He emphasizes "not" by moving the subject ("that wisdom") after the verb "is." This implies that some readers may have thought the behavior that James characterizes as "bitter

---

144. 1 Cor. 3:3–4; 2 Cor. 12:20; Gal. 5:20.
145. BDAG, 392.
146. E.g., 2 Cor. 12:20; Gal. 5:20.
147. See also Vlachos 2013, 122.
148. Mayor 1913, 128; Hiebert 1979, 230–31.
149. Laws 1980, 160–61; Martin 1988, 131; Painter and deSilva 2012, 130; Moo 2015, 169–70.

jealousy and self-centeredness" (3:14) was "wise." The verb for jealousy (ζηλόω, verb; ζῆλος, noun) occurs again in 4:2, suggesting that at least the materialistic desires of chapter 4 are illustrations of the type of conduct James repudiates. James then describes "the wisdom from above coming down": what it is not (3:15–16) and what it is (3:17–18). The image of "from above coming down" has appeared earlier in the letter when describing the perfect gifts from the Father of lights. The same word for "above" (ἄνωθεν) appears in 1:17 and 3:15, while synonyms for "coming down" appear in both verses (καταβαίνω, κατέρχομαι, 1:17; 3:15). One such gift is "wisdom," for which James has already exhorted the listeners to ask (1:5–8). God's gifts are from "above" (ἄνωθεν),[150] which is a euphemism for God's presence,[151] and not from within, from the heart (1:14; 3:14), or from below, which are sources of what is "earthly, worldly, demonic" (3:15). The earlier image (see 1:17–18) alludes to a sun-shower. The blessing of rain falls down from above, while at the same time the sun or moon is shining. A present participle is used in both verses ("coming down), which indicates that God's wisdom is continuous, since its source is outside of one, "above" humans who are lower.[152] God is a generous God (1:5) who never holds back on wisdom.

In contrast, in 3:15, the source of "jealousy and self-centeredness" is "earthly, worldly, demonic."[153] The three synonyms have increasingly negative connotations.[154] Ἐπίγειος ("**earthly**"), a combination of "upon" (ἐπί) and "earth" (γῆ), may simply refer to the earth as opposed to heaven,[155] but for James the context clearly is negative (and metaphorical), as in Philippians 3:19, "the ones thinking about *earthly things*," who are "enemies of the cross of Christ" (Phil. 3:18). This type of wisdom is not heavenly.

If ἐπίγειος refers to the earth (γῆ), ψυχικός refers to life ("**worldly**," 3:15). Ψυχικός comes from ψυχή, "life, earthly life," and alludes to Genesis 2:7, where God breathed on the formed dust of the earth "the breath of life and the human became a living being" (ψυχὴν ζῶσαν).[156]

---

150. Literally, a higher place, or the top, e.g., Matt. 27:51; Mark 15:38; John 19:23.
151. James 1:17; John 3:3, 7, 31; 19:11.
152. Thayer, 339.
153. This is an asyndeton, a list not ending with "and," thus creating a never-ending sequence. Since the three words are synonyms, they are also a pleonasm.
154. See also Ropes 1916, 248; Hiebert 1979, 231.
155. E.g., John 3:12; 1 Cor. 15:40; Phil. 2:10.
156. See also James 1:8; Acts 20:10; 1 Cor. 15:45.

Thayer defines ψυχή as "the breath of life, the vital force which animates the body and shows itself in breathing."[157] BDAG defines the adjective ψυχικός as pertaining "to the life of the natural world and whatever belongs to it, in contrast to the realm of experience whose central characteristic" is "spirit" (πνεῦμα).[158] Thus, ψυκικός may simply refer to what is perishable and physical as opposed to what is imperishable or spiritual (1 Cor. 15:44–46). But Paul and Jude also define the "natural" or "worldly" person as one who does not possess God's Spirit and is therefore not able to understand spiritual things (1 Cor. 2:14; Jude 19). For Paul, such a person has received the "spirit of the world" (πνεῦμα τοῦ κόσμου), words taught by human wisdom (1 Cor. 2:1, 12–13). James would describe such a person as a "friend of the world" (φιλία τοῦ κόσμου) but an enemy of God (4:4), someone "worldly" and not "spiritual" (3:15).

The third synonym is clearly negative ("**demonic**," δαιμονιώδης, 3:15)[159] and suggests that the source of wisdom is "hell" (3:6), a euphemism for the devil (4:7). James has mentioned "demons" already in 2:19 as those who know that God is one. Demons also knew who Jesus was when he was on earth—the Holy One of God, the Son of God, the Messiah.[160] For ancient Greeks, demons (or "daemons") were semidivine beings, spirits, or higher powers who might even be worshiped.[161] But for New Testament writers, demons are always evil, malignant, malevolent, unclean, deceitful, and hostile.[162] The Gospels have numerous references to persons who want demons to be cast out.[163] To cast them out is part of the apostolic mission, including also to heal the sick, raise the dead, cleanse the lepers and, of course, preach about God's reign.[164] Demons possessed people, resulting in human harm. For example, one boy suffered greatly, being cast into fire and water (Matt. 17:15–18; Luke 9:39). An adult man lived naked in the tombs, seized by demons with extraordinary strength (Luke 8:27–29). Demons were understood by Jesus and the ancient Jews as coming from Satan (Luke 11:15–20). Demons could do impressive signs and encourage their own

---

157. Thayer, 677.
158. BDAG, 1100. See also Hiebert 1979, 232.
159. Δαιμονιώδης is a combination of δαιμόνιον plus εἶδος, signifying "resembling or proceeding from an evil spirit" (Thayer, 124).
160. E.g., Mark 1:34; Luke 4:34, 41; 8:28.
161. E.g., Acts 17:18; Rev. 9:20; BDAG, 210.
162. BDAG, 210; James 3:16; Luke 4:33.
163. E.g., Matt. 7:22; 9:32–34; 12:24–28; 17:15–18.
164. Matt. 10:8; Mark 3:14–15; Luke 9:1–2.

teachings (1 Tim. 4:1; Rev. 16:14). James suggests that the wisdom his readers were proposing came at some point from such messengers of Satan. They were harmful and so was their "wisdom."

How can one recognize the presence of such wisdom? It is located wherever there is "jealousy and self-centeredness." In the same place will be found "restlessness and every evil deed" (3:16). Ὅπου ("where") and ἐκεῖ ("there") are both adverbs denoting place.[165]

"**Restlessness**" (ἀκαταστασία, 3:16) and "restless" were already used in James several times (see 1:8; 3:8), referring to a beastlike quality wreaking havoc wherever it goes. It causes evil deeds. What kind of evil deeds has James mentioned outside of jealousy and self-centeredness? Accusing God of tempting one instead of taking responsibility for one's own evil desires (1:13–15), anger (1:19), not doing God's word (1:22–23), partiality to the rich (2:1–9), lack of mercy (2:13), not caring for the poor (2:15–16), and not bridling the tongue (3:2–8).

In the center of his letter, closing this section on wisdom (1:5–8, 19–26; 3:1–18), James tells the readers in detail what qualities characterize the wisdom from above: "But the from above wisdom, on the one hand, first is pure, then peaceable, reasonable, persuadable, full of mercy and good fruits, not partial, not hypocritical. Then a fruit of righteousness in peace is sown by the ones doing peace" (3:17–18). The "from above" wisdom has eight characteristics that flow down from God's presence, beginning with **purity**. Water is pure when it comes from above, external to oneself. If it were not pure, it would sully all the rest of the contents.[166] By the time it reaches the fifth characteristic, the rainfall overflows ("*full of* mercy") and a harvest of "good **fruits**" is growing (3:17). "Fruits" is plural because emphasis is on the product of good gifts (1:17) with its many manifestations. The final verse (3:18) summarizes James's key point, while continuing the imagery of farming. "**Righteousness**" is the final harvest from above, but done in cooperation with humans and the manner of sowing. The sower has to be doing peace and sowing in a peaceful manner: "a fruit . . . in peace is sown by the ones doing peace" (3:18). All these activities and characteristics contrast with the earlier ones described in 3:14–16 and 3:6: being righteous instead of unrighteous; purifying instead of defiling; building up instead of being destructive; being truthful instead of false; acting mercifully instead of jealously, heavenly instead

---

165. Ἐκεῖ refers "to a position in the immediate vicinity" (BDAG, 301, 717).
166. The rabbinic laws agreed that a liquid poured out from a clean to an unclean vessel does not serve as a connective making the upper vessel unclean (m. Maks. 5:9).

of earthly, generously instead of selfishly, humbly instead of boastfully, godly instead of demonic, and peaceably instead of pugnaciously; and producing good instead of evil.

"**Pure**" (ἁγνός, 3:17) may relate to sexual purity (e.g., 4 Macc. 18:7–8), worship of only one God (e.g., 2 Cor. 11:2–3; 4 Macc. 5:37), not sinning with others (1 Tim. 5:22), and resembling purity of metals, as in Psalm 12:6: "The words of the Lord are pure words, as silver tried in the fire, proved in a furnace of earth, purified seven times." God is pure, without any evil (1 John 3:3). Purity itself has no evil. In contrast to the tongue, purity does not defile (James 3:6; 4 Macc. 5:37). It is like sweet water that brings health and life (3:12).[167] It is unadulterated with selfish ambition or self-seeking (James 3:16; Phil. 1:17). Thus, the fount of wisdom from above is God's own purity or holiness.

Then James follows with four qualities, all beginning with the same letter, epsilon, and the first three in alphabetical order: ἔπειτα ("then") εἰρηνική, ἐπιεικής, εὐπειθής . . . ἐλέους ("peaceable, reasonable, persuadable . . . mercy," 3:17). After a break in the rhythm ("full of mercy and good fruits"), James continues with another alliteration, three qualities that begin with alpha, in alphabetical order: ἀγαθῶν, ἀδιάκριτος, ἀνυπόκριτος ("good . . . , not partial, not hypocritical," 3:17). What is the function of the alliteration and asyndeton (not having "and" at the end of the series)? Possibly, the repetition of sound sounds like the blessing of rain slowly dripping down, since these qualities are all of the same nature. James as a teacher created a verse easy to memorize.[168]

The adjective "pure" is followed by another adjective, "**peaceable**" (3:17). There can be no peace with self-centeredness or jealousy. Εἰρηνικός ("peaceable") comes from εἰρήνη ("peace"),[169] an important Hebrew concept. "Peace be with you" was a common greeting.[170] At a literal level, "peace" is the opposite of fighting. For example, a king who cannot defeat his enemy will send a delegation and ask for the terms of peace (Luke 14:31–32). Someone who is "peaceable" stops people fighting, as Moses attempted between two Israelites: "Men, you are brothers; why do you wrong each other?" (Acts 7:26 NRSV).[171] But "peace" can be much more. When the poor are fed and clothed, then indeed they are given "peace" (James 2:16). When the sick, physically and

---

167. E.g., Ezek. 47:8–10; Matt. 5:3–10.
168. See also Blomberg and Kamell 2008, 175.
169. Robertson 1933, 47.
170. E.g., Matt. 10:12–13; Luke 24:36; John 14:27; 20:21, 26.
171. See also Acts 12:20; 24:2.

spiritually, are healed, then, indeed, they can be sent off in "peace."[172] Jesus accomplished the archetypal peacemaking act through his blood on the cross (Col. 1:20). James brought peace between the warring parties at the Jerusalem council on the issue of how to "purify" Gentiles by allowing each faction to speak, hearkening back to the Old Testament basis for Gentile conversion, working with this group in its decision-making process, and coming out with a consensus—in this case, a compromise of behavior required for the newly converted Gentiles in order not to offend fellowship with Jews. This agreement was then circulated and communicated with the rest of the church (Acts 15:1–33). Afterward, there was peace. The reason jealousy and self-centeredness cannot result in peace is because others' interests are not affirmed and others' gifts are not welcomed (3:16). Of course, one cannot have peace if one is not making peace oneself. James in 3:17–18 alludes to Jesus's Sermon on the Mount: "Blessed are the peacemakers, for they will be called children of God" (Matt. 5:9 NRSV).

The third characteristic is ἐπιεικής ("**reasonable**," 3:17). Two different meanings have been found, but they can be reconciled. In the New Testament, ἐπιεικής appears to signify "gentle" in contrast to quarrelsome and violent, such as in 1 Timothy 3:3 ("not pugnacious, but *gentle*, not contentious").[173] It is a synonym of πραΰτης ("gentle, humble"),[174] the way one should receive the implanted word, and the type of wisdom a learned person should have. It is a synonym of "mercy" and, like the other qualities, descriptive of God.[175]

Ἐπιεικής can refer to the opposite of δίκαιος and, therefore, "not according to the letter of the law," "reasonable," "not insisting on every right of letter of law or custom," "tolerant," "yielding."[176] Ἐπιείκεια and ἐπιεικής may be defined as "a fairness that corrects anything that might be odious or unjust in the strict application of the letter of the law."[177] How might these two meanings coalesce? The type of gentleness in the New Testament is one that opposes the quarrelsome nature that always insists on its own way. It is not yielding to evil or

---

172. E.g., Mark 5:34; Luke 7:50; 8:48.
173. See also Titus 3:2 and 1 Pet. 2:18.
174. James 3:13; 1:21; 2 Cor. 10:1.
175. Ps. 85[86]:5 LXX; 2 Macc. 10:4.
176. LSJ, 632; BDAG, 371.
177. *TLNT* 2, 35. For example, the NIV, JB, and REB translate it "considerate," while the NRSV, KJV, ESV, CEB, NLT, TEV, and CEV translate it "gentle." "Respect for the feelings of others, being willing to wave all rigor and severity in its dealings with others" (Hiebert 1979, 235).

to force, but rather to the intention of the law, because sometimes pushing the letter of the law can undermine its intention. It is "reasonable." For example, one judge in court required a man I knew who was engaged in drinking to attend Alcoholics Anonymous meetings for a few months. Instead, the defendant decided to attend a full year of an Adult and Teen Challenge program. He did much more than the judge wanted. The defending lawyer explained that he was fulfilling the *intention* of the judge's ruling, which was not the letter of his ruling but much more effective.

The fourth quality of the wisdom from above is that it is "**persuadable**" or "compliant" (εὐπειθής, 3:17). Ceslas Spicq summarizes, "It refers not to passive obedience but to an inclination to accept suggestions and conform to them willingly." He adds, it includes a willingness to be convinced or persuaded without any compulsion.[178] For example, Paul tells King Agrippa that he was "*not disobedient* to the heavenly vision" (ἀπειθής, Acts 26:19). It is a good type of persuasion[179] or a willing obedience, in James's context, to God's commands.[180]

Peaceable, reasonable, and persuadable—how might these three qualities fit this letter? First, they are a further explanation of what is entailed in a "gentle wisdom" (3:13). It is peaceable, reasonable, and persuadable. Second, these qualities hearken back to many comments already stated in the letter, such as: a wise person must be willing to ask for wisdom (1:5), be compliant and trusting of God (1:6), be humble in respect to themselves (1:9, 13, 19–20), be humble toward God (1:17–18), be willing to change (1:21, 24–25), be willing to treat others well (1:27–2:4, 15–16), be merciful (2:13), and be tamable (3:8).

The rhythm of the verse (three parallel words) is broken by the next phrase (a pleonasm) ("full of **mercy** and good fruits"). It is as if the dripping rainfall has now gathered together and filled up with "mercy and good fruits" (3:17). James has already mentioned the importance of mercy in 2:13, involving good will toward the poor and afflicted and repentant persons. If one receives one's wisdom from above, then one will be thoroughly filled with the characteristic of mercy. Mercy is an important quality in this letter, one that was lacking in the readers who were not merciful in their treatment of the poor. Mercy was also important to Jesus, who challenged the scribes and Pharisees not to neglect the "weightier matters of the law: justice and mercy and faithfulness" (Matt. 23:23).

---

178. *TLNT* 2, 130.
179. Εὖ ("good") and πείθω ("persuade") (Robertson 1933, 47).
180. See also Titus 1:16.

"**Good fruits**" (3:17) summarizes the main purpose of the letter: "The twelve tribes in the dispersion, having laid aside all evil deeds, should receive in humility the implanted word." Doers of the implanted word reflect their faith in good actions. James also refers to "good conduct" (ἀναστροφή) in 3:13 and to "firstfruits" (ἀπαρχή) in 1:18. Believers are a firstfruit producing fruits. "Fruit" (καρπός) may refer literally to the harvest of seeds or trees or of crops in general,[181] as James had referred earlier to the fruits from a variety of trees (figs, olives, grapes, 3:12). Or, "fruit" may refer to a metaphor. Jesus used similar illustrations in his own communications: "Every good [ἀγαθός] tree bears good fruit [καρπός], but the bad tree bears bad fruit. A good tree cannot bear bad fruit, nor can a bad tree bear good fruit" (Matt. 7:17–18 NRSV). Also, he said, some seed fell into "the good [ἀγαθός] earth and when it grew, it produced a crop [καρπός] a hundred times as much" (Luke 8:8). Jesus explains the latter parable: "The seed on good soil stands for those with a noble and good [ἀγαθός] heart, who hear the word, retain it, and by persevering produce a crop [καρποφορέω]" (Luke 8:15 NIV). That verse summarizes James's whole letter and in particular the phrase "good fruits." "Fruit" or "fruits" was often used metaphorically of deeds, the visible evidence of a life.[182] This visible evidence, James specifies, must be "good" (ἀγαθός), the same adjective used earlier of "gifts" from the Father of lights (1:17).

James then continues with the pouring down of the last two qualities that describe the wisdom from above: "**not partial** [ἀδιάκριτος], not hypocritical [ἀνυπόκριτος]" (3:17). Both begin and end with the same two components: "not"[183] and κρίνω ("to judge"). A κριτής is a "judge." Judgment is a major theme in this letter.[184] It addresses faith and doubt (1:6) and treatment of the poor and wealthy (2:4, 6, 12–13) and of others in general (4:11–12), and eventually centers on judgment by God (2:12–13; 3:1; 5:9, 12). Judging is something teachers must do

---

181. Matt. 13:8; 21:19, 34, 41; Mark 11:14; Luke 12:17; 1 Cor. 9:7; 2 Tim. 2:6.
182. E.g., "fruits" are a sign of a repentant life (Matt. 3:8; Luke 3:8–9), show the "fruits of the kingdom" (Matt. 21:43) or of the Spirit (Gal. 5:22–23), come from following Jesus (John 12:24–26; 15:1–8, 16), or reveal a false prophet (Matt. 7:15–16).
183. A privative gives a negative sense to the word to which it is prefixed (Thayer, 1; Robertson 1933, 47).
184. The word family (κρίνω ["I judge"], κριτής ["judge"], κρίμα ["judgment"], κρίσις ["judgment"], κριτήριον ["court"], διακρίνω ["I judge"], ἀδιάκριτος ["without partiality"], ἀνυπόκριτος ["genuine"]) occurs in 1:6; 2:4, 6, 12, 13; 3:1, 17; 4:11, 12; 5:9, 12. See also discussion under 2:4.

as they evaluate their students. Judges must "differentiate" (διακρίνω) and express opinions or pass judgments (κρίνω) upon the lives and actions of other people.[185] In these two final adjectives, James tells his readers not to make judgments of two different kinds. The first word ἀδιάκριτος is composed of ἀ plus διακρίνω (διακρίνω may be found in 1:6 and 2:4). Διακρίνω basically signifies to choose between two options. In 2:4, someone chooses between the poor and wealthy, but makes a choice not commensurate with God's values. Interpreters have leaned toward one or the other verse as background for their translation of ἀδιάκριτος in 3:17, someone who does *not* διακρίνω: "not being uncertain, unwavering"[186] (relates to 1:6) or "not being judgmental or divisive, nonjudgmental, not divisive, impartial" (relates to 2:4).[187] Is the meaning "unwavering" or "impartial"? The most likely sense of the word in 3:17, I think, is "without partiality," "impartial," or "without distinction."[188] It is the more common meaning at its time and is a close synonym to some of the other words in the verse—peaceable (not discriminating), merciful, and truthful (not hypocritical)—and it contrasts with the major theme of partiality in chapter 2.

The second word (ἀνυπόκριτος, **"not hypocritical,"** 3:17) has three components: ἀ ("not") plus ὑπό ("under") and κρίνω ("to judge") or ἀ ("not") plus ὑποκρίνομαι ("to impersonate any one, play a part," "pretend").[189] Ὑποκριτής is a "stage-player," especially the Greek comic player, "pretender, hypocrite."[190] "Hypocrite" is a word Jesus frequently used to name the religious leaders who pretended to be genuinely interested in his message, but in reality were out to find reasons to harm him (Matt. 22:18). The term also describes those who appeared to be one way outside, but were different inside. To others they appear righteous, but in reality they are evil (Matt. 23:28). They might give, pray, or fast simply so others would see and approve them (Matt. 6:2, 5, 16). They would have different criteria for judging themselves versus

185. BDAG, 231, 567.
186. E.g., NASB; Ropes 1916, 250; McCartney 2009, 202; *TDNT* 3, 950.
187. BDAG, 19. E.g., "without partiality, and without hypocrisy," KJV; "fair," CEB; "shows no favoritism," NLT; "free from prejudice," TEV, NRSV, NIV, JB, ESV, and HCSB.
188. *TLNT* 1, 134; LSJ, 22.
189. Kohlenberger, Goodrick, and Swanson 1995, 86; Thayer, 52, 643; Robertson 1933, 47.
190. Ὑπόκρισις is the "acting of a stage-player" or "hypocrisy" (Thayer, 643; *TLNT* 1, 134).

judging others.[191] Their words were false (1 Tim. 4:2). In other words, their pretense did not further God's kingdom. James has written in chapter 3 about taming the tongue. One way to tame it is to have one's words (and actions) be truthful and loving.[192] James would certainly not want his readers to pretend to have gentle wisdom or to affirm a counterfeit wisdom (3:13, 15).

The final harvest ("fruit") turns out to be "righteousness"[193] (3:18). Δέ ("then") connects verse 18 with verse 17 as the climax of what comes from above.[194] **"Fruit"** (καρπός) is collective.[195] It is singular because it has only one seed, the one from "above."[196] James emphasizes the prepositional phrase "in peace" by placing it before the verb, indicating that the manner of sowing is crucial.[197] **"Peacemakers"** (NIV) or literally "the ones doing peace" is a present active participle indicating that peacemaking is a continual process. It is not simply a title or position ("Peacemaker") but indicates one who does continuous actions promoting peace.

Righteousness (δικαιοσύνη) is another significant word family for James.[198] It is a quality of God, synonymous with holiness (1:20). "Righteousness" is the demonstration of faith through moral and just action while trusting God's good and sovereign nature (see 2:23). It includes holiness and justice. "Righteousness" summarizes all the qualities cited in 3:17. The righteous person, we will learn in 5:6, can be oppressed or persecuted by other people, as Elijah was by Ahab, but yet God rewards such a person with effective prayer (5:16–18).

---

191. Matt. 7:5; 23:13, 15, 23; Luke 6:42; 13:15.
192. See also Rom. 12:9; 2 Cor. 6:6; 1 Pet. 1:22.
193. As a genitive of quality, righteousness is the type of fruit produced or "the fruit that consists in righteousness" (Laws 1980, 165; Blomberg and Kamell 2008, 177; McCartney 2009, 203.
194. See also Blomberg and Kamell 2008, 176.
195. BDAG, 509. E.g., James 5:7, 18.
196. In both Philippians 1:11 and Hebrews 12:11, "fruit" of "righteousness" is a quality that comes later in the Christian life, as in James 3:18. It is the harvest in Hebrews that results from God's discipline and in Philippians that results from the growth of love and knowledge (Phil. 1:9). In Philippians 1:11, Jesus is the vehicle for obtaining righteousness, while in James 3:17–18 it comes from "above." See also Prov. 11:30. Cf. James 1:20; 3:14.
197. See also Hiebert 1979, 237.
198. James 1:20; 2:23; 3:18—δικαιοσύνη(noun); 5:6, 16—δίκαιος (adj.); 2:21, 24, 25—δικαιόω (verb).

THEOLOGICAL AND HOMILETICAL
TOPICS IN CHAPTER 3

The overall goal of the letter of James is for readers in humility to receive the implanted word. One way believers do not evidence an "implanted" word is by uttering worldly speech. That is why wisdom is needed (1:5–8). That may be why at the end of the letter James offers confession as a vehicle for change (5:16). So how does God measure learning? It is not by degree attained, information assimilated, big technical words learned, or by integrations or connections achieved. Rather, it is by one's life. True learning is the ability to use or restrain speech and to integrate speech and action. Education is evaluated by behavior, not by speech alone. And we need to evaluate the source of the behavior—is it earthly? We need to ask God to help us accept the truth and to give us pure gifts, flowing down like rain from above, and to remove demonic jealousy and fighting. We need to be set apart but yet be a part of the world; bringing peace because we are peacemakers; being merciful and reasonable because we have received mercy; being open to being persuaded and without favoritism because everyone is created in God's image; not intending to show off our faith but, yes, intending to show we have faith. When disorder, untruthfulness, selfishness, jealousy, and evil deeds result, in God's estimation, an educated person is a fool, a doctor of deceit. When a life like James's—famed for righteousness, good acts, and meekness—results, God is pleased. Our world desperately needs people whose learning results in a life of good actions, bringing unity because we do not disguise the truth; showing concern for others on the basis of mercy, tolerance, and lack of favoritism, where love for people supersedes love for exactness or preciseness; obeying when we too expect to be obeyed; and being gentle and genuine.

As always, James has integrated theology with practice. He has explained what not to do and what to do to be a God-pleasing teacher. This chapter is helpful for sermons or lessons to train teachers and others in a congregation, Christian college, or seminary setting. Case studies on harmful or peaceable words might help parishioners become more skilled in controlling their tongues. People who ride horses, sail boats, or serve as forest rangers can add their own personal illustrations. Prayer for inner cleansing can help. Children or artists may want to sketch the different images. The goal is to encourage oneself and others to demonstrate one's wisdom in godly actions.

BECOMING A WISE TEACHER

It is easy to agree verbally with James's exhortations, but not so easy to do. If one is honest, being a teacher who exhibits her (or his) wisdom in good conduct characterized by gentleness is rarely one of the attributes needed for promotion. Such attributes in a teacher will appeal to wise students, but many other students might instead esteem more the entertaining or contentious or easy-grading teacher. For example, even though schools in which I have taught seek faculty who are spiritually mature, competent to teach, committed to the local and global church, student-oriented, and collegial, in practice many Christian faculty and administrators have appeared to be impressed more by power to influence, ability to promote oneself while appearing humble, ability to attract many students to one's classes, and facility with scholarly lingo and names. Being different on the outside may be an asset, only if one then speaks and acts in the approved academic style. Broader academic news is filled with accusations of sexual abuse, fighting between the far right and the far left, ethnic minorities and immigrants complaining about treatment, preferred treatment of tenure-track versus part-time adjunct professors, academic favoritism to students in popular sports, and financial embezzlement.[199] Academia is not always wise and learned.

Thus, the first step the biblical teacher must take is to be willing to value what James values—no matter the cost. The cost of discipleship affects academia too. Promotions may take longer, but it is well worth receiving God's affirmation first. In one's heart, one must choose relationships over ambition.

Speaking and conduct affect many spheres of educational influence: (1) classroom and academia; (2) outsiders, such as those to whom one speaks in the community; (3) church and friends; and (4) home. The most difficult is the home, where one seeks a break from outside pressures by becoming "natural" or without any controls. In all these environments, what can one do to become more of the gentle, wise teacher whom James extols?

1. Pray each morning before one teaches that God will empower one's words so they advance God's reign, and pray that God will help oneself and one's students to grow in the virtues of James 3:17–18.

2. Make sure to take daily, weekly, and semester sabbath rests. If one is tired and stressed out, it is almost impossible to be patient, peaceable, reasonable, persuadable,

---

199. Example of issues in one newspaper: *The Chronicle of Higher Education* 64, no. 3 (Sept. 15, 2017): 3.

merciful, and impartial. Furthermore, when we tire, whatever our potential weakness is will flair up. Better to try to avoid the pitfall by the way we structure our lives. If we overwork to appeal to administrators, they will not be happy with our overstressed inefficiency, and we will not be happy either (and we also might be keeping someone else from earning a little bit of money they sorely need).

3. A study once noted that most faculty allow only one second for students to respond. If we simply wait three seconds, quieter (and international) students will have time to think and respond as well. The three-second wait is also helpful to curb one's own tongue when one is ready to criticize a student with a skillfully worded barb. The three-second wait might also help a teacher to listen to another's point of view before criticizing it.

4. Everyone must be respected, even if different. Make a point of looking for potentially gifted leaders in a variety of categories: women as well as men, persons of color as well as Caucasians, slower and quiet students as well as verbal and bright students. This is not merely "political correctness" but rather an opportunity to affirm students and faculty who may have different styles but important gifts for God's kingdom. A quiet student who appears unimpressive from a hardly known country might be very bright and able to go back to that country and reach hundreds of unreached nonbelievers.

5. Education involves criticism by its very nature. Therefore, we need to complement it consciously with gentleness and tolerance.

6. Expect to be misunderstood. Teachers regularly misunderstand others; why should not students misunderstand teachers? Allow for redoings of assignments during the semester.[200] Education is more important than competition.

7. Do not evaluate your effectiveness by the achievement of other faculty. This can result in envy, not joy, when others

---

200. See W. Spencer 2014, 34–44.

achieve.[201] I have found that in every area of academic achievement, some other faculty member has done better: number of publications, number of students enrolled in classes, number of speaking engagements, salary received, and so on. And I often have felt the pull to compare myself with not just one other faculty member but with all the faculty. One can never be satisfied. Compete only with yourself; do the best you can with the time and gifts you have. Always seek to please God first and to grow in God's word implanted in you, as a unique person.

8. Yield to others' genuine concerns and God's peace, but never yield to falsehood or to any forces antithetical to God. Students and faculty may be easily inadvertently hurt. Be gentle and reasonable with them, but do not let yourself be persuaded by forces not in agreement with God's laws or kingdom.

9. Be merciful with yourself. Do not torture yourself! We all fail frequently. Our good actions do *not* justify us before God—only Jesus Christ can do that. Know that you are loved by God. In the sphere of God's approval, you can gradually work to be more skillful in pleasing God. I have taught more than forty years and expected I would get better and better. But instead, I am sad to admit, I still make new errors every year! God is a merciful God; therefore, God can be merciful with me.

---

201. 1 Cor. 12:26. As the contemporary proverb summarizes: "Comparison is the thief of joy" (attributed to Theodore Roosevelt).

JAMES 4:1-17

TRANSLATION AND GRAMMATICAL ANALYSIS[1]

4:1a Whence are wars and whence are battles among you?[2] (initial sentence; main clause)

4:1a Are they not from this: from your pleasures, the ones waging war among your members? (explanatory sentence; main clause)

4:2a You desire (explanatory sentence; main clause)

4:2b and you do not have, (main clause)

4:2c you kill (main clause)

4:2d and you are filled with jealousy (main clause)

4:2e and you are not able to obtain, (main clause)

4:2f you battle (main clause)

4:2g and you make war, (main clause)

4:2h you do not have (main clause)

---

1. See "Definition of Terms in Grammatical Analysis."
2. The compound elliptical verbs are both modified by the final "among you."

4:2i because you do not ask; (subordinate adverbial clause; causal)

4:3a you ask (explanatory sentence; main clause)

4:3b and you do not receive, (main clause)

4:3c because you ask wrongly, (subordinate adverbial clause; causal; answers why)

4:3d in order that in your pleasures you might spend. (subordinate adverbial clause; final; purpose)

4:4a Adulteresses, do you not know (explanatory sentence; main clause)

4:4b that the friendship of the world is enmity against God? (subordinate noun clause; direct object)

4:4a Therefore whoever might desire to be a friend of the world (alternative sentence; subordinate noun clause; subject)

4:4b is constituted an enemy against God. (main clause)

4:5a Or, do you think (explanatory sentence; main clause)

4:5b that to no purpose the writing says: (subordinate noun clause; direct object)

4:5c "the spirit that yearns for envy (subordinate noun clause; direct object)

4:5d settled among us," (subordinate adjectival clause; modifies "spirit")[3]

4:6a but he gives greater grace; (adversative sentence; main clause)

4:6a therefore it says: (illative sentence; main clause)

4:6b "God to [the] haughty is opposed, (subordinate noun clause; direct object)

---

3.   KJV. See exposition for other options.

4:6c but to [the] lowly gives grace.[4] (subordinate noun clause; direct object)

4:7a Therefore submit to God, (illative sentence; main clause)

4:7b but take a stand against the devil, (main clause)

4:7c and he will flee from you; (main clause)

4:8a draw near to God (alternative sentence; main clause)

4:8b and he will draw near to you. (main clause)

4:8a Cleanse hands, sinners, (alternative sentence; main clause)

4:8b and purify hearts, two-willed ones. (main clause)

4:9a Be miserable (alternative sentence; main clause)

4:9b and mourn (main clause)

4:9c and weep. (main clause)

4:9a Your laughter turn around to mourning (alternative sentence; main clause)

4:9b and joy [turn around] into gloominess. (main clause)

4:10a Be humble before the Lord (illative sentence; main clause)

4:10b and he will lift you up. (main clause)

4:11a Do not keep slandering one another, brothers and sisters. (initial sentence; main clause)

4:11a The one slandering brother or judging his brother slanders [the] law and judges [the] law;[5] (explanatory sentence; main clause)

4:11b but, if you judge [the] law, (subordinate adverbial clause; conditional)

---

4. Appears to be compound verbs with the same subject "God."
5. Compound verbs are modified by the same subordinate clause.

4:11c you are not a doer of [the] law but [you are] a judge.[6] (main clause)

4:12a One is lawgiver[7] and Judge, the One being able to save and to destroy; (explanatory sentence; main clause)

4:12b but who are you, the one judging the neighbor? (main clause)

4:13a Come now the ones saying: (initial sentence; main clause)

4:13b "Today or tomorrow we will go into such and such a city (subordinate adjectival clause; answers which "one"?)

4:13c and we will be active there a year (subordinate adjectival clause)

4:13d and we will carry on business (subordinate adjectival clause)

4:13e and we will make a profit," (subordinate adjectival clause)

4:14a which [indeed][8] you do not understand (explanatory sentence; subordinate adjectival clause)

4:14b what kind of tomorrow is your life—(main clause)

4:14c for a mist you are, the one for a little appearing, then also disappearing. (subordinate adverbial clause; causal; answers why)

4:15a Instead you should say: (adversative sentence; main clause)

4:15b "If the Lord might will (subordinate noun clause; direct object)

4:15c then we will live (subordinate noun clause)

4:15d and we will do this or that." (subordinate noun clause)

---

6. Compound verbs have the same subject.
7. There is good Alexandrian manuscript support to include the article before "lawgiver" (fourth- and fifth-century codices Sinaiticus and Alexandrinus), but omitting the article has even earlier support (third-century papyrus[100], fourth-century Vaticanus, and seventh-century papyrus[74]. The rest of the support for both variants is ninth-century and later. Thus, I have omitted the article.
8. BDAG, 729–30.

4:16a But now you boast in your arrogance; (adversative sentence; main clause)

4:16a every such boast is evil. (explanatory sentence; main clause)

4:17a Therefore knowing to do good and not doing it is sin to him. (illative sentence; main clause)

OUTLINE

IV. Lay aside fighting as the world fights; rather, humble yourself before the Lord and God will exalt you (ch. 4).
   A. Instead of fighting, which makes you God's enemy, humble yourself before the Lord (4:1–10).
   B. Fighting makes you a judge—a person who speaks evil of brothers and sisters; rather, be a doer of the law (4:11–12).
   C. Do not do business as the world does because such arrogance is inappropriate to humans whose lives are temporary and dependent on God's will (4:13–17).

LITERARY STRUCTURE

James's letter has three major themes (trials, wisdom, wealth) that interrelate with the larger theme of becoming doers of the word. James 1:21 can serve as a thesis sentence: James exhorts the twelve tribes in the dispersion, having laid aside all evil deeds, to receive in humility the implanted word. After James's extensive description of true wisdom in 3:13, 17–18, which contrasts with its opposite (3:14–16), James tackles in more detail the sinful actions that have been occurring among the dispersed Jewish Christians. In other words, he further describes "evil deeds" that need to be laid aside (1:21) and the wisdom from below that motivates them (3:15–16).[9] James 4:1–17 hearkens back to the theme of trials (1:2–4). These include avoidable "trials" from sinful internal desires (1:12–18).[10] These desires, which cause worldly fighting, can result

---

9. See also Martin 1988, 142; Blomberg and Kamell 2008, 182–83.
10. Martin (1988) relates this chapter to misuse of the tongue (derogatory words and arrogant plans). Accumulation of wealth is also a subtheme (159–63, 169–70; McKnight [2011, 359–60] describes speech ethics in 3:1–4:12. Blomberg and Kamell [2008, 203–4] relate 4:13–5:18 to trials). I have placed the whole section (4:1–17) under trials because of the connection of "desires" in 1:12–18 to the many synonyms of "desire," "pleasures," "friendship of the world," and "envy" in 4:1–5. "Slander" (4:11) does refer to misuse of the

in one becoming God's enemy. Such "evil deeds" do not help one receive the implanted word, as does humility. Fighting can also make one the wrong kind of judge, someone who speaks evil of other believers. A doer of God's law does not speak evil or falsehood against others. James 4:11–12 appears to be unrelated to what precedes it,[11] but it fits as another aspect of worldly fighting:[12] "Do not keep slandering one another, brothers and sisters" (4:11a). James explains why not to slander in the verses that follow (4:11b–12). With the imperative "come," James moves to a different but related theme (4:13), a third aspect of worldly fighting[13] and another way to speak falsehoods against others and usurp God's place: worldly planning in business (4:13–17). James's basic statement comes in verse 13, is explained in verses 14–16, and is summarized in verse 17. The group in 4:13–16 is comparable to the earlier groups described in the third person ("if *any*"): if any lacks wisdom (1:5), hears but does not do the word (1:23), thinks they are religious but does not bridle one's tongue (1:26), says that one has faith but not works (2:14), or wanders from the truth (5:19). As James does not want his readers to take God's place in judgment (4:10–12), so too he does not want them to take God's place in business practices (4:13–16).

EXPOSITION

Lay Aside Fighting as the World Fights; Rather, Humble Yourself before the Lord and God Will Exalt You (ch. 4)

Instead of Fighting, Which Makes You God's Enemy, Humble Yourself before the Lord (4:1–10)
James had previously written of trials (1:12–18). These "trials" may be called "temptations" when they come from sinful internal desires. James now returns to this theme, warning his readers of wrong desires that can result in one becoming God's enemy. Humility is the needed antidote.

James had used the imagery of a sun shower that yields a harvest for the wisdom that comes from above (3:15, 17–18; 1:17–18). In contrast,

---

tongue, and the rich merchants (4:13–17) relate to the theme of the use of wealth. Nevertheless, the cause of the difficulties is inward (desires), although it is reflected in the use of the tongue and the attitude to accumulation of wealth. See also table "Themes in James" in introduction.

11. E.g., Townsend 1994, 84.
12. See also Hiebert 1979, 266.
13. See also Hiebert 1979, 272.

he uses war to describe the wisdom from below (4:1–3; 3:14–16). To highlight the concept of "war" in the first sentence, he omits the verb ("are"—ellipsis) and repeats synonyms for "fighting" (pleonasm): "Whence [are] wars and whence [are] battles among you?" He follows with another question: "[Are they] not from this: from your pleasures, the ones waging war among your members?" (4:1). These rhetorical questions are really statements in the form of questions, so as to call forth a response from the readers. He emphasizes the interrogative adverbs "whence" (πόθεν, "from where" or "from what source")[14] by placing them first in the sentence and repeating them. What is the real source of their fights? he asks.

Images of "**war**" are developed in these verses: "wars," "battles," "waging war," "kill," "battle," "make war," "enmity," "enemy," "is opposed," "submit," "take a stand," "flee" (4:1–2, 4, 6–7).[15] Πόλεμος usually refers to "war" but also signifies "battle, fight," even of a "single combat."[16] Μάχη refers to "battle, combat," usually of armies, and the verb (μάχομαι) refers to "armies and persons fighting as parts of armies" but sometimes also to a "single combat."[17] "War" and "battle" imply communal efforts. In other words, even a single combat is enacted in the midst of a larger campaign. Similar war imagery is used elsewhere in the Bible. For example, a king about to wage war (πόλεμος) against another king will first sit down and consider whether he is able with ten thousand to oppose the other who comes against him with twenty thousand (Luke 14:31). A bugle will sound so the soldiers get ready for battle (1 Cor. 14:8). Horses can be equipped for and participate in battle (Rev. 9:7, 9). For instance, forty thousand Israelites *fought* against Jericho (Josh. 4:13). Ultimately, the battles mentioned in James 4 are instigated by the devil,[18] but James emphasizes here (4:1), as he did in 1:13–15, human responsibility: the source being human "pleasures" (4:1, 3—ἡδονή).[19]

James refers earlier to one's own **desire** (ἐπιθυμία) as the basis for temptation that leads to sin (1:14–15). In 4:1, 3, he uses a synonym (ἡδονή) to describe further the basis for fighting. Ἡδονή properly

---

14. BDAG, 838.
15. Πόλεμος, μάχη, στρατεύω, φονεύω, μάχομαι, πολεμέω, ἔχθρα, ἐχθρός, ἀντιτάσσομαι, ὑποτάσσω, ἀνθίστημι, φεύγω.
16. LSJ, 1432; BDAG, 844. Πόλεμος pictures the chronic state or campaign, while μάχη presents the separate conflicts in the war (Robertson 1933, 49; Hiebert 1979, 242).
17. LSJ, 1085. E.g., Acts 7:26.
18. James 3:15; Rev. 12:9; 13:7; 16:14; 19:19; 20:7–8.
19. Proverbs 26:20 says "With much wood fire increases; but where there is not a double-minded person [δίθυμος], strife [μάχη] ceases."

refers to "sensual pleasures," pleasures involving one's senses, such as taste or flavor,[20] or the pleasure from sleep (Wis. 7:2) or from peace (Prov. 17:1). But in the New Testament, ἡδονή is not good. James has alluded earlier to Jesus's parable of the sower (e.g., 1:18, 21; 3:17–18) and this verse too may contain a similar allusion. The seeds that fall among thorns, according to Jesus, refer to people who hear the word of God but eventually do not continue to obey the word because they get choked "by cares and riches and *pleasures* of life," and, as a consequence, their fruit does not mature (Luke 8:14). Paul describes these passions as ones that enslave, causing "malice and envy" (Titus 3:3). Peter focuses on sexual passions: "Their idea of *pleasure* is to carouse in broad daylight. . . . With eyes full of adultery, they never stop sinning; they seduce the unstable; they are experts in greed" (2 Pet. 2:13–14 NIV). Like Peter, James will refer to adultery (4:4).

To what other "pleasures" (4:1) does James refer? Later he refers to moneymaking (4:13) and riches (5:2–3), as he did earlier (1:11). Greed related to possessions may very well be where his readers may spend their resources (4:3). "Pleasure" may also refer to friendship with the world (4:4) and coveting what another has (4:2–3). Painter and deSilva remind us of the tenth commandment in Exodus 20:17: "You shall not covet."[21] Are the wars in oneself or between members of the Christian community? **"Member"** (4:1, μέλος) is primarily a "limb" of the body,[22] such as the tongue as a small member of the body (3:5–6).[23] Paul uses "member" in the context of sexual immorality, as does Jesus (1 Cor. 6:15–16; Matt. 5:27–30). "Member" can refer to one individual body (e.g., Matt. 5:29–30; Col. 3:5) or to several individuals who are part of a larger Christian community, the body of Christ.[24] Although the context of James 4 may be financial, other physical pleasures might be appropriate applications, similar to the way Paul groups together earthly passions that depend on the senses: "sexual immorality, impurity, lustful desire, evil desire, and greed, which is idolatry" (Col. 3:5).[25]

These sensual pleasures (ἡδονή) wage war (στρατεύω) among the members (4:1). Στρατεύω signifies to "advance with an army or fleet,

---

20. LSJ, 764; e.g., Num. 11:8; Wis. 16:20.
21. Painter and deSilva 2012, 137–38.
22. LSJ, 1099; BDAG, 628.
23. Other examples of "members" of the body are: eye, hand (Matt. 5:29–30); and foot, hand, ear, eye, head (1 Cor. 12:14–21).
24. E.g., 1 Cor. 6:15–16; Eph. 4:15–16, 25; 5:30.
25. "Greed" is both financial and sexual injustice. See also Eph. 5:3–5 (Spencer 2015, 33–34).

wage war," referring to "rulers, officers, or men." The army can be military or naval (στρατός).[26] For instance, two thousand of Herod's old soldiers *fought* against the king's troops (*Ant.* 17.10.4.270).

James probably refers to fighting among believers,[27] rather than simply within one individual.[28] War and battles literally are between people. "Jealousy" is also between people (4:2). How does the imagery of warfare help us understand James's intent? Warfare is destructive. It is often caused by wanting what belongs to another, as one country might want the resources in another country's borders. Warfare itself expends an enormous amount of resources, energy, and time. Wars rarely result in peace, which is James's desire (3:18). Warfare is not "gentle," and rarely reasonable, merciful, or impartial (3:13, 17). An individual desire may begin the war (1:14–15), but eventually it includes the amassing of armies to fight. Fighting is not a way to "hear" with the result of doing God's word (1:23–25).

Moreover, fighting does not bring satisfaction: "You desire and you do not have, you kill and you are filled with jealousy and you are not able to obtain, you battle and you make war, you do not have" (4:2). In contrast to 4:1, where the verb is omitted (three times, the verb "to be"), in 4:2–3a a series of present-tense verbs (12) in short main clauses is presented as descriptive of its readers. Using battle actions, they accomplish nothing. The clauses are connected by "and," making the actions of the verbs of equal importance and accentuating each. The first two clauses ("You desire and you do not have," 4:2) are parallel to the last set of clauses ("You ask and you do not receive," 4:3), creating two units. The first unit is modified by two additional sets of clauses that are parallel ("You kill and you are filled with jealousy" is parallel to "you battle and you make war," 4:2). All these actions relate to getting something, which is not obtained: "You do not have," "you are not able to obtain," "you do not have," "you do not receive" (4:2–3). What they want is unclear, but what is clear is that they covet what belongs to others.

It all begins with desire (4:1–2). Desire precedes action, is individual, and leads to sin and death. Ἐπιθυμέω (verb) and ἐπιθυμία (noun) signify to keep the θυμός (passion or strong feeling) turned upon a thing. (See 1:14–15.) When the desire does not result in possession, this person may quickly jump to murder.

"Do not **murder**" has already been mentioned (2:11) and will be repeated in 5:6. Φονεύω ("to murder," 4:2) occurs only twelve times in

---

26. LSJ, 1651, 1653.
27. See also Ropes 1916, 253; Martin 1988, 144.
28. See Laws 1980, 168; Davids 1982, 157; Tasker 1957, 85.

the New Testament,[29] as opposed to ἀποκτείνω ("to kill"), which occurs seventy-four times. Normally in the Bible, φονεύω refers to "murder" (the opposite of love of the neighbor), when someone rises up against his or her neighbor; in that case, the killer is worthy of death.[30] For example, the wicked "killed the widow and orphan and *murdered* the stranger. And they say, 'the Lord does not see'" (Ps. 94:6–7). The natives of Malta thought Paul was being punished as a murderer because a viper fastened itself on his hand (Acts 28:3–4). Peter warned his readers to suffer as Christians, not as criminals: murderers or thieves (1 Pet. 4:15). Ἀποκτείνω, on the other hand, is more general: "to kill in any way whatever," "so as to put out of the way."[31]

Certainly literal murder is included. For instance, because King Ahab wanted the ancestral home of Naboth for a vegetable garden, Queen Jezebel had Naboth falsely accused and stoned to death. The Lord accused Ahab of stealing from and murdering Naboth (1 Kings 21:1–19). But murder, according to Jesus, also includes insult and anger without cause (Matt. 5:21–22). Those whose possessions one covets can be destroyed in many ways outside of depriving them of their physical lives, such as by theft.[32] The rich who drag the poor into court and slander their names (James 2:6–7) may also steal their property. If field owners do not pay the harvester, the harvester and family may starve (5:4). Thus "murder," along with "wars" and "battles," may be figurative in the context of chapter 4. For James, though, both its literal and metaphorical senses are "evil deeds."

To murder is paired off with **jealousy** (4:2). One would surmise that jealousy would precede murder in the sentence because murder appears to be a greater destruction.[33] James has mentioned jealousy already in chapter 3. It is synonymous with self-centeredness, restlessness, and evil deeds (3:14, 16). Ζηλόω refers to intense feelings (see 3:14),

---

29. One-third (four) of the New Testament uses of φονεύω ("to murder") occur in James.
30. Num. 35:21, 30–31; Lev. 19:18; Deut. 22:26; Rom. 13:8–10; "to commit murder" (Thayer, 657). All the New Testament references are negative (φονεύω [verb], φονεύς [noun]) and most of the Old Testament references. The LXX usually employs φονεύω negatively (e.g., Neh. 4:11). It can also refer to someone accused of murder (e.g., Num. 35:6, 12, 19, 25–27). But it has some references to God-approved killing in war (Josh. 10:28, 30, 32, 35).
31. Thayer, 64.
32. E.g., Deut. 24:6; Davids 1982, 159.
33. Ropes (1916, 254) calls it "anticlimax."

here to pursue evil and to harm. People want what belongs to others. Not to covet and not to murder are two of the Ten Commandments (Exod. 20:13, 17; Deut. 5:17, 21). For someone, even murder may not be enough and jealousy may continue to harm. For example, someone might murder in order to receive an inheritance, but upon finding that only part of the inheritance was obtained the miscreant could murder more heirs. A business that covets another company's financial success might murder its CEO without appropriate punishment in a corrupt society. But, then, overtaking one business might not be enough, and more companies' key executives might be eliminated. Murder might be a onetime act, but coveting or greed has no end. How much is enough, anyway?

James gives two reasons why readers do not obtain what they want in the adverbial clauses "because you do not ask" and "because you ask wrongly, in order that in your pleasures you might spend" (4:2, 3). **Asking** contrasts with killing and coveting to reach one's desires. God grants wisdom to those who ask (1:5), but God does not grant harmful or covetous sensual pleasures (4:1, 3). To ask "wrongly" or "badly" is to ask simply to "spend"[34] on self-centered and harmful pleasures. To ask well is to ask for the wisdom from above, good conduct, gentleness, purity, reasonableness, persuasibility, mercy, good fruits, impartiality, genuineness, righteousness, and peacemaking (3:13, 17–18).

Fighting to obtain what is not ours is the way of the world (4:4). James challenges the readers: "Adulteresses, do you not know that the friendship of the world is enmity against God?" (4:4a). **"Adulteress"** (μοιχαλίς) is feminine, while "adulterer" (μοιχός) is masculine. This is a rare use of the feminine for the generic (cf. 1:8).[35] James may use the feminine generic in the letter (rather than the masculine) because he describes the feminine word φιλία ("friendship, 4:4); he may also allude to the readers described with the feminine word φυλή ("tribe,"

---

34. Δαπανάω (4:3) signifies to "spend freely," to "use up or pay out material or physical resources" (BDAG, 212). James 4:3 is similar to Luke 15:14, where the younger son squandered his inheritance and was left with nothing.

35. The later Codex Sinaiticus (6th–7th c.) appears to be the earliest manuscript wherein the masculine (μοιχοί) is added to the feminine (μοιχαλίδες). However, the original fourth-century Codex Sinaiticus as well as the earliest papyri (p[100]; 3th–4th c.) and Codex Vaticanus (4th c.) all simply have the feminine. The earliest Western text (*italic*[s]), the earliest Syriac version (*syr*[p] 5th–6th c.), the Caesarean version (*geo*), and Augustine all cite only the feminine.

1:1) and to feminine "pleasure" (ἡδονή, 4:3). In addition, he may allude to Jesus's own use of the same feminine metaphor. Jesus uses "adulteress" metaphorically to complement the feminine noun "generation" (γενεά): "an evil and adulterous generation." The scribes and Pharisees insist on Jesus giving them a miraculous sign (Matt. 12:39; 16:4), however, they already did not welcome Jesus's healing of the demon-possessed man who was blind and mute (Matt. 12:22) or Jesus's other signs. Instead, Jesus offers them the sign of Jonah, judgment only ("Forty days more, and Nineveh shall be overthrown," Jon. 3:4). Similar in content to James is Mark 8:34–38, where Jesus admonishes the "adulterous and sinful" crowd not to save their own lives and gain the whole world (κόσμος), for they would end up forfeiting their lives. Instead, they should lose their lives for Jesus.

"Adultery" has also been used in the Old Testament to describe love and obedience to pagan gods. For instance, the Lord has Hosea son of Beeri "love a woman who has a lover and is an adulteress, just as the LORD loves the people of Israel, though they turn to other gods" (Hos. 3:1 NRSV). The Lord also laments to Israel: "How can I pardon you? Your children have forsaken me, and have sworn by those who are no gods. When I fed them to the full, they committed adultery" (Jer. 5:7 NRSV).[36]

Normally, adultery is used literally in the New and Old Testaments.[37] Writers presuppose the commandment "You shall not commit adultery" (Exod. 20:14; Deut. 5:18). The opposite of adultery is faithfulness to one's spouse for life.[38] Adultery refers both to physical and attitudinal lack of fidelity, because Jesus broadens "adultery" to include a man looking at a woman lustfully. The cause is not the other person, but oneself.[39] Giving credit to pagan gods for one's sustenance God calls "adultery" (e.g., Jer. 5:7; Hos. 2:5).

Thus, "adultery" is an apt metaphor to describe the pursuit of greed[40] or coveting what others have to the benefit of one's own sensual pleasures,[41] demonstrations of the worldview of wisdom from below (3:14–16). The image is one of love misdirected and thus is personal, not impersonal, as one might think of war.

The twelve tribes do not know the truth "that the friendship of the world is enmity against God" (4:4). **"Friendship of the world"**

---

36. See also Jer. 3:6–9; 13:27; Ezek. 16:28–36; 23:37–45; Hos. 4:13–14.
37. E.g., Matt. 5:32; 19:18; 1 Cor. 6:9; Hos. 4:2.
38. E.g., Luke 16:18; Rom. 7:3.
39. Matt. 5:27–28; 15:19; Mark 7:21.
40. See also 2 Pet. 2:13–14.
41. See also Hos. 7:4.

signifies asking and pursuing goals that are simply pleasurable to oneself. These goals do not help one draw near to God (4:8). They do not help one's neighbor. They include seeking profit merely for the sake of profit (4:13) and slandering a Christian brother or sister in order to pursue one's own self-enhancing, others-destroying goals (4:11; 3:14). The "world" symbolizes a lifestyle of battling for what one covets (4:1–3); it is a "world of unrighteousness" (3:6), what one should guard oneself against (1:27).

The more abstract "friendship" (φιλία) quickly turns to the more concrete and personal "friend" (φίλος, 4:4). The genitive ("of the world") defines the kind of friendship referred to.[42] It is not the friendship described earlier when Abraham was called friend *of God* (2:23), where faith was demonstrated by actions (2:22, 25). These actions demonstrate a different friend: the "world."

A friend, as illustrated in the New Testament, is someone one wants to be with, no matter what others think (Matt. 11:19; Luke 7:34), someone hospitable to oneself,[43] someone who rejoices with one when good news is received,[44] someone who does not want one harmed (Acts 19:31), and someone who may even relay messages for one (Luke 7:6). That kind of friend is an equal. But a friend may also be an inferior, who obeys one (see James 2:23), such as a friend of Caesar. The ruler in James 4:4 is the "world." The "world" is an enemy of God, so, therefore, the friend of the "world" is also an enemy of God: "Therefore, whoever might desire to be a friend of the world is constituted an enemy against God" (4:4). One cannot be a friend of the world *and* a friend of God, according to James. As Jesus said, you are either with him or against him (Matt. 12:30; Luke 11:23). One cannot live in a worldly lifestyle with worldly goals[45] while claiming to be approved by God.

James illustrates 4:4 with the following quotation: "Or, do you think that to no purpose the writing says: 'the spirit that yearns for envy settled among us'" (4:5).

---

42. Ropes (1916, 260) classifies the phrase as objective genitive: "friendship for the world"; also Hiebert 1979, 250; Blomberg and Kamell 2008, 190.
43. Luke 11:5–6; 14:10; Acts 27:3.
44. Luke 15:6, 9, 29; John 3:29; Acts 10:24.
45. Hiebert 1979 defines friendship with the world as "an egocentric world-system that is hostile to God. Its central aim is self-enjoyment and self-aggrandizement" (251). Painter and deSilva (2012, 140) refer to 1 John 2:15–17. Brosend defines friendship with the world as "to affirm the values, choices, and priorities of a meaning system that grounds meaning in material possessions, status, and regard" (2004, 115).

Different Translations of the Quotation in James 4:5 Literally, in original order: "For envy, he/it/she yearns, the spirit, which settled among us."				
Translation	Subject of "settled" κατοικίζω	Subject of "yearns" ἐπιποθέω	Type of "spirit" πνεῦμα	Type of jealousy φθόνος	OT references
1.	spirit	human	human (subject)	bad	Prov. 21:10 MT; e.g., Num. 12:1–15
2.	God	human	human (subject)	bad	Eccl. 12:7; Isa. 42:5; 63:10–11
3.	God	God	human (object)	good	Zech. 8:2; Pss. 51:11–12; 103:8–9
4.	God	God	Holy Spirit (object)	good	Zech. 8:2; Exod. 20:5
5.	God	Spirit	Holy Spirit (subject)	good	Acts 5:32; Rom. 8:11; Gal. 4:6; 2 Tim. 1:14

1. "The spirit that dwelleth in us lusteth to envy" (KJV, NTME, Wycliffe); "the spirit that yearns for envy settled among us" (author's trans.).[46]

2. "The spirit which God implanted in us is filled with envious longings" (REB); "the spirit he caused to live in us envies intensely" (NIV 1984, NET).[47]

3. "He yearns jealously over the spirit which he has made to dwell in us" (RSV, NRSV, NIV 2011, ESV, NLT).[48]

---

46. See also Laws 1980, 176–78; Anderson and Keating 2017, 84; Brosend 2004, 110.
47. Moo 2015, 183–85; Painter and deSilva 2012, 141; Adamson 1976, 172–73; Townsend 1994, 80. Davids (1982, 163–64) sees this view as having "problems."
48. Dibelius 1976, 224; Ropes 1916, 263–64; Martin 1988, 150–51; Davids 1982, 163–64; Blomberg and Kamell 2008, 191–92; Carpenter 2001, 193.

4. "He jealously desires the Spirit which He has made to dwell in us" (NASB, CEV).[49]

5. "The Spirit that God made to live in us wants us for himself alone" (NCV).[50]

In the Greek, James emphasizes the purpose by placing the prepositional phrase "for **envy**" before the verb at the beginning of the sentence.[51] The closest antecedent to the adjectival clause "which/that settled among us" is "the spirit." Grammatically, "spirit" (πνεῦμα) can serve as subject (nominative case) or direct object (accusative case), since it is a neuter noun.

My own preference is the first of the five options, but the second one is also possible. Why? First, φθόνος and φθονέω always have a negative connotation in the New Testament and the Apocrypha (it does not occur in the Old Testament). For example, "Let us not become conceited, competing against one another, *envying* one another" (Gal. 5:26 NRSV).[52] Liddell and Scott's *Lexicon* agrees that φθόνος signifies "ill-will or malice, esp. envy or jealousy of the good fortune of others."[53] When God is called a "jealous" God in the Old Testament, a different Greek word is used (ζηλόω).[54] For instance, when Jesus commands the sellers to stop selling at the temple, his disciples recall Psalm 69:9: "*Zeal* for your house will consume me" (ζῆλος, John 2:17). However, the same word family in James's letter always has negative connotations (3:14, 16; 4:2). Thus, the concept of envy or jealousy is always negative in James's letter.

Second, this translation fits well in the immediate context. The **"spirit"** refers to the human spirit that is a friend of the world, an enemy of God that loves the world created by infighting (4:1–4). "Friendship of the world" and "friend of the world" describe the human seeking self-pleasure (4:1–4).[55] The contrast comes with the "but" in

---

49. McCartney 2009, 211–14. Hiebert (1979, 257) sees this translation as "highly improbable."
50. Hiebert 1979, 257.
51. See also Hiebert 1979, 255.
52. See also Matt. 27:18; Mark 15:10; Rom. 1:29; Gal. 5:21; Phil. 1:15; 1 Tim. 6:4; Titus 3:3; 1 Pet. 2:1.
53. LSJ, 1930.
54. E.g., Exod. 20:5; 34:14; Deut. 4:24.
55. Carpenter (2001,192) also mentions the creation imagery in 3:7–9, which suggests that "spirit" in 4:5 is the "life principle" God gave humans.

4:6: God gives greater grace to the person who submits to God, *not* to the spirit colonizing the world.

Third, **"yearn"** (ἐπιποθέω) is synonymous with "pleasure" (ἡδονή, 4:1, 3, 5). "Yearn" or "long" relates to the senses and to feelings, for example: "Like newborn infants, *long for* the pure, spiritual milk . . . you have tasted" (1 Pet. 2:2–3 NRSV). "Pleasure" (ἡδονή) can be a positive, neutral, or negative concept, as also "yearn" can be positive, neutral, or negative.[56] Paul uses ἐπιποθέω several times to describe one Christian longing to see another Christian in person.[57] In that case, the use of ἐπιποθέω in James 4:5 would be personification: the "spirit," an aspect of a person, longing not for human companionship but rather for jealousy. Coveting feeds more coveting.

Thus, the literary context strongly supports the first two translation options. The difficulty with the first option is the unique verb κατοικίζω, a combination of κατά ("down") and οἰκίζω ("build a house").[58] BDAG's *Lexicon* suggests it has a causative sense: "cause to dwell, establish, **settle**."[59] However, Liddell and Scott's *Lexicon* simply defines the verb as "settle, establish."[60] In the Old Testament, κατοικίζω in the aorist active indicative (which is the same in James) always has a causative sense; for instance, Pharaoh tells Joseph to *settle* his father and brothers in the best part of the land of Egypt (Gen. 47:6). However, every aorist active verb in the Old Testament also has a direct object. For example, Joseph caused *his father and brothers* to settle.[61] In contrast, in the Old Testament, κατοικίζω in the passive voice may signify "settle" without a direct object, as in "Moses was content to dwell with [Reuel]."[62] Therefore, since the verb in James 4:5 has no direct object after it, it is not definite that James used the causative sense of κατοικίζω.[63] James thus used the verb in a fresh manner (the active voice without a direct object): "it/he settled among us" (4:5). This spirit with an

56. A negative example of ἐπιποθέω ("yearn") is Sirach 25:21.
57. Rom. 1:11; 2 Cor. 9:14; Phil. 1:8; 1 Thess. 3:6; 2 Tim. 1:4.
58. Newman 2010, 100, in UBS 2014. The preposition κατά gives the verb perfective force (Robertson 1934, 605–6); i.e., it intensifies the verb.
59. BDAG, 535; Thayer, 341.
60. LSJ, 928. And with the accusative case, "colonize, people a place" or middle voice "establish oneself, settle."
61. Other examples: Gen. 3:25 LXX; 47:11; Lev. 23:43; Josh. 6:25 LXX; 1 Sam. 12:8; 2 Kings 17:6; 2 Chron. 8:2; Pss. 4:8; 68:6; 107:36; 113:9.
62. Exod. 2:21; Deut. 2:12, 21–23; 2 Kings 17:24; Ezek. 26:19–20.
63. Some later ancient manuscripts (A-5 c; K, L, P-9c) changed the verb to κατοικέω for its more common significance: "he/she/it settled."

envious yearning or longing settled or became a permanent inhabitant among us. It affected everyone! If κατοικίζω is causative, it could allude back to "the friendship of the world": "the spirit which [the friendship of the world] caused to dwell among us yearns for envy" (4:5).

To what passage does James 4:5 refer? In the other Old Testament quotations in James's letter, the reference is quite clear, although some of these may come through indirectly by way of James quoting Jesus.

Summary of Old Testament and New Testament Quotations in James			
James	Old Testament	New Testament	Introduction
2:8	Lev. 19:18 LXX/MT	Jesus: Matt. 22:39	τὴν γραφήν ("the Scripture")
2:11	Exod. 20:13–14	Jesus: Luke 18:20	ὁ εἰπών ("the one saying")
2:23	Gen. 15:6 LXX		ἡ γραφὴ ἡ λέγουσα ("the Scripture, the one saying")
4:6	Prov. 3:34 LXX		λέγει ("it says")
4:5			ἡ γραφὴ λέγει ("the Scripture says")

No one has found a word-for-word Old Testament quotation for 4:5; however, several allusions have been suggested.[64] An allusion would be a rephrasing of the content of an Old Testament passage in James's own words. If the "spirit" refers to the human spirit, James could be alluding to a passage such as Proverbs 21:10, which in the Hebrew says: "the spirit [breath/soul] of the wicked desires evil." James quotes from Proverbs again in 4:6, and he uses "spirit" to refer to the human spirit in 2:26. An example of the harm created by envy would be when Miriam and Aaron become jealous of Moses (Num. 12:1–15).

Or, the implied subject of κατοικίζω might be "God": "the spirit which [God] caused to dwell among us yearns for envy." "God" (θεός) has been mentioned in 4:4: "an enemy against *God*." "God" is the explicit subject of the next quotation: "God to the haughty is opposed . . . submit to God" (4:6–7). At creation, God places within everyone

---

64.   Moo (2015, 186), and others, notes that John 7:38 is also an allusion.

breath or the spirit, that part of oneself that hearkens to God and self-examines.[65] This usage is causative. Thus, option two would continue the negative connotation of jealousy in the passage but assume the readers know that it is God who gives one the spirit of life: "the spirit which he caused to dwell among us yearns enviously." "God," though, is not mentioned until the next sentence, after the adversative "but."

The third and fourth options might allude to a passage such as Zechariah 8:2: "Thus says the Lord Almighty: 'I have been jealous for Jerusalem and for Zion with great jealousy, and I have been jealous for her with great fury.'" God could take his Spirit away (Ps. 51:11–12) if readers continue their friendship with the world. Of course, the Greek Old Testament uses a different word for "jealousy," and it would then have a positive connotation in James 4:5. What we do not want to conclude is that God placed in humans an evil spirit that is envious, because the good God gives only good gifts (James 1:13–17) and James has throughout stressed human culpability for sinful behavior (e.g., 4:1).

Edmond Hiebert concludes that James refers not to a specific Old Testament passage, but to the teaching of the Scriptures as a whole.[66] William Brosend suggests that James may refer to a Jesus saying or "Jesus material" or tradition. The Scripture could be a saying by Jesus not in the Gospels, similar to Acts 20:35. Brosend states that James never quotes Jesus.[67] However, I have shown how his scriptural quotations have twice repeated Jesus word for word (see James 2:8, 11). I agree that more often James alludes to Jesus's teachings but does not quote them word for word. But in this instance (4:5) James refers to a "writing," not to a verbal quotation.

Craig Carpenter defends "the Scripture says" (4:5) as referring forward to Proverbs 3:34 in James 4:6. James 4:5 is a paraphrase of, an indirect statement, or an interpretive introduction to Proverbs 3:34. Carpenter interprets 4:5b–6a, "God jealously desires the spirit which he has caused to dwell in us but he gives greater grace," as a paraphrase of 4:6c–d, the direct quotation: "The Lord opposes the proud but he gives grace to the humble." These sentences echo Psalm 103:8–9 in reverse sequence. Carpenter turns the first sentence into a question

65. 1 Cor. 2:11; Isa. 42:5; Eccl. 12:7.
66. Hiebert 1979, 254; also Tasker 1957, 91.
67. Brosend 2004, 11, 114.

that demands the answer "no." His view is carefully defended, but it has some difficulties.[68]

Commentators have attempted to interpret James 4:5 with due respect to biblical inspiration. Clearly 4:5 contrasts to 4:6, the greater grace that God gives. The implied subject (4:6a) is cited in Proverbs 3:34 (LXX): *"God* to the haughty is opposed, but to the lowly gives grace." God is opposed to the human spirit that longs for envy and friendship with the world, those who, when they desire but do not have, will kill, be filled with jealousy, and wage war for their pleasures (4:1–5).

Greater than all the sinful behavior mentioned in 4:1–5 is God's grace (χάρις, 4:6). **"Grace"** is part of a larger word family: χαρά ("joy") and χαίρω ("rejoice"). James uses this word family only four times (1:1, 2; 4:6, 9), yet it is a very important concept. It is a synonym of "mercy" (ἔλεος), which is the approved way to judge, and a quality of the "wisdom from above" (2:13; 3:17). The author of Hebrews relates grace and mercy together as well: "Let us therefore approach the throne of grace with boldness, so that we may receive mercy and find grace to help in time of need" (4:16 NRSV). Χάρις is "that which affords joy, pleasure, delight, *sweetness, charm, loveliness.*"[69] In the New Testament, it refers to "loving-kindness" or "steadfast love"—in the Hebrew, חֶסֶד. God is known for having grace and truth, steadfast love and faithfulness.[70] When the Word became flesh in Jesus, humans saw glory, and, like the Father, Jesus was overflowing with grace and truth (John 1:14, 17). "Grace" includes great love,[71] generosity, gift-giving,[72] thanksgiving, and forgiveness.[73] God's grace is at work in people's salvific transformation[74] and continues at work in their ministry and lives.[75] Its evidence

---

68. Carpenter 2001, 197–205. The difficulties with this view are the unnecessary dual introduction ("the Scripture says . . . it says"); rare use of "that" (ὅτι) in indirect discourse—normally the quotation follows the introduction "the Scripture says"; moving the end of the question to 6a (" . . . grace?"); and omission of an adverb (μή) to indicate the answer to the question is "no." See also McCartney 2009, 216–17, and Blomberg and Kamell 2008, 192.
69. Thayer, 665.
70. Exod. 34:6. See further Spencer and Spencer 1998, 30–34. "Grace" may also be exhibited by humans (e.g., Acts 2:47; 7:10, 46; 24:27; 25:3, 9).
71. 2 Cor. 8:9; 2 Thess. 2:16–17; 1 Tim. 1:12–16; Heb. 2:9.
72. Rom. 5:15; 11:6; 2 Cor. 9:8, 14–15; Eph. 3:7–8; 2 Tim. 1:8–10.
73. Rom. 6:17; 1 Cor. 15:57; 2 Cor. 2:14; Col. 3:16; Heb. 12:15, 28.
74. Acts 15:11; 18:27; Rom. 3:22–24; 1 Cor. 15:10; 2 Cor. 4:15; Eph. 1:5–8; 2:4–8; Titus 2:11–12; 3:6–7.
75. Acts 4:33; 14:26; Rom. 1:5; 12:3; 15:15–16; 1 Cor. 3:10; 2 Cor. 8:1–2.

may be seen in new believers and results in joy (Acts 11:22–23). God's forgiving grace is not a license for immorality (Rom. 6:1–2, 14–15; Jude 4), but rather is a continually available antidote to sin (James 4:6).

The basis for James's statement that God continues to give "grace" (forgiveness and strength for transformation) is Proverbs 3:34: "God to the haughty is opposed, but to the lowly gives grace" (James 4:6). The larger context of Proverbs 3 discusses wisdom, which is also developed in James's letter (3:13–18). Proverbs, like James, is concerned for the poor, exhorting the wise not to ask the poor to come back another day (Prov. 3:27–28; James 2:15–16). Proverbs 3 also exhorts not to do evil against one's neighbor, nor to quarrel without cause, nor to covet the ways of evil people (Prov. 3: 29–32; James 1:19–20; 3:14–16; 4:1–5). Thus, in Proverbs, the **"haughty"** refers to those who do evil and admire others who do evil. In James, the "haughty" are those who fight among each other impelled by their own pleasures and coveting (4:1–5).

James 4:6 highlights the contrast between the "haughty" versus the "lowly" by placing these indirect objects before their verbs ("is opposed," "gives grace"). The attitude of a human affects God's responsive action. "Haughty" (ὑπερήφανος) refers to "showing one's self above others."[76] It refers to attitude and action that begin inside oneself, in one's inmost will or heart (Luke 1:51; Mark 7:22–23, ὑπερηφανία) and characterizes those who do not acknowledge God (Rom. 1:28–30). For Mary, the haughty are synonymous with rulers and the rich (Luke 1:51–53) and, for Peter, with those who are greedy for money and lord it over others (1 Pet. 5:1–3). Haughtiness is self-exaltation rather than exaltation by God (James 4:6–8; 1 Pet. 5:6).

Those who fight in a worldly manner will find God **opposing** them. Ἀντιτάσσω (4:6) signifies to "range in battle against," as if God, on one side, faces a line of human soldiers, on the other side, drawn out in battle array.[77] This metaphor is commonly used in the Bible to signify opposing or resisting another, such as the unbelieving Jews who opposed Paul in Corinth (Acts 18:6) or those who oppose governmental authorities (Rom. 13:2). Devout Jews (men, women, and children) complained against Emperor Gaius Caligula's mandate to place his statue in every city including the temple in Jerusalem. They did not carry arms against the Romans but assembled as a crowd to protest (*J.W.* 2.10.3.194). In the Old Testament, God opposed Solomon because of his syncretism by appointing Jeroboam to take away ten tribes from

76. Ὑπέρ ("above") plus φαίνομαι ("show one's self") (Thayer, 641).
77. LSJ, 164. It is an "old military term" (Robertson 1933, 52; Hiebert 1979, 260–61).

Solomon's kingdom (1 Kings 11:29–34). The contrast to opposition is mercy. When God opposes, he does not save (Hos. 1:6–7). It is difficult to fight human beings, but who would dare to fight God?

Much better it is to become humble or "**lowly**" (ταπεινός), not showing oneself above others (ὑπερήφανος, 4:6). In James 1:9–10, the lowly person is the poor Christian; while in 4:6, 10, the lowly person does not covet other's possessions. Humble persons do not engage in the battles going on (4:1–4). They are willing to be submissive to God, resist the devil, draw near to God, and be purified by God from the inside out (4:7–8).

James repeats twice, at the beginning and ending of the verse, that God "gives grace." That is James's emphasis: grace, not judgment. The humble know they need God's grace and, thus, God gives it to them daily.[78]

If one does not want to be opposed by God and wants rather to receive grace, one must "submit to God" (4:7). Instead of being opposed by God (ἀντιτάσσω), one must oppose or **take a stand** (ἀνθίστημι) against the evil one, the devil (4:7). James continues the military imagery to encourage the lowly Christian to fight the wars occurring around him or her.[79] The first two clauses form a perfect antithetic parallelism in Greek:

submit, therefore, to (the) God,
withstand, however, (to) the devil [4:7a]

indicating the two contrasting actions: **submission** pertains to God, while resisting pertains to the devil. God is one's friend (2:23), while the devil is one's enemy (4:4).[80]

In an ancient Roman army, soldiers volunteered to work under a general.[81] In the Macedonian army, the ὑπόταξις refers to the lightly armed infantry drawing up *behind* the phalanx. They are "submitted" (ὑποτάσσω) to the phalanx,[82] which indicates that they support or

---

78. "Give" is in the present tense.
79. The ten aorist imperatives in verses 7–10 function like "curt military commands" to "demand incisive action" (Hiebert 1979, 260): submit, take a stand, draw near, cleanse, purify, be miserable, mourn, weep, turn around, be humble.
80. The devil is the archetype of pride who "fosters jealousy and ambition" and "murderous envy" (McCartney 2009, 217).
81. Hammond and Scullard 1970, 120.
82. LSJ, 1897. Another "military term" (Robertson 1933, 52; Hiebert 1979, 261).

protect the phalanx.[83] In James, the passive voice is used to indicate that Christians "subject themselves"[84] to the commander of *their* choice. Christians need to cooperate with God, their general.[85] And who is their commander? God is the Father of lights, the very good, generous, consistent, and compassionate commander, who provides the good harvest, seeks peace, frees, and gives grace.[86]

While cooperating with (submitting to) God's good and healthy will, they must also "stand against, especially in battle, [or] withstand"[87] (ἀνθίστημι) the devil (4:7). To stand against someone sounds as if it is a passive act. However, it can be quite active. For example, Paul "stood against" Peter in Antioch face-to-face because of Peter's inconsistent behavior. Peter had been eating with the Gentiles, but when the circumcision party representatives arrived, Peter would no longer eat with them. Paul explained to him why his actions were wrong (Gal. 2:11–21).

James has used the passive voice about oneself ("submit yourself") and the active voice toward another ("take a stand"); now he uses the middle voice ("he will himself flee") (4:7). One can **flee** "from" (4:7) or flee "to" (e.g., Matt. 24:16). Simply by submitting to God and withstanding the devil, then, the devil will himself run away from the believer. In a battle, no act could be more victorious than to have the enemy simply run away. Those who obey the Lord's covenant are promised, "The LORD will cause your enemies who rise against you [ἀνθίστημι] to be defeated before you; they shall come out against you one way, and flee [φεύγω] before you seven ways" (Deut. 28:7 NRSV). The battle has been won when the devil flees! The devil flees when the human is submitted to God. Only God can defeat the devil because "the Lord is strong and mighty, the Lord is mighty in battle" (Ps. 24:8 [v. 9 LXX].)

That is why a Christian must "**draw near** to God" (4:8). When someone resists the devil, the devil flees away. The counterpart is that when someone draws near to God, God draws near to the believer (4:8). Normally, "draw near" (ἐγγίζω [verb] and ἐγγύς [adv.]) can describe location (e.g., "near Jerusalem," Matt. 21:1) or time (e.g., "summer is near," Matt. 24:32). Location can include coming near a person (e.g.,

---

83. Adkins and Adkins 2005, 94–95, 99, 102, 106.
84. BDAG, 1042. The passive voice functions like the middle, "calling for their voluntary subordination to God and His will" (Hiebert 1979, 261).
85. According to Painter and deSilva, "to submit to God is to acknowledge God as God and to recognize that humans are the work of God's hands" (2012, 143).
86. James 1:5, 17, 25, 27; 2:5, 23; 3:17–18; 4:6; 5:4, 11.
87. LSJ, 140.

Jesus came *near* the two disciples going to Emmaus, Luke 24:15), which is what James writes. God can be as close, if not closer, as Jesus walking with the disciples on the road to Emmaus. God is "near" to give wisdom and to answer our prayers (1:5; 5:17–18). Paul describes God's nearness as "over all and through all and in all" (Eph. 4:6). God is very close, close over us and close between us and close within or among us to help us live loving lives. Psalm 139 describes God's nearness as: "behind and before you press me in and you place upon me your palm" (Ps. 139:5). God walks behind, before, and next to us. God is spirit and, therefore, omnipresent (Ps. 139:7).[88]

James's promise is that God "*will* draw near"[89] to us (4:8). The prophet Malachi has a similar message: "Return to me, and I will return to you" (Mal. 3:7). In Malachi, people return by being obedient to God in their tithes (3:8–10). The Spirit gave Azariah son of Oded a similar message for King Asa: "The Lord is with you, while you are with him. If you seek him, he will be found by you, but if you abandon him, he will abandon you" (2 Chron. 15:1–2 NRSV).[90] Asa returned to God by putting away all the idols and repairing the temple (2 Chron. 15:8–15). For James, as well, drawing near to God who is holy[91] entails not sinning but repenting, and purifying oneself: "cleanse hands, sinners, and purify hearts, two-willed ones" (4:8).[92]

"**Hands**" ($\chi\epsilon\acute{\iota}\rho$) in the New Testament are symbols of judgment and arrest,[93] healing and blessing,[94] protection, authority, power,[95] and work and behavior. In James 4:8, hands are a synecdoche for the behavior of a person,[96] because most often people use their hands to work.

---

88. See Spencer, Hailson, Kroeger, and Spencer 1995, 136–39. The right to draw near to God distinguishes God's people (Deut. 4:7) (Tasker 1957, 93).
89. The future indicative is fundamentally and usually punctiliar in idea. This future is predictive or prophetic, God's promise to the person who draws near (Robertson 1934, 353, 872–73).
90. See also Zech. 1:3.
91. In Exodus 19:22 and 24:2, "drawing near" is associated with priests consecrating themselves and Moses approaching God. On God as holy, see Lev. 11:44–45; 19:2; 20:26; Josh. 24:19–23; 1 Sam. 2:2–4; Isa. 6:3; 43:15.
92. In Greek, this is a perfect synonymous parallelism, which mirrors the parallel thought.
93. E.g., Matt. 17:22; 26:45, 50; Mark 9:31; 14:41, 46; Heb. 10:31.
94. E.g., Matt. 19:13, 15; Mark 5:23; 6:5; 7:32; 8:23, 25; 10:13.
95. E.g., Luke 4:11; 23:46; John 3:35; 10:28–29; 13:3; Acts 8:18–19; 13:3; 19:6; 1 Tim. 4:14; 5:22.
96. A synecdoche is a part (hand) representing a whole body in action. The tongue is another synecdoche (1:26; 3:5–12) representing the opening

For example, Paul tells the Thessalonians "to work with your hands" (1 Thess. 4:11) and he reminds the Ephesian elders: "You yourselves know that these *hands* of mine have supplied my own needs and the needs of my companions" (Acts 20:34 NIV).[97]

Cleansing of hands was, in addition, especially symbolic for the Jews because the holy place of the temple had a bronze basin for washing. With the water, the priests washed their hands and feet before they made an offering by fire (Exod. 30:17–21). The devout Pharisees, who wanted to extend the practices of purity of the priests in the temple to daily life, practiced the liturgical washing of hands before eating.[98] The rabbis concluded that hands were "susceptible to uncleanness, and they are rendered clean by the pouring over them of water up to the wrist" (m. Yad. 2:3). This practice is evident in the Gospels (e.g., Matt. 15:1–20; Mark 7:2–5). James may allude to this practice by referring to "hands" and the need for cleansing, but in his case, cleansing is done by transformed behavior, not mere water. As with Jesus, James wants change in their "hearts," not merely their "lips."[99]

The first two clauses of James 4:8 should remind the Jewish readers of Psalm 24:4.[100] Who shall stand in the Lord's holy place? "Those who have clean hands and **pure hearts**." In the psalm, such people do not support falsehood, swearing deceitfully to their neighbor, nor taking the Lord's name in vain (Ps. 24:3–4).[101] James wants change in outward behavior ("hands") and inward thoughts and attitudes ("hearts").[102]

By ending the sentence with **"two-willed ones"** (4:8), James reiterates his concern for a fully integrated personality. Δίψυχος is the same word used earlier in 1:8 for someone who is inclined in two different directions, one will acting as a sinner and desiring to be a friend of the world, the other will desiring to be pure and a friend of God.

---

between inward impurity and the outside world. See also 1 Tim. 2:8; Rev. 9:20.

97. See also Acts 7:41; 19:26; 1 Cor. 4:12; Eph. 4:28; Rev. 9:20.
98. Only water about the size of one or two eggs was used for cleansing (m. Yad. 1:1). M. Ber. 8:2, 4, discusses in what sequence to wash hands and mix the cup or sweep the room. See also Tasker 1957, 94.
99. Matt. 15:8, 17–20; Mark 7:6, citing Isa. 29:13.
100. See also Dibelius 1976, 226. Other similar passages are Job 17:9; 22:30; Isa. 1:16–17; Jer. 4:14; Matt. 5:8.
101. These are also concerns of James in 3:9; 5:12.
102. Purifying hearts involves removing everything from one's thoughts and actions that keep one from "single-mindedly pursuing God and his will in the world" (Blomberg and Kamell 2008, 194–95).

James wants the Jewish Christians to be wholeheartedly submitted to God,[103] to draw near to God, while fighting the evil one.

The crucial step in change is genuine repentance: "Be miserable and mourn and weep. Your laughter turn around to mourning and joy into gloominess" (4:9). James continues his series of commands to his readers. He considers their sin great. By using three synonymous commands, each joined by "and,"[104] James hammers home his point—be serious about changing your behavior!

The first verb, "**be miserable**" (ταλαιπωρέω), is a strong verb that refers to difficulties experienced, which in turn result in giving expression to grief.[105] In James 4:9, James commands readers to express their grief at their sin now, to avoid the experience of God's judgment (ταλαιπωρία, 5:1). How burdensome that grief is can be seen in some examples. A woman who had been raped by a group of men experienced "great *affliction* at what had happened" (*Ant.* 5.2.8.146–47). Some Jews who had been captured and bound, expecting infuriated elephants to trample them, were "*miserable* victims" (3 Macc. 5:2–5). It is the opposite of the joy one feels when blessed.[106] When David regrets his own sin, all day long he mourns, feeling *miserable*, but still he hopes in the Lord's affirming answer (Ps. 38:6, 15). According to Ceslas Spicq, his is "the cry of a broken heart."[107]

The next two verbs, like ταλαιπωρέω ("be miserable"), can serve to express deep regret at sin or judgment for unrepented sin. For instance, the Corinthians should have mourned when they learned of sexual immorality in their presence, rather than having become arrogant (1 Cor. 5:1–2).[108] "**Mourn**" (πενθέω, πένθος) occurs twice in 4:9, as a verb and a noun. "Mourn" and "weep" (κλαίω) also occur in the Sermon on the Plain: "Blessed are the ones weeping [κλαίω] now, for you will laugh [γελάω]. . . . Woe to the ones laughing [γελάω] now, for you will mourn [πενθέω] and weep [κλαίω]" (Luke 6:21, 25). The former "weeping" may express repentance, the latter one judgment.[109] The context in Jesus's sermon, as in James's letter, also relates to the wealthy versus the poor (Luke 6:20–21, 24–25). Mourning and

---

103. "Purity of heart is identified with 'single-minded' commitment" (Painter and deSilva 2012, 144).
104. Polysyndeton; see also NRSV.
105. BDAG, 988.
106. BDAG, 988.
107. *TLNT* 3, 368.
108. See also 2 Cor. 12:21.
109. See also Rev. 18:8.

weeping occur together,[110] for example, in the end times when merchants mourn because they no longer have anyone to buy their cargo, inhibiting their goal to become rich (Rev. 18:11, 15). BDAG's *Lexicon* defines πενθέω as "to experience sadness as the result of some condition or circumstance, *be sad, grieve, mourn.*"[111] In James 4:9, the condition is sin and the sadness expresses regret for current sinful behavior.

Grief and sadness result in verbal expression: **weeping audibly** (κλαίω, 4:9).[112] The weeping is audible because the sadness is deeply and genuinely felt. For example, in the New Testament, people cry at the death of a loved one (a young girl [Mark 5:38–39], an only son [Luke 7:12–13], an only brother [John 11:31–33], a special widow [Acts 9:39], an apostle [Acts 21:13], and Jesus [John 16:20; 20:11–15]); they cry at the death of many loved and innocent children (Matt. 2:16–18), or the realization of one's own betrayal (Matt. 26:75). As with the other two verbs, crying can express deep repentance, as the woman who had been a sinner. Her sins were forgiven and she was saved by her faith (Luke 7:37–39, 48–50). Weeping can also occur during a time of disaster caused by judgment.[113]

Like Jesus, James wants the **laughter** or happiness of those who are friends with the world to turn to mourning and gloominess (4:9). James is not against all joy. The letter begins with a greeting of joy and a discussion of joy in the midst of persecution (1:1–2). Genuine joy flows from God's "grace" or steadfast love (4:6). But as Solomon explains: There is "a time to weep [κλαίω], and a time to laugh [γελάω]; a time to mourn, and a time to dance" (Eccl. 3:4 NRSV). The readers who were involved in self-seeking warfare with their Christian family needed to "turn around" (μετατρέπω) their laughter[114] and joy to behavior expressing repentance: mourning and gloominess (4:9). When it comes to acting for God, one should *not* change or turn around one's behavior,[115] but when it comes to acting *against* God, change is indispensable (James 4:9).

"**Gloominess**" (κατήφεια, 4:9) is related to the adjective κατηφής ("of a downcast look"). Κατήφεια properly is "a downcast look expressive of sorrow; hence shame, dejection, gloom."[116] "Gloominess" is the

---

110. See also 2 Sam. 19:1; Neh. 8:9.
111. BDAG, 795.
112. Thayer, 347, compares κλαίω ("to weep") to its synonyms.
113. James 5:1; Luke 19:41–44; 23:28–31.
114. E.g., Prov. 10:23. Laughter refers to "loud, unseemly gaiety as pleasure-loving friends of the world" (Hiebert 1979, 265).
115. E.g., 4 Macc. 15:11, 18.
116. Thayer, 340.

opposite of joy (4:9). This "gloominess" is the silent shame expressed outwardly by downcast eyes.[117] It is regret of one's past actions.[118]

James began the series of commands in 4:7–10 with the command to submit oneself (ὑποτάσσω) to God (4:7), and now he returns to a synonym of "submit": "**Be humble** (ταπεινόω) before the Lord and he will lift you up" (4:10). Submission to God, therefore, includes fighting the evil one, drawing near to God, cleansing and purifying one's outward behavior and inward self, and expressing one's genuine feelings and intentions of repentance.[119] The end result—the Lord will **lift** one back up! In James 1:9, the "humble" or "lowly" brother is the poor Christian, not being powerful in a worldly sense (see 1:9–10). But in 4:10 we learn that anyone can choose to become "lowly";[120] as a matter of fact, it is a command for all. Before the Lord, all humans are lowly. We merely need to acknowledge that fact to God and live accordingly with God as our "Lord." The selfishness, scheming, envy, and disputing involved in worldly fighting (4:1–3) that results in arrogance toward others ultimately comes from arrogance toward God. In contrast, humility and purity of actions comes from desiring to please God.

The Lord in turn "will lift you up" (ὑψόω, 4:10). Peter summarizes Proverbs 3:34 in the same way James does: "Therefore humble yourselves [ταπεινόω] under the mighty hand of God, so that he might exalt [ὑψόω] you in due time" (1 Pet. 5:6). James does not clarify how God will exalt the person in the immediate context, but earlier James explained how the lowly person already has been exalted as "rich in faith" and become one of the "heirs of the kingdom" (1:9; 2:5). Both James and Peter remind their readers that those who persevere will receive "the crown of life" (James 1:12) or "the never-fading glorious crown" (1 Pet. 5:4). Ultimately, that "high position" (ὕψος) is God's very presence, where God the Trinity presides.[121]

Exaltation of the humble (and the humbling of the arrogant) is a repeated teaching by Jesus. He criticizes the teachers of the law who practice their piety simply for others to see and to honor[122] and warns

117. E.g., Luke 18:13. MM, 337; LSJ, 927; Robertson 1933, 53.
118. E.g., *Ant.* 13.16.1.406.
119. See also Ropes 1916, 272: "Humble yourselves" "sums up" the acts directed in verses 7–9. This is called an "inclusio" (Blomberg and Kamell 2008, 185; Vlachos 2013, 142).
120. "The passive here has almost the middle or reflexive sense": "humble yourselves" (Robertson 1933, 53).
121. Luke 24:49; Acts 2:32–33; 5:30–31.
122. Matt. 23:2–12; Luke 14:7–11; 18:9–14.

them of the forthcoming punishment by position reversal between the humble and the arrogant. Instead, Jesus calls the greatest in heaven those who become as humble as children and welcome such in his name (Matt. 18:1–5).

Fighting Makes You a Judge—A Person Who Speaks Evil of Brothers and Sisters; Rather, Be a Doer of the Law (4:11–12)

James's letter has three major themes (trials, wisdom, wealth) that interrelate with the larger theme of becoming doers of the word (see introduction). James 4:1–17 hearkens back to the theme of trials (1:2–4). These include avoidable "trials" from sinful internal desires (1:12–18). These desires, which cause worldly fighting, can result in one becoming God's enemy. Such "evil deeds" do not help one receive the implanted word, as does humility. Fighting can also make one the wrong kind of judge, someone who speaks evil of other believers. A doer of God's law does not speak evil or falsehood against others. James 4:11–12 appears to be another aspect of worldly fighting: "Do not keep slandering one another, brothers and sisters" (4:11a). James explains why not to slander in the verses that follow (4:11b–12).

After ten aorist imperatives, the present imperative stands out, highlighting the ongoing[123] nature of the activity: "do not keep slandering" (4:11). Καταλαλέω ("**slander**") in the New Testament is always negative, literally signifying "to speak" (λαλέω) "against" (κατά) another, thus, to speak falsehoods against someone (e.g., Hos. 7:13). Λαλέω signifies properly "to utter a sound," "to utter or form words with the mouth," referring to the sound, pronunciation, and form of what is uttered; whereas λέγω refers to the meaning and substance of what is spoken.[124] For example, James uses λαλέω to describe the words spoken by the prophets in the name of the Lord (5:10) or the words too easily uttered which replace listening (1:19). The preposition κατά ("against") signifies the negative nature of these words. Paul uses καταλαλέω to describe the Corinthian church context, which had some of the same difficulties as had the twelve tribes in their diaspora: jealousy, anger, selfishness, slander, and disorder.[125] At a time of persecution, Peter warns his readers to have honorable conduct and deeds to counteract the slander of Christians by Gentiles

---

123. See also Hiebert 1979, 266.
124. Λαλέω is onomatopoetic: la-la (Thayer, 368). E.g., Romans 3:19 and Matthew 13:3 show the different uses of the two verbs.
125. 2 Cor. 12:20; James 1:19–20; 3:14, 16; 4:11. See also Exod. 20:16; Lev. 19:16.

(1 Peter 2:12; 3:16). During the exodus, Miriam and Aaron "spoke against" Moses, jealous that the Lord spoke only through Moses and directly to him (Num. 12:1–8). Slander includes complaining unfairly against someone in anger, as when the Israelites complained against God and Moses: "Why have you brought us up out of Egypt to die in the wilderness?" (Num. 21:5 NRSV).[126] James does not want the expressions coming out of the twelve tribes in diaspora to be negative ones against other believers.

James uses **"judging"** (κρίνω) as a synonym for "slander" (καταλαλέω): "The one slandering [καταλαλέω] brother or judging [κρίνω] his brother slanders [καταλαλέω] the law and judges [κρίνω] the law; but, if you judge the law, you are not a doer of the law but you are a judge. One is Lawgiver and Judge, the One being able to save and to destroy; but who are you, the one judging [κρίνω] the neighbor?" (4:11–12). The judgment that James describes is not truthful, but rather false, unhelpful, and destructive. He has already complained about evil judgment (2:4, 13) and special seating for the wealthy and powerful (see 2:4). Moreover, the rich "slandered" (βλασφημέω) or disrespected the good name of the poor when they brought them to court (2:7). Are all these wars (4:1–2) caused by the rich wanting more and using others, especially the less powerful poor, merely to fulfill those selfish wants? James could also be referring to the rich being envious of the possessions of other wealthy people or even of the poor being envious of those less poor. Focusing on sensual pleasures is a foundation to the problem (4:3).

What **law** is being slandered or judged (4:11)? Earlier James has mentioned the "royal law": "love your neighbor as yourself" (2:8, citing Lev. 19:18 and Jesus in Matt. 22:39). This is a summary of the Ten Commandments. If James in 4:11 refers back to this law,[127] which seems likely, he is explaining that speaking falsely against a Christian brother or sister implies that one speaks falsely against a tenet of God that prohibits such action. For a negative example, if the government establishes a law that one cannot worship God in a Christian setting, but Christians still insist on worshiping God, then, in their actions they are protesting the governmental law. They are judging that law by not doing it. The principle also applies to God's law: if the twelve tribes are *not* loving their neighbors when they speak against them, they are in effect criticizing God's law to love their neighbor as themselves. They

126. See also Ps. 50:19–20.
127. Many commentators agree: Ropes 1916, 274; Hiebert 1979, 268–69, 271; Laws 1980, 187; Martin 1988, 159, 163; McKnight 2011, 363.

are not doing the law. For Jewish Christians, this accusation by James would be very serious because of their high view of the law.

James then reminds them that only one being is the true **Lawgiver** and Judge: "One is Lawgiver and Judge, the One being able to save and to destroy; but who are you, the one judging the neighbor?" (4:12). In other words, how could any mere human try to take God's place, by judging his or her neighbor?[128] God as lawgiver (νομοθέτης) and judge (κριτής) has a rich Old Testament background. The Lord calls Moses up Mount Sinai, where the Lord says: "I will give you the tablets of stone, the law and the commandments, which I have written to give them laws [νομοθετέω]" (Exod. 24:12). There the Lord teaches Moses many different laws, including the Ten Commandments, to teach the Israelites (Exod. 25:1–31:18).[129] The specific law to which James refers is the one just mentioned (4:11; 2:8): the summary of the Ten Commandments, love your neighbor as yourself. The Jews thought they were a distinctive people because of the giving of the law (Rom. 9:4; Heb. 7:11). In the new covenant, God's laws are implanted by the Holy Spirit in believers' inner beings (Heb. 8:6–11; Jer. 31:31–34). But, believers need to remember that God is the source of these laws.

Similarly, only God is the perfect and ultimate **Judge** (4:12).[130] God appoints human judges who have derivative authority (Rom. 13:1–2). For example, God appointed judges in the Old Testament to rule (Acts 13:20). The Roman procurators, such as Governor Felix, also were rulers and judges (Acts 24:10) with the power to save someone's life or have them killed. Certainly unjust judges existed then, as now, but God is always just and merciful (e.g., Luke 18:2–8; Ps. 85:8–11). The functions of judging, ruling, saving, and destroying are all related, as Isaiah states: "the LORD is our judge, the LORD is our ruler, the LORD is our king; he will save us" (Isa. 33:22 NRSV). God both gives the laws and judges by them. Human judges might sentence a person to physical death, but only God can sentence someone to eternal death or life (Matt. 10:28).

God as the ultimate lawgiver and judge also always[131] has the power "to save and to destroy"[132] (James 4:12). Literally, **salvation** has

---

128. Emphatic "you" (σύ) begins the final sentence in 4:12, accentuating human arrogance (Robertson 1933, 54; McKnight 2011, 366).
129. See also Ps. 25:8; 27:11; 119:33, 102; 4 Macc. 5:25.
130. See also 1 Cor. 4:4–5.
131. The present participle is used for δύναμαι ("being able") in 4:12.
132. The aorist infinitive ("to save," "to destroy") has a sense of totality here, treating the ability to save and to destroy as single whole acts (Robertson 1934, 832).

to do with the prevention of death and potential death, or healing. For example, when a great windstorm caused the boat to be swept over by waves in the Sea of Galilee, Jesus's disciples woke him up, shouting: "Lord, save [σῴζω] us! We are perishing [ἀπόλλυμι]!" (Matt. 8:25). When Jesus calmed the winds and waves, they were "saved." The woman who had been bleeding for twelve years, whom no physician could heal, hoped that, if she touched Jesus's cloak, she would be "saved" or "healed." Jesus did heal (σῴζω) her (Matt. 9:20–22; Mark 5:25–34). God has the power to save from death, by healing (e.g., James 5:15).

"Salvation" is also spiritual. The word σῴζω may be used metaphorically to describe real spiritual events. Salvation can refer to freedom from condemnation or judgment for sins,[133] the granting of eternal life (which follows forgiveness by God),[134] transformed behavior and knowledge (e.g., Luke 19:7–9; 1 Tim. 2:4), and the redemption of the heirs' bodies (Rom. 8:23–24; Eph. 2:5–8). The implanted word and faith demonstrated by deeds will spiritually save someone (James 1:21; 2:14) by transforming their life into one that God will affirm at the judgment day. God has the power of life now and eternally (e.g., James 5:20).

God also has the power to take away life. To take away life can be expressed with different verbs in Greek. Φονεύω, for instance, was used to describe "murder" in James 4:2 and 2:11. Ἀποκτείνω signifies "to kill in any way whatever."[135] Θύω can signify to sacrifice or kill, as in John 10:10.[136] But ἀπόλλυμι (James 4:12) signifies "to **destroy**," in other words, "to put out of the way entirely, abolish, put an end to," including to kill.[137] For example, the beauty of a flower will eventually be ruined and totally end (James 1:11). A hair on one's head can die and fall off (Luke 21:18; Acts 27:34). Riches and gold can disintegrate (1 Pet. 1:7; Rev. 18:14). The heavens will eventually perish, in the same way as a garment falls apart (Heb. 1:10–11).[138] God can destroy life or save it.[139] Or, God can make null or of no effect the influence of some people (e.g., 1 Cor. 1:19). James refers to all these aspects of "destroy" in 4:12.

The twelve tribes have made their own laws by which they judge their neighbors (4:12). They have taken onto themselves God's exalted

---

133. E.g., Matt. 1:21; John 3:17; Rom. 5:9–10; 1 Thess. 2:16; 1 Tim. 1:15; 1 Pet. 4:18.
134. E.g., Matt. 24:13; Mark 13:13; Luke 13:23; Acts 2:21; Heb. 5:7; Jude 21–23.
135. Thayer, 64; "to deprive of life" (BDAG, 114).
136. Thayer, 294; BDAG, 463.
137. Thayer, 64–65.
138. See also Matt. 9:17; Mark 2:22.
139. E.g., Deut. 32:39; 1 Sam. 2:6; 2 Kings 5:7; Matt. 10:28; 1 Cor. 10:9–10; Jude 5.

position, using their worldly ways as means to lift themselves above other believers and trying to condemn and destroy them (4:1–6, 11–12).

Do Not Do Business as the World Does, Because Such Arrogance Is Inappropriate to Humans Whose Lives Are Temporary and Dependent on God's Will (4:13–17)

With the imperative "come," James moves to a different but related theme (4:13), a third aspect of worldly fighting,[140] and another way to speak falsehoods against others and usurp God's place: worldly planning in business (4:13–17). His basic statement in verse 13 is explained in verses 14–16 and is summarized in verse 17.

James uses the command (**"come"**) to catch the readers' attention as he tries to help them understand how their actions in business are wrong.[141] He speaks to a specific group: "the ones saying: 'Today or tomorrow we will go into such and such a city and we will be active there a year and we will carry on business and we will make a profit'" (4:13). Another related but different group will be addressed in 5:1, "the wealthy."[142] The group in 4:13–16 is comparable to the earlier groups described in the third person ("if *any*" [εἰ, ἐάν τις]): if any lacks wisdom (1:5), hears but does not do the word (1:23), thinks they are religious but does not bridle one's tongue (1:26), says that one has faith but does not have works (2:14), or wanders from the truth (5:19). These words introduce negative attitudes and actions.[143] James allows the readers in these instances to include themselves in the group if they fit in the group. He will do a similar technique at the end of the letter for neutral or unavoidable actions: *any* (τις) who suffer, are cheerful, or are sick (5:13–14).

Does James complain against all businesspeople who make future plans to make a profit? No. There is nothing inherently wrong in planning for the future or making a profit.[144] Proverbs 6 directs people to plan ahead and to work: "Go to the ant, you lazybones; consider its ways, and be wise. . . . It prepares its food in summer, and gathers its sustenance in harvest. How long will you lie there, O lazybones? When will you rise from your sleep? A little sleep, a little slumber, a little folding

---

140. See also Hiebert 1979, 272.
141. Ἄγω signifies "to direct the movement of an object from one position to another" or "to move away from a position," to go (BDAG, 16–17).
142. Both groups are introduced by the plural article used as a pronoun, "the ones" (οἱ).
143. Εἴ τις ("if any") in James 3:2, in contrast, is positive: "if any does not stumble in word."
144. Κερδαίνω ("I profit"), κέρδος ("profit").

of the hands to rest, and poverty will come upon you like a robber, and want, like an armed warrior" (Prov. 6:6, 8–11 NRSV). The capable wife described by King Lemuel's mother in Proverbs 31 is a merchant who brings her food from far away. She buys fields and makes and sells fine linen.[145] However, she is also trustworthy, kind, wise, and provides for the poor. Joseph is blessed by God. At thirty years of age, he becomes the second-in-command in Egypt and builds on God's foretelling by accumulating and then selling Pharaoh's crops (Gen. 41:33–57). Jesus also uses a businessperson as a positive model for those who seek the kingdom of God (Matt. 13:44–46). The slaves who invest the five and two talents (a talent is equal to more than $1,000—more than fifteen years of wages in that day) and thereby double the master's money are lauded by Jesus (Matt. 25:16–27). What is not lauded is "shameful profit" (Titus 1:11).

As James does not want his readers to take God's place in judgment (4:10–12), so too he does not want them to take God's place in business practices (4:13–16). Future planning has several contingencies that cannot be ignored: what happens tomorrow is unknown to ourselves, for we are temporal (4:14), and the Lord's will for us is not fully known (4:15). Not taking these contingencies seriously results in arrogant boasting (4:16). McKnight explains that the merchants "think their time, the locations to which they can go, their business activities, and their profits are all under their control." Their sin is "presumptuous planning and arrogant confidence that they can control life and profits."[146] These activities are part of friendship with the world—wanting something and not having it and therefore fighting for it by organizing one's life to obtain it (4:1–3, 13).

James addresses those who "carry on business" (4:13).[147] **"To do business"** is to trade, buy, and sell. James speaks to the world-traveling businessperson, "one on a journey, whether by sea or by land," a "merchant," not so much the local retailer (κάπηλος). Jesus told his

---

145. Prov. 31:11–14, 16, 18, 20, 24, 26, 31.

146. McKnight 2011, 377.

147. The verb used is ἐμπορεύομαι. In the word family is included ἔμπορος ("merchant"), ἐμπορία ("business"), ἐμπόριον ("market"). BDAG, 324, agrees that ἐμπορεύομαι in general literature signifies "both in the sense of travel and of traveling for business reasons." Travel is also included in James 4:13. LSJ, 547, 876, defines it as "travel" and travel for business, to be a merchant, while it defines κάπηλος as "retail-dealer," especially tavern-keeper. The opposite is merchant (ἔμπορος) or producer (αὐτοπώλης). Adkins and Adkins 2005, 200; Thayer, 208. Πορεύομαι ("go") emphasizes the activity of motion. Cf. 2 Cor. 2:17: καπηλεύω ("peddle for profit").

listeners about a wedding banquet for a king's son to which were invited farmers and merchants (ἐμπορία). While a third group grabbed the messengers and killed them—the merchants did not actively persecute the messengers—yet they still sinned by being so consumed with their work that they ignored attending the banquet, symbolic of the greatest event of all time—the celebration of God's Son coming to earth (Matt. 22:2–6). Merchants sold doves in the temple in Jerusalem, and by doing so changed its purpose from a house of prayer to a house of business or merchandise (John 2:16, ἐμπόριον). Revelation 18 describes some of the items that merchants would trade: gold, silver, jewels, pearls, fine linen, purple garments, silk, scarlet, scented wood, ivory, costly wood, bronze, iron, marble, cinnamon and other spices, incense, myrrh, frankincense, wine, olive oil, flour, wheat, cattle, sheep, horses, chariots, and slaves (Rev. 18:3, 11–13, 15–17). Ezekiel 27 describes additional items that Tyre, renowned for trade, sold: iron, tin, lead, mules, ebony, turquoise, coral, rubies, elephants' teeth, honey, wool, cane, camels, and lambs (Ezek. 27:3, 12–24). In other words, James is writing about any person doing business with any kind of product.[148]

The business persons join together a series of clauses with "and" (polysyndeton), thereby accentuating the continual nature of the work, each step just as important as the last one. They only use the future tense, not the more doubtful or hesitant subjunctive tense: "we will go . . . and we will be active . . . and we will carry on business and we will make a profit" (4:13).[149] The actions are all communal ("we, we, we, we"). This might even be a whole company or the household head telling the workers what they are going to do, or it could be one person telling another of his or her plans for the next year. The future tense is almost like a command. The future tense states positively what will occur and what they will do. The clauses are in sequence. First they go, then they stay, then they trade, and finally they make a profit. There is a purpose to their lives. What is the appeal? Life appears secure. The goal is concrete: financial security. Moreover, travel might be exciting to some.

---

148. See further on commerce in Judea, Jeremias (1962, 31–51). He mentions that "the profession of a merchant was held in great respect" (31); Martin 1988, 162. Adkins and Adkins (2005) add that the major imports and exports of Hellenistic Greece were grain, wine, olive oil, timber, fish, hides, marble, textiles, metals, pottery, and slaves (200–3); Harland 2002, 517–19.
149. In Luke 12:18–20, the future tense and "and" are repeated also in the boasting of the rich person who suddenly dies that night (Brosend 2004, 123).

But the problem, outside of the fact of whether their business goals please God, is that life is not as secure as one might want. We cannot be sure what tomorrow is going to look like. We do not even know whether we are going to be alive! "Which indeed you do not understand what kind of tomorrow is your life, for a mist you are, the one for a little appearing, then also disappearing" (4:14).[150] What is a **mist** (ἀτμίς)? A mist is not a cloud (νέφος),[151] a visible collection of particles of water or ice suspended in the air, usually high up above the earth's surface. In contrast, a mist is on the earth's surface. It is close up, but it is only "cloud-like." It is a onetime appearance of minute globules of water or simply a fine spray.[152] In the Bible, ἀτμίς refers to smoky vapor (Acts 2:19) or vapor from a furnace or pan[153] or to the mist or smoke from incense[154] or even to the haze before one's eyes from tears (Hos. 13:3 LXX). Jesus son of Sirach uses ἀτμίς to describe the "fiery vapors" that the sun sends forth as bright beams (Sir. 43:4). It is the type of mist or vapor that appears for a little then no longer appears. In the Bible it is often dependent on an external cause. Whether you are wealthy (James 1:11) or you are poor, you are still a "mist." What does this mean practically? We humans are not going to live forever. After the flood, God appears to have set a maximum of 120 years of age (Gen. 6:3; Deut. 34:7). According to Moses, people can expect to live until seventy or eighty years of age (Ps. 90:10), if ill health or persecution or an accident or war do not intervene. We may have eternity in our hearts, but, because of a fallen world, our bodies live in a world of mortality (Eccl. 3:11).

What does James suggest that businesspersons do? "Instead, you should say: 'If the Lord might will then we will live and we will do this or that'" (4:15). Plans are a necessary part of life, but they should be hypothetical because God is in control of our lives. We expect our plans to happen, but we have some doubt. Our future plans should be subsumed in a subjunctive attitude ("the Lord might will"), describing what is likely to occur in an attitude of expectation or anticipation. The subjunctive is a mood of doubt, hesitation, and hope.[155] Under the

---

150. See also Job 7:16; Ps. 39:4; Prov. 27:1; Matt. 6:34. Other biblical images used for the transience of life are a cloud (Job 7:9), grass (James 1:11; Pss. 102:11; 103:15–16); a spider's web (Ps. 39:11; 90:9), breath (Job 7:9), a flower (Job 14:2), and a shadow (1 Chron. 29:15; Ps. 102:11; Eccl. 6:12).
151. Thayer, 83, 424.
152. *Random House Webster's* 2001, 390, 1231.
153. Gen. 19:28; Sir. 22:24; 38:28; 2 Macc. 7:5.
154. Lev. 16:13; Ezek. 8:11; Sir. 24:15.
155. Robertson 1934, 927–78.

umbrella of "if the Lord might will" comes our future plans: "We will live and we will do this or that" (4:15). What is the result? The readers will be less arrogant and boastful about future accomplishments (4:16). One way to humble oneself before the Lord (4:10) is to make tentative plans. Then we trust the Lord to lift us up because we trust the Lord who is the good Parent who gives every good gift (1:17). We commit our work to the Lord and our plans can then be established by God (Prov. 16:3). Proverbs 16:9 explains: "The human mind plans the way, but the LORD directs the steps" (NRSV). Placing one's plans under God's will helps one receive the implanted word that has the power to save. It pleases God. It helps one be a doer of the word and mature as a Christian (James 1:21–22). On the other hand, once a businessperson understands this good concept, *not* to do it is "sin" (4:17).[156]

James applies this principle to believers in business. However, the apostle Paul used similar wording in all his plans of travel. For instance, when the Ephesians asked Paul to stay longer, he told them he would return—"God willing" (Acts 18:21). He did return (Acts 19). Even when Paul wrote to the Corinthians that he would visit them, he clarified "if the Lord might will" (1 Cor. 4:19; 16:7). He did make a quick trip to Corinth, but he did not make a second promised visit because, after deliberating, he concluded that the Lord did not want him to go to Corinth at that time (2 Cor. 1:15–17; 2:1–4). Paul also told the Romans that he hoped to visit them, "praying . . . by God's will to come" to them (Rom. 1:10). He asks the Romans to pray so that by God's will he might visit them (Rom. 15:32). He did visit them, but on his way to prison (Acts 28:14–16)! Then, Paul told the Philippians that he hoped to leave prison in Rome and visit them "in the Lord" (Phil. 2:24). By saying "if the Lord wills," travelers and merchants[157] are reminded, as are others to whom they communicate, that the Lord is ultimately in control and that they want ultimately to please God more than to make a profit in their work.

THEOLOGICAL AND HOMILETICAL
TOPICS IN CHAPTER 4

James concerns himself with soteriology, the process of salvation, and theology, the nature of God. He is interested in salvific transformation, the transformation of behavior, knowledge, and attitude. He wants a fully integrated personality with a Christlike worldview and lifestyle. Such Christian worldviews are desperately needed today in

---

156. "Sin" is emphasized, the object being placed before the verb (Hiebert 1979, 280).
157. See also Heb. 6:3.

Christianity because, instead of desiring to please God, Christians who only talk about faith but do not act on it serve their own desires and worldly friendship. Many business entrepreneurs go into business only to achieve financial security,[158] not to thank and honor God. For example, John Henry Womack, who founded and was the president and CEO of three businesses, first began his businesses as solely a means for him to provide for his family. But later he realized God had a bigger plan for his companies: to serve and build capability within communities and, specifically, to develop the economic opportunities for African Americans. Every meeting was begun in prayer, even among the board of directors, where participants were not all Christian. Notwithstanding, in 1989–90 his business was rated as one of the top one hundred African American owned and operated companies in the United States by *Black Enterprise Magazine*.[159]

God provides the resources to transform greedy and embattled business practices. God's grace responds to us when we draw near to God. Humans should not strive to take God's place in judgment and business. Whether recognized or not, God is in control of life's events, and humans need to be humble if they want to honor God.

James relies on the Ten Commandments and Jesus's teachings as the basis for Christian living: not to covet what others have in order to benefit one's own sensual desires, not to murder and fight to obtain what is not ours, and not to worship worldly ideals in wanting more than what is ours. Instead, James wants us to ask well and to fulfill the summation of the Ten Commandments, which is to love our neighbor as ourselves, in all aspects of our lives.

This is what we need to strive for with one another, to present friendship with the world as unattractive and friendship with God as attractive and worthwhile. We get there by way of personal and group exhortation, education, and entreaty to God.

JAMES SHOWS CHRIST

Martin Luther is renowned for his comment regarding James's letter in his 1522 introduction to his first edition of his German New Testament. He writes that Saint James's epistle is a "right strawy epistle in comparison with" Saint John's gospel, Saint Paul's epistles, and Saint Peter's first epistle because it does not "show thee Christ" and it "has no gospel character to it." However, we have seen how James echoes many of Jesus's teachings. James is interested in numerous topics that

---

158. Lesonsky 2001, 17.
159. Spencer 2015, 45–46; Womack 2016, ch. 6.

interest Jesus, and his perspective on those topics is similar to Jesus's perspective. No wonder—since James is Jesus's half-brother. They had the same mother and human father, Mary and Joseph. Furthermore, it is likely that James heard Jesus preach. We are told that Mary and Jesus's siblings were sometimes present at Jesus's teaching.[160] James may not have fully accepted Jesus's claims for himself during Jesus's lifetime, but he could not keep away from Jesus's preaching and certainly accepted his claims later.

James shows the reader Christ by developing many concepts taught by Jesus.[161] For example, James develops an important parable Jesus used: the parable of the sower.[162] The parable illustrates perseverance and the demonstration of understanding by movement from hearing to doing.[163] For James the "word" that is sown in different soils is Jesus's teachings.

Jesus and James also place priority on applying the Ten Commandments to the disciples' lives. Both refer to the summary of the Ten Commandments: love your neighbor as yourself[164] and to the sixth, seventh, and tenth commandments, not to commit adultery, murder, or coveting.[165]

James, like Jesus, employs the analogy of defining a tree by its fruit.[166] Actions define what someone believes. Both are teachers[167] who warn their listeners that teachers have to guard the words they say.[168] They both warn against hypocrisy[169] and the danger of demons and hell[170] and falling under God's judgment.[171]

---

160. See introduction. Matt. 12:46–50; Mark 3:20–35; Luke 8:4–21; John 2:1–12; 7:3–10.
161. For similar comparisons, see McKnight 2011, 25–27; Mayor 1913, lxxxv–lci; McCartney 2009, 49–52; Brosend 2004, 11; Painter and deSilva 2012, 34–39.
162. Matt. 13:3–23; Mark 4:3–20; Luke 8:5–15.
163. James 1:2, 12, 18–19, 21–22; 2:14, 17–26; 4:1–3; Matt. 5:16; 7:21, 24; 11:15; 13:16, 43; 21:28–32, 43; 23:3; Luke 11:27–28.
164. James 2:8, 11; Matt. 7:12; 22:36–40; Luke 18:20.
165. James 2:11; 3:14; 4:2–4; 5:6; Matt. 5:21–22, 27–28; 12:39; 16:4; 19:18; 22:37–40; Mark 10:19; Luke 18:20.
166. James 3:12, 18; Matt. 7:16–18, 12:33; Luke 6:44–45.
167. James 3:1; Matt. 23:7; Luke 20:21; John 1:38.
168. James 3:1, 9; Matt. 5:19; 7:2, 24; 12:36–37; Luke 20:47.
169. James 3:17; Matt. 22:18; 23:28; 24:51; Luke 12:2.
170. James 3:6; 4:7; Matt. 4:1–11; 9:32–34; 10:8; 13:39, 42, 50; 17:15–18; 18:8; 25:40, 45; Luke 11:15–20.
171. James 4:12; 5:7–9; Matt. 10:28; 24:33; 25:46.

James and Jesus center on several similar and important concepts, including humility and gentleness;[172] self-identification as a slave;[173] perfection or maturity;[174] reversal of positions;[175] evil coming from within, therefore, transformation having to begin with the inside;[176] asking in faith without doubt to a generous God;[177] joy;[178] impartiality;[179] peace;[180] righteousness;[181] purity (James 3:17; 4:8; Matt. 5:8); grace (James 4:6; John 1:14, 17); forgiveness (James 5:15–16; Matt. 6:14–15; 9:2–8; 12:32); mercy (James 2:13; 3:17; Matt. 9:13; 12:7); and having a similar attitude to the future (James 4:13–15; Matt. 6:34) and toward judgment (James 2:4, 13; 4:11–12; Matt. 7:1–2).[182] James emphasized in his letter what Jesus considered to be the "weightier matters of the law" (justice and mercy and faith) (Matt. 23:23), that God is good and generous (James 1:5, 17; Matt. 7:11), and that Jesus is the Lord of glory (James 2:1; Matt. 24:30; 25:31; Luke 9:29–32; John 1:14). Both Jesus and James are very sympathetic to the poor and critical of the rich;[183] neither are sympathetic to anger and swearing.[184]

Both enjoy using a variety of images from nature in their teaching: sowing seeds, sunlight, rain, birds,[185] the wavering sea as a vehicle for doubt (James 1:6–8; Matt. 8:23–27; 14:24–31), the temporary nature of wild flowers (James 1:11; Matt. 6:28–30), vineyards (James 3:12; Matt. 20:1–8; 21:28–41), fig trees (James 3:12; Matt. 21:19–21), salt (James 3:11–12; Matt. 5:13), laughing and mourning (James 4:9; 5:1; Matt. 5:4; Luke 6:21, 25), and "above" as a synecdoche for God's presence (James

---

172. James 1:9, 11; 3:13, 17; Matt. 11:28–30; 18:2–4; 23:12.
173. James 1:1; Matt. 20:26–28; 23:11–12; Mark 10:43–45.
174. James 1:1–4; 3:2; Matt. 5:47–48; 12:35.
175. James 1:9–10; 4:6–10; Matt. 10:39; 23:12; 25:29; Luke 6:20–26; 12:48; 18:14.
176. James 1:14–15; 2:9, 4:1–8; Matt. 12:34–35; 15:8, 11, 17–20; 19; 23:25–28; Mark 7:20–23.
177. James 1:3, 5–8, 17; 4:2–3; Matt. 7:7–11; 9:2, 22, 28–29; 13:58; 14:31; 15:28; 17:20–21; 18:18–20; 21:22; Luke 11:9–13.
178. James 1:2; Matt. 5:10–12; Luke 10:17–20.
179. James 2:1; Matt. 7:2; Luke 20:21; John 7:24.
180. James 3:17–18; Matt. 5:9; 10:12–13, 34–38.
181. James 1:20; 3:18; 5:6; Matt. 3:15; 5:6, 20; 6:33.
182. James 2:13; 3:17; 5:11; Matt. 5:7; 9:10–13; 12:7; 18:21–35; 20:31–34; 25:34–45.
183. James 1:9–11, 27; 2:1–9, 15–16; 5:1–6; Matt. 5:3; 6:11, 19–21, 25–32; 8:20; 11:5; 19:21–24; Mark 12:41–44; Luke 4:18; 6:20–26; 12:33; 20:45–47.
184. James 1:19–21; 5:12; Matt. 5:21–22, 33–37; 23:16–22.
185. James 1:17–18; 3:7; 5:7, 17–18; Matt. 6:26–30; 7:25–27; 13:24–43.

1:17; John 8:23). They both use the terms "brother" and "sister" (James 1:14–15; Matt. 12:49–50) and "twelve tribes" (James 1:1; Matt. 19:28). In illustrations, both employ the masculine for the concrete and the generic for the abstract (James 1:6–8; Matt. 7:24–26), and use many rhetorical questions to engage their listeners. Like other Jews, they consider Abraham and Elijah to be model believers and esteem being friends of God.[186]

Both of them treat synagogues as important[187] and are called to minister to the "lost sheep of Israel" (James 1:1; Matt. 10:5–6; 15:24). Not only were James and Jesus both teachers, but they also furthered healing, prayer, and transformation. But for James, healing was done in *Jesus*'s name.[188]

Thus, James shows Christ by alluding to and developing Jesus's teachings. Jesus preached, "Repent, for God's reign has come near," proclaiming good news to the poor, healing to the needy, and freedom to the oppressed, and, consequently, James taught God's royal law (James 2:5, 8; Matt. 11:5; Luke 4:18, 43). What Jesus taught was "gospel," and James applies that gospel to his own context.

---

186. James 2:21–23; 5:17–18; Matt. 3:9; 8:11; 11:14; 17:11–12; 22:32; 27:47–49; Luke 4:25–26; 13:16, 28: 16:22–30; 19:9; John 8:39–40, 56–58; 15:15–16.
187. James 2:2; Matt. 6:5; 13:54; 23:6; Luke 4:16; John 18:20.
188. James 5:14–20; Matt. 4:23; 6:5–13; 8:14–17; 18:10–15; 21:13; Luke 19:10.

TRANSLATION AND GRAMMATICAL ANALYSIS[1]

5:1a Come, now, rich ones, (initial sentence; main clause)

5:1b weep crying aloud for your coming miseries. (main clause)

5:2a Your riches have rotted (explanatory sentence; main clause)

5:2b and your clothing has become moth-eaten; (main clause)

5:3a your gold and silver have become corroded (main clause)

5:3b and their corrosion will be a witness against you and will eat your flesh as fire.[2] (main clause)

5:3c You stored up [as treasures] in the last days. (explanatory sentence; main clause)

5:4a Behold (illustrative sentence; main clause)

---

1. See "Definition of Terms in Grammatical Analysis."
2. These are compound verbs with the same subject "rust."

5:4b the wages of the laborers, the ones having reaped your fields, the one being withheld[3] from you, shout,[4] (subordinate noun clause or main clause)

5:4c and the cries of the ones harvesting have come to the ears of the Lord of Hosts. (subordinate noun clause or main clause)

5:5a You live a life of luxury on the earth (explanatory sentence; main clause)

5:5b and you live luxuriously, (main clause)

5:5c your hearts are fattened in a day of slaughter, (main clause)

5:6d You condemn, (main clause)

5:6e you kill the righteous, (main clause)

5:6f he does not resist you. (main clause)

5:7a Therefore, persevere, brothers and sisters, until the arrival of the Lord. (initial sentence; main clause)

5:7a Behold (main clause)

5:7b the farmer awaits the precious fruit of the earth being patient upon it (subordinate noun clause or main clause)

5:7c until he might receive early and late rains. (subordinate adverbial clause; temporal)

5:8a Persevere also you, (alternative sentence; main clause)

5:8b strengthen your hearts, (main clause)

---

3. Some ancient Greek manuscripts (fifth century and later) have ἀπεστερημένος ("defraud"). However, the earliest and best quality Greek manuscripts (codexes Sinaiticus and Vaticanus, fourth century) support ἀφυστερημένος ("withhold"). The same Greek word is used in Nehemiah 9:20.
4. See 3:4a, b.

5:8c since the arrival of the Lord draws near. (subordinate adverbial clause; causal; answers why)

5:9a Do not keep murmuring, brothers and sisters, against one another, (adversative sentence; main clause)

5:9b lest you might be judged; (subordinate adverbial clause; causal; answers why)

5:9a behold[5] (explanatory sentence; main clause)

5:9b the judge before the doors stands. (subordinate noun clause or main clause)

5:10a [For] an example of suffering and perseverance, brothers and sisters, take the prophets, (illustrative sentence; main clause)

5:10b who spoke in the Lord's name. (subordinate adjectival clause)

5:11a Behold (illative sentence; main clause)

5:11b we consider blessed the ones enduring; (subordinate noun clause or main clause)

5:11a you heard of the endurance of Job (illustrative sentence; main clause)

5:11b and you saw the outcome of the Lord, (main clause)

5:11c that greatly compassionate is the Lord and merciful. (subordinate adverbial clause; causal; answers why)

5:12a And above all things, my brothers and sisters, do not make an oath either heavenly or earthly or any other oath; (initial sentence; main clause)

5:12a but let your yes be yes (adversative sentence; main clause)

5:12b and [let your] no [be] no (main clause)

---

5. See 3:4a.

5:12c lest you might fall under judgment. (subordinate adverbial clause; causal; answers why)[6]

5:13a Are any among you suffering? (initial sentence; main clause)

5:13a Let that person keep praying. (illative sentence; main clause)

5:13a Are any among you cheerful? (illustrative sentence; main clause)

5:13a Let that person keep singing! (illative sentence; main clause)

5:14a Are any sick among you? (illustrative sentence; main clause)

5:14a Let him call for him/herself the elders of the church (illative sentence; main clause)

5:14b and let them pray for that person, having anointed him/her with oil in the name of the Lord. (main clause)

5:15a And the prayer of faith will save the one being sick (illative sentence; main clause)

5:15b and the Lord will raise that one; (main clause)

5:15a and, if he may have committed sins, (explanatory sentence; subordinate adverbial clause; condition; third class)

5:15b it will be forgiven to him/her. (main clause)

5:16a Therefore, keep confessing your sins to one another (illative sentence; main clause)

5:16b and keep praying for one another, (main clause)

---

6.   Robertson (1933, 63) calls a subordinate clause "negative purpose."

5:16c so that you may be healed. (subordinate adverbial clause; final; purpose/result)

5:16a The prayer of a righteous person has much strength in its working. (explanatory sentence; main clause)

5:17a Elijah was a human of like nature to us, (illustrative sentence; main clause)

5:17b and he prayed fervently that it might not rain, (main clause)

5:17c and for three years and six months it did not rain on the earth. (main clause)

5:18a Then he prayed again, (illustrative sentence; main clause)

5:18b and the heaven gave rain (main clause)

5:18c and the earth yielded its harvest. (main clause)

5:19a My brothers and sisters, if anyone among you might be led astray[7] from the truth (initial sentence; subordinate adverbial clause; conditional)

5:19b and someone might turn him/her back,[8] (subordinate adverbial clause; conditional)

5:20c let that person know (main clause)

5:20d that the one having turned back a sinner from his erroneous way will save his life from death (subordinate noun clause)

5:20e and will cover a multitude of sins. (subordinate noun clause)

---

7. In passive voice, "to proceed without a sense of proper direction" (BDAG, 821–22).
8. "To return to a point where one has been" (BDAG, 382).

OUTLINE

V. Lay aside wealth (5:1–12).
   A. The rich will be judged (5:1–6).
   B. Therefore, be patient and be ready because the Judge is standing at the doors (5:7–11).
   C. Do not swear oaths (5:12).

VI. Receive the implanted word by being mature in actions (5:13–20).
   A. Deal wisely with suffering, joy, and illness (5:13–18).
   B. Deal wisely with those led astray (5:19–20).

LITERARY STRUCTURE

James addresses two related but different groups in 4:13–17 and 5:1–6. Both sections discuss issues related to wealth. In 4:13–17, James addresses the world-traveling businesspersons who boast in their plans. In 5:1–6, James addresses the unjust wealthy. The same introductory command introduces each section, the imperative "come" (ἄγε, 4:13; 5:1). The first "come now" is a warning providing the opportunity to change, while the second "come now" is a warning predicting judgment to come. In chapter 5, the three themes discussed in the letter conclude: the rich who oppress the poor will be judged (wealth, 5:1–6), the laborer must persevere through trials (from the rich) because the judge is near, and the listeners should not murmur or give oaths (wisdom and the tongue) (5:7–12). Laying aside evil deeds is discussed in 5:1–12 and receiving the implanted word is discussed in 5:13–20. The final conclusion (5:13–20) explains how to persevere in the midst of different trials. Prayer and community can address experiences of joy, suffering, illness, and deception. In contrast to the unrepentant wealthy, doers of the word care for the innocent poor (1:27), do not favor the wealthy over the poor (2:1–13), act to assist the poor (2:14–17), pay the wages of laborers (5:4), and reach out to those led astray (5:19–20).

EXPOSITION

Lay Aside Wealth (5:1–12)

The Rich Will Be Judged (5:1–6)
The dramatic call "come now" is addressed to the wealthy. In ancient Judea, the wealthy included merchants (4:13), landowners

(5:4–5), tax collectors, bankers, priestly aristocracy, and persons of private means.[9] Some commentators[10] wonder whether the "**rich ones**" (πλούσιος) are believers in James's letter. In 5:1, they are commanded to "weep crying aloud for your coming miseries." Κλαίω ("weep audibly," 5:1) may be a sign of genuine repentance (see 4:9). However, the modifying participle "**crying**" (ὀλολύζω) suggests this weeping is a sign of judgment.[11] Ὀλολύζω is onomatopoetic. It sounds like what it describes (*o-lo-lu-zo*), a loud repeating cry of grief. Among the Greeks, it is mostly used to refer to women crying aloud to the gods in prayer.[12] In the Old Testament, God exhorts the idols in Jerusalem to "howl" when they fall (Isa. 10:10) and Isaiah exhorts the Israelites: "*Howl ye, for the day of the Lord is near, and destruction from God shall arrive*" (Isa. 13:6).[13] The Lord warns Lebanon: "Let the pine howl [ὀλολύζω], because the cedar has fallen; for the mighty men have been greatly afflicted [ταλαιπωρέω]: howl [ὀλολύζω], ye oaks of the land of Bashan; for the thickly planted forest has been torn down" (Zech. 11:2). Howling occurs at defeat—God's punishment.[14] The cry of the rich might as well be this repeating *o-lo-lu-zo*, which the pagans cry out to false gods or the Jews cry when in despair and judgment, because they will not be able to avoid the miseries coming upon them. This is a hopeless cry.[15]

In contrast with 5:1–6, 1:10–11 suggests that the rich can be believers. The "lowly brother" is contrasted with the "rich one" ("brother" being a metaphor for a Christian believer). If the rich were to boast in their lowly position, they would not rely on the temporary state of their

9.   Jeremias 1969, 95–98.
10. E.g., Townsend (1994, 90) concludes that the rich in 5:1 "are not members or prospective members of the community, but its enemies." Davids (1982, 174) agrees that the landholding class is "clearly outside the community" as opposed to the merchant class in chapter 4 (also Hiebert 1979, 283; Moo 2015, 201; Vlachos 2013, 158). According to Ropes (1916, 282), the rich in 1:10 are Christians, but not in 2:2–6 and 5:1–6. McKnight (2011, 381) concludes neither 4:13–17 nor 5:1–6 refer to the messianic community, yet the "rich" are directly addressed.
11. Yet, even though Jonah preached only impending judgment, the Ninevites repented (Painter and deSilva 2012, 153).
12. LSJ, 1217.
13. See also Isa. 14:31; 15:2–3; 16:7; 23:1, 6, 14; 24:11; Jer. 48:20, 31; Ezek. 21:12; Hos. 7:14.
14. For the combination of defeat and judgment, see also Jer. 4:13 LXX. Cf. James 4:9, which has misery but not necessarily judgment.
15. Cf. πενθέω ("mourn") in James 4:9; Luke 6:21 and στενάζω ("to express grief by inarticulate or semi-articulate sounds") in James 5:9.

riches and thus they too would be God's heirs. When James indicates that God chose the poor to be rich in faith, nothing is said of the spiritual state of the wealthy. The "poor" are those who love God in word and deed (2:5). However, Joseph of Arimathea is described as a "rich" person and a "disciple of Jesus" (Matt. 27:57). Zacchaeus was a "rich" chief tax collector who gave away half of his possessions to the poor and paid back four times as much as he defrauded (Luke 19:2–10). Paul exhorts the rich believers not to be haughty and not to hope upon the uncertainty of riches, but rather to hope on God, do good, be rich in good deeds, and give (1 Tim. 6:17–19).[16] In effect, we find in James stages of indictment among the wealthy that eventually lead to condemnation if behavior and attitude are not changed.[17]

James, who himself was not reared in a wealthy home, was partial to the poor. He reminded his hearers that the rich oppress poor believers, drag them into court, slander their name, and do not pay their wages (2:5–6; 5:4). The rich are given preferential treatment, even though they oppress the poor. James and Jesus see wealth more as an impediment than an asset.[18] The danger of wealth is to then assert, as did the church in Laodicea: "I am rich and I have acquired wealth and I have need of nothing" (Rev. 3:17). No one ever has need of nothing from God. In contrast, Jesus who is rich became poor for the sake of humans (2 Cor. 8:9).

What are the "**miseries**" (ταλαιπωρία, 5:1)? "Your riches have rotted and your clothing has become moth-eaten; your gold and silver have become corroded and their corrosion will be a witness against you and will eat your flesh as fire" (5:2–3). James connects "rich ones" (5:1) with "riches" (5:2) by repetition (pleonasm) and alliteration.[19] The riches are destroyed by age or are worn out.[20] Clothing is now "moth-eaten." In 5:2–3, James appears to allude to illustrations Jesus used in the Sermon on the Mount when he said, "Do not store up for yourselves treasures on earth, where moth and rust consume and where thieves break in and steal; but store up for yourselves treasures in heaven, where neither moth nor rust consumes and where thieves do not break

---

16. See also Spencer 2013, 161–63.
17. See also Adamson 1976, 183; McKnight 2011, 397.
18. See exposition of James 2:5–6. E.g., Matt. 19:23–24; Luke 6:24; 12:15–21; 16:19–31; 18:22–25.
19. Alliteration is created by repetition of initial syllabi (πλου-) in πλούσιοι ... πλοῦτος ("rich ones ... riches") and initial consonants of the action (σε + ση) in σέσηπεν ... σητόβρωτα ("rotted ... moth-eaten").
20. Thayer, 568, 574.

in and steal" (Matt. 6:19–20 NRSV). Jesus's point is that "where your treasure is, there your heart will be also" (Matt. 6:21). James continues, what happens when your treasure is on the earth, even if you have hired guards to prevent stealing? It still becomes destroyed.

Moths (σής) are well known as consumers of clothing. Moths are the second largest group of insects. Especially in the larva or caterpillar stage some moths are very destructive, feeding on plants, grains, fruits, fruit trees, and clothing of wool and fur. The moths deposit many eggs from which emerge caterpillars. They are voracious eaters that destroy the foliage, stems, roots, and wood of growing plants; they invade and devour stored food products and ruin fibers. Larvae enter fruit and feed internally, just below the surface. Damage to an orchard can reach up to 90 percent.[21] Thus, from the outside a fruit might look healthy, but on the inside it is dying (cf. Prov. 25:20).

Moths spoiling garments (5:2) is a persistent image of destruction and mortality,[22] analogous to the withering of a flower (Job 13:28–14:2; cf. James 1:11). Job complains about the rich: "Even if he should gather silver as earth, and prepare gold as clay . . . his house is gone like moths, and like a spider's web" (Job 27:16, 18 LXX). **Corruption** (σήπω) is used for the destruction of clothes (Ep. Jer. 71–72), plants (Ezek. 17:9), and even human flesh.[23] The pseudepigraphal Epistle of Jeremiah (c. first century BC) describes the gods of wood laid over with silver and gold and regal clothing: "Ye shall know them to be no gods by the bright purple that *rotteth* upon them" (72). Riches are transient, James warns. They may be attractive for a while and from a superficial perspective, but from the inside out they will become destroyed.

"Riches" (πλοῦτος, 5:2) is a general term that includes clothing, money ("gold and silver"), and "a life of luxury" (5:3, 5). As early as Abrahamic times, gold, silver, and clothing were combined together to be special gifts by Abraham's estate manager to the prospective bride, Rebekah (Gen. 24:22, 53). Abraham was very rich (πλούσιος) in silver and gold (Gen. 13:2). Clothing is more ephemeral than gold and silver. And yet even gold and silver can become corroded.[24] I once hid some gold coins in our basement for my mother. When our basement was flooded, we forgot they had been stored there. Years later, when we

---

21. Beer 1987, 586–87, 590; EPPO 2011, 2.
22. E.g., Job 4:19–21; Isa. 50:9; 51:8; 32:22 LXX; Mic. 7:4 LXX.
23. Job 13:27–14:2; 16:8 LXX; 19:20 LXX; 33:21.
24. Peter agrees that silver and gold are perishable (1 Pet. 1:18). See also Lam. 4:1; Ep. Jer. 12, 24. Cf. Brosend 2004, 133.

rediscovered the coins, most of them were damaged and their value had greatly diminished.

Gold and silver (5:3) were rare metals in Greece and Rome; they were imported from Spain.[25] Both were used as coinage and for ornaments. They were melted in fire in order to be purified.[26] These valuable metals[27] were used to decorate many items in the tabernacle/temple, such as the ark of the covenant.[28] Merchants would sell these special items (Rev. 18:12). Sometimes idols would be made of gold and silver.[29] Even Jesus's family was given gold by the magi (Matt. 2:11). Although gold and silver have to be refined, both are resistant to corrosive materials. Gold is not attacked by any single acid except hot selenic.[30] Silver is resistant to corrosive materials, such as acetic acid and alkali.[31] Thus, when James refers to "gold and silver" (5:3), he refers to highly valued items that do not easily corrode. But, even as riches and clothing can come into a destroyed state, so too can even gold and silver, as we learned: "your gold and silver have become corroded and their corrosion will be a witness against you and will eat your flesh as fire" (5:3).

James uses two words that are interrelated: κατιόω ("to **corrode**") and ἰός ("corrosion" or "**rust**," 5:3). Κατιόω, made of several words (κατά ["down/over"] and ἰός ["corrosion"]), signifies "to rust over," "rust through," "become rusty, tarnished, corroded."[32] Ἰός, which also means "poison, venom,"[33] was already used in James 3:8 to describe the "restless" tongue, "full of deadly *poison*." Now a similar poison has corroded their valuables. Although silver is resistant to corrosion and does not oxidize easily, it readily forms a surface of silver sulfide that can tarnish. Gold too can darken and tarnish from perspiration, perfumes, storage, leaching of acid, and acidic vegetables. This film or coating can be called "rust" or "corrosion." Strabo writes about the Dead Sea that it is full of asphalt, from which arises smoky soot that "tarnishes copper and silver and anything that glistens, even gold" (*Geogr.* 16.2.42).

---

25. E.g., Isa. 60:9; Hammond and Scullard 1970, 471, 990; *J.W.* 2.374.
26. E.g., Prov. 10:20; 17:3; 27:21; Ezek. 24:11–12.
27. E.g., 1 Cor. 3:12; 2 Tim. 2:20.
28. E.g., Exod. 25:11–12; 27:11; Matt. 23:16–17; Heb. 9:4.
29. E.g., Exod. 20:23; Acts 17:29; 19:24; Rev. 9:20.
30. Hopkins 1987, 198; Corrosion Doctors n.d., "Gold Corrosion."
31. Levy 1987, 33.
32. Thayer, 340; BDAG, 477, 534; Robertson 1933, 58; Kohlenberger, Goodrick, and Swanson 1995, 522.
33. LSJ, 832.

Corrosion is "the deterioration of a material, usually a metal, that re-sults from a reaction with its environment."[34]

James now moves to personification to indicate the shocking next stage (5:3). The very items one has valued—inanimate gold and silver—have themselves produced a product ("corrosion") that becomes incarnate and a human enemy, a **"witness** against" one, which will not simply remain on the metals but will metathesize onto one's own flesh and consume it "as fire" (5:3). **"Fire"** ($\pi\hat{\upsilon}\rho$) is another image to describe the tongue, as was "poison" (James 3:5–6). Fire affects the whole body; now it destroys the person (3:6; 5:3). The user of fire is eventually destroyed by it. Thus, judgment is self-inflicted, the result of one's own values, choices, and behavior. These were the treasures stored up[35] ($\theta\eta\sigma\alpha\upsilon\rho\acute{\iota}\zeta\omega$, 5:3), probably alluding to Jesus's warning not to store up treasures ($\theta\eta\sigma\alpha\upsilon\rho\acute{\iota}\zeta\omega$) on earth where "moth and rust destroy" (Matt. 6:19–20).

Another witness against them at their judgment is their injustice against their laborers (5:4). By repeating the article (four times) be-tween each adjective, James emphasizes the subject: *"the* wages of *the* laborers of *the* ones having reaped *the* fields" (5:4). He tells us three things about the wages: whose wages they are ("the laborers"); what the owners have done with the wages (they have withheld them); and how, through personification, the wages have responded (they shout in complaint!). As a result, the harvesters too cry, and the God of war ("hosts") hears them.

James begins with the imperative "behold" (5:4, as he also did in 3:4, 5, with the illustrations of the ships and forests) to call the atten-tion of his readers[36] to this amazing but dismaying picture of wages shouting because the landowners have not been paying their workers.[37]

---

34. *Random House Webster's* 2001, 1685; Corrosion Doctors n.d., "Gold Cor-rosion": 1; "Silver Corrosion": 1; "What Corrosion Is!": 3; Levy 1987, 33–34; Robertson (1933, 58) summarizes: silver corrodes and gold tarnishes. BDAG (477) adds that the ancients praised gold for "being rustproof," but "if not adequately refined or subject to chemical pollution some metals in a gold object would be subject to oxidation."
35. Hiebert 1979 explains that the aorist tense "states the historical fact with no reference to the duration of the activity, now viewed as termi-nated by the judgment" (287–88).
36. BDAG, 468. See also Davids 1982, 177.
37. Even though Jesus exhorted his disciples not to practice their piety for earthly rewards (Matt. 5:12; Luke 6:23, 35), but rather for heavenly ones, yet he commanded the seventy-two workers to expect room and board as

In Judea,[38] outside of the urban centers, most people were involved in agriculture.[39] God had taught that the real owner of the land was God (Lev. 25:23) and that humans were hereditary tenants. Even if land were sold, in the year of Jubilee all land was to be returned to its original owners or heirs (Lev. 25:10–34). However, during the monarchy and thereafter, land became concentrated in large estates among a wealthy minority. For example, the high priest Rabbi Eleazar ben Harsum inherited from his father one thousand villages and one thousand ships, and had so many slaves that they did not know their own master.[40] The exile broke up some of these large estates, but still, before the AD 70 war, after the time of Herod, the number of landless tenants increased. Many of the small plots of land were sold to large landowners. Droughts, poor harvests, famines, and heavy taxation[41] might cause a small peasant landowner to mortgage fields to the wealthy and become a hired laborer or tenant farmer on them. The powerful tried to keep the peasants perennially in debt.[42] Landlords in Judea tended to hire free laborers rather than slaves to work the land.[43] A day laborer would earn about a denarius a day (Matt. 20:2, 9). In contrast, for example, the marriage settlement of Miriam, daughter of Nicodemus ben Gorion, was a million gold denarii. One widow received four hundred gold denarii a day simply for luxuries.[44]

The Old Testament laws were very strict about paying workers their wages on time. James certainly presupposes such laws as Deuteronomy 24:14–15 (NRSV): "You shall not withhold the wages of poor and needy laborers, whether other Israelites or aliens who reside in your land in one of your towns. You shall pay them their wages daily before sunset, because they are poor and their livelihood

---

payment for sharing the good news because "the worker is worthy of his wages" (μισθός, James 5:4; Luke 10:7; 1 Tim. 5:17–18).
38. "Judea" is the official name of the province. After AD 139 it became Syria Palestine (Schürer 1973–79, 1:514).
39. Some estimate 80–90 percent. The seven staples in Judea were wheat, barley, grapes, figs, pomegranates, olives, and honey (Deut. 8:8; Hanson and Oakman 1998, 104–5; Harland 2002, 515–6, 520–22).
40. Jeremias 1969, 97, 99.
41. Taxation consumed approximately one quarter to one half of production, which was given to Rome and Herod, and more for the Jerusalem temple (Hanson and Oakman 1998, 108, 114; Harland 2002, 522).
42. Hanson and Oakman 1998, 120.
43. Hengel 1974, 14–16; Davids 1982, 32–33; Blomberg and Kamell 2008, 222, 225.
44. Jeremias 1969, 94–95.

depends on them; otherwise they might cry to the LORD against you, and you would incur guilt."[45] But in preexilic times some wealthy landowners did not follow God's laws. They seized lands that were not theirs (e.g., Mic. 2:2; Isa. 5:8) and did not pay their workers (e.g., Jer. 22:13). These practices continued even after the exile (Mal. 3:5; Luke 20:47). These landowners would owe money but be remiss in paying what they owed.[46] If the laborers were not paid, they and their families could not eat or pay their bills.

Several synonyms for "cry out" are used: "**shout**" (κράζω, κραυγή) and "**cries**" (βοή, βοάω, 5:4). Κράζω may be onomatopoetic to signify a "croak," such as "the cry of the raven," and "to cry out harshly," including with inarticulate sounds. To "shout" is to cry aloud vociferously.[47] It can be a shout of complaint, of fear, of pleading for healing, or of joy.[48] Βοή (noun) and βοάω (verb) also signify "to use one's voice at a high volume," even as loud as the roar of a lion. But, they emphasize more a "cry out as a manifestation of feeling."[49] Feeling would be expressed by Jesus's shout at the cross: "My God, my God, why have you forsaken me?" (Mark 15:34), or when the chosen ones cry out to God day and night for help (Luke 18:7). Βοάω can refer to shouting out a proclamation (Matt. 3:3–4), crying for healing (Luke 9:38–40; 18:38), complaining (Acts 17:6; 25:24), or expressing joy (Gal. 4:27).[50] The wages shout harshly with outrage at the injustice,[51] personifying the cry with dismay and pleading for help for the harvesters.

God is not a human, but human characteristics are sometimes used to describe God in order to communicate aspects of God's character (anthropomorphism). The "**ear**" (οὖς, 5:4) is a synecdoche, a part to represent hearing and response to pleas. Jesus would often repeat "the one having ears, let him/her hear" to signify that listeners need to be willing to understand and respond positively.[52] These cries of the

45. See also Lev. 19:13; m. B. Mes. 9:11–12.
46. Unlike God, who did not *withhold* the manna he promised the Israelites, Neh. 9:20 ἀφυστερέω ("withhold"); BDAG, 159; Thayer, 90.
47. Thayer, 104, 358; BDAG, 563.
48. Complaint: Matt. 8:29; 27:23; fear: Matt. 14:26, 30; healing: Matt. 9:27; 15:22–23; 20:30–31; joy: Matt. 21:9, 15.
49. Thayer, 103–4; BDAG, 180.
50. See further Spencer and Spencer 1990, 140–43.
51. Campbell 2017 claims Old Testament writers almost exclusively use κράζω to move God to action, never simply to accept a situation (130–31).
52. Matt. 11:15; 13:9, 43; Mark 4:9, 23; 8:18; Luke 8:8; 14:35; Isa. 6:9–10.

"wages of the laborers" will be heard, understood, and responded to by "the Lord of Hosts."[53]

"The Lord of Hosts" (5:4) or "Sabaoth" is a Greek transcription of the Hebrew for "armies" or "hosts" (Σαβαώθ; צבאות). [54]"Hosts" are army troops. The Lord's army consists of angels. Elisha was surrounded by such angelic "horses and chariots of fire" when he was attacked by the Arameans (2 Kings 6:16–18).[55] James alludes to Isaiah's prophecy: "Woe to them that join house to house, and add field to field, that they may take away something of their neighbor's. . . . For these things have reached *the ears of the Lord of hosts*: for though many houses should be built, many and fair houses shall be desolate, and there shall be no inhabitants in them" (Isa. 5:8–9 LXX). When complaints reach the Lord of Hosts, the God who champions justice, they have reached a holy, righteous, just, and powerful Judge,[56] demonstrated when young David challenged the giant Goliath: "You come to me with sword and spear and javelin; but I come to you in the name of the LORD of hosts, the God of the armies of Israel, whom you have defied. This very day the LORD will deliver you into my hand" (1 Sam. 17:45–46a NRSV). "The LORD of hosts has a day against all that is proud and lofty, against all that is lifted up and high" (Isa. 2:12). That day is forthcoming for the unrepentant, unjust wealthy (James 5:5). The harvesters' Redeemer is the Lord of Hosts, the Holy One of Israel (Isa. 47:4).

James then continues his condemnation of these wealthy with five aorist (past or completed tense) indicative parallel verbs describing further why they are condemned: "You live a life of luxury on the earth and you live luxuriously, your hearts are fattened in a day of slaughter, you condemn, you kill the righteous" (5:5–6). The first two verbs are synonyms (pleonasm) ("You live a life of **luxury**" [τρυφάω] and "you live luxuriously" [σπαταλάω]). The repetition emphasizes to what extent they indulge themselves. Jesus said that, unlike John the Baptist, those who wear expensive garments and live in luxury (τρυφή) are in palaces (Luke 7:25). The first word family could have positive connotations. Eden is called the "Garden

---

53. See also 1 Pet. 3:12, citing Ps. 34:15.
54. BDAG, 909; Thayer, 565.
55. Also Ps. 103:21; see further Spencer and Spencer 1998, 29.
56. E.g., "Lord of Hosts" describes God as judge: Isa. 1:9, 24; 5:16, 24–25; 10:16; 13:4, 13; 14:22; 19:16–18; 22:5, 12, 14; 28:22; 29:5–6; holy: Isa. 6:3; 18:7; 45:13; powerful: Isa. 9:7; 10:24, 33; 14:24; 19:4, 12, 24–25; 31:4–5; 37:16, 31–32; 51:15; 54:5; just: Isa. 25:6; 28:5–6.

of Delight" (τρυφή, Gen. 3:24 LXX) and, like Eden, after the exile, Israel too would be a garden of delight (Ezek. 36:35 LXX). When the Israelites were given the land of the Canaanites, they were given a rich land with "houses filled with all sorts of goods, hewn cisterns, vineyards, olive orchards, and fruit trees in abundance; so they ate, and were filled and grew fat, and *delighted themselves* [τρυφάω] in [God's] great goodness" (Neh. 9:25). Nevertheless, they became disobedient (Neh. 9:26). Micah prophesizes against "the leaders of my people" who "shall be cut forth from their *luxurious* houses" (LXX) because they "covet fields, and seize them; houses, and take them away; they oppress householder and house, people and their inheritance" (Mic. 2:2, 9 NRSV). Ezekiel writes about Sodom and her daughters who also "lived in pleasure, in fullness of bread and in *abundance*" (σπαταλάω/σπατάλη), but they did not help the "poor and needy"; instead they were "haughty" (Ezek. 16:49–50).

Τρυφάω (verb) and τρυφή (noun) refer to living in pleasure, which can turn to living *for* pleasure, or self-indulgence,[57] while σπαταλάω (verb) and σπατάλη (noun) refer to living luxuriously in self-indulgence "beyond the bounds of propriety," akin to "riotous living."[58] The luxury that could come from God's good blessings turns into self-indulgence that harms others.

The "**hearts**" of these wealthy have become "**fattened**" (5:5). Animals might become fattened before they are slaughtered.[59] Sheep, goats, lambs, and calves were slaughtered as offerings to God at the tabernacle.[60] Even the Messiah's death is described as like a lamb to the slaughter (Isa. 53:7; Acts 8:32). But, the "**slaughter**" (σφαγή) James describes is the slaughter of judgment, as in, "The LORD has a sword; it is sated with blood, it is gorged with fat, with the blood of lambs and goats, . . . a great slaughter in the land of Edom," for a people "doomed to judgment" (Isa. 34:5–6 NRSV). Jeremiah complains against the guilty who prosper: God is "near in their mouths yet far from their hearts." In contrast, Jeremiah's "heart" is with God. Therefore, Jeremiah pleads: "Pull them out like sheep for the slaughter, and set them apart for the day of slaughter" (σφαγή, Jer.

---

57. See BDAG, 1018; Thayer, 631.
58. BDAG, 936; Thayer, 583; from σπάω to "suck in, e.g. wine" (BDAG, 936). Ropes (1916, 290) agrees σπαταλᾶν has worse associations in secular use than τρυφάω "suggesting lewdness and riotousness." E.g., Luke 15:13.
59. The life of luxurious pleasure was in reality the "fattening of the ox" for slaughter (Ropes 1916, 290).
60. E.g., Exod. 12:6; 29:11, 16; Lev. 1:5.

12:1–3). Those who continue to oppress the worker will be judged. Their luxurious living flows from their inner selves, their "hearts." These hearts are fattened with self-indulgence. Envy and selfish ambition are in the hearts of those whose wisdom comes from below (James 3:14–15). Their hearts are deceived (1:26). Instead, James has already warned his readers that their hearts need to be purified and become fully submitted to God (4:7–8).

James continues with the last two descriptive verbs of these wealthy ("You condemn, you kill the righteous" [5:6]), which appear to hearken back to chapter 2 to the rich who oppress and drag the poor into court (2:6). To **"condemn"** (καταδικάζω) is to "pronounce guilty," to make a formal and official judgment against someone—in this case, the innocent righteous person.[61] For example, the unbelieving Jews asked Festus to pronounce a sentence of condemnation or guilty verdict against Paul (Acts 25:15). The irony in James is that the unjust wealthy pronounce others guilty, but they are the ones who are themselves guilty!

The last two verbs in 5:6 seem to be related: "You kill **the righteous**, he does not resist you." Why does James use the singular rather than the plural "the righteous *ones, they*"? In contrast, the next verse continues with the second person plural: "persevere, brothers and sisters" (5:7). The answer has several levels. James has chosen to use the representative singular, "the singular with the article to signify the whole class."[62] "The righteous" then refers back to the oppressed laborers whose wages are being withheld (5:4, 6). The landowners' actions are akin to murder (φονεύω) because of the result in the laborers' lives.[63] "Righteous" (δίκαιος) has been an important concept for James, referring both to morality or holiness and justice.[64] Righteousness is the demonstration of faith through moral and just action while trusting God's good and sovereign nature, exemplified by those like Abraham, Rahab, and Elijah.[65] These righteous

---

61. Thayer, 331; BDAG, 516; Matt. 12:7.
62. Robertson 1934, 408, 757.
63. See exposition James 2:11; 4:2; "He who defrauds a worker of his wages sheds blood" (Sir. 34:22 REB).
64. See exposition James 3:18.
65. The New Testament cites other "righteous" (δίκαιος) people: John the Baptist (Mark 6:20); Zechariah and Elizabeth (Luke 1:5–6); Simeon (Luke 2:25); Joseph of Arimathea (Luke 23:50); Cornelius (Act 10:22); Lot (2 Pet. 2:7–8); and Abel (Matt. 23:35; 1 John 3:12).

farm laborers have done their harvesting with integrity, and they rely upon God to vindicate their injustice.

Righteousness is, of course, a characteristic of God,[66] from whom humans ultimately derive their own righteousness. The "Righteous One" is a distinctive term used to describe the Messiah and those persecuted in his name. Jesus accuses the teachers of the law for their persecution of the righteous (Matt. 23:35). Jesus in particular is the archetype of the person who is righteous and yet persecuted. For example, Peter preached that Jesus who was killed and disowned by his own people is "the Holy and Righteous [δίκαιος] One" (Acts 3:14). Ananias tells Paul that Paul saw and heard "the Righteous One" (Acts 22:14). Stephen challenged his listeners that their ancestors killed those who predicted the coming of "the Righteous One" (Acts 7:52).[67] The Messiah is called "the righteous one, [the Lord's] servant" who "shall make many righteous" and "bear their iniquities" (Isa. 53:11 NRSV). "He was oppressed, and he was afflicted, yet he did not open his mouth; like a lamb that is led to the slaughter, and like a sheep that before its shearers is silent, so he did not open his mouth" (Isa. 53:7 NRSV).[68] He was "stricken for the transgression of [God's] people" (Isa. 53:8). In the same way as the laborers do not "resist" (ἀντιτάσσω) or fight back the landowners, Jesus did not fight back against his enemies at his crucifixion.[69] Jesus is an archetypal model for the laborers to inspire them. It is also true, as Dan McCartney adds, that "when rich people oppress the poor, they are participating in the attack on God himself that culminated in the cross."[70] However, unlike Jesus, the laborers do not bear the sins of others (Isa. 53:11–12; 1 Pet. 3:18). Thus, "the righteous" alludes to the righteous laborers, but also to the righteous believers who have been mistreated in the past—and ultimately, to Jesus himself, as one who was falsely accused but did not retaliate against his oppressors.

---

66. E.g., James 1:20. See also John 17:25; Rev. 15:3; 16:5, 7; 19:2; Isa. 26:7; 45:21; 61:8.
67. John and pagan observers also refer to Jesus Christ as "righteous" in Matt. 27:19, 24; Luke 23:47; 1 John 2:1, 29; 3:7.
68. See also Isa. 42:2.
69. Cf. Matt. 5:39.
70. McCartney 2009, 237. James himself also becomes for others a type of "the Righteous One," in his life and martyrdom (*Hist. eccl.* 2.23.4).

EMPLOYERS STILL WITHHOLD WAGES FROM WORKERS

Today some employers still withhold wages from employees. How might this be done? In the United States, for example, they can:

1. Misuse bankruptcy laws so as not to pay debts. For example, Chapter 11 bankruptcy allows the company to pay creditors only a percentage of what is owed. Chapter 7 bankruptcy allows the owner to start a new business with no burdens or obligations from the one closed. In a bankruptcy, an employee may lose his/her job and, as well, pension benefits if the benefits are not in a separate account.[71] Workers' pay has a relatively low priority in bankruptcy codes.[72]

2. Claim the work was not good quality or was completed too late, although the subcontractor has an excellent reputation.[73]

3. Not pass tips on to servers.

4. Claim salaried employees are not entitled to overtime, even if they earn less than $455 per week. Normally, any hours worked over forty in one week entitles employees to time and a half. (In 2011, compared to 2008, lawsuits for not being paid overtime increased 32 percent.)

5. Fail to keep proper time records for employees—for instance, by requiring them to log in hours "off the clock" or requiring them to wait before clocking in.

71. Bill Herrfeldt, "The Effects of Bankruptcy on Employers," *Chron*, https://smallbusiness.chron.com/effects-bankruptcy-employees-17068.html; Sam Ashe-Edmunds, "The Positive Effects of Bankruptcy on a Business," *Chron*, https://smallbusiness.chron.com/effects-bankruptcy-employees-61798.html, accessed Sept. 4, 2018.
72. Reich 2015, 61–62.
73. Steve Reilly, "USA Today Exclusive: Hundreds Allege Donald Trump Doesn't Pay His Bills," *USA TODAY*, June 9, 2016, updated April 25, 2018, https://www.usatoday.com/story/news/politics/elections/2016/06/09/donald-trump-unpaid-bills-republican-president-lawsuits/85297274, accessed Sept. 4, 2018.

6. Require off-hours duties without pay, expecting employees to be on call without paying overtime, or expecting workers to do work from home without pay. (Most Americans do an extra thirty hours of work per month from home.)

7. Require workers to volunteer.

8. Pretend not to notice workers toiling through lunch.[74]

Therefore, Be Patient and Be Ready Because the Judge Is Standing at the Doors (5:7–11)

What then is James's advice for the oppressed laborers? Ἀντιτάσσω (**"resist,"** 5:6) does not imply complete passivity. Rather, these laborers have decided not to "range in physical battle against" the landlords,[75] as opposed to some disaffected peasants who did resort to banditry.[76] Because the workers are in prayer (5:4) we can assume that they had complained unsuccessfully to the owners about their maltreatment. The "wages" certainly complained, but the workers received no positive response. They could go to their local judge or procurator, even as the widow who kept coming to her local judge in Jesus's parable, pleading: "Grant me justice against my opponent" (Luke 18:2–3). But, James warns his readers the wealthy have already been victorious. The workers were "condemned" already (5:6),[77] and therefore it is unlikely for the poor to defeat the wealthy in court any more. Basically, in 5:6–11, James advises the workers to persevere[78] and not to complain against one another. He last used ἀδελφοί ("brothers and sisters") as a term of endearment in 4:11; now he repeats this address five times in thirteen verses to encourage the righteous believers as he closes his letter (5:7, 9, 10, 12, 19).

The verb μακροθυμέω (**"persevere"**) begins 5:7 and 5:8 and the cognate noun μακροθυμία ("perseverance") is used in 5:7 and 5:10. The synonym word family ὑπομένω and ὑπομονή ("enduring," "endurance") are used in 5:11. Often the concept of "patience" is used to translate these

74. Donna Ballman, "Ten Tricks Employers Use to Cheat Workers out of Overtime," *Aol.*, July 11, 2012, https://www.aol.com/2012/07/11/10-tricks-employers-use-to-cheat-workers-out-of-overtime, accessed Sept. 4, 2018.
75. See exposition of James 4:6.
76. Hanson and Oakman 1998, 87–91, 95.
77. Robertson 1960, 60; Ropes 1916, 291; Hiebert 1979, 293; McKnight 2011, 396; cf. Ps. 10:7–10.
78. See exposition of James 1:2–4.

words.[79] "Patience" in English is "the bearing of provocation, annoyance, misfortune, or pain, without complaint, loss of temper, irritation, or the like."[80] However, the examples James uses appear not to fit that concept to present-day readers. The prophets and Job did plenty of complaining to God (e.g., "Today also my complaint is bitter; his hand is heavy despite my groaning," Job 23:2 NRSV). Job and the prophets lost their temper at times and were certainly irritated (e.g., "You will be in the right, O LORD, when I lay charges against you; but let me put my case to you" and "You have overpowered me, and you have prevailed," Jer. 12:1; 20:7 NRSV). Rather, I think what James is calling for is perseverance and endurance. "Perseverance" in English is "steady persistence in a course of action, a purpose, a state, etc. esp. in spite of difficulties, obstacles, or discouragement." It is resolute and unyielding in holding on in following a course of action or activity, maintained in spite of difficulties; a steadfast and long-continued application.[81] James's "twelve tribes" readers had many difficulties. They endured the diaspora that caused them to leave Jerusalem (Acts 8:1–3)[82] and also suffered the mistreatment from the rich affecting their dignity and economic status. It could be easy for them to give up on their Christian walk.

Μακροθυμέω (verb) and μακροθυμία (noun) are composite words derived from μακρός ("long" or "lasting long") and θυμός ("feeling and thought, esp. of strong feeling and passion").[83] Literally, the word family refers to the holding of strong feelings over a long time.[84] The writer of Hebrews uses the verb to describe Abraham's waiting for the fulfillment of God's promise for him and Sarah to be blessed with a child (Heb. 6:15). That took about twenty-five years, and in the midst of those aging years Abraham and Sarah were ready to settle for Eliezer or Ishmael as heirs (Gen. 12:2; 15:2–5; 16:1–3, 11). Μακροθυμία includes the allotting of time for people to repent or to learn.[85] It may refer to compassion and forgiveness (1 Tim. 1:16). The Lord's "compassion" results in salvation (2 Pet. 3:15). It includes being of "a long spirit," not losing heart, hence "to persevere patiently and bravely" in "enduring misfortunes and troubles."[86]

---

79. E.g., NRSV; NIV.
80. *Random House Webster's* 2001, 1421.
81. *Random House Webster's* 2001, 1441.
82. See Introduction.
83. Thayer, 387; LSJ, 810.
84. Spencer and Spencer 1990, 60.
85. E.g., Rom. 2:4; 2 Tim. 4:2; 2 Pet. 3:9.
86. Thayer, 387.

In the midst of their difficulties, James commands his beloved brothers and sisters to persevere (5:7–8). At the start of the letter, James exhorted his diaspora Jewish Christian readers to endure, to hold out or bear up (ὑπομονή, 1:3, 4) in the face of difficulties, or trials: those external, unavoidable events that happen to one. If they endure (ὑπομένω), they will become mature and they will be rewarded (1:12).[87] Now, at the end of his letter, James comes back to this theme of perseverance under trials and applies it specifically to the challenging situation of the impoverished workers. God will surely bring judgment to the greedy oppressors (5:7–9). It may be at the end of time or before that time, but it can also happen at any time, imminently. Certainly the war with Rome in AD 66–70 was a judgment against the unjust, powerful wealthy.

James gives many illustrations that develop the meaning of "perseverance." One is being sure of the coming of the Lord, following the example of the **"farmer"** (5:7). Γεωργός[88] often refers to someone who does agricultural work on a contractual basis, such as a tenant farmer.[89] For example, Jesus describes the landowner who plants a vineyard but then leases the property to tenant farmers who would keep their share of the crops but were supposed to give the rest of the produce to the owner of the property (Matt. 21:33–41; 2 Tim. 2:6). The farmer had to wait for the rains to produce the "precious fruit of the earth" (5:7). A weather phenomenon limited to the eastern Mediterranean is the "early and late **rains**" (5:7), mentioned several times in the Bible (Deut. 11:14; Jer. 5:24; Joel 2:23). As a rule, the first rain begins in October and the late rain falls at the end of March or in early April. Early and late rains are the first and last installments of the winter rains. The early rain softens the ground and prepares it for plowing and seeding, while the late showers help bring crops to maturity.[90] In the Mediterranean zone of Israel, seventeen to forty inches a year is normal, which is enough to support field crops, vineyards, and orchards.[91] Rain is crucial because Israel is situated at the "very rim of the Afro-Asian desert belt." Precipitation is uncertain not only in amount but also in distribution. The sown land and the desert are separated by a belt or border changing in width from year to year.[92]

---

87. See exposition of James 1:2–3.
88. Someone who works (ἔργον) the ground (γῆ) (LSJ, 347).
89. BDAG, 196.
90. *IDB*, 3:621, 623, 625. See also Hiebert 1979, 298; Laws 1980, 211.
91. Alon 1969, 53.
92. Zohary 1982, 26.

James's illustration emphasizes waiting for something special (the rains, 5:7) that affects one's whole livelihood but is not under one's control. Rather, the rains are under God's control (Jer. 5:24). The farmer keeps doing his or her work but must wait for the rainy season to be complete to realize the final harvest (April–June).[93] So, too, James's readers need to be patient and persevere. Vindication will come through God's hand. Meanwhile, the believers' goal is maturity (1:4). They should not lose sight of that goal.

Therefore, they need to **"strengthen"** their hearts, to be ready themselves for the appearance of the Lord (5:8). They do not want to be found with "fattened" hearts ready for slaughter, but rather with purified and strengthened hearts (4:8; 5:5). A "strengthened" heart is stable and well supported.[94] When Jesus *"set* his face to go to Jerusalem," he knew he was going to his crucifixion (Luke 9:44, 51). He set a goal, albeit a difficult one, and worked toward it by sending disciples ahead to each city he was about to enter (Luke 9:52). He was the opposite of the "two-willed" person (James 1:8). Like the farmer who aims to reap a harvest (5:7), believers should set goals and steps to those goals so that their inner beings are prepared for the Lord's arrival, pleasing in God's sight and purified from evil.[95]

Meanwhile, when outside forces overwhelm, the temptation is to turn feelings of discontentment inward toward those close to us (5:9). Στενάζω (**"murmur"/groan"**) normally is a neutral[96] word signifying the expression of grief by "inarticulate or semi-articulate sounds."[97] It is built from the adjective στενός ("narrow"),[98] implying that going through a narrow space is difficult (e.g., Luke 13:24). Job is an appropriate example for the listeners (James 5:11) because he complains with groans about the sufferings he was experiencing (στενάζω, Job 23:2), even though he was innocent (Job 1:8; 42:7–8).[99] Sometimes this

---

93. Daniel-Rops 1962, 233.
94. Στηρίζω signifies "to make stable, place firmly, set fast," as in "he *set* the stone *fast* in the ground" (Thayer, 588; LSJ, 1644). The stone was well supported.
95. James 1:27; 1 Thess. 3:13; 2 Thess. 2:17; 3:3.
96. E.g., στενάζω may refer to the groans of experiencing mortality and suffering from a fallen world while looking with expectation to redemption (Rom. 8:22–23; 2 Cor. 5:2, 4).
97. Thayer, 347; see also Job 9:27 LXX.
98. Kohlenberger, Goodrick, and Swanson 1995, 902.
99. I.e., he was *not* suffering in punishment because of his sins (e.g., Ezek. 21:6–7).

type of "sighing" or "groaning" can be done in sympathy with those suffering,[100] as did Job who defends himself: "Yet I wept over every helpless person; I *groaned* [στενάζω] when I saw a man in distress" (Job 30:25 LXX). It can be a type of prayer (e.g., Mark 7:34, στενάζω; Acts 7:34, στεναγμός). What makes James's use unique is that he uses στενάζω to refer to "groaning against" (κατά) other people, even one's own Christian family ("brothers and sisters," 5:9). James refers to a negative type of complaint or judgment (κρίνω, 5:9). Job ends his self-defense pleading "If my land *has cried out* [στενάζω] against me, and its furrows have wept together; if I have eaten its yield without payment, and caused the death of its owners" (Job 31:38–39 NRSV), then indeed Job deserves to suffer. Unlike the landowners in James's time, Job did not withhold any wages. In Job 31, the sighing or crying is a just complaint, but in James 5:9 the complaining or expression of discontentment[101] against other people is not valid or just. Στενάζω has been translated in James 5:9 as blaming one's troubles on others (REB) or grumbling against others (NIV, NRSV)[102] or murmuring.[103] Στενάζω does *not* refer to articulate and logical complaints. The present active imperative suggests these express ongoing negative feelings. Similar to partiality toward the rich and against the poor (2:3–4), these complainers have become "judges with evil thoughts" (2:4). Their grumblings or murmurings may imply "slander" or speaking falsehoods against others (4:11–12).

As in James 4:11–12, after the command not to speak falsely against one another, James then, by proximity, compares their actions to those of God the Trinity, the true and perfect judge (4:12; 5:9).[104] This judge "before the doors stands" (5:9). The plural **"doors"** (θύρα) is used for the double or folding doors before a dwelling.[105] In a first-century house, as in Simon Peter's house in Capernaum, the gate or entrance was outside the courtyard. Rooms would open onto the courtyard, not to the outside.[106] James emphasizes the prepositional phrase "before the doors" (5:9) to highlight the imminence of the knocking.

---

100. E.g., Job 18:20 LXX; Nah. 3:7.
101. BDAG, 942.
102. "Grumble" signifies to "murmur or mutter in discontent; complain sullenly" (*Random House Webster's* 2001, 846).
103. Thayer, 587; "murmur" signifies "to complain in a low tone or in private" (*Random House Webster's* 2001, 1266).
104. See exposition James 4:12.
105. LSJ, 811; Thayer, 293. E.g., John 20:19, 26; Acts 5:23; 16:26; 21:30.
106. McRay 1991, 80–81.

The judge is about to knock. For example, Jesus explains imminence by an analogy employing the fig tree: "Whenever [the fig tree's] branch becomes tender and its leaves grow, you know that summer is near. So also, whenever you might see all these things, you know that [the Son of Humanity[107]] is near, at the doors" (Matt. 24:32–33). Summer is not here yet. The judge is not yet knocking, but he is in the position to knock. The perfect tense **"stands"** (ἵστημι, 5:9) has the sense of an action that begins at a specific time (punctiliar) and continues[108] (durative) ("has stood," "stands," or "is standing"). The length of time is undisclosed, but the judge can enter at any time. As James said: "The arrival of the Lord draws near" (5:8). Those who think they are righteous may look forward to the punishment of those they consider wicked but forget that they themselves will be judged.

Who is the **judge** (5:9)? In Matthew 24, the judge clearly is Jesus, "the Son of Humanity coming upon the clouds of heaven with power and great glory" (Matt. 24:30; Mark 13:29). This same "Son of Humanity," when he returns in glory, will sit on the judge's throne and judge all the nations (Matt. 25:31–33). Paul tells the Corinthians that "all of us must appear before the judgment seat of Christ, so that each may receive recompense for what has been done in the body, whether good or evil" (2 Cor. 5:10 NRSV). Peter writes that the Father "judges all people impartially according to their deeds" (1 Pet. 1:17 NRSV). God is "judge of all" (Heb. 12:23). Paul adds that every knee will bow before God to give an account.[109]

Peter tells Cornelius and the gathering in Caesarea that God appointed Jesus as "judge of the living and dead,"[110] possibly alluding to Jesus's teaching that the Father has "entrusted all judgment to the Son" (John 5:22, 27).[111] Paul combines both ideas: the "day when God will judge the secret thoughts of humans . . . through Christ Jesus" (Rom. 2:16). Ultimately, "whatever [the Father] may do, that also the Son likewise does" (John 5:19). James does not clearly specify who is the Lord who arrives, draws near, and judges (5:7–9), but the rest of the New Testament teaches that God will judge all through the Son at the close of time.

James then gives two more illustrations of other believers who persevered: the prophets and Job (5:10–11). Ὑπόδειγμα is a positive

---

107. The generic ἄνθρωπος ("humanity") is used.
108. Robertson 1934, 893.
109. Rom. 14:11–12, citing Isa. 45:23; Rom. 3:6; James 4:11–12.
110. Acts 10:42; also Paul in Acts 17:31; 2 Tim. 4:1, 8.
111. See also John 13:3.

example to be followed or a negative example to be avoided, being used for purposes of moral instruction.[112] For instance, Jesus models how he as Teacher and Lord washed his disciples' feet (as a slave might) so that they also would do as he did (John 13:12–15).[113] In contrast, God, by burning Sodom and Gomorrah, made them a negative example of what is going to happen to the ungodly (2 Pet. 2:6).[114]

One might expect the **prophets** "who spoke in the Lord's name" (5:10) never to have any difficulties. But instead they had to suffer and persevere. **Suffering** (κακοπάθεια [noun], κακοπαθέω [verb]) is a general term used here and in 5:13. It can refer to the labor (hard work and late nights) entailed in writing a book (2 Macc. 2:26–27), the hardships of military service (2 Tim 2:3),[115] or being unjustly imprisoned for the sake of Jesus Christ (2 Tim. 2:8–9). Countless Old Testament prophets could serve as examples of suffering as a result of speaking in the Lord's name but nevertheless persevering through it. Two examples are John the Baptist and Jeremiah. John had been imprisoned and eventually killed by Herod because John had told Herod that his marriage to Herodias was not according to God's laws.[116] Jeremiah too had to preach an unpopular message.[117] As a result, even his own relatives and neighbors from Anathoth tried to kill him to keep him from prophesying.[118] When Jeremiah complained, God challenged him to more difficult labors: "If you have raced with foot-runners and they have wearied you, how will you compete with horses?" (Jer. 12:5 NRSV). Jeremiah could not marry (16:1–4). His enemies plotted to charge Jeremiah (18:18–19). The priest Pashhur son of Immer struck Jeremiah and put him in the stocks (20:1–2). He had conflict with other prophets (28:1–11). Eventually, he was confined to the court of the guard and prevented from entering the temple, falsely accused, beaten, and imprisoned in a cistern, and, at the end, forcibly taken to Egypt.[119] He complained: "I have become the laughingstock of all my people, the object of their taunt-songs all day long. . . . I have forgotten what happiness is" (Lam. 3:14, 17 NRSV). He cried out: "Those who were my

---

112. See also BDAG, 1037. The verb ὑποδείκνυμι is properly "to show by placing *under* (i.e. before) the eyes," to teach or warn (Thayer, 643).
113. See also 2 Macc. 6:28–31; 4 Macc. 17:23.
114. See also Heb. 4:6, 11; Jude 7 (δεῖγμα, "example"); *J.W.* 2.397.
115. Thayer, 320 (κακοπαθέω).
116. Matt. 14:3–12; Luke 3:19–20; 7:26–27; 9:9.
117. E.g., Jer. 23:33; 26:11; 29:5–9; 38:1–6.
118. Jer. 1:1; 11:18–23; 12:6; 20:10.
119. Jer. 33:1; 36:5; 37:11–16; 38:6; 43:2–7.

enemies without cause have hunted me like a bird; they flung me alive into a pit and hurled stones on me; water closed over my head; I said, 'I am lost'" (Lam. 3:52–54 NRSV). However, Jeremiah was sustained over his fifty-year ministry by the knowledge that "the steadfast love of the LORD never ceases, his mercies never come to an end; they are new every morning; great is your faithfulness. 'The LORD is my portion,' says my soul, 'therefore I will hope in him'" (Lam. 3:22–24 NRSV).

James calls the readers to attend to ("behold") his next illustration, the **"endurance"** of **Job** (5:11). Endurance (ὑπομένω [verb], ὑπομονή [noun]) is the capacity to hold out or bear up in the face of difficulties or trials, external unavoidable events that happen to one—in this case, being tested for the genuineness of one's faith. Job was tested for his faith, as had been Abraham and Rahab (James 2:20–25).[120] The testing of one's faith produces endurance, which results in maturity (1:3–4), the confidence in God to resolve injustice because God is compassionate and merciful. The person who endures to the end is rewarded (1:12). Job did not give up. James has tied together the theme of persistence and endurance with trials by repeating this important word family at the end of his letter (ὑπομένω, ὑπομονή).

The book of Job begins with God's repeated declaration that Job is "blameless and upright, one who fears God and turns away from evil" (1:1, 8; 2:3 NRSV). Job practices many of James's virtues: care of widows and orphans,[121] care of the poor (31:19), not trusting in gold (31:24), understanding that life is fleeting (14:1–2), righteous anger at those who steal (e.g., 24:2)—in other words, integration of practice and doctrine. Job will not accept any falsehood (27:4). Job is *not* a two-willed man!

Job is blessed by God at the beginning with many children, workers, possessions, and a good reputation. He is "the greatest of all the people of the east" (1:3, 10). The accuser, Satan, challenges God that if Job's possessions and family are harmed, Job would curse God to his face (1:11). When God allows Satan to harm Job's family, workers, and possessions, Job still blesses the Lord (1:21). And, when Job himself is afflicted with painful inflammations or boils[122] throughout every part of his body, he still does not curse God, though his suffering is great (2:7, 13) and his complaints are many. Job's face is "red with weeping, and deep darkness is on" his eyelids (16:16). His spirit is broken (17:1). Like Jeremiah, he is bereft: "I

---

120. See exposition of James 1:2–4, 12.
121. E.g., Job 22:9; 24:3, 9; 31:16–17, 21.
122. "Boil" is ἕλκος = שְׁחִין (BDB, 1006).

am a laughingstock to my friends; I, who called upon God and he answered me, a just and blameless man, I am a laughingstock."[123] Job never curses God, but he does curse the day of his birth.[124] Job's three friends Eliphaz, Bildad, and Zophar come to comfort him, but their only theodicy is to assume that all human suffering is caused by human sin (e.g., 4:7–8). Thus, both Job and even God conclude they are all "miserable comforters."[125]

Job never doubts the nature of God as just, wise, mighty, omniscient, and the creator and sustainer of the world.[126] Yet Job persists in defending his innocence and repeatedly desires to present his case to God.[127] But even the righteous Job grows in understanding and maturity when God confronts him: God is even greater than Job imagined and more responsive than he thought. Job concludes: "I have uttered what I did not understand, things too wonderful for me, which I did not know. ... [N]ow my eye sees you; therefore I despise myself, and repent in dust and ashes" (Job 42:3, 5–6 NRSV). God then vindicates and rewards Job at the end. To Eliphaz, Bildad, and Zophar, God declares: "You have not spoken of me what is right, as my servant Job has," and promises Job will pray for them (42:7–8). Job's family, servants, possessions, and reputation are restored at the end (42:10–17).[128] God challenges Job: "Shall a faultfinder contend with the Almighty?" (40:2), but yet God allows Job to present his case. Furthermore, God vindicates him, even if Job was "righteous in his own eyes" (32:1). The τέλος (James 5:11, **"outcome"** or conclusion of the process)[129] was to reconfirm the good nature of God: the Lord is "compassionate" and "merciful" (James 5:11).[130]

James stresses the first attribute:[131] πολύσπλαγχνος (πολύς ["full of"] and σπλάγχνον ["**compassion**," 5:11]). Σπλάγχνον literally refers to the intestines or bowels (heart, lungs, liver, etc.).[132] According to Joseph Thayer, the σπλάγχνον were regarded by Greek poets as the seat of the more violent passions, such as anger and love, but by

---

123. Job 12:4 NRSV; see also 17:6; 19:13–19; 30:1, 9.
124. Job 3:1–3, 11; 10:18–19.
125. Job 16:2; 21:34; 42:7–8.
126. E.g., Job 9:1, 4, 19, 32; 10:8, 12; 12:10, 13–16; 26:13; 28:24.
127. Job 9:15–16, 21; 10:1, 7; 13:3; 23:3–4.
128. See also Spencer and Spencer 1994, 142–50.
129. BDAG, 998.
130. "Compassionate" and "merciful" is a pleonasm made of two synonyms.
131. Emphasis in 5:11 is done by placing the first attribute ("compassionate") before the verb and noun of the clause ("is the Lord").
132. Thayer, 530, 584; e.g., Acts 1:18.

the Hebrews as the seat of the tenderer affections, especially kindness, benevolence, and compassion.[133] These are "gut-level feelings." According to physician Michael Gershon, "There is essentially a brain in the gut," an "independent nervous system in the small intestine: the enteric nervous system." He adds that "95 percent of the body's serotonin—the neurotransmitter that plays a role in mood—is in the gut, which uses it to send messages to the brain." These messages can alter mood and change personality.[134] In other words, these feelings are not logical deeds of obedience; they arise from deep within. God's very nature is deep compassion (e.g., Luke 1:78). Jesus exhibited such compassion when he saw people in need: the blind, the leper, the mournful, the hungry, the directionless, and the repentant.[135] God's compassion is illustrated by the father who saw his prodigal son "still a long way off . . . and *was filled with compassion* for him; he ran to his son, threw his arms around him and kissed him" (σπλαγχνίζομαι, Luke 15:20 NIV). Even though the son had demanded his part of the father's property early and wasted it, when he returned, the father treated him regally and celebrated (Luke 15:22–24). This is what James's readers should feel for the needy (James 2:14–16; 1 John 3:17, σπλάγχνον). This was God's attitude to Job. God is *greatly* (πολύς) compassionate.

God also is "**merciful**" (5:11). Οἰκτιρμός (noun), οἰκτίρμων (adj.), οἰκτείρω (verb) originates from the "viscera, which were thought to be the seat of compassion." Οἰκτίρος comes from the root idea of "oh!" (οἴ), an exclamation of pain, grief, pity, astonishment.[136] The plural shows the ongoing character of the pity.[137] This is the first characteristic that God reveals to Moses in self-revelation: "The LORD, the LORD, a God merciful [οἰκτίρμων] and gracious [ἐλεήμων], slow to anger [μακρόθυμος], and abounding in steadfast love and faithfulness [ἀληθινός]" (Exod. 34:6 NRSV). Four of these attributes of God have been mentioned by James, three of them in the passage 5:7–11. God is the "Father of compassion" (2 Cor. 1:3) who calls all to "become merciful just as also your Father is merciful" (Luke 6:36). These traits, according to James, were all evident in the outcome of Job's long discourse.

---

133. Thayer, 584–85.
134. "Digestive Health," *CVS Health Extra* 12, no. 4 (2006): 60.
135. Matt. 9:36; 14:14; 15:32; 18:27; 20:34; Mark 1:41; 6:34; 8:2; Luke 7:13, σπλαγχνίζομαι ("be moved with compassion").
136. Thayer, 442; LSJ, 1200.
137. See Spencer 2001, 29.

Do Not Swear Oaths (5:12)

James concludes this section by warning the Christians against judgment by the Lord, so that they avoid negative condemnation when the Lord arrives (5:3–5, 8–9, 12).[138] James does not want them to murmur or grumble against one another or make oaths (5:12). Πρὸ πάντων (**"above all things"** or "especially") is a "marker of precedence in importance or rank."[139] Peter uses a similar phrase (πρὸ πάντων) near the end of his letter in a context of future judgment and the end of all things. What Peter considers most important is to "maintain constant love for one another, for love covers a multitude of sins" (1 Pet. 4:8 NRSV). Why does James see making an **oath** as so wrong? Is this not a particular temptation for those who are oppressed? This was Job's temptation: to feel so depressed that he would want to curse God and then die. The unpaid workers themselves might end up using oaths, as Job was tempted to do, to dishonor God's name in anger. When Peter was accused of being with Jesus of Nazareth, he denied it with an oath: "I do not know that person!" (Matt. 26:71–74; Mark 14:71). In effect, such an oath makes "wrongful use" of God's name (Exod. 20:7). God's name is used to tell a falsehood to promote sin or to be disrespectful, which is what Job's wife recommended to Job's ultimate peril (Job 2:9). Making such an oath, then, takes one out of the Lord's mercy into the Lord's judgment.

An oath (ὀμνύω [verb], ὅρκος [noun]) affirms "the veracity of one's statement by invoking a transcendent entity, freq[uently] w[ith] implied invitation of punishment if one is untruthful, *swear, take an oath*."[140] Oaths can be used for positive or negative reasons. The author of Hebrews states that human beings "swear [ὀμνύω] by someone greater than themselves, and an oath [ὅρκος] given as confirmation puts an end to all dispute" (Heb. 6:16 NRSV). When God made a promise to Abraham "because he had no one greater by whom to swear, he swore by himself" (Heb. 6:13 NRSV). God, therefore, would never change his mind because of the oath (Heb. 7:21; Ps. 110:4).[141] Oaths were regularly used in ancient Jewish society as a guarantee one is telling the truth.[142]

---

138. Cf. Dibelius (1976, 248), who sees no relation of 5:12 with the context.
139. BDAG, 864; e.g., Christ is "before all things" (Col. 1: 17).
140. BDAG, 705.
141. E.g., when Herod promised Herodias to give her anything she wanted, he regretted having to kill John the Baptist as she requested but had to do so "because of his oaths and for the guests" (Mark 6:23–26; Matt. 14:7–10).
142. E.g., m. Seqal. 2:1; Ketub. 8:5; 10:5; Git. 4:3; B.Mes. 3:2; 6:8.

For example, the hired laborer had to take an oath in order to be paid wages if the landowner claimed already to have paid.[143]

The Old Testament enjoins the Hebrews to keep their oaths or promises: "If you make a vow to the LORD your God, do not postpone fulfilling it; for the LORD your God will surely require it of you, and you would incur guilt. But if you refrain from vowing, you will not incur guilt. Whatever your lips utter you must diligently perform, just as you have freely vowed to the LORD your God with your own mouth" (Deut. 23:21–23 NRSV).[144] Leviticus exhorts them not to "swear falsely by [God's] name, profaning the name of your God; I am the Lord" (Lev. 19:12). God is as much against false swearing as against those who oppress the widow, the orphan, or the hired workers in their wages (Mal. 3:5). The *Mishnah* even claims that "noisome beasts come upon the world because of false swearing and the profaning of the Name" (m. 'Abot 5:9).

James follows Jesus, who in his teaching modifies Leviticus 19:12. They do not want *any oaths*: "neither heavenly nor earthly" (James 5:12; Matt. 5:34–36). For example, Jesus criticizes the Pharisees who swear by the "gold of the sanctuary" but not the sanctuary, or the gift on the altar but not the altar (Matt. 23:16–22).[145] In contrast, James and Jesus simply want believers to let their "yes be yes and no, no" (James 5:12; Matt. 5:37). Jesus adds: "Anything more than these is from the evil one" (Matt. 5:37). What might make it evil? Possibly, it is the reducing of God and God's creations to objects to be manipulated to one's own desires, including using oaths to equivocate on promises.[146]

Receive the Implanted Word by Being Mature in Actions (5:13–20)

Many ancient Hellenistic letters ended with a health wish and/or oath formula.[147] Thus, the command not to swear fits well at the

---

143. M. Sebu. 7:1. See also m. B. Mes. 9:12; m. Ned. 1:1; m. Sebu. 1:1; 3:1.
144. See also Num. 30:1–2; Eccl. 5:4.
145. A sampling of such vows can be found, such as swearing "May it be to me" as the "lamb," as the "Temple-sheds," as the "wood for burning on the altar," as the "Fire-offerings," as the "Altar," as "Jerusalem," or as "utensils of the Altar." But, according to Rabbi Judah, "May it be Jerusalem!" is *not* valid because it omits "as," the particle of comparison (m. Ned. 1:3). M. Ned. 2:1–3:4 describes kinds of vows not binding. The tractate Nedarim explains in detail how and how not to make a vow or oath for it to be valid legally.
146. See also Eccl. 5:2; McCartney 2009, 247 ("people use oaths to compensate for the lack of truthfulness"); Laws 1980, 221.
147. Francis 1970, 125.

end, followed by the injunctions for a healthy community. In this last chapter, James has gathered up his three different themes, in a different order from the start. Chapter 1 discussed trials (1:2–4), wisdom and the tongue (1:5–8), and wealth (1:9–11); in chapter 5, he has dealt with wealth (5:1–6), trials (5:7–11), and the tongue (5:12). He writes about the danger of judgment for the unjust wealthy (5:1–6) and the oppressed workers (5:7–12). He closes the letter with a summary of injunctions that help believers who are suffering, joyful, ill, or deceived (5:13–20) to receive the implanted word by being mature in actions.

Deal Wisely with Suffering, Joy, and Illness (5:13–18)

James begins with three questions; the first two words of each question are parallel.[148] Each question is answered by a one-word command in Greek: "Are any among you suffering? Let that person keep praying. Are any among you cheerful? Let that person keep singing! Are any sick among you? Let him call . . . " (5:13–14a). The last question breaks the one-word answer (προσευχέσθω . . . ψαλλέτω). In other words, James offers three different categories for the reader to choose which one is appropriate for himself or herself at that time. The first two clearly are opposites: suffering versus joy.

To what kinds of suffering does James refer? James has already described some of the **sufferings** or difficulties (κακοπαθέω [verb], κακοπαθία [noun]) that might confront someone, such as those experienced by the prophets and Job or those caused by hard work, unjust persecution, and testing (but *not* from one's own sin).[149] James probably includes the suffering caused by oppression (5:1–5, 13). He has called the believers to persevere by having confidence in God's good, compassionate, and just nature (5:7–11). Now he gives a further manner to enable them to persevere: prayer (προσεύχομαι).

James, himself renowned as a man of **prayer**,[150] employs in 5:13–18 several synonyms for different kinds of prayer. Προσεύχομαι and προσευχή are the most common words for prayer in the New Testament.

---

148. The verb ("are") + τις ("any").
149. James 1:2–3; 5:10–11. See exposition on James 5:10.
150. *Hist. eccl.* 2.23; see introduction.

Frequency of Different Words for Prayer in the New Testament					
Word families	Concept	James	Total of each word in NT[151]	Total of word family in NT	Omitted refs: words used but not for prayer to God
1. Προσεύχομαι (verb)	reverently pray	5:13, 14, 17, 18	85	=121	
Προσευχή (noun)		5:17	36[152]		
2. Εὐχαριστέω (verb)	thank		35	=49	3: Luke 17:16; Rom. 16:4; 1 Cor. 1:14
Εὐχαριστία (noun)			14		1: Acts 24:3
3. Δέομαι (verb)	need		10	=28	12: Luke 5:12; 8:28, 38; 9:38, 40; Acts 8:34; 21:39; 26:3; 2 Cor. 5:20; 8:4; 10:2; Gal. 4:12
Δέησις (noun)		5:16	18		
4. Εὔχομαι (verb)	vow	5:16	6	=7	1: Rom. 9:3
Εὐχή (noun)		5:15	1		2: Acts 18:18; 21:23
5. Ψάλλω (verb)	sing	5:13	5	=12	
Ψαλμός (noun)			7		

---

151. The frequency count comes from Kohlenberger, Goodrich, and Swanson 1995, 188, 192, 379–80, 854–55, 1018.
152. The noun προσευχή can also refer to a place of prayer, as in Acts 16:13, 16.

Προσεύχομαι is limited to communication with God,[153] for example, this word family describes Jesus's lessons on prayer: "In this way you yourselves *pray*: 'Our Father, the One in the heavens . . . '" (Matt. 6:9, and, "Whenever you *pray*, say: 'Father, let it be praised your name . . .'" (Luke 11:2). Προσευχή is etymologically a vow (εὐχή) addressed to (πρός) God.[154] It stresses the One addressed and the sacred nature of the act.[155]

Prayer can sustain an individual while suffering, or it can be used to pray for others, as Job did.[156] For example, Jesus teaches his disciples to pray for those who persecute them (Matt. 5:44; Luke 6:28). Prayer can keep the individual focused on God's "hallowed" and praiseworthy nature and on obedience to God (to do God's will), or on asking for the necessary food for living (give today our daily bread), for forgiveness, and for rescue.[157] As well, God can provide the suffering person with guidance,[158] persistence (Luke 18:1–8), empowerment,[159] healing (Acts 9:40), and enlightenment.[160] The prayer (εὐχή) for the sick is one kind of prayer for one type of suffering, one that James will later address (James 5:14–16). Elijah's prayer illustrates the power of prayer even over the forces of nature (5:16–18). The goal of prayer is *not* a show of piety;[161] rather, its essence is communication with a loving God, exemplified by communication within the Trinity, demonstrated by Jesus when on earth.[162]

James also addresses the opposite condition: **cheerfulness** (5:13). Εὐθυμέω is a composite of εὖ ("well" or "good") and θυμός ("passion" or "strong feeling").[163] If ἐπιθυμέω refers to keeping the θυμός (passion or desire) focused on something,[164] εὔθυμος is a good passion or strong

---

153. "Everywhere of prayers to the gods, or to God," in contrast with δέησις (Thayer, 545).
154. Thayer, 545.
155. See Spencer and Spencer 1990, 131–39.
156. See the intercessional nature of prayer also in Romans 15:30–32; Ephesians 6:18; Colossians 4:12; 1 Thessalonians 1:2; 5:25; and 1 Timothy 2:1–2.
157. Matt. 6:9–13; Luke 11:2–4; 18:10–13; Acts 12:12; 1 Cor. 14:15–16; Col. 1:3; Philem. 22.
158. Matt. 26:39–42; Luke 6:12–13; 22:42; Acts 1:24–25; 22:17–18.
159. Acts 6:6; 8:15; 9:40; 13:3; 14:23; 20:36; 21:5; 1 Cor. 14:13; Eph. 6:19; Phil. 1:9–11; Col. 1:9–12; 4:3; 2 Thess. 1:11; 3:1; Heb. 13:18–19.
160. E.g., Acts 10:30–33.
161. Matt. 6:5–7; Mark 12:40; Luke 20:47.
162. Matt. 14:23; Mark 1:35; 6:46; Luke 3:21; 5:16; 6:12; 9:18.
163. Thayer, 256, 258, 293; LSJ, 810.
164. See exposition of James 1:14–15.

feeling. For example, in contrast to the despair the officers and travelers felt when their ship was driven by violent winds and the cargo was lost, Paul encourages them to have a "good feeling" or "be cheerful" because he was told that no one would die (Acts 27:22–25).

This may be a time for another kind of prayer: **singing** (ψάλλω, 5:13). Ψάλλω refers literally to playing on a stringed instrument, to play the harp, and so on, and to sing to the music of the harp.[165] The verb normally in the Bible refers to praise of God. It first appears in the song of praise to God by Deborah and Barak—"I will sing a psalm [ψάλλω] to the Lord the God of Israel" (Judg. 5:3)—after their victory over the Canaanite rulers. In the book of Psalms, it is used in praise of God by playing the harp,[166] including making a loud noise (Ps. 33:3). It is also used of the singing that might accompany a stringed instrument.[167] These songs were songs of praise or thankfulness for God's mighty acts.[168] Songs were sometimes sung as background for a prophet to hear and speak God's revelation (2 Kings 3:15) or to calm a disquieted person and keep away evil spirits (1 Sam. 16:16, 23). In the New Testament, songs of praise become almost metaphorical as a means by which Christians communicate with one another so as to teach one another and be filled with the Spirit. For example, Paul exhorts, "Be filled with the Spirit, speaking to one another in psalms [ψαλμός] and hymns and spiritual songs, singing and making melody [ψάλλω] in your heart to the Lord" (Eph. 5:18b–19).[169] Thus, "singing" or "playing" may be literal or metaphorical, but in the Bible the result is praise of God. Whether someone is suffering or someone is cheerful, one should direct one's attention appropriately in communicating with God and one another. While a believer does not always have to express sadness or joy, Christians are counseled to weep with the sad, and rejoice with the cheerful (Rom. 12:15).

James speaks next to those who are **sick**: "Are any sick among you?" (5:14). Literally, ἀσθένεια refers to "want of strength."[170] It is the opposite of power (1 Cor. 15:43; Heb. 11:34). One type of lack of

---

165. Also, ψάλλω literally means to cause to vibrate by touching, to twang (Thayer, 675).
166. Ps. 68:25; 70:22; 98:5; 144:9; 147:7; 149:3. Psalm 69:12 is *not* in praise of God.
167. Ps. 7:17; 9:2, 11; 57:7, 9; 59:17; 61:8; 68:4, 32; 92:1; 135:3.
168. Ps. 13:6; 21:13; 27:6; 30:4; 71:22; 105:2.
169. See also Col. 3:16.
170. Included in the word family are ἀσθενέω (verb), ἀσθένεια (noun), ἀσθενής (adj.), and ἀσθένημα (noun). They are a composite of ἀ ("not") and σθένος

strength is caused by physical disability, such as blindness, lameness, and paralysis.[171] Sometimes it refers to illnesses that could or do lead to death.[172] The New Testament also uses the ἀσθενέω word family metaphorically for human imperfection (Heb. 5:2–3; 7:28), for "weak" faith,[173] for unimpressive rhetorical skills (1 Cor. 2:3–4; 2 Cor. 10:10), or for the difficulties an individual might have in following Jesus.[174] The New Testament separates illness from possession by evil spirits (e.g., Luke 8:2; Acts 5:16). James addresses those who are physically ill but well enough to act on remedying their illness by calling for help.

James uses the present imperative for "pray" (5:13) and "sing" but the aorist imperative for "**call to one's self**; to bid to come to one's self"[175] (προσκαλέω, 5:14) implying that prayer and singing are ongoing activities but calling the elders is not. In other words, one does not call the elders every time when one has a brief symptom of illness but rather when one has an ongoing sickness (ἀσθενέω also is present tense). When individual prayer has not sufficed (5:13), the sick person then invites the elders to come or brings to their attention his/her need for prayer. This is the sick person's action of faith: asking for wellness (e.g., John 5:6; Mark 2:5).

James specifies who should be called: "the elders of the **church**" (5:14). In the Greco-Roman world ἐκκλησία referred to the "assembly duly summoned" or a "regularly summoned legislative body."[176] For example, the legislative assembly for Ephesus was *not* duly called during the riot (Acts 19:32–41). God through Jesus began his own "church" (ἐκκλησία) built on the foundation of Jesus as the Messiah, Son of the Living God.[177] Jesus, the savior and source of the church, loves it and cares for it.[178] Even though God has appointed in the church those with spiritual gifts of miracles and healing (1 Cor. 12:28–30), he also has given the **elders** (two or more) in their official capacity the gift of healing to enact their office. The readers of the letter were meeting in

("strength, might, esp. bodily strength") (Thayer, 80, 574; LSJ, 256, 1595). E.g., 1 Pet. 3:7.
171. John 5:3; Luke 13:11; Acts 3:2.
172. John 11:1–6, 11; Acts 9:37; Phil. 2:26–27; 2 Tim. 4:20.
173. Rom. 4:19; 8:26; 14:1–2; 1 Cor. 8:11–12; Heb. 4:15.
174. 2 Cor. 11:30–33; 12:5, 9–10.
175. Thayer, 546.
176. LSJ, 509; BDAG, 303. See also *Ant.* 4.8.45.309; Ps. 22:22; Deut. 4:10; 9:10; 18:16; 31:30.
177. Matt. 16:16–18; 1 Cor. 10:32; 11:22; 15:9; Gal. 1:13; 1 Tim. 3:5, 15.
178. Eph. 1:22; 5:23, 25, 29–30.

a Jewish synagogue (συναγωγή, 2:2), but they also had their own ecclesial Christian structure. *God's* church was commissioned to watch, oversee, and shepherd the Christian "flock."[179] One function they have in their care of the church is to have faith in Jesus's name to pray for healing (James 5:14–15).[180]

Πρεσβύτερος is the comparative or adjectival form of the root noun πρέσβυς (an old person or **elder**, usually then sixty years of age or over), literally, "the older one" or "elder of two," as in Luke 15:25. Elders in Greco-Roman times had authority in religious and civic matters. They handled city administration and jurisdiction. The establishment of elders is modeled by Moses, following Jethro's advice, who chose trustworthy and honest judges over groups of a thousand, hundred, fifty, and ten to judge the minor cases while he handled the difficult cases (Exod. 18:13–26). These judges were chosen by the tribes themselves and were trained by Moses (Deut. 1:9–18). The Jewish Christians appear to have adapted the Jewish leadership format. Christian elders first appear in Acts (Acts 11:29–30). Paul and Barnabas oversaw the election of elders in every city (Acts 14:23). The Christian elders were also called overseers (Titus 1:5, 7) because, as stewards or managers of a household, they were stewards of the church (Acts 20:28). Elders were teaching ministers with gifts of organization and hospitality (1 Tim. 3:1–2; Titus 1:9).[181]

The elders themselves were to pray for the sick person after they anointed the person with oil (5:14).[182] They follow the example of the Lord Jesus in whose name they pray. Jesus was concerned with physical health as a way to promote God's reign on earth. Jesus healed many simply by pronouncement[183] or by touch and laying hands on the sick.[184] Jesus commissioned the Twelve and seventy-two apostles to "heal the sick."[185] After the Twelve preached that people should repent, they cast out demons and anointed with oil many who were sick

---

179. Acts 20:28; 1 Tim. 3:1–4; Titus 1:5, 7–9.
180. See further Spencer and Spencer 1994, 237–38.
181. See Spencer 2014b, 10–20, 33–41, 47–48; Spencer 2013, 78–94, 121, 135–36; Spencer and Spencer 1994, 179–83.
182. Normally the aorist participle ("having anointed," ἀλείψαντες) signifies an action that precedes the main verb ("let them pray") (Robertson 1934, 860–61). In addition, it is physically difficult to anoint with oil while praying.
183. John 4:46–52; 5:7–9; 11:43.
184. Matt. 19:13; Mark 6:56; Luke 4:40; 13:12–13. Possibly ἐπί ("over") in James 5:14 may imply hands were laid *on* the sick person (Moo 2015, 223; Davids 1982, 193).
185. Matt. 10:7–8; Luke 9:2; 10:9.

and cured them (Mark 6:12–13). Peter and Paul also healed in Jesus's name by pronouncement, touch, prayer, and laying of hands on the sick.[186] James institutionalized for elders the practice employed by the twelve apostles in Mark 6:12–13.[187]

Olive oil (ἔλαιον), mentioned already in 3:12, was an everyday commodity of ancient society.[188] It was mixed into and poured onto foods,[189] used to light lamps,[190] and applied to the skin after a bath or before exercise.[191] Some merchants sold only oil.[192] Olive oil was used in ancient times as part of the healing process,[193] as by the Samaritan who poured oil and wine on the wounds of the attacked man before he bandaged him (Luke 10:34). In the ancient Greek play *Georgos* ("Farmer"), when one character received a deep cut in his leg while hoeing, another character kept anointing him with olive oil to cleanse and heal him. Today, its health benefits in preventing cancer and healing skin ailments are promoted.[194] But it does not heal *all* illnesses. Thus, olive oil in James 5:14 could represent the natural medicines that can be used in healing, or it is a physical symbol of the healing that will follow. Combined with God's sovereign care, natural medicine works to its maximum.[195] The key to healing is that the oil is applied in the "name of the Lord," followed by prayer. God is the Divine Healer (Exod. 15:26) who has the power to heal.

Oil has other significances in the Bible. Priests and rulers were anointed to symbolize holiness or dedication. This type of anointing

---

186. Acts 3:4–7; 4:10; 5:15; 9:40; 19:12; 28:8.
187. James himself was an apostle (Gal. 1:19).
188. E.g., Rev. 6:6. For more examples of the use of oil in the Bible and in ancient society, see Spencer and Spencer 1994, 238–39.
189. E.g., Exod. 29:2, 40.
190. E.g., Matt. 25:3–10.
191. Deut. 28:40; 2 Sam. 14:2; Mic. 6:15.
192. LSJ, 527–28. See also Spencer 1994, 238–39.
193. Isa. 1:6; Ezek. 16:9; Mark 6:13.
194. Olive oil has antioxidants, deeply cleanses, and enhances exfoliation of the skin (Edward Group, "Benefits of Olive Oil for Skin," *Global Healing Center*, Jan. 26, 2015, https://www.globalhealingcenter.com/natural-health/benefits-of-olive-oil-for-skin). Olive oil consumption protects the heart, fights cancer, aids weight loss, supports brain memory and focus, aids mood regulation, protects skin from environmental toxicity, prevents and treats diabetes, and balances hormones ("Top 8 Benefits of Using Olive Oil," http://dietsok.info/top-8-benefits-of-using-olive-oil/, accessed August 7, 2018.
195. MacNutt 1977, 37, 53.

may be combined with χρῖσμα, χρῖσις, or χρίω ("anoint" or consecrate for special service).[196] However, James does not indicate the anointed person is "set apart." Anointing can also symbolize celebration[197] and restoring the person to a "cheerful" state (James 5:13). But the symbol of healing seems most appropriate in the context of illness.[198]

James then promises: "And the prayer of faith will save the one being sick and the Lord will raise that one; and, if he may have committed sins, it will be forgiven to him/her" (5:15). The prayer in 5:15 refers back to the prayer of the elders in 5:14; thus, it is the faith of the elders that is effective "to save the one being sick." Here, James uses another synonym for **"prayer"** (εὐχή). Εὐχή mainly signifies a "vow," "a solemn promise with the understanding that one is subject to penalty for failure to discharge the obligation."[199] Such vows were integral aspects of the Old Testament offerings.[200] For example, Jacob made a vow: "If God will be with me, and will keep me in this way that I go, and will give me bread to eat and clothing to wear, so that I come again to my father's house in peace, then the LORD shall be my God, and this stone, which I have set up for a pillar, shall be God's house; and of all that you give me I will surely give one-tenth to you" (Gen. 28:20–22 NRSV). Hannah also made a vow: "O LORD of hosts, if only you will look on the misery of your servant, and remember me, and not forget your servant, but will give to your servant a male child, then I will set him before you as a nazirite until the day of his death. He shall drink neither wine nor intoxicants, and no razor shall touch his head" (1 Sam. 1:11 NRSV). God affirmed both these vows and agreed to do them (Gen. 31:13; 1 Sam. 1:17–20). A Nazarite vow was institutionalized (Num. 6:2–21). Unlike the "oath" (ὅρκος) of 5:12, in a "vow" (εὐχή, 5:15) God's name is not profaned. Desire, need, and faith melt into prayer to God, as when Paul wrote to the Corinthians, "This also we pray/desire [εὔχομαι]—your perfection" (2 Cor. 13:9).[201] Thus, these elders agree to a joint "vow" or prayer for the wellbeing of the sick person. "Faith" modifies the prayer or vow: it is full of faith. The nature of the prayer is faithful[202] or the source of the prayer is faith, a united agreement among two or more elders for healing presented in assurance

---

196. E.g., BDAG, 1090–91; Exod. 29:7, 21; Lev. 21:10; 1 Kings 1:39; 2 Kings 9:1–3; Ps. 104:15; LSJ, 2007. See also McCartney 2009, 253–54.
197. 2 Sam. 14:2; Eccl. 9:8; Luke 7:46.
198. Spencer and Spencer 1994, 123–24.
199. BDAG, 416.
200. E.g., Lev. 7:6 LXX; 22:21; 27:2; Acts 18:18; 21:23.
201. Acts 26:29; Rom. 9:3; 2 Cor. 13:7; 3 John 2.
202. Genitive of quality—faith is an attribute of this prayer.

to God.[203] It is similar to the way one ought to ask God for wisdom: "in no way wavering" (1:6).

The faith-full prayer will have two consequences: it will save the one being sick and the Lord will raise him or her (5:15). To **"save"** (σῴζω) someone, according to the Bible, is to act on the person's behalf,[204] protecting him or her from a person, thing, or event that could destroy the person physically, emotionally, or spiritually. Some of the potential causes of "death" are illness, demonic possession,[205] sins,[206] natural disasters,[207] and political oppression.[208] Death can be temporal[209] or eternal.[210] Elsewhere in James, σῴζω appears to refer to protection or prevention of eternal *spiritual* death, as "the implanted word, the one being able to *save* your lives" (1:21), and "the one having turned back a sinner from his erroneous wandering will *save* his life from death and will cover a multitude of sins" (5:20). However, James 4:12 could refer to temporal and eternal death: God is "Lawgiver and Judge, the One being able to *save* and to destroy."[211] "Save" (σῴζω) refers to healing in several New Testament passages. For instance, the woman who had been bleeding for twelve years, tells herself: "If only I touch his cloak, I will be *saved*" (σῴζω), implying she will be healed (Matt. 9:21). Jesus told her: "Take heart, daughter; your faith has saved [σῴζω] you," and the woman "was saved [σῴζω] from that hour" (Mark 5:22).[212] Clearly, the woman was healed.[213] Jairus, too, asked Jesus to put his hands on his daughter so that "she may be saved [σῴζω] and live" (Mark 5:23).[214] Jesus uses the same verb in response when he is about to resurrect her from the dead: "Only believe, and she will be saved" (σῴζω, Luke 8:50–55). She does live.

The object of "salvation" is "the one who is **sick**" (5:15, κάμνω). Again, the illness is not a brief one, but is ongoing.[215] Κάμνω may simply refer to

---

203. Subjective genitive—faith produces the prayer.
204. Judg. 6:31; 1 Sam. 23:2, 5; 25:31.
205. E.g., Luke 8:36.
206. E.g., Matt. 1:21.
207. Gen. 19:17; Matt. 8:25; 24:22; Acts 27:20, 31; 1 Cor. 3:15.
208. Jude 5; Judg. 2:16, 18; 6:14–15, 36–37; 7:7; 8:22; 10:12–14; 12:2–3; 13:5.
209. Gen. 19:20; 32:30; 47:25; Matt. 27:40, 49; John 12:27.
210. E.g., Matt. 10:22; 16:25; 19:25.
211. See also Mark 3:4.
212. See also Luke 8:43–48.
213. Eusebius notes the statues the woman had constructed, depicting Jesus healing her, that she set up in front of her home (*Hist. eccl.* 7.18).
214. See also Acts 4:9; 14:9–10.
215. Κάμνω is present participle (κάμνοντα).

work or labor; to the "effect of continued work, to *be weary*"; to be "hard pressed"; or to "those whose work is done, who have met with disaster."[216] Hebrews uses this verb as a synonym of losing heart (12:3). Job describes his own desire to die as a *weariness* of soul (Job 10:1; 17:1–2). In extracanonical literature, the Wisdom of Solomon describes those already dead (4:16). Josephus uses the verb to describe the child of Jeroboam who is ill and about to die.[217] Thus, James describes the person who is extremely weary, possibly near death: he "will be saved" and the Lord "will **raise** him" (5:15) by the faith-filled prayer of the elders. The sick can rise up (ἐγείρω) by getting up out of bed and walking, as Peter's mother-in-law did.[218] A synonym for healing is used in 5:16 (ἰάομαι). But, for all humans comes a time when they will die. And, for those people, to "rise up" refers to the resurrection from the dead. Jesus himself was killed and on the third day raised to life.[219] Jesus explains that "just as the Father raises the dead and gives them life, so also the Son gives life to whomever he wishes."[220] Thus, the "Lord" refers either to Jesus, God the Son, who has been given all authority, or to God the Father. My husband, Rev. Dr. William David Spencer, summarizes: "The resurrection is God's ultimate answer to suffering, and the work the church does to alleviate it now is God's temporal answer."[221] God's ultimate answer to suffering is foretold in Revelation 21, when God dwells with humans: then, God "will wipe every tear from their eyes. There will be no more death or mourning or crying or pain, for the old order of things has passed away" (Rev. 21:4 NIV).

James ends the sentence with a conditional adverbial clause: "and, if he may have committed sins, it will be forgiven to him/her" (5:15). The conditional clause ("if . . . ") with the present subjunctive ("may") indicates that all illnesses are not caused by sin, but that continued sin may be an issue for this particular sick person.[222] The perfect participle

216. LSJ, 872.
217. *Ant.* 8.11.1.266, 273. See also Hippocrates, *Morb.* 3.16.148.
218. Matt. 8:15; Mark 1:31. See also Matt. 9:5–7, 25. Even in the NT, not all believers are healed, e.g., 2 Cor. 12:8–9; 1 Tim. 5:23; 2 Tim. 4:20. The Second Vatican Council "restored the original practice" of the Roman Catholic Church of "administering the sacrament as a prayer for healing" (Anderson and Keating 2017, 115).
219. Matt. 16:21; 17:23; 20:19; 1 Cor. 15:4, 12–15, 42.
220. John 5:21 NRSV; Acts 26:8; 2 Cor. 1:9.
221. Systematic Theology 3 lecture notes, Gordon-Conwell Theological Seminary, Boston, MA, August 1, 2018.
222. The subjunctive mood is a mood of doubt. As a third-class condition, the condition is stated as doubtful but with some expectation of realization (Robertson 1934, 927–28, 1004, 1016).

("may have committed sins") highlights that these potential sins would have begun in the past and continued over time. They would not be new or fleeting sins. The main clause is in the definitive future ("it will be forgiven to him/her"), asserting positively what will occur.[223] Thus, the elders "in the name of the Lord" (5:14) can be instruments of physical and spiritual salvation. James does not clarify who will forgive the sins.[224] Ultimately, only God has the power to forgive sins.[225] Humans participate in this process.[226] But forgiveness is not possible without confession of sins (5:16).

"Therefore" (οὖν, 5:16) indicates that what follows is the result of or an inference from what precedes it.[227] In order not to develop any illness from sins,[228] James commands two continual actions: "Therefore, keep confessing your sins to one another, and keep praying for one another, so that you may be healed" (5:16). **Confession** and prayer done communally are two key actions for the church. Ἐξομολογέω signifies to confess or profess "forth from the heart, freely, or publicly, openly."[229] It is a synonym at times for "to sing,"[230] as in "Therefore will I *confess* [ἐξομολογέω] to thee, O Lord, among the nations, and sing [ψάλλω] to your name" (Ps. 18:49).[231] A similar type of public praise of God the Father was done by God the Son: "I publicly praise you, Father, Lord of the heaven and the earth, for having hidden these things from wise and intelligent people, and having revealed them to babies" (Luke 10:21; Matt. 11:25). This confession of sins is to "one another" (5:16). Thus, prayer is not simply vertical (elders for the sick, 5:14) or private (for oneself, 5:13), but also horizontal (5:16). Here is the priesthood of all believers in action (1 Pet. 2:5, 9),[232] confessing publicly what is within, and praying prayers of faith for one another. In the Old Testament,

---

223. Robertson 1934, 925.
224. "It" probably refers to "the sinning." The singular verb ("is forgiven") is according to traditional phrasing, as in Leviticus 4:26, 31, 35 LXX (Vlachos 2013, 188).
225. Matt. 6:12; 9:6; Mark 2:7–12; Luke 5:20–26; 7:48–49; 11:4; 1 John 1:9; 2:12.
226. Matt. 6:14–15; 18:21–35; Luke 17:1–4; John 20:23. McKnight (2011, 446) agrees that this passage presupposes the priesthood of all believers.
227. BDAG, 736.
228. E.g., 1 Cor. 11:29–32. See Spencer and Spencer 1994, 55–72.
229. Ἐξομολογέω is a composite word from ἐκ ("from out of, out from, forth from") and ὁμολογέω ("to confess," "profess," "declare openly, speak out freely") (Thayer, 189, 224, 446).
230. Pss. 7:17; 30:12; 33:2; 70:22; 138:1.
231. See also Rom. 15:9.
232. See also Exod. 19:5–6; Isa. 61:6; Rev. 1:5–6; 5:10; 20:6.

people brought guilt and sin offerings to the priest, but, since Jesus has become the perfect sin offering,[233] expiation offerings are no longer necessary, nor are professional priests needed in the process of atonement (e.g., Heb. 9:11–10:18).

Confession of one's sins is essential in becoming a Christian, as when believers confessed their sins before being baptized by John the Baptist (Matt. 3:6; Mark 1:5). But, believers should also confess sins that were not terminated when becoming a Christian. At Ephesus, for instance, such confession and consequent dramatic transformation of behavior caused the church to grow powerfully (Acts 19:18–20). Confession may include asking forgiveness of a person or persons sinned against (e.g., Matt. 5:23–24; 6:12–15). Scot McKnight adds that sins mentioned in the letter would be included: mistreatment of poor, verbal sins, violence, judgmentalism, and greed.[234] Confession is also important as preparation for the judgment to come.[235] James does not require confession of sins to everyone, but he does mean to another human being; confessing to God alone is not always enough.[236] This is *not* a forced confession. It is freely done from the heart and expressed outwardly.[237]

The response to confession is forgiveness (5:15) but also faith-full prayer[238] on behalf of one another. Often people need God's support and communal support to persevere. The overall purpose (ὅπως) is **healing** (ἰάομαι, 5:16), a synonym for σῴζω (5:15). Σῴζω can refer to physical healing, but it also has many other uses.[239] In contrast, ἰάομαι principally refers to physical healing, but it can also refer to spiritual healing. Jesus "healed" (ἰάομαι) many in his ministry: those who were paralyzed,[240] had dropsy (Luke 14:2–4), leprosy (Luke 17:13–15), a cut ear (Luke 22:51), hemorrhaging (Mark 5:29; Luke 8:47), demon possession,[241] and those near death (Luke 7:2–20; John 4:47–53). He commissioned the Twelve, too, to heal (Luke 9:2). Paul also healed the

---

233. E.g., Rom. 5:8–10; 2 Cor. 5:21; 1 Pet. 2:24.
234. McKnight 2011, 446, 454.
235. James 5:8, 12; Isa. 45:22–23; Rom. 14:10–11; 2 Cor. 5:10.
236. "Confession" does not have to be to all people, as the verb is used when Judas spoke only to the officers of the temple (Luke 22:4–6).
237. Spencer and Spencer 1990, 120–21.
238. Εὔχομαι ("to pray"), 5:16, is the verb form of εὐχή ("prayer"), 5:15. "Mutual confession must culminate in sympathetic intercession," for otherwise "confessions may prove to be harmful" (Hiebert 1979, 325).
239. See exposition of James 5:15.
240. Matt. 8:8, 13; Luke 5:17–26; 6:18–19; John 5:5–11.
241. Matt. 15:22–28; Luke 9:42; Acts 10:38.

ill (Acts 28:8–9). The Holy Spirit also gives "gifts of healing" (ἴαμα) to some (not all) in the church (1 Cor. 12:9, 28–30). But ἰάομαι may also refer to spiritual healing of repentant sinners.[242] James mentions two means of physical healing, through the elders and through the Christian community. But in 5:16, he does not promise that all will be healed;[243] rather, he uses the aorist subjunctive. The subjunctive mood is the attitude of future expectation and anticipation. It is the mode of "doubtful statement" or hesitation (in contrast to the indicative, the mode of positive assertion, or the imperative, that of commanding statement).[244] Thus, believers are to pray unwaveringly for physical and spiritual healing, as God is the all-powerful Healer, but healing of all people is not guaranteed in this passage.[245]

James explains and encourages with the closing sentence: "The prayer of a righteous person has much strength in its working," or "Much can accomplish a working prayer of a righteous person" (5:16). James begins with "**much**" (πολύ), accentuating the adverb.[246] "Much" what? Much strength or power (ἰσχύω). Then, he indicates what or who has this strength—it is the prayer of a righteous person (δέησις δικαίου). James does not limit the power to the elders[247] or to men only (cf. KJV, which does). James emphasizes at the end (using pleonasm, repeating the idea of the first word—"much") the effectiveness of such a prayer ("in its working"—ἐνεργουμένη). A. K. M. Adam suggests that "the participle in the emphatic position probably serves to remind readers that a righteous person's prayer can accomplish much."[248] James uses the singular number (a righteous person) as a prelude to the illustration to follow of the individual Elijah (5:17–18).[249]

Another synonym for "prayer" (προσεύχομαι, εὐχή) is δέησις (5:14–16). Δέησις (noun) and δέομαι (verb) come from δέω, "to want, need" and "to stand in need of."[250] This word family emphasizes forceful requests or urging in regard to some need.[251] Paul's prayer to see the Romans is described with δέομαι (Rom. 1:10). For example, a prayer for

---

242. Matt. 13:15; John 12:40; Acts 28:27; 1 Pet. 2:24; Isa. 6:9–10.
243. E.g., future indicative tense.
244. Robertson 1934, 927–28.
245. See Keener 2011 for examples of contemporary healing.
246. See also Vlachos 2013, 189.
247. See also Vlachos 2013, 189.
248. Adam 2013, 103.
249. The same technique is used in 1 Timothy 2:11–15 (Spencer 2013, 58).
250. Thayer, 129.
251. See Spencer and Spencer 1990, 112–15.

deliverance from deadly perils would be a forceful request,[252] as would prayers for healing (Luke 5:12; 9:38, 40), for a child to be born (Luke 1:13), for urgently needed harvesters (Matt. 9:36–38; Luke 10:2), or for forgiveness of wicked actions (Acts 8:22, 24). This forceful request for a need is illustrated by Elijah, who prayed for no rain and then for rain (James 5:17–18). James wants the mutual prayers for members of the community to have this level of importance, for the need is especially keen at this time when laborers are working but not being paid (5:4–5), when perseverance and love are needed (5:7–11), and when some are very ill (5:13–14).

The character of the person praying is most important: "**righteous**" (δίκαιος, 5:16), which comes from a significant word family in James's letter. James, himself renowned as "righteous,"[253] desires righteousness in others as well. For James, a "righteous" person is holy and just with wisdom from above (3:17–18), demonstrating her or his faith through moral and just action while trusting God's good and sovereign nature.[254] God rewards the prayers of such people (James 5:16; 1 Pet. 3:12). Peter quotes Psalm 34:12–16 (1 Pet. 3:10–12), but James alludes to Psalm 34 throughout the letter, especially in chapter 5. In addition to "keep your tongue from evil" (Ps. 34:13) being similar to James 5:12, the rest of the psalm has many similarities: "The eyes of the LORD are on the righteous, and his ears are open to their cry. The face of the LORD is against evildoers, to cut off the remembrance of them from the earth. When the righteous cry for help, the LORD hears, and rescues them from all their troubles. The LORD is near to the brokenhearted, and saves the crushed in spirit. Many are the afflictions of the righteous, but the LORD rescues them from them all" (Ps. 34:15–19 NRSV). James has been urging the twelve tribes to become doers of the word, throwing off filth and evil, while receiving the implanted word (1:21–22). Such an integration of faith with action is pleasing in God's sight and is rewarded in response to one's requests to God.

The example of a righteous person accomplishing much through prayer is described: "Elijah was a human of like nature to us, and he prayed fervently that it might not rain, and for three years and six months it did not rain on the earth. Then he prayed again, and the heaven gave rain and the earth yielded its harvest" (5:17–18). James lists six main (independent) clauses all connected by "and" (καί,

---

252. E.g., Luke 21:36; Acts 4:31; 2 Cor. 1:11; Phil. 1:19.
253. *Hist. eccl.* 2.23.
254. See exposition of James 2:24; 3:18.

polysyndeton) to present in sequence the narrative of events. James begins by emphasizing Elijah's **human** nature by presenting "human" before its verb, literally: "Elijah, a human, was" (5:17), then he repeats "of like nature to us" (ὁμοιοπαθής, a pleonasm).[255] Paul also uses these words (ὁμοιοπαθής + εἰμι + ἄνθρωπος) to keep worshipers of Zeus from treating him and Barnabas as gods: "We ourselves, *we are of like nature to you, humans,* bringing you good news" (Acts 14:15). Thus, James wants to encourage the praying community to identify with Elijah, not treat him as uniquely gifted.

Elijah the Tishbite prophesized in the 800s (ninth century BC), during the reigns of Ahab and Ahaziah in Israel. Both Ahab and his son Ahaziah did much evil, "more than all who were before."[256] For instance, Ahab built a place of worship in honor of Baal in Samaria (1 Kings 16:32). During this time of syncretism and heresy, Elijah was totally committed to the Lord God of Israel no matter what other people did or said. He believed there was only one God and obeyed whatever God commanded; in other words, he had faith *and* action (James 2:18–19). He is the only person, according to the Bible, whose death was an ascension in a whirlwind into heaven (2 Kings 2:11). He and Moses appear when Jesus is transfigured.[257] God promises to send Elijah to Israel before the "great and terrible day of the Lord" (Mal. 4:5).[258] Jesus sees John the Baptist as Elijah personified (Matt. 11:13–14; 17:10–13; Luke 1:17). Jesus, like James, refers to Elijah "during the time of the drought" (Luke 4:25–26), and Paul uses Elijah as an example of intercessory prayer (Rom. 11:2–4).

James emphasizes Elijah's proactive intercession, as opposed to 1 Kings 17–18, which focuses on Elijah's prophetic proclamations. The later (c. AD 100)[259] pseudepigraphal 4 Ezra mentions Elijah's prayer for rain.

255. Ὁμοιοπαθής is a composite of ὅμοιος ("like") and πάσχω ("to suffer" or "to feel") signifying "suffering the like with another, of like feelings or affections" (Thayer, 445, 494).
256. 1 Kings 16:30–33; 21:25–26; 22:51–53.
257. Matt. 17:3–4; Mark 9:4–5; Luke 9:30–33.
258. Many Jews expected Elijah to return: Matt. 16:13–14; 27:47, 49; Mark 6:15; 8:27–28; 9:11–13; 15:35–36; John 1:21, 25; m. Seqal. 2:5; Sotah 9:15; B. Mes. 1:8; 2:8; 3:4–5; 'Ed. 8:7.
259. Metzger 1983, 520.

References to Elijah and the Drought			
James	Jesus	1 Kings	Apocrypha & Pseudepigrapha
He prayed fervently that it might not rain (5:17)		Elijah declares to Ahab: "As the Lord lives, the God of Israel, who I stand in [the] presence of, there shall not be these years light rain nor rain but according to my word" (17:1)	
3½ years no rain on earth	3½ years no rain (Luke 4:25)	In the third year God tells Elijah to go to Ahab: "I will send rain on the earth" (18:1)	"By the word of the Lord [Elijah] shut up the heaven" (Sir. 48:3)
He prayed again (5:18)		Elijah "bowed himself down upon the earth and put his face between his knees" (18:42).[260]	Elijah prayed "for those who received the rain" (4 Ezra 7:109)
Heaven gave rain		It rains (18:44–45)	
Earth yielded its harvest			

It is unclear from the Bible what came first (Elijah praying or God's revelation to Elijah), but the sequence probably is as follows: God reveals to Elijah there would be no rain. Elijah declares to Ahab: "As the Lord lives, the God of Israel, who I stand in [the] presence of, there shall not be these years light rain nor rain but according to my word" (1 Kings 17:1). This verse indicates that Elijah had been in the

---

260. Some scholars (e.g., Moo [2015, 232]) think 1 Kings 18:42 refers to prayer. However, the action in 18:42 *follows* Elijah's declaration that "there is the sound of abundance of rain" (18:41) and precedes his commands to his servant to see the rain cloud coming from the sea (18:43–44). Thus, 18:42 more likely refers to Elijah listening for rain (although he could have been praying simultaneously).

presence of God, the amount of time for the drought is undetermined
("these years"), and Elijah tells Ahab there will be no rain.[261] Elijah
prays there be no rain, and then there is no rain. God then tells Elijah
how God will take care of Elijah during this severe drought: by going
to the Wadi Cherith and being fed by ravens there (1 Kings 17:2–4).
Eventually, even this stream dries up (1 Kings 17:7). Then God has
Elijah go to Sidon where God miraculously takes care of Elijah, the
widow of Zarephath, and her household (1 Kings 17:9–16). The drought
went on for three and a half years. God then tells Elijah he will send
rain on the earth (1 Kings 18:1). Did Elijah pray before this declaration? That would make 18:1 an answer to prayer. Eventually a "heavy
rain" descends (1 Kings 18:45).

One might expect James to have chosen as his illustration Elijah
reviving the son of the widow of Zarephath, since the topic is healing
(1 Kings 17:17–24), but instead he chose a larger set of events (1 Kings
17:1–18:45): the prayer for drought and rain, in which the healing is
encased. The rain eventually yields a "harvest" or "fruit" (James 5:18),
which alludes back to the "fruit of righteousness" in 3:18 and to the
illustration of the farmer waiting for "the precious fruit of the earth"
(5:7).[262] James has also used imagery from nature in chapter 1: "Every
good gift and every perfect present is *from above, coming down* from
the Father of *lights*. . . . We may be a kind of *firstfruit* of his *creations*.
. . . Receive the *implanted* word" (1:17–18, 21). Rain and harvest are
day-by-day issues for the farmers (5:4) who are reading the letter. The
giving of rain is an allusion to the Giver of rain, the Father of lights,
who has created the heavens and the earth, and therefore is all powerful, including over the recreating and restoration of human bodies
and spirits. This example is one all can see. Within the narrative is the
illustration of a faithful widow who takes care of Elijah in the midst of

---

261. Drought is the threatened punishment for national idolatry: "Take care,
    or you will be seduced into turning away, serving other gods and wor-
    shiping them, for then the anger of the LORD will be kindled against you
    and he will shut up the heavens, so that there will be no rain, and the
    land will yield no fruit; then you will perish quickly off the good land that
    the LORD is giving you" (Deut. 11:16–17 NRSV) (Jamieson, Fausset, and
    Brown 1961, 263). In addition, the oath is a "challenge to Baal, who was
    represented by Ahab. If the Lord withheld the rain, rendering Baal—
    considered the god of fertility and lord of the rain clouds—powerless, he
    would be proven the true God and Elijah the true prophet of his word"
    (*NIV Archaeological Study Bible* 2005, 513).
262. See also McCartney 2009, 260.

the drought (1 Kings 17:9–16). Thus, this illustration unites the letter and, as well, communicates the possibility of a response to prayer from God even greater than physical healing.

What kind of prayer did Elijah do? He **"prayed fervently"** (προσευχῇ προσηύξατο, 5:17). He prayed reverently (προσεύχομαι).[263] James uses a pleonasm, the noun form προσευχή ("with a prayer") to intensify the verb form προσεύχομαι ("he prayed").[264] Jesus uses a similar technique to express his deep interest: *"I have eagerly desired* to eat this Passover with you" (ἐπιθυμίᾳ ἐπεθύμησα, Luke 22:15).[265] Elijah had no doubts when he prayed (James 1:6–8). One reason he had no doubts was because he had been in God's very presence and was sure of his mission. The Lord responded to his prayer.

James uses two synonyms for **"rain"** (βρέχω, 5:17; ὑετός, 5:18).[266] Βρέχω (verb) and its noun βροχή[267] can be used in a variety of contexts, such as, the "Father in heaven . . . *sends rain* [βρέχω] on the righteous and unrighteous" (Matt. 5:45). It is also used for heavy tears (Luke 7:38, 44; Ps. 6:6) and fire and sulfur raining down from heaven (Luke 17:29; Gen. 19:24; Exod. 9:23). It can signify heavy rain: the rain fell, the floods came, and the winds blew (Matt. 7:25, 27). Ὑετός in the New Testament is used for rain that results in a harvest, as in James 5:18. For example, Paul describes to the Lycaonians God's general gifts to humanity as One who gives rains (ὑετός) from heaven and fruitful seasons that result in food and joyful hearts (Acts 14:17). God had promised the Hebrews that the land of Canaan, unlike Egypt, has "rain of heaven," the early and latter rains (Deut. 11:11, 14), but, if Israel served other gods, the Lord would restrain heaven, not give rain, and no harvests would result (Deut. 11:17).[268] Thus, James alludes to God's covenant promise of blessing to encourage perseverance in prayer among the twelve tribes.

---

263. See exposition James 5:13.
264. Vlachos (2013, 190–91) sees the repetition as likely reflecting the Semitic infinite absolute construction. Nevertheless, he agrees the form intensifies the verb.
265. See also Deut. 7:26.
266. Both words are used in Isaiah 5:6 and Ezekiel 22:24.
267. Thayer, 106.
268. See also Deut. 28:12; Heb. 6:7. First Kings 18:44–45 LXX employs ὑετός.

SUMMARY OF ACTION STEPS IN HEALING
BY ELDERS (JAMES 5:14–16)

I. Sick persons call for help for ongoing illness (faith is exhibited in call)

We need to educate people about the need to ask for prayer from elders. Sick people should ask for elders' prayer when their own prayer and prayer from two or three others is not answered.

II. Church elders are ready to pray in faith for the sick

We need to train and educate elders in every church to work with pastor(s) in the healing process. Two or three elders are the minimum needed to represent the church (Deut. 17:6). The elders' faith or trust is exhibited in jointly agreed confidence in God's power to heal and to produce the wellbeing of the sick person. God decides if the healing is now or at the resurrection. Let one or more elders anoint the sick person with olive oil in the name of the Lord and ask the sick person if he/she wants to confess any ongoing sin and then forgive that sin in the Lord's name. The elders should be righteous, not doing any ongoing sins themselves, and they should pray in conjunction with the medical treatment of the illness.

III. Church helps in healing process

Church leaders should organize regular opportunities for communal confession and prayer for one another.

IV. Some frequent questions

Is this kind of prayer by elders necessary? The skin of one student I knew was becoming jaundiced due to continuing kidney problems. I asked her if she ever asked the elders of her church to pray for her. She mentioned that she had enough prayer partners: Christians throughout the world and at the school. I suggested that following James's precepts in 5:14–18 was a matter of obedience to God. Even if it made no sense to her, she should give James's injunctions a try. How could it hurt? Eventually, she went ahead and asked her church elders to pray for her, and immediately she began to improve and eventually was healed.

Are all prayers by elders the same? My husband Bill has had prayer for his Crohn's health condition several times over the years. One group of elders he asked for prayer from were not too sure of the possibility of healing, with the results that he was healed only slightly. A second group of elders he asked had much practice in such prayer and were fully confident of God's power. This time, Bill was healed overnight. Later, when he was hospitalized for several months after surgery, he invited different elders to come in every day to pray for the specific medical need suggested by the doctor. This prayer took several months but resulted in healing. By watching his diet, regular rest, prayer, and minimal medication, his health has been excellent.

What types of healing are there? When I was diagnosed with breast cancer in 2004, I asked the elders and pastors of our church to come to my home for prayer. They gladly agreed. I, of course, wanted total healing for all cancer to disappear and for no surgery to be required. I did have to undergo surgery, but the surgery was effective, and the recovery was quick. I asked for prayer for every step needed in the healing process. No cancer has returned for the last fifteen years.

Around the same time, an intensive viral attack resulted in my receiving an essential head tremor condition. Again, I asked for prayer from the elders and other faithful Christians. I also read that sometimes caffeine can accentuate tremors so I eliminated that from my diet. Between the prayer and avoiding all caffeine, I have avoided tremors for over a decade, although I still have the potential to get tremors (e.g., caused by tiredness or loud sounds).

Francis MacNutt mentions various degrees of improvement from prayer: cessation of pain, removal of side effects of treatment, stabilization of sickness, return of physical function without healing of the illness, and bodily healing. He concludes: we should be ready to praise God "for all the levels of healing that are steps on the way to perfect life and wholeness." He adds: "Healing is a mystery—that it's complicated and not all that simple . . . should free us from any need to give simplistic answers to people who wonder why they are not totally healed."[269]

Deal Wisely with Those Led Astray (5:19–20)

James now ends with the last category of reader: "If anyone among you might be led astray from the truth" (5:19). He has already dealt with three other categories of readers:[270] the suffering, the cheerful, and the sick (5:13–18). The last category is the deceived. He introduces these final verses with "my brothers and sisters" (ἀδελφοί μου). He has employed this metaphor (ἀδελφός, ἀδελφή) of equality twenty times in the letter.[271] In James, the vocative "brothers and sisters" indicates the addition of a new

---

269. MacNutt 1977, 57–62.
270. See exposition of James 5:13–14.
271. See exposition of James 1:16.

topic[272] or it draws the reader's attention to what follows.[273] This final address closes the letter and calls the readers to pay attention.

Unlike Paul, James uses no final greeting or signature; rather, his format is similar to Hebrew letters before the Bar Kosiba period (AD 132–35). David Aune writes that the Hebrew documentary letters before AD 132 that he and others have studied have "no final greetings, dates, or signatures."[274] For instance, Jonathan writes the Spartans with no closing formula but with a prescript and greeting: "From Jonathan the High Priest, the Senate of the Jews, the priests, and the rest of the Jewish people, to our brothers of Sparta. Greeting" (1 Macc. 12:6 REB).

James goes back in 5:19–20 to a theme he introduced in chapter 1: deception (1:16). In 1:16, he warns the readers not to be **led astray** (πλανάω) from the correct path by following a wrong desire.[275] Now, at the end of the letter, as part of the directions for the community to care for each other, James raises concern for someone led astray from the path of truth to a false path: "My brothers and sisters, if anyone among you might be led astray away from the truth and someone might turn him/her back, let that person know that the one having turned back a sinner from his erroneous way will save his life[276] from death and will cover a multitude of sins" (5:19–20). Sheep are a recurrent biblical example of animals who wander off (e.g., Matt. 18:12–14; 1 Pet. 2:25). If indeed the church is the priesthood of all believers,[277] then, like priests, believers need to "deal gently" with "those who are ignorant and are going astray" (Heb. 5:2 NIV). Jesus warns his disciples to stay on the narrow path that leads to life (Matt. 7:14), even as Moses taught the Israelites: "Deviate neither to right nor to left from all the things which I command you this day, and do not go after other gods to serve them" (Deut. 28:14 REB).[278]

James begins (5:19) addressing two groups:

(1) the person led astray (singular) from among them (plural) and
2) the person (singular) who turns the person led astray back to where he or she had been.[279]

---

272. James 1:2, 19; 2:1, 14; 3:1; 4:11; 5:7, 12.
273. James 1:16; 2:5; 3:10, 12; 5:9, 10. Cf. McCartney 2009, 247.
274. Aune 1987, 175–77. Francis (1970, 125) adds that many Hellenistic letters of all types have no closing formulas. Also see introduction.
275. See exposition of James 1:14–16.
276. On ψυχή ("life"), see exposition of James 1:21.
277. See exposition of James 5:16.
278. See also Deut. 5:32.
279. BDAG, 382 (ἐπιστρέφω ["to turn back"]).

Then, James makes his main point: "let that person know," referring again to (2) the person who turns back the sinner from his erroneous way (5:20). That person "will save" and "will cover" (5:20), but
who will be saved or covered? To whom does *"his* life from death" refer?
And, whose "multitude of sins" are covered? The first direct object "his
life" seems most likely to refer to the person led astray (1) because
leaving the correct path would lead to death, like a sheep falling into
a pit.[280] That would complete the chiastic order: 1, 2, 2, 1. But then,
whose sins are covered? Certainly the person sinning has many sins,[281]
but so also would the person restoring the sinner.

In this context, I think "will cover a multitude of sins" (5:20) refers to the person who turns back the wayward sinner (2).[282] Why?
The sinner (1) has one sin, albeit major. He or she was led astray
from the truth and is on an erroneous path, while, in a general way,
all believers have many sins (3:2). The key to understanding James's
point is in the verb **"cover"** (καλύπτω). Καλύπτω may literally refer
to the way storm waves may cover a boat (Matt. 8:24) or a jar cover
a light (Luke 8:16). James may be alluding to a practice mentioned
in Leviticus 16:13. When Aaron the high priest entered the holy of
holies in the temple once a year to make atonement for the people
(Lev. 16:17), he had to carry incense. The "smoke of the incense *shall
cover* the mercy-seat over the tables of testimony and he shall not
die" (Lev. 16:13). God made himself known at the ark of the covenant
(Exod. 25:22). In other words, the incense "covered" or obscured the
mercy-seat so that Aaron's own sins would be less obvious when he
went to make atonement for other people's sins. Aaron still had to
make offerings for himself, his household, the people, the sanctuary,
the tent of meeting, the altar, and the other priests.[283] But the incense
obscured Aaron's sinful nature. After Jesus's perfect sacrifice, however, all need for temple offerings ended. Even though James lived
while the temple sacrifices were still ongoing, according to tradition
(*Hist. eccl.* 2.23), he still prayed in the temple, but his letter took
to heart Jesus's teachings that Jesus was greater than the temple

---

280. See also James 1:15.
281. The last clause refers to the sins of the wanderer: Hiebert 1979, 336–37;
Martin 1988, 220; Vlachos 2013, 199; Tasker 1957, 143–44; Townsend
1994, 111; McKnight 2011, 459–60.
282. See also Ropes 1916, 315–16; Brosend 2004, 157; Dibelius 1976, 259;
Adamson 1976, 203–4.
283. Lev. 16:6–11, 15–18, 20–21, 24, 30, 33–34. "Covering" of sin also was a
symbolic way to describe the forgiving of sins (Neh. 4:5; Ps. 85:2 LXX).

(Matt. 12:6) and Jesus's own body is the perfect holy place (ναός, John 2:19–22).[284] The "incense" of the Old Testament now symbolically is the loving effort of one believer to bring back another erring believer. That action "covers" or obscures the intercessor's own many sins. This reference rounds off the earlier discussion (5:13–18) on the community functioning as the priesthood of all believers. James had told his hearers to confess their sins to one another; now, he encourages them to help each other out of sin.

James 5:19–20 also reminds the readers of many themes in the letter, including James's many references to mercy, for example, "mercy triumphs over judgment" (2:13), God's wisdom being "full of mercy and good fruits" and doing "peace" (3:17–18), and the Lord being "greatly compassionate" and "merciful" (5:11). The thesis of the letter includes the concept of receiving "the implanted word, the one being able to save your lives" (1:21). Thus, James at the end of his letter emphasizes the importance of salvation (5:20). James's Old Testament illustrations all participated in restoration and intercession. Elijah's confrontation with King Ahab brought even Ahab to a point of repentance (1 Kings 21:20–29). Job interceded for his friends (42:8–9). Abraham rescued Lot and his family and interceded for Sodom (Gen. 14:12–16; 18:23–33). Rahab participated in the restoration of herself and her household (Josh. 2:8–14).

The commandment to love your neighbor as yourself (James 2:8) is now displayed in action. Such love includes turning back those who are deceived (5:19–20). Peter appears to allude to James 5:20. He repeats "covers a multitude of sins" (καλύπτει πλῆθος ἁμαρτιῶν) but specifies it is love for one another that covers one's sins (1 Pet. 4:8). Jude too encourages believers to "save others by snatching them out of the fire" (23 NRSV).[285] A similar thought may be found in Proverbs: "Hatred stirs up strife, but love covers all offenses" (10:12 NRSV). The rabbis agreed: "If any man has caused a single soul to perish from Israel, Scripture[286] imputes it to him as though he had caused a whole world to perish; and if any man saves alive a single soul from Israel, Scripture imputes it to him as though he had saved alive a whole world" (m. Sanh. 4:5).

---

284. See also 1 Cor. 3:16–17; 6:19; 2 Cor. 6:16; Eph. 2:21.
285. See also Gal. 6:1–2.
286. The Scripture is Genesis 4:10. Because the plural "bloods" is used, therefore that implies the blood of the brother Abel and the blood of his posterity has perished.

Thus, James, who himself was known as an intercessor for his people and who died praying that the Lord would forgive the very people who were stoning him (*Hist. eccl.* 2.23), has subtly tied together thematically at the conclusion of his letter many of his interests and topics: the importance of Old Testament principles enlightened by Jesus's teachings on mercy, mutual love, salvation, and restoration, while giving an example of a faithful person proven righteous from her/ his actions (2:24).

THEOLOGICAL AND HOMILETICAL
TOPICS IN CHAPTER 5

In chapter 5, James refers to many important theological concepts: soteriology (the road to maturity and salvation), eschatology (preparation for judgment), theology (the nature of God the Trinity as just, holy, powerful, compassionate, merciful, righteous, forgiving, peacemaking, and loving), and ecclesiology (the function or activity of the church). The literary themes throughout the letter appear again in discussion of the topics of wealth, trials, and wisdom. James continues to discuss the laying aside of evil deeds and the receiving of the implanted word (1:21). The letter's structure is subtle, the commands are direct, and the images are creative. The human expression of emotions is treated as normal, but destructive ones are not affirmed. James connects the readers to the Old Testament and to Jesus's teachings. The models of Job, Elijah, the prophets, and Jesus are educational.

This chapter suggests poignant sermons on wealth (5:1–6): the unjust acquisition of wealth, wealth as a temporary and unstable source of security, and warnings against self-indulgence. James is concerned for justice, the just treatment of workers, and empathy for the innocent poor. Many related images can be summoned from ancient and contemporary times. A message that is always timely is to encourage perseverance and endurance in the Lord in the midst of difficulties and to work on maturity, the integration of doctrine and practice. The careful use of God's name is always relevant. Especially during Lent, sermons and classes on the different types of prayers are of interest. A sermon on the office of elders' prayer for healing can be followed by a service on healing. Humility for a Christian is important. A message on the importance of confession, forgiveness, intercession, and faith in God as functions of the priesthood of all believers can also be applied in small group practice.

Chapter 5 certainly has significant lessons for theology and ecclesiology, relevant for any age.

JAMES'S TRANSFORMATIVE LETTER
AS A BASIS FOR ALCOHOLICS ANONYMOUS

One example of the transformative nature of James, and especially the end of chapter 5, may be found in the early years of Alcoholics Anonymous (AA), when at least a 75 percent success rate was claimed among those who committed fully to the program. The Twelve Steps are an elaboration of six original steps and four basic ideas.[287] The book of James was deeply studied by AA's cofounders. Many thought the book of James was so important that they favored calling the AA fellowship the "James Club." In effect, James was their favorite book of the Bible.[288] The original six steps and four basic ideas, as well as the current Twelve Steps, can all be found in James.

"Trust in God" is the overarching idea for the first three of the Twelve Steps. The original first step was "We admitted that we were licked, that we were powerless over alcohol."[289] They saw themselves as "two-willed" persons (James 1:8) who needed to surrender the ego. They needed to submit themselves to God and humble themselves before the Lord (James 4:7, 10). In effect, they came to believe that a Power greater than themselves could restore them to sanity (step 2 of Twelve Steps).[290]

The second big idea was "cleaning house." Steps 4 through 8 all relate to this idea, and all of them may be found in James. In step 4, Dick B. recounts, "[we] made a searching and fearless moral inventory of ourselves." The cofounders were inspired by James 2:8, 14, 17; 3:17; 4:11–12, and 5:9 not to judge others falsely or grumble against them, but to love them. Loving their neighbor included practicing their faith by their actions. This moral inventory was then followed by action: "We admitted to God, to ourselves, and to another human being the exact nature of our wrongs" (step 5). James 3:14–16 and 5:16 are crucial, especially the confessing of sins to one another.[291] Confession of sins is mentioned again and again in the guiding ("Big") book.

---

287. B. 1995, 7, 166, 174–75.
288. B. 1995, 86, 88.
289. B. 1995, 166. This original step has developed into three steps: The participants admit they were powerless over alcohol—that their lives had become unmanageable; they came to believe that a Power greater than themselves could restore them to sanity; they made a decision to turn their will and their lives over to the care of God as they understood Him (121, 130, 132).
290. B. 1995, 89, 97, 128, 130, 171.
291. B. 1995, 95, 97–102, 136, 139, 141, 143, 167, 170, 175.

Surrendering prayer is crucial in step 6: "We were entirely ready to have God remove all these defects of character," and James 5:14–15 was most helpful. In Cleveland some recovered AAs would have a "newcomer get down on his knees, [pray] over him, [anoint] him with oil, and [have] him make his request in the name of Jesus Christ that alcohol be taken out of his life and that he be healed."[292]

James 4:7–8 and 10 were also helpful for step 7: "We humbly asked God to remove our shortcomings." A conversion experience by the power of God was an early AA idea that sadly seemed to vanish in later AA language. Step 8 alluded to the need for forgiveness for sins committed with reference to James 5:15: "We made a list of all persons we had harmed, and became willing to make amends to them all." Examples of such harms could be found listed in James 1:19–20; 3:8; 4:11–17; and 5:1–6.[293]

"Love" was the third key idea, loving your neighbor as yourself (James 2:8), which was developed in steps 9 and 10: "We made direct amends to such people wherever possible, except when to do so would injure them or others," and "We continued to take personal inventory and when we were wrong promptly admitted it."[294]

Step 11 focused on love of God, which is also found in James: "We sought through prayer and meditation to improve our conscious contact with God as we understood Him, praying only for knowledge of His will for us and the power to carry that out." Recovering alcoholics need to ask for wisdom (James 1:5; 3:17), not for their own selfish desires (4:3). They need to pray for themselves and for others (5:13–16). Love of God is then flushed out with love for others or "service": "Having had a spiritual awakening as the result of these steps, we tried to carry this message to alcoholics, and to practice these principles in all our affairs" (step 12). This step again hearkens to James 1:22–23; 2:8, 20, and 26: becoming doers of the word, not merely hearers.[295] They saw alcoholism as a physical, mental, and spiritual problem.[296] If the biblical principles behind the Twelve Steps are practiced not only by recovering alcoholics but by all in the church, possibly then the church can be revived, and it can affect its society more.

---

292. B. 1995, 100, 144, 176.
293. B. 1995, 90, 94, 97–98, 145–47, 170, 174.
294. B. 1995, 149–150, 170–71, 174–75.
295. B. 1995, 89–90, 92–93, 96, 151–54, 156, 159, 162, 164, 172–75.
296. B. 1995, 123.

GLOSSARY OF STYLISTIC TERMS

Addition sentence changes is a general term for rhetorical devices that add letters, syllables, words, phrases, and clauses to a sentence to achieve a certain effect, such as chiasm, parallelism, pleonasm, and polysyndeton.[1]

Alliteration is recurrence of an initial consonant or vowel sound (e.g., James 3:17; 5:2). A synonym is *homoeoprophoron*, "similar in pronunciation." *Assonance* is the use of identical or similar sounds between internal vowels in neighboring words. Alliteration and assonance have the same function: to intensify.[2]

Anadiplosis is the repetition of the last word of one line or clause to begin the next (e.g., James 1:3–6, 26–27).

Anthropomorphism is the ascribing of human form or attributes to a being or thing not human, especially to a deity, such as "the ears of the Lord" (James 5:4).[3]

Asyndeton is the deliberate omission of conjunctions between a series of related words, phrases, or clauses separated by commas (e.g., James 1:9).

---

1. See also Lanham 1991, 182; Spencer 1998a, Appendix 2.
2. Lanham 1991, 1–2, 24, 82.
3. *Random House Webster's* 2001, 88.

Chiasm is a reverted type of parallelism, an inversion of the second of two parallel phrases, clauses, etc. It is diagonal arrangement, usually of one to four clauses or phrases in sequences in a well-rounded sentence or period. The first clause corresponds with the last, and the second with the second-to-last, as in the sequence ABBA, ABCDDCBA, or even ABCBA. A theme may be developed in a chiastic pattern of thought in larger contexts. A *period* in rhetoric is a well-rounded sentence in which one to four clauses have a circular form.[4]

Ellipsis is the deliberate omission of a word or words necessary to complete or clarify a construction but which is implied by the context (e.g., James 1:10; 4:1).

Hendiadys is the expression of an idea by two nouns in the same case connected by "and" functioning as a noun and its qualifier, such as 1 Timothy 2:9 where "not in braided hair and gold" becomes "gold-braided hair."[5]

Metaphor is an implied or implicit comparison between two things of unlike nature that yet have something in common so that one or more properties of the first are attributed to the second, such as "Adulteresses" in James 4:4. Development of a metaphor is the extent to which the author works out the ramifications of a certain comparison. (See expositions of James 1:6–8, 11–12, 14–18, 23–26; 3:2–3, 5–8; 4:6.)

Onomatopoeia is the use or invention of words that sound like their meaning. A word is formed by imitation of a sound made by or associated with its referent (e.g., James 5:1).[6]

Parallelism is the repetition of a syntactic or structural pattern. Demetrius (*Eloc.* 23) notes that like corresponds with like throughout: article opposed to article, "connective to connective, like to like, everything is parallel," from the beginning to the end. Ideas may also be presented in a parallel thought structure. In *antithetic parallelism* the thought of the first line is echoed negatively (e.g., James 4:7), while in *synonymous parallelism*, the thought of the first line is echoed positively (e.g., James 2:26).

4.   Spencer 1998a, 199–201; Lanham 1991, 112–13.
5.   Spencer 2013, 57.
6.   Lanham 1991, 105; *Random House Webster's* 2001, 1354.

Personification (prosopopoeia) invests abstractions (qualities, ideas, or general terms), inanimate objects, or nonhuman living things with human qualities or abilities, especially with human feelings, such as "the wages . . . shout" (James 5:4; see also 1:14–15; 4:5; 5:3).

Pleonasm, as well as of all forms of addition, is the doubling and repetition of words of similar meaning, or of thoughts of similar content, such as "wise and learned" (James 3:13). (See expositions of James 1:4–5, 11–12, 17, 21, 27; 3:2–4, 6, 14, 17; 4:1; 5:1–2, 5–6, 16–17.)

Polysyndeton is the deliberate use of the same or even different conjunctions or connecting particles two or more times in close succession between each clause, word, or phrase (e.g., James 1:11, 24; 3:6; 4:9, 13; 5:17).

Simile is an explicit comparison using a word such as "like" or "as" between two things of unlike nature that yet have something in common so that one or more properties of the first are attributed to the second (James 1:6, 10–11, 22–23; 2:26).

Substitution sentence changes is a general term for rhetorical terms that neither add nor subtract letters, syllables, words, phrases, or clauses to a sentence, but rather, substitute a figurative term for a literal term, such as metaphor, personification, simile, and synecdoche.

Subtraction or *omission sentence changes* is a general term for rhetorical terms which subtract or omit letters, syllables, words, phrases, or clauses from a sentence, such as asyndeton and ellipsis.

Synecdoche is substitution of a part (a less inclusive term) for the whole (a more inclusive term) or vice versa, such as "the tongue" representing speech (James 3:5–10; see also 1:10, 17, 23; 2:7; 3:6, 15; 4:8; 5:14).

UNUSUAL WORDS AND PHRASES IN JAMES

1:6[1] ἀνεμίζω:[2] to blow

1:8; 4:8 δίψυχος:[3] two-willed

1:13 ἀπείραστος:[4] untemptable

1:17 πατρὸς τῶν φώτων:[5] Father of lights

---

1. Painter and deSilva (2012, 58) refer to ten words first known in James. My deep appreciation to James Darlack, head librarian of Goddard Library, and Jihyung Kim, teaching assistant, Gordon-Conwell Theological Seminary, Hamilton, MA, who double-checked all references in the TLG 2018.
2. Mayor 1913, 240; Robertson 1933, 14.
3. Mayor 1913, 243; BDAG, 253; Robertson 1933, 15; Hiebert 1979, 87; Blomberg and Kamell 2008, 53; Ropes 1916, 143; Davids 1982, 74; MM, 166. See also 1 Clem. 11:2; 23:3; 2 Clem. 11:2.
4. Mayor 1913, 241; Robertson 1933, 17–18. Adjective form is from verb πειράζω ("to tempt"). Possibly also used in 3th–2nd century BC fragments, one by Chrysippus (*Phil. Fragmenta moralia*, frag. 632) quoted by Clement of Alexandria (*Strom.* 7.7), according to J. von Arnim, *Stoicorum veterum fragmenta* (Leipzig: Teubner, 1903), 3:3–191, and another by Demetrius Lacon (*Phil. Opus incertum*, col. 6), according to E. Puglia, *Aporie testuali ed esegetiche in Epicuro* (P. Herc. 1012) (Naples: Bibliopolis, 1988), 151–86.
5. Laws 1980, 73: "No certain precedent for this title has been found in Jewish literature"; McCartney 2009, 112. The phrase is also found in some variants of the LAE 36.5 and T. Ab. 7.5 re. B, which are dated 100 BC–AD 200, but most likely they are late first century AD.

1:17 ἀποσκίασμα:[6] turning

1:21 ῥυπαρία:[7] filth

1:21 τὸν ἔμφυτον λόγον:[8] the implanted word

1:26 θρησκός:[9] religious

1:26; 3:2 χαλιναγωγέω:[10] to bridle

2:2 χρυσοδακτύλιος:[11] with a gold ring

2:9 προσωπολημπτέω:[12] act with partiality

---

6. Mayor 1913, 241; Ropes 1916, 165. The term possibly was employed in 5th–4th century BC fragments by Democritus (*Phil. Testimonia*, frag. 90) and Theopompus (*Hist. Fragmenta*, frag. 400), according to H. Diels and W. Kranz, *Die Fragmente der Vorsokratiker*, vol. 2, 6th ed. (Berlin: Weidman, 1952), 81–129 and F. Jacoby, *Die Fragmente der griechischen Historiker*, no. 115 (Leiden: Brill, 1923–58).
7. Mayor 1913, 255. The term is possibly used in 5th–3rd century BC fragments, one by Critias (*Eleg. Phil. et Trag. Fragmenta*, frag. 56), Pseudo-Hippocrates (*Med.*, 36), and Teles of Megara (*Phil*, pp. 33, 37), according to Diels and Kranz, *Die Fragmente der Vorsokratiker*, 375–399; C. E. Ruelle, *Les lapidaires de l'antiquité et du Moyen Age*, vol. 2.1 (Paris: Leroux, 1898), 185–90, and O. Hense, *Teletis reliquiae*, 2nd ed. (Tübingen: Mohr, 1909), 33–44. See also Barn. 9:9.
8. First known occurrence of phrase.
9. Mayor 1913, 247; *TLNT* 2, 200; Laws 1980, 88; Dibelius 1976, 121.
10. Some say this first appears in James (Mayor 1913, 257; Robertson 1933, 24–25; Davids 1982, 101; MM, 682). "In our lit. only fig[urative]" (BDAG, 1076). However, it appears also in Philo, *Creation* 86 (20 BC–AD 50). Also see Pol. *Phil.* 5:3.
11. Mayor 1913, 258; Robertson 1933, 28; Adam 2013, 36; Davids 1982, 108; Painter and deSilva 2012, 87.
12. Davids 1982, 15; Mayor 1913, 255; Painter and deSilva 2012, 87. In LXX and Luke 20:21 (πρόσωπον λαμβάνειν). Προσωπολημψία ("partiality") is found also in Romans 2:11; Ephesians 6:9; and Colossians 3:25, but probably James 2:1 is the earliest of these letters. Προσωπολημπτέω (verb), προσωπολημψία (noun), and προσωπολήμπτης (noun) (Acts 10:34) have been "found only in Christian writers" (BDAG, 887) and "may be reckoned amongst the earliest definite Christian words" (MM, 553).

2:13 ἀνέλεος:[13] without mercy

3:15 δαιμονιώδης:[14] demonic

5:11 πολύσπλαγχνος:[15] greatly compassionate

13. Mayor 1913, 240; Painter and deSilva 2012, 87, 98; Robertson 1933, 33; Ropes 1916, 201. Attic spelling is ἀνηλεής (BDAG, 77). The word appears in T. Ab. 16.3 re. A, which is dated late first century AD.
14. Mayor 1913, 242; Painter and deSilva 2012, 127. The word may be found in ancient fragments (4–2 BC) of Aristophanes (*Gramm. Ceteri Aristophanis libri* 2, frag. 1) and Apollodorus (*Gramm. Fragmenta*, frag. 67c), according to A. Nauck, *Aristophanis Byzanti grammatici Alexandrini fragmenta*, 2nd ed. (Halle: Lippert and Schmid, 1848), 264, 271, 273–77, 279–82, and K. Müller, *Fragmenta historicorum Graecorum* 1 (Paris: Didot, 1853), 1:428–69; 4:649–50).
15. Mayor 1913, 254; Hiebert 1979, 306; Painter and deSilva 2012, 160; MM, 527. See also Herm. Vis. 1.3.2; 2.2.8 (πολυσπλαγχνία [noun]).

IMPERATIVES IN JAMES

1:1 χαίρειν: greetings[1]

1:2 ἡγήσασθε: consider

1:4 ἐχέτω: let

1:5 αἰτείτω: ask

1:6 αἰτείτω: ask

1:7 μὴ οἰέσθω: not suppose

1:9 καυχάσθω: boast

1:13 μηδεὶς λεγέτω: let no one say

1:16 Μὴ πλανᾶσθε: do not deceive yourselves

1:19 Ἴστε . . . ἔστω: understand . . . let

1:21 δέξασθε: receive

1:22 Γίνεσθε: become

2:1 μὴ ἔχετε: have

---

1.   UBS 5th ed. is employed for this study.

2:3 κάθου . . . στῆθι: stay seated . . . stand

2:5 Ἀκούσατε: listen

2:8 Ἀγαπήσεις: love

2:11 Μὴ μοιχεύσῃς . . . Μὴ φονεύσῃς: do not commit adultery . . . do not murder

2:12 λαλεῖτε . . . ποιεῖτε: speak . . . act

2:16 Ὑπάγετε . . . θερμαίνεσθε . . . χορτάζεσθε: go . . . warm yourself . . . be satisfied

2:18 δεῖξόν: show

2:24 ὁρᾶτε: see

3:1 Μὴ γίνεσθε: let not

3:4 ἰδοὺ: behold

3:5 Ἰδοὺ: behold

3:10 οὐ χρή: it is not appropriate

3:13 δειξάτω: let him/her show

3:14 μὴ κατακαυχᾶσθε καὶ ψεύδεσθε: do not boast against and lie against

4:7 ὑποτάγητε . . . ἀντίστητε: submit . . . take a stand against

4:8 ἐγγίσατε . . . καθαρίσατε . . . ἁγνίσατε: draw near . . . cleanse . . . purify

4:9 ταλαιπωρήσατε . . . πενθήσατε . . . κλαύσατε . . . μετατραπήτω: be miserable . . . mourn . . . weep . . . turn around

4:10 ταπεινώθητε: be humble

4:11 Μὴ καταλαλεῖτε: do not keep slandering

4:13 Ἄγε: come

4:15 τοῦ λέγειν ὑμᾶς: you should say

5:1 Ἄγε . . . κλαύσατε: come . . . weep

5:4 ἰδού: behold

5:7 Μακροθυμήσατε . . . ἰδού: persevere . . . behold

5:8 μακροθυμήσατε . . . στηρίξατε: persevere . . . strengthen

5:9 μὴ στενάζετε . . . ἰδού: do not keep mourning . . . behold

5:10 λάβετε: take

5:11 ἰδού: behold

5:12 μὴ ὀμνύετε . . . ἤτω: do not make an oath . . . let

5:13 προσευχέσθω . . . ψαλλέτω: keep praying . . . keep singing

5:14 προσκαλεσάσθω . . . προσευξάσθωσαν: call for him/herself . . . let pray

5:16 ἐξομολογεῖσθε . . . εὔχεσθε: keep confessing . . . keep praying

5:20 γινωσκέτω: let know

REFERENCES

ANCIENT

Bruce, Barbara J., trans. 2002. *Origen: Homilies on Joshua*. FC. Edited by Cynthia White. Washington, DC: Catholic University of America Press.

Charlesworth, James H., ed. 1983–85. *The Old Testament Pseudepigrapha*. 2 vols. Garden City, NY: Doubleday.

Colson, F. H., trans. 1959. *Philo. VI*. LCL. Cambridge, MA: Harvard University Press.

———. 1962. *Philo. X*. LCL. Cambridge, MA: Harvard University Press.

———, and G. H. Whitaker, trans. 1930. *Philo. III*. LCL. Cambridge, MA: Harvard University Press.

Danby, Herbert. 1933. *The Mishnah*. Oxford: Oxford University Press.

Grenfell, Bernard P., and Arthur S. Hunt. 1889–1941. *The Oxyrhynchus Papyri*. 18 vols. London: Egypt Exploration.

Feldman, Louis H., trans. 1965. *Josephus Antiquities XVIII–XIX*. LCL. Cambridge, MA: Harvard University Press.

Hennecke, Edgar, ed. 1963. *New Testament Apocrypha*. Vol. 1. Edited by Wilhelm Schneemelcher. Translated by R. McL. Wilson. Philadelphia: Westminster.

Hicks, R. D., trans. 1925. *Diogenes Laertius: Lives of Eminent Philosophers*. LCL. 2 vols. New York: Putnam's.

Holmes, Michael W., ed., trans. 2007. *The Apostolic Fathers: Greek Texts and English Translations*. 3rd ed. Grand Rapids: Baker.

The Holy Scriptures, according to the Masoretic Text: A New Translation. 1955. Philadelphia: Jewish Publication Society of America.

311

Jones, Horace Leonard, trans. 1923–30. *The Geography of Strabo*. 8 vols. LCL. New York: Putnam's.

Lake, Kirsopp, and J. E. L. Oulton, trans. 1926–32. *Eusebius: The Ecclesiastical History*. 2 vols. LCL. Cambridge, MA: Harvard University Press.

Maier, Paul L. 1999. *Eusebius: The Church History*. Grand Rapids: Kregel.

Mair, A. W. trans. 1928. *Oppian, Colluthus, Tryphiodorus*. LCL. Cambridge, MA: Harvard University Press.

Oldfather, W. A., trans. *Epictetus*. 1925–28. LCL. 2 vols. Cambridge, MA: Harvard University Press.

Rahlfs, Alfred. 2006. *Septuaginta*. Edited by Robert Hanhart. Stuttgart, Germany: Deutsche Bibelgesellschaft.

Roberts, Alexander, and James Donaldson, trans. 1869. *The Writings of Tertullian*. Vol. 1. Ante-Nicene Christian Library 11. Edinburgh: T&T Clark.

———, and W. H. Rambaut, trans. 1880. *The Writings of Irenaeus*. 2 vols. Ante-Nicene Christian Library. Edinburgh: T&T Clark.

The Septuagint Version of the Old Testament and Apocrypha: Greek and English. n.d. London: Samuel Bagster.

Thackeray, H. St. J., trans. 1926. *Josephus: The Life. Against Apion*. LCL. Cambridge, MA: Harvard University Press.

———. 1927–28. *Josephus: The Jewish War*. 3 vols. LCL. Cambridge, MA: Harvard University Press.

Whiston, William, trans. 1987. *The Works of Josephus*. Peabody, MA: Hendrickson.

CONTEMPORARY

Adam, A. K. M. 2013. *James: A Handbook on the Greek Text*. BHGNT. Waco, TX: Baylor University Press.

Adamson, James B. 1976. *The Epistle of James*. NICNT. Grand Rapids: Eerdmans.

Adkins, Lesley, and Roy A. Adkins. 2005. *Handbook to Life in Ancient Greece*. 2nd ed. New York: Facts on File.

Alon, Azaria. 1969. *The Natural History of the Land of the Bible*. New York: Hamlyn.

Anderson, David A. 1979. *All the Trees and Woody Plants of the Bible*. Waco, TX: Word.

Anderson, Kelly, and Daniel A. Keating. 2017. *James, First, Second, and Third John*. Catholic Commentary on Sacred Scripture. Grand Rapids: Baker.

REFERENCES

Aune, David E. 1987. *The New Testament in Its Literary Environment.* LEC. Philadelphia: Westminster.

B., Dick. 1995. *The Good Book and the Big Book: A.A.'s Roots in the Bible.* San Rafael, CA: Paradise Research.

Barker, Kenneth L., ed. 2006. *Zondervan TNIV Study Bible.* Grand Rapids: Zondervan.

Barnes, Albert. 1949. *Notes on the New Testament, Explanatory and Practical: James, Peter, John, and Jude.* Edited by Robert Frew. Grand Rapids: Baker.

Bateman IV, Herbert W. 2013. *Interpreting the General Letters: An Exegetical Handbook.* Handbooks for New Testament Exegesis. Grand Rapids: Kregel.

———. 2017. *Evangelical Exegetical Commentary: Jude.* Bellingham, WA: Lexham.

Bauckham, Richard. 1999. *James: Wisdom of James, Disciple of Jesus the Sage.* New Testament Readings. New York: Routledge.

Beer, Robert. 1987. "Moth." *Collier's Encyclopedia.* Vol. 16, edited by William Halsey and Bernard Johnston. New York: Macmillan: 586–90.

Blomberg, Craig L., and Mariam J. Kamell. 2008. *James: Zondervan Exegetical Commentary on the New Testament.* Grand Rapids: Zondervan.

Boring, M. Eugene. 2012. *An Introduction to the New Testament: History, Literature, Theology.* Louisville: Westminster John Knox.

Brosend II, William F. 2004. *James and Jude.* New Cambridge Bible Commentary. Cambridge: Cambridge University Press.

Bruce, F. F. 1990. *The Acts of the Apostles: The Greek Text with Introduction and Commentary.* 3rd ed. Grand Rapids: Eerdmans.

Büchsel, Friedrich. 1965. "θυμός, ἐπιθυμία, ἐπιθυμέω, ἐπιθυμητής, ἐνθυμέομαι, ἐνθύμησις." *TDNT* 3:167–72.

Calvin, John. 1960. *Institutes of the Christian Religion.* LCC. Edited by John T. McNeill. Translated by Ford Lewis Battles. 2 vols. Philadelphia: Westminster.

———. n.d. *Ephesians–Jude.* Vol. 12 of *Calvin's Commentaries.* Wilmington, DE: Associated Publishers & Authors.

Campbell, Keith D. 2017. "Lament in James and Its Significance for the Church." *JETS* 60, no. 1 (March): 125–38.

Cargal, Timothy. 1999. "Review of *Glaube zwischen Vollkommenheit und Verweltlichung: Eine Untersuchung zur literarischen Gestalt und zur inhaltlichen Kohärenz des Jakobusbriefes,* by Manabu Tsuji." *JBL* 118 (3): 567–69.

Carpenter, Craig B. 2001. "James 4.5 Reconsidered." *NTS* 47, no. 2 (April): 189–205.

Carson, D. A. 1998. *The Inclusive Language Debate: A Plea for Realism*. Grand Rapids: Baker.

Carter, Philippa. 2002. "Joshua." *The IVP Women's Bible Commentary*. Edited by Catherine Clark Kroeger and Mary J. Evans, 112–27. Downers Grove, IL: InterVarsity.

Casson, Lionel. 1964. *Illustrated History of Ships and Boats*. Garden City, NY: Doubleday.

———. 1971. *Ships and Seamanship in the Ancient World*. Princeton, NJ: Princeton University Press.

———. 1994. *Travel in the Ancient World*. Baltimore: Johns Hopkins University Press.

Comfort, Philip Wesley. 1992. *The Quest for the Original Text of the New Testament*. Grand Rapids: Baker.

Corrosion Doctors. n.d. "Gold Corrosion." Accessed July 11, 2018. http://www.corrosion-doctors.org/MatSelect/corrgold.htm.

———. n.d. "Silver Corrosion." Accessed July 11, 2018. http://www.corrosion-doctors.org/MatSelect/corrsilver.htm.

———. n.d. "What Corrosion Is!" Accessed July 11, 2018. http://www.corrosion-doctors.org/Principles/What-is.htm.

Daniel-Rops, Henri. 1962. *Daily Life in the Time of Jesus*. Translated by Patrick O'Brian. Ann Arbor, MI: Servant.

Davids, Peter. 1982. *The Epistle of James: A Commentary on the Greek Text*. NIGTC. Grand Rapids: Eerdmans.

Dibelius, Martin. 1976. *James: A Commentary on the Epistle of James*. Hermeneia: A Critical and Historical Commentary on the Bible. Edited by Helmut Koester and Heinrich Greeven. Translated by Michael A. Williams. 11th ed. Philadelphia: Fortress.

Ehrman, Bart D. 2004. *The New Testament and Other Early Christian Writings: A Reader*. 2nd ed. New York: Oxford University Press.

Eisenman, Robert. 1997. *James the Brother of Jesus: The Key to Unlocking the Secrets of Early Christianity and the Dead Sea Scrolls*. New York: Penguin.

EPPO (European and Mediterranean Plant Protection Organization). 2011. "*Thaumatotibia leucotreta* (Lepidoptera: Tortricidae)": 1–4. Accessed July 10, 2018. https://www.eppo.int/QUARANTINE/Alert_List/insects/thaumatotibia_leucotreta.htm.

Finegan, Jack, and Alexander Melamid. 1987. "Jerusalem." *Collier's Encyclopedia*. Vol. 13, edited by William Halsey and Bernard Johnston, 542–48. New York: Macmillan.

Fiorello, Michael D. 2012. "The Ethical Implication of Holiness in James 2." *JETS* 55, no. 3 (September): 557–72.

Foster, Robert J. 2014. *The Significance of Exemplars for the Interpretation of the Letter of James*. WUNT. Tübingen: Mohr Siebeck.

Francis, Fred O. 1970. "The Form and Function of the Opening and Closing Paragraphs of James and 1 John." *ZNW*, no. 61, 110–26.

Gardiner, E. Norman. 1930. *Athletics of the Ancient World*. Chicago: ARES.

Goswell, Gregory. 2016. "The Place of the Book of Acts in Reading the New Testament." *JETS* 59, no. 1: 67–82.

Guthrie, Donald. 1970. *New Testament Introduction*. 3rd ed. Downers Grove, IL: InterVarsity.

Hammond, N. G. L., and H. H. Scullard, eds. 1970. 2nd ed. *The Oxford Classical Dictionary*. Oxford: Clarendon.

Hanson, K. C., and Douglas E. Oakman. 1998. *Palestine in the Time of Jesus: Social Structures and Social Conflicts*. Minneapolis: Fortress.

Harland, Philip A. 2002. "The Economy of First-Century Palestine: State of the Scholarly Discussion." In *Handbook of Early Christianity: Social Science Approaches*, edited by Anthony J. Blasi, Jean Duhaime, and Paul-André Turcotte, 511–27. New York: Altamira.

Harrison, R. K. 1985. "Nazareth." In *Major Cities of the Biblical World*, edited by R. K. Harrison: 170–79. Nashville: Thomas Nelson.

Hartin, Patrick J. 2004. *James of Jerusalem: Heir to Jesus of Nazareth*. Interfaces. Collegeville, MN: Liturgical.

Hengel, Martin. 1974. *Property and Riches in the Early Church: Aspects of a Social History of Early Christianity*. Philadelphia: Fortress.

Herman, Christine. 2017. "A Lesson in Listening: Why the Best Witnesses Use Their Ears First and Their Mouths Later." *CT* 61, no. 6 (June): 40–43.

Hiebert, D. Edmond. 1979. *The Epistle of James: Tests of a Living Faith*. Chicago: Moody.

Hopkins, B. Smith. 1987. "Gold." In *Collier's Encyclopedia*. Vol. 11, edited by William Halsey and Bernard Johnston, 198–99. New York: Macmillan.

James, Arthur. 2005. "James." In *South Asia Bible Commentary*, edited by Brian Wintle, et al., 1732–38. Rajasthan, India: Open Door Publications.

Jamieson, Robert, A. R. Fausset, and David Brown. 1961. *Commentary: Practical and Explanatory on the Whole Bible*. Rev. ed. Grand Rapids: Zondervan.

Jeremias, Joachim. 1969. *Jerusalem in the Time of Jesus: An Investigation into Economic and Social Conditions during the New Testament Period.* Philadelphia: Fortress.

Johnson, Luke Timothy. 2004. *Brother of Jesus, Friend of God: Studies in the Letter of James.* Grand Rapids: Eerdmans.

Keener, Craig. 2011. *Miracles: The Credibility of the New Testament Accounts.* Grand Rapids: Baker.

Keil, C. F., and F. Delitzsch. 1973. *The Pentateuch.* Vol. 1 of *Commentary on the Old Testament in Ten Volumes,* translated by James Martin. Grand Rapids: Eerdmans.

Kistemaker, Simon J. 1986. *New Testament Commentary: Exposition of the Epistle of James and the Epistles of John.* Grand Rapids: Baker.

Kohlenberger III, John R., Edward W. Goodrick, and James A. Swanson. 1995. *The Exhaustive Concordance to the Greek New Testament.* Zondervan Greek Reference Series. Grand Rapids: Zondervan.

Lang, Friedrich. 1968. "πῦρ, πυρόω, πύρωσις, πύρινος, πυρρός." In *TDNT* 6:928–52.

Lanham, Richard A. 1991. *A Handlist of Rhetorical Terms.* 2nd ed. Berkeley: University of California Press.

Laws, Sophie. 1980. *A Commentary on the Epistle of James.* HNTC. Peabody, MA: Hendrickson.

Lea, T. D. 1991. "Pseudonymity and the New Testament." In *New Testament Criticism and Interpretation,* edited by David Alan Black and David S. Dockery, 535–59. Grand Rapids: Zondervan.

Lenski, R. C. H. 1946. *The Interpretation of the Epistle to the Hebrews and of the Epistle of James.* Columbus, OH: Wartburg.

Lesonsky, Rieva. 2001. *Start Your Own Business.* Irvine, CA: Entrepreneur.

Levy, Alan D. 1987. "Silver." *Collier's Encyclopedia.* Vol. 21, edited by William Halsey and Bernard Johnston, 33–34. New York: Macmillan.

Lohse, Eduard. 1968. "Προσωπολημψία, προσωπολήμπτης, προσωπολημπτέω, ἀπροσωπολήμπτως." In *TDNT* 6:779–80.

MacNutt, Francis. 1977. *The Power to Heal.* Notre Dame, IN: Ave Maria.

Manton, Thomas. 1693. *A Commentary on James.* Geneva Series Commentary. Edinburgh: Banner of Truth Trust.

Martin, Ralph P. 1988. *James.* Vol. 48 of *Word Biblical Commentary.* Waco, TX: Word.

Marxsen, Willi. 1970. *Introduction to the New Testament: An Approach to Its Problems.* Translated by G. Buswell. Philadelphia: Fortress.

REFERENCES

Maynard-Reid, Pedrito U. 1987. *Poverty and Wealth in James.* Maryknoll, NY: Orbis.

Mayor, J. B. 1913. *The Epistle of St James.* 3rd ed. Minneapolis: Klock & Klock.

McCartney, Dan G. 2009. *James.* BECNT. Grand Rapids: Baker Academic.

McGavran, Donald A. 1980. *Understanding Church Growth.* Edited by C. Peter Wagner. 3rd ed. Grand Rapids: Eerdmans.

McKnight, Scot. 2011. *The Letter of James.* NICNT. Grand Rapids: Eerdmans.

McRay, John. 1991. *Archaeology and the New Testament.* Grand Rapids: Baker.

Metzger, Bruce M. 1983. "The Fourth Book of Ezra." In *The Old Testament Pseudepigrapha.* Vol. 1, edited by James H. Charlesworth, 517–59. Garden City, NY: Doubleday.

———. 2002. *A Textual Commentary on the Greek New Testament.* 2nd ed. New York: United Bible Societies.

Millard, Alan. 2001. *Reading and Writing in the Time of Jesus.* The Biblical Seminar 69. Sheffield: Sheffield Academic.

Mitton, C. Leslie. 1966. *The Epistle of James.* London: Marshall, Morgan & Scott.

Mongstad-Kvammen, Ingeborg. 2013. *Toward a Postcolonial Reading of the Epistle of James: James 2:1–13 in Its Roman Imperial Context.* BibInt 119. Boston: Brill.

Moo, Douglas J. 2015. *James.* 2nd ed. TNTC 16. Downers Grove, IL: InterVarsity.

NIV Archaeological Study Bible. 2005. Grand Rapids: Zondervan.

Nolland, John. 2005. *The Gospel of Matthew: A Commentary on the Greek Text.* NIGTC. Grand Rapids: Eerdmans.

Olson, Everett C. 1987. "Horse." In *Collier's Encyclopedia.* Vol. 12, edited by William D. Holsey and Bernard Johnston, 255–64. New York: Macmillan.

Painter, John, and David A. deSilva. 2012. *James and Jude.* Paideia Commentaries on the New Testament. Grand Rapids: Baker.

Perkins, Pheme. 1995. *First and Second Peter, James, and Jude.* IBC. Louisville: John Knox.

Poythress, Vern, and Wayne Grudem. 2000. *The Gender-Neutral Bible Controversy: Muting the Masculinity of God's Words.* Nashville: B&H.

Ramsay, William M. 2001. *St. Paul: The Traveler and Roman Citizen.* Edited by Mark Wilson. Grand Rapids: Kregel.

Random House Webster's Unabridged Dictionary. 2001. New York: Random House Reference.

Reich, Robert. 2015. *Saving Capitalism: For the Many, Not the Few.* New York: Alfred A. Knopf.

Robertson, Archibald Thomas. 1930a. *The Gospel according to Matthew, The Gospel according to Mark.* Vol. 1 of *Word Pictures in the New Testament.* Nashville: Broadman.

———. 1930b. *The Acts of the Apostles.* Vol. 3 of *Word Pictures in the New Testament.* Nashville: Broadman.

———. 1933. *The General Epistles and the Revelation of John.* Vol. 6 of *Word Pictures in the New Testament.* Nashville: Broadman.

———. 1934. *A Grammar of the Greek New Testament in the Light of Historical Research.* Nashville: Broadman.

Ropes, James Hardy. 1916. *A Critical and Exegetical Commentary on the Epistle of St. James.* ICC. Edinburgh: T&T Clark.

Runesson, Anders, Donald D. Binder, and Birger Olsson. 2010. *The Ancient Synagogue from Its Origins to 200 C.E.: A Source Book.* Boston: Brill.

Schürer, Emil. 1973–79. *The History of the Jewish People in the Age of Jesus Christ (175 B.C.–A.D. 135).* 2 vols. Edited by Geza Vermes, Fergus Millar, and Matthew Black. 2nd ed. Edinburgh: T&T Clark.

Shah, Anup. 2013. "Poverty Facts and Stats." *Global Issues.* Accessed January 8, 2020. http://www.globalissues.org/article/26/poverty-facts-and-stats.

Shepard, Francis P. 1987. "Ocean." In *Collier's Encyclopedia.* Vol. 18, edited by William D. Holsey and Bernard Johnston, 58–65. New York: Macmillan.

Spencer, Aída Besançon. 1985. *Beyond the Curse: Women Called to Ministry.* Grand Rapids: Baker Academic.

———. 1998a. *Paul's Literary Style: A Stylistic and Historical Comparison of II Corinthians 11:16–12:13, Romans 8:9–39, and Philippians 3:2–4:13.* Lanham, MD: University Press of America.

———. 1998b. "Exclusive Language—Is It Accurate?" *RevExp* 95, no. 3 (Summer): 383–95.

———. 2001. *2 Corinthians.* The People's Bible Commentary. Abingdon: Bible Reading Fellowship.

———. 2005. "Jesus' Treatment of Women in the Gospels." In *Discovering Biblical Equality: Complementarity without Hierarchy.* 2nd ed, edited by Ronald W. Pierce and Rebecca Merrill Groothuis, 126–41. Downers Grove, IL: InterVarsity.

———. 2007. "The Denial of the Good News and the Ending of Mark." *BBR* 17 (2): 269–83.

REFERENCES

———. 2013. *1 Timothy*. NCCS. Eugene, OR: Cascade.

———. 2014a. "Position Reversal and Hope for the Oppressed." In *Latino/a Biblical Hermeneutics: Problematics, Objectives, Strategies*, edited by Francisco Lozada Jr. and Fernando F. Segovia, 95–106. Atlanta: SBL.

———. 2014b. *2 Timothy and Titus*. NCCS. Eugene, OR: Cascade.

———. 2015. "Toppling the Silent Idol: Assessing Greed as Part of an Idolatrous Meta-System and Promoting Holiness as an Antidote to Greed." *AfrJ* 7, no. 2 (November): 29–47.

———. 2017. "Review article of *Paul and Money: A Biblical and Theological Analysis of the Apostle's Teachings and Practices* by Verlyn D. Verbrugge and Keith R. Krell." *AfrJ* 9, no. 1 (April): 26–31.

———, Donna F. G. Hailson, Catherine Clark Kroeger, and William David Spencer. 1995. *The Goddess Revival: A Biblical Response to God(dess) Spirituality*. HPA. Eugene, OR: Wipf & Stock.

Spencer, William David. 2014. "Intentional Teaching." *AfrJ* 6, no. 2 (November): 34–44.

Spencer, William David, and Aída Besançon Spencer. 1990. *The Prayer Life of Jesus: Shout of Agony, Revelation of Love, a Commentary*. Lanham, MD: University Press of America.

———. 1994. *Joy through the Night: Biblical Resources on Suffering*. HPA. Eugene, OR: Wipf & Stock.

———, eds. 1998. *The Global God: Multicultural Evangelical Views of God*. Grand Rapids: Baker.

Stapleton, A. 1885. *Natural History of the Bible*. Evangelical Normal Series. Cleveland: Evangelical Association.

Stephens, William H. 1987. *The New Testament World in Pictures*. Designed by Paula A. Savage. Nashville: Broadman.

Strauss, Mark L. 1998. *Distorting Scripture? The Challenge of Bible Translation and Gender Accuracy*. Downers Grove, IL: InterVarsity.

Sukenik, E. L. 1934. *Ancient Synagogues in Palestine and Greece*. Schweich Lectures of the British Academy 1930. Oxford: Oxford University Press.

Tasker, R. V. G. 1957. *The General Epistle of James*. The Tyndale New Testament Commentaries. Grand Rapids: Eerdmans.

Townsend, Michael J. 1994. *The Epistle of James*. Epworth Commentaries. London: Epworth.

Trimmer, Joseph F. 2004. *The New Writing with a Purpose*. 14th ed. Boston: Houghton Mifflin.

Tuoti, Gerry. 2017. "Seniors Frequent Targets of Financial Abuse." *The Hamilton-Wenham Chronicle*, July 13, 2017, A1, A8.

Verbrugge, Verlyn B., and Keith R. Krell. 2015. *Paul and Money: A Biblical and Theological Analysis of the Apostle's Teachings and Practices*. Grand Rapids: Zondervan.

Villiers, Alan. 1963. *Men, Ships, and the Sea*. Washington, DC: National Geographic Society.

Vlachos, Chris A. 2013. *James*. Exegetical Guide to the Greek New Testament. Nashville: Broadman & Holman.

Wallace, Daniel B. 1996. *Greek Grammar beyond the Basics: An Exegetical Syntax of the New Testament*. Grand Rapids: Zondervan.

Whitlark, Jason A. 2010. "Έμφυτος Λόγος: A New Covenant Motif in the Letter of James." *HBT* 32, no. 2 (January): 144–65.

Wilson, James T. 1987. "Spring." In *Collier's Encyclopedia*. Vol. 21, edited by William Halsey and Bernard Johnston, 461–62. New York: Macmillan.

Wiseman, D. J. 1964. "Rahab of Jericho." *Tyndale* 14 (June): 8–11.

Witherington III, Ben. 2007. *Letters and Homilies for Jewish Christians: A Socio-Rhetorical Commentary on Hebrews, James and Jude*. Downers Grove, IL: InterVarsity.

Womack, John Henry. 2016. *Sharecropper to Entrepreneur to Pastor: Looking Back and Giving Thanks*. Eugene, OR: Resource Publications.

Wright, N. T. 2009. *Justification: God's Plan and Paul's Vision*. Downers Grove, IL: InterVarsity.

Zohary, Michael. 1982. *Plants of the Bible: A Complete Handbook to All the Plants with 200 Full-Color Plates Taken in the Natural Habitat*. Cambridge: Cambridge University Press.